Controlled Drinking

To Jean

To Anne and John Robertson

NICK HEATHER and IAN ROBERTSON

Controlled Drinking

METHUEN

LONDON AND NEW YORK

First published in 1981 by
Methuen & Co. Ltd
11 New Fetter Lane, London EC4P 4EE
Published in the USA by
Methuen & Co.
in association with Methuen, Inc.
733 Third Avenue, New York, NY 10017

© 1981 Nick Heather and Ian Robertson

Photoset by Inforum Ltd, Porstmouth

Printed in Great Britain at
the University Press, Cambridge

British Library Cataloguing in Publication Data

Heather, Nick
  Controlled drinking.
  1. Alcoholism – Treatment
  I. Title
  362.2'92   HV5276

ISBN 0-416-71970-8

Contents

Foreword

That some people who have become dependent on alcohol, even to the point of harm, should subsequently come to use that substance innocuously, ought not in itself to cause surprise. What is rather more important is to establish whether or not this does in fact occur, to what extent, and in which people. In that way further knowledge would inform the actions and thinking of all concerned with the problems of dependent and harmful drinking.

Oddly enough, the demonstration that a similar phenomenon does occur in Vietnam veterans in relation to heroin has aroused none of the heat and disputation attaching here.

Whether one calls this phenomenon 'controlled drinking' or uses some other term, the facts are to hand, and are marshalled here more completely than ever before.

Seen in this way, the return to problem-free drinking is a relatively unimportant part of ethanology. There is so much more of interest and value in other areas, such as for example prevention, that controversy over this issue should not hold us back. Yet so strong are entrenched ideological views on this issue, that the argument waxes ever more fiercely, recalling the nineteenth-century battles between wets and drys, using indeed the very language and thoughts of early nineteenth-century temperance workers, with the same preoccupation with the moral and religious aspects of 'the first drink', and the role of divine help.

There have been two valuable sequelae of this controversy. It has focused our attention on our basic concept of the condition we call alcoholism. It has enabled us to look again at what Jellinek said, for example, and to question simplistic beliefs about 'disease', 'illness', and 'constitutional predisposition'.

Additionally, it has inaugurated an era of diversification in the treatment of alcoholics, which is very fully documented here. This has brought many talented people with special skills, into this field for the first time, and made this a most exciting period in the long history of this topic.

This book had to be written if ever the argument could be allowed to rest. For that we are indebted to the authors. If they are successful in their task, as is very likely, then the thinking of us all will be emancipated from the deadening influence of nineteenth-century morality and the way will be fully open to these new ventures in treatment, and above all in prevention, which have hitherto been made very difficult for us to pursue. It could well make ethanology as a scientific discipline as free from the constraints of those who divine on mystical and moral grounds, as is astronomy from astrology. All the evidence needed is to hand, and is critically evaluated here by the authors.

D.L. Davies,
London.
25.5.80

Authors' preface

This is not intended as a polemical book. We are not opposed to polemic in principle; it can sometimes serve a useful function in the development of ideas. However, we feel the time for polemic has passed. As recently as three or four years ago, the mention of controlled drinking in alcoholism circles was liable to arouse vehement feelings. But at a conference on New Directions in Alcoholism Treatment held at the Institute of Psychiatry in London in April 1979, the mood had clearly changed to one of reconciliation and a desire to progress beyond repetitive disputes. As the results of a recent survey (Robertson and Heather, 1980*b*) have shown, most treatment centres now accept the principle of controlled drinking and few experts in the alcoholism field would insist that the disease theory was immune to criticism. Clearly, controlled drinking treatment is here to stay.

These remarks do not mean that nothing we have written in this book will be found controversial by some. In particular, we regret the tendency to relegate the new methods to a minor and ancillary role in the range of traditional treatment services – as being applicable, for example, to *only* those with less serious problems. The controlled drinking treatment goal has a much more important part to play than this. We also detect an unfortunate inclination to avoid facing up to the implications of the scientific evidence related to controlled drinking for the overall theory of alcoholism, and we have dealt at some length with these wider implications in Chapter 8.

It might still be asked why an entire book devoted to the topic of 'controlled drinking' needed to be written, since the effect might be to distract attention from more fundamental and more human questions. We take this point, but it has been our intention to provide as comprehensive a review as possible of all the relevant evidence in order to stimulate and encourage future research, treatment and educational developments. Nevertheless, we sincerely hope that this evidence will now become fully integrated into the main body of knowledge on alcoholism and that this will be the last time a book such as this needs to be compiled.

In regard to terminology, we have used 'alcoholism' in the widest and least specific sense possible and as roughly equivalent to Jellinek's 'any use of alcoholic beverages that causes any damage to the individual or to society or both'. Although 'alcoholism' was pronounced to be 'dead' at the London conference referred to above, alternative circumlocutions are too clumsy for convenient employment. We trust that the meaning of other terms, such as 'alcoholic', 'alcohol abuser' and 'problem-drinker', will become clear in their specific contexts. The problem of what to call drinking in former alcoholics which does not appear to be doing them harm is addressed in

Chapter 4. However, while we are aware that some object to the term, we have used 'controlled drinking' for the title of this book because of its juxtaposition with the concept of loss of control which remains central to the modern understanding of alcoholism.

The book has been written primarily for workers in the alcoholism field – for psychiatrists, general practitioners, sociologists, social workers and counsellors of all sorts. One particular readership we have in mind is psychologists, both clinical and academic, whom we hope to persuade to take a greater interest in alcoholism when they see how relevant their knowledge and skills can be. Because of this somewhat heterogeneous readership, the book can be read selectively if so desired. For example, parts of Chapter 1, especially those describing earlier disease models, will be highly familiar to many psychiatrists and may be omitted. (Nevertheless, we thought it important to arrive at what Jellinek actually said, and not what he is commonly thought to have said.) Psychiatrists may find more of value in the account of the learning theory foundations of behavioural treatments offered in Chapter 5. On the other hand, psychologists and those approaching the subject with relatively few preconceptions may not find the opening chapter too elementary for their purposes. We also recognize that Chapters 2, 3 and 6, containing as they do long strings of detailed description and criticism of scientific evidence, may be difficult to read in one sitting. Some readers may therefore find it more convenient to restrict attention to the summary sections included in these chapters. However, should the reader wish to make a personal assessment of the evidence on which our conclusions are based, then it will obviously be necessary to read the entire chapter. As we implied above, the chapters in question are intended to provide as comprehensive a review as possible in the limited space available of the most important and most recent evidence bearing on a particular area of enquiry and we hope that they will serve as points of reference for research workers in the alcoholism field.

One kind of reader we have definitely *not* written for is the person who is currently experiencing, or has experienced in the past, problems connected with drinking. We will not be appalled if such a person does read the book; on the contrary, we have more confidence in peoples' ability to arrive at a sensible judgement based on evidence than some others appear to have. But it has not been our aim to have a direct influence on drinking behaviour by means of the book. However, lest there be any misunderstanding on this score, let us make two things clear. It could not be further from our intentions to persuade someone who has achieved a contented life through total abstinence from alcohol to return to drinking. And if anyone should, for whatever reason, be encouraged by the contents of this book to attempt normal drinking, either as an alternative to abstinence or to present harmful drinking, they should seek professional advice before doing so.

Many people have made valuable contributions to this book. First of all we should like to thank all those who replied by letter or in personal conversation to our enquiries: Bill Acker, Lynn Alden, Helen Annis, Glen Caddy, Jonathon Chick, David Foy, Ray Hodgson, Alastair Keddie, Peter Lewis, Ron McKechnie, William Miller, Jim Orford, Mansell Pattison, Howard Rankin, Martha Sanchez-Craig, Bill Saunders, Mark Sobell, Anthony Thorley, Fred Yates. The following read and made valuable comments on parts of earlier drafts of the manuscript: David Davies, Douglas Fraser, Ray Hodgson and Stephen Rollnick. Our special thanks must go to Isabel Ormerod for great patience and dedication in typing the manuscript. We must not forget to thank also the library staff at Ninewells Medical School for their unfailing courtesy and efficiency. Finally we would like to express our gratitude to all our friends and colleagues in the *New Directions in the Study of Alcohol Group* for the stimulation and encouragement they have provided over the past few years. During part of the period in which this book was prepared, the first author was supported by a grant from the Scottish Home and Health Department and the second author by a grant from the Medical Research Council.

We and the publishers thank the following for permission to use copyright material: the Editors of *Behaviour, Research and Therapy* and Pergamon Press Ltd for Table 2.1; The Rand Corporation and Dr Polich for Tables 2.2 and 2.3; the Editor of *Psychological Reports* and Dr Miriam Cohen for Figure 3.1; The American Psychological Association and Dr Marlatt for Table 3.1 (© 1973 The American Psychological Association); the Editor of *Archives of General Psychiatry* and Dr Lidwig for Table 3.2 (© 1978 The American Medical Association); The Addiction Research Foundation for Table 4.1.

Nick Heather,
Ian Robertson,
Dundee.
30.6.80

1 Introduction: disease conceptions of alcoholism

This book is about 'controlled drinking'. It is centrally concerned with issues relating to the acquisition or resumption of patterns of harmfree drinking by persons previously identified as alcoholics or problem-drinkers and with a critical evaluation of controlled drinking treatment methods. Before proceeding to the empirical evidence which bears upon these matters, however, it is first necessary to undertake a brief review of disease conceptions of alcoholism.

This review will be necessary because the traditional treatment goal of total abstinence continues to be the major therapeutic response to the individual suffering caused by alcohol abuse in our society. The claim that some alcoholics can return to harmfree drinking has been seen as controversial only because it runs counter to this widely accepted and, in some circles, sacrosanct treatment objective. For this reason, no sensible discussion of controlled drinking can take place without first considering the historical development of, and theoretical justification for, its powerful and pervasive alternative. This does not mean that these two solutions to the problem of alcoholism are necessarily antagonistic or that they may not one day achieve a stable and peaceful co-existence. But it does mean that the background to the debate about controlled drinking cannot be fully appreciated without first understanding why it is that abstinence has for so long been regarded as essential to the alcoholic's recovery and why controlled drinking impossible.

It may well be feasible to arrive at a conceptualization of alcoholism as a disease which does not entail the therapeutic requirement of total abstinence and, indeed, this is one of the questions to which this chapter will address itself. The fact remains, nevertheless, that the dominant and most influential disease formulations do make such a demand. This is because alcoholism is viewed in these dominant conceptions as an *irreversible* disease. Other prominent and common properties of disease conceptions, such as the assumption of a unitary phenomenon with qualitative differences between alcoholics and nonalcoholics and the postulation of a relatively inexorable progression of symptoms through a distinct sequence of phases (see Pattison *et al.*, 1977), are intimately linked with this central feature of irreversibility. Moreover, as we will argue in the concluding chapter, irreversibility represents that property of disease conceptions which has had by far the greatest practical significance for society's response to the problems caused by alcohol and now constitutes the only remaining justification for a scientific explanation of alcoholism in disease terms. Therefore, the question whether alcoholism is or is not an irreversible condition is crucial, not only for the possibility of controlled drinking treatment methods, but also for the future status of the disease perspective of alcoholism as a whole.

THE HISTORICAL CONTEXT

The origins of the disease theory of alcoholism are popularly thought to have coincided with the beginning of the alcoholism treatment movement following the repeal of Prohibition in the United States. However, Levine (1978) makes clear that the modern understanding of alcoholism as a disease was anticipated as long ago as the late eighteenth and early nineteenth centuries. In order to appreciate the full significance of the change in thinking which led to the emergence of the first disease conception of alcoholism, it may be useful to contrast it with the classical view of human nature which had dominated the seventeenth and most of the eighteenth centuries. In the classical understanding, man was set apart from the natural world, including all lower forms of life, as being a creature uniquely endowed with reason. Human behaviour, therefore, was not regarded as susceptible to natural, scientific explanations since it was assumed that men acted freely in accordance with rational principles of self-interest. If some men acted in a way contrary to the law of the land or to accepted canons of proper conduct, they had done so in full knowledge of the adverse consequences which might follow from such behaviour. In regard to excessive drinking, for example, it was taken for granted that people drank and got drunk because they wanted to, not because they were compelled to. As Levine puts it, 'drunkenness was a choice, albeit a sinful one, which some individuals made'.

The kernel of the new disease conception of habitual drunkenness, which was worked out fully in the early years of the nineteenth century, was the concept of addiction. Indeed, it is a surprising fact that alcohol was seen as an inherently addicting substance long before opium was so regarded (see Levine, 1978). Two physicians, Benjamin Rush in America and Thomas Trotter in Britain, were chiefly responsible for developing the novel concept of addiction by paying attention to the reports of many drunkards that they experienced irresistible and overpowering desires for alcohol. Rush diagnosed inebriety as 'a disease of the will' and described the drunkard's behaviour in terms closely similar to modern depictions of 'loss of control'. Moreover, abstinence was prescribed unequivocally by Rush and others as the only cure for the disease. Rush is usually credited with being the founder of the Temperance Movement in the United States and we may note in passing the intimate links between early temperance advocates and the medical profession. Abstinence was enthusiastically adopted as the solution to inebriety by the majority of temperance supporters in America and from there the idea spread to Britain and other parts of Europe.

In addition to a correspondence between early and modern views of alcoholism on a conceptual level, there also exist striking similarities between the organizational forms adopted in response to the problem of drunkenness. The Washingtonian movement of the 1840s, described by Maxwell (1950), consisted of a fraternal association of reformed drunkards whose self-imposed task was to rescue fellow sufferers from their plight. Meetings typically took the form of autobiographical accounts of the individual's struggles with alcohol and recitals of the events leading to the eventual victory over the unnatural appetite for drink. This 'repentant role', characterized by repeated public confessions of guilt and repentance, is related in turn to a cultural tradition embedded in evangelistic Protestantism (Trice and Roman, 1970). The early parallels with Alcoholics Anonymous, as well as the deeper cultural roots of AA group behaviour, are obvious. Similar precedents in Victorian Britain are well illustrated by Harrison (1970).

These similarities should not be pressed too far. In particular, there is one important difference between early and later disease conceptions of alcoholism, to do with the proposed location of the source of addiction. In the temperance perspective, the origin of addiction was situated in the nature of the substance itself; anyone who drank alcohol was putting himself at risk of contracting the disease. While there exist recent statements of the position that alcohol dependence is caused by nothing more than the regular and excessive ingestion of alcohol, many modern disease conceptions, including the Alcoholics Anonymous model of alcoholism, locate the source of addiction in the individual person. For a variety of hypothesized reasons, it is claimed that only some individuals are capable of becoming addicted to alcohol; moderate or heavy usage by those not so predisposed does not lead on to addiction.

Despite the lack of agreement between these two versions of addiction, the present argument is that the core of modern disease conceptions of alcoholism, the concept of addiction itself and the loss of control over drinking which is alleged to follow from addiction, has been inherited from the early nineteenth-century medical thought which gave impetus to the Temperance Movement, and that the recent preference for total abstinence as a cure for alcoholism has its roots in temperance ideology. Moreover, the organizational forms adopted by Alcoholics Anonymous show it to be a more modern counterpart of the temperance societies which proliferated during the last century and which used the Washingtonians as their prototype. Contrary to the suggestion of Jellinek (1960), most temperance supporters were far from hostile to the notion that habitual drunkenness was a disease and to the consequent exoneration from blame of the drunkard; the attitude to the inebriate was, in large measure, one of sympathy and not of condemnation; it was the moderate drinker for whom most disapproval was reserved (Levine, 1978). The later antagonism between temperance supporters and those concerned with the treatment of alcoholics arose because of a shift in emphasis in the Temperance Movement in the late nineteenth and early twentieth centuries from 'moral suasion' to 'legislative coercion' (Harrison, 1970) and its subsequent dedication to the legal prohibition of alcohol. After the repeal of the 18th Amendment in the United States, no rediscovered disease conception of alcoholism was likely to attract widespread public support if it warned against the dangers of moderate consumption, and this partly explains the appeal to the vulnerability of the few rather than the many. Even so, several prominent temperance workers were enthusiastic about the formation of the alcoholism treatment movement by Alcoholics Anonymous and the Yale Center of Alcohol Studies in the 1930s and 1940s, as Rubin (1979) demonstrates. Later, temperance societies came to perceive common interests between their natural enemy, the liquor industry, and the treatment movement owing to the implication that, if only some individuals were vulnerable to the disease of alcoholism, there could be no harm in drinking for the majority. Indeed, there is some evidence to suggest that the industry did regard the new approach to alcoholism in this light (Rubin, 1979). An unfortunate consequence of these disputes was to obscure the continuity between the new disease view of alcoholism and the mainstream of temperance ideology.

THE AA MODEL OF ALCOHOLISM

Room (1972a) has argued convincingly that the rediscovery of a disease conception of alcoholism forty years ago, in which Alcoholics Anonymous played a major part in collaboration with medical sympathizers, was motivated by practical rather than theoretical considerations (see also Seeley, 1962). As Room puts it, 'the promulgation of disease concepts of alcoholism has been brought about essentially as a means of getting a better deal for the "alcoholic" rather than as a logical consequence of scholarly work and scientific discoveries'. The legal code retains an adherence to the classical view of human nature and continues to be fundamentally at odds with medical and social sciences presenting deterministic accounts of behaviour. Therefore, the main thrust of the rediscovered disease conception was an effort to remove the alcoholic's behaviour from the realm of choice and moral obligation and to absolve him from responsibility for his deviant actions in law. Moreover, in terms of Talcott Parsons' (1951) classic description of 'the sick role', the sick alcoholic was now provided with a defence against accusations of defaulting on the everyday responsibilities of family, work and friendship. It was hoped that he would now enjoy a more humane response from society and be provided with access to treatment services, sick leave, insurance benefits and the like; in return he was expected merely to co-operate with the treatment offered him. The disease formulation was also intended to improve the public image of the alcoholic by removing the stigma associated with public drunkenness. In the light of these sociopolitical objectives, it is perhaps not surprising that the presentation of alcoholism as a disease was characterized by the considerable vagueness deplored by Wexberg (1951). As Room (1972*a*) again points out, this vagueness may well have served to conceal potentially divisive differences in outlook between those attempting to improve the alcoholic's position, and lack of specificity over the nature of the disease in question may have helped to distance the alcoholic from other groups, such as drug addicts and the mentally ill, with more obviously spoiled social identities. It is essential to note that, in the cultural climate of the 1930s and 1940s, these objectives could be achieved only by an appeal to a disease model. The crucial question of whether this remains true today will be discussed in Chapter 8.

The Alcoholics Anonymous model begins with the assertion of a qualitative difference between the alcoholic and all other types of drinker. In the *Big Book of AA* (Alcoholics Anonymous, 1939), the real alcoholic is unambiguously set apart from the moderate drinker, 'who can take it or leave it alone', and from the hard drinker who, although he may be impaired both physically and mentally through drinking, can stop or moderate if he finds sufficiently strong motivation, 'even though he may find it difficult or troublesome and may even need medical attention'. In contrast, it seems that the drinking of the alcoholic is beyond the influence of environmental contingencies and cannot be changed by such life-events as 'ill-health, falling in love, change of environment or the warning of a doctor'. Despite its lack of precision, the enigmatic concept of the 'real alcoholic' informs all AA views on alcoholism and is especially important for the AA reaction to the possibility of teaching alcoholics to control their drinking. The real alcoholic is someone who, by definition, cannot do so. It should be noted in passing that this implied definition of the real alcoholic is circular. If the individual has in fact failed to control his drinking and has not been influenced by ill-health, marriages, doctors' warnings and the like, then he is a real alcoholic. And a real alcoholic is defined as someone who cannot control his drinking, etc. . . . Conversely, as we shall see in the next chapter, if a person has succeeded in controlling his drinking, then he cannot have been a 'real' alcoholic, no matter how serious his drinking problem might have appeared and no matter how much damage it may have caused.

Alcoholics, then, are different from other people in that they cannot handle alcohol safely. A further crucial element of the AA model is the idea that this special vulnerability, whatever exactly it might be, is present before the first intake of alcohol. In the early days of Alcoholics Anonymous, the vulnerability was thought of as an inborn, constitutional deficit, and here AAs took notice of contemporary evidence that alcoholism tended to run in families (e.g. Wall, 1936). Although it must be stressed that his book is not part of official AA literature, Kessel (1962) attributes to AAs the belief that 'one does not become an alcoholic, one is born an alcoholic'. More specifically, the deficit in question was originally described as an allergy to alcohol. In 'The Doctor's Opinion' which begins the *AA Big Book* (AA, 1939), the 'patron saint' of Alcoholics Anonymous, William D. Silkworth, states that 'the action of alcohol on these chronic alcoholics is a manifestation of an allergy . . .' and 'these allergic types can never safely use alcohol in any form at all'. It seems that the term allergy was not meant in any exact sense, but referred merely to some kind of abnormal reaction to alcohol specific to alcoholics. In more recent times the allergy concept has become less popular, owing probably to criticisms from medical authorities (e.g. Jellinek, 1960; Kessel and Walton, 1965) and many AAs would now disavow the notion of an inherited predisposition of any sort. If influenced by reverberations of Freudian psychology, they may refer instead to the results of early learning experiences which give the pre-alcoholic an overwhelming attraction to dependence on alcohol. Or they may appeal to some ill-defined general 'sensitivity' which distinguishes the future alcoholic in his potential reaction to drink (cf. Mann, 1968).

Perhaps the most essential element of the model is precisely what is of main interest in this chapter, the notion of irreversibility. Prominent in all AA publications is the statement that alcoholism is a disease, a progressive disease, which can be arrested by total abstinence but which cannot be cured. While the pious hope is sometimes expressed that medical science may one day discover the nature of the crucial physiological defect, this is not presented as a realistic possibility. Much of the initial response to the new recruit is devoted to persuading him of the uncomfortable truth of this assertion and to a discussion of the problems which will undoubtedly arise from a life without alcohol. Thus AAs continue to call themselves alcoholics even though they may have been abstinent for twenty years or more; they are 'recovering alcoholics'. All this is condensed, of course, into the well-known maxim 'once an alcoholic, always an alcoholic'.

The fourth element which may be isolated from the AA model is concerned with the behavioural consequences of the pre-existent and permanent vulnerability to alcohol. In the *AA Big Book* (AA, 1939) it is explained that 'alcoholics have one symptom in common; they cannot start drinking without developing the phenomenon of craving'. Although accounts of the underlying cause may vary, 'craving' or 'a compulsion to drink regardless of the consequences' (Mann, 1968) appear as the subjective accompaniment of an objectively observable loss of control over drinking. In a famous passage, which as Pattison *et al.* (1977) point out, is often misquoted as though it were the opinion of the author being expressed, Jellinek (1960) characterizes the AA view of loss of control as follows:

> Recovered alcoholics in Alcoholics Anonymous speak of 'loss of control' to denote that stage in the development of their drinking history when the ingestion of one alcoholic drink sets up a chain reaction so that they are unable to adhere to their intention to 'have one or two drinks only' but continue to ingest more and more – often with quite some difficulty and disgust – contrary to their volition.

Jellinek's reference to 'the ingestion of one alcoholic drink' attributes to AA the loss of control concept in its purest form, what may legitimately be described as the 'one drink, one drunk' hypothesis. It is likely that some AAs now entertain more complex and sophisticated notions of loss of control as a result of changes in medical thinking on the topic.

AA thinking may have changed in certain respects over the years, but in relation to the final element in this synopsis of the AA model, there has been no suggestion of any change whatever. This is the necessity for total and lifelong abstinence on the part of the 'real' alcoholic. Abstinence is the most widely recognized part of AA ideology among the general public and quotations in support of its attribution to AA would be superfluous. Total abstinence is made all the more indispensable by the fact that alcoholism is said to be a *progressive* disease; if drinking is continued, further deterioration is inevitable.

JELLINEK'S FIRST DISEASE CONCEPTION

It is difficult to overestimate the influence of Alcoholics Anonymous on medical theory and practice in the field of alcoholism. The fellowship has always been interested in popularizing its creed among the medical profession, as several AA pamphlets attest (e.g. Alcoholics Anonymous, 1955; 1965); the conclusion can only be that this effort has been remarkably successful. A great many hospital rehabilitation programmes consist of little more than a formalized version of AA principles or make attandance at AA meetings compulsory (Moore and Buchanan, 1966). Jones and Heldrich (1972) showed that a majority of physicians who agreed that alcoholism was a disease believed that referral to AA was the wisest professional strategy. On a more theoretical level the parallelism between AA and dominant medical conceptions may be illustrated by the fact that Jellinek's (1946; 1952) seminal description of the phases of alcoholism was based on replies to a questionnaire constructed by AAs and sent out to members through the official AA publication *Grapevine*.

Jellinek (1952) begins by restricting the concept of alcoholism to those excessive drinkers characterized by physical or psychological pathology and whose rehabilitation primarily requires medical-psychiatric treatment. Among those who may legitimately be called alcoholics, there are two distinct types, namely, 'alcohol addicts' to whom the disease concept of alcoholism attaches, and 'habitual symptomatic excessive drinkers' to whom it does not. The differentiating criterion between these types is 'loss of control' which occurs only among alcohol addicts and then only after many years of excessive drinking. Jellinek does not wish to deny that the habitual symptomatic excessive drinker, or 'nonaddictive alcoholic', is also a sick person; however, 'his ailment is not the excessive drinking, but rather the psychological or social difficulties from which alcohol intoxication gives temporary surcease'. These difficulties are originally present in both types but with alcohol addicts the process of loss of control, which is 'a disease condition *per se*', is superimposed on psychological pathology. Whether this superimposed process is itself psychological or physical in nature is not known. Nor has it been established whether loss of control originates in 'a predisposing X factor' or is acquired in the course of excessive drinking – for example in acquired nutritional habits. This agnosticism marks an obvious departure from AA insistence on a predisposing factor. Nevertheless, the basic dichotomy of alcohol addicts and habitual symptomatic excessive drinkers clearly reflects the AA distinction between 'real alcoholics' and 'hard drinkers', especially since, as in the case of the hard drinker, the nonaddictive alcoholic is said to experience most of the major symptoms of alcoholism without acquiring loss of control.

Jellinek's description of the emergence of alcohol problems may be thought of as a series of barriers which less serious types of problem-drinkers successively fail to surmount, leaving only the alcohol addict at the finishing line. Beginning with drinking which reflects the culture to which the individual belongs, an unknown proportion of drinkers sometimes take advantage of the tension-reducing properties of alcohol for the relief of major individual stresses and become 'occasional symptomatic excessive drinkers'. Some of these in turn, more particularly those who are 'definitely deviating personalities', come to take constant recourse to alcohol and become 'habitual symptomatic excessive drinkers'. Finally, a further unknown proportion of these develop loss of control and become alcohol addicts. Thus, up to the point of discontinuity introduced by loss of control, Jellinek provides a basis for relating normal and abnormal functional uses of alcohol.

The phases of alcohol addiction itself consist of groups of sequential symptoms which are said to be characteristic of each phase, 'although not all symptoms . . . occur necessarily in all alcohol addicts, nor do they occur in every addict in the same sequence'. In the Prealcoholic Symptomatic Phase, the future addict cannot be distinguished from other symptomatic drinkers, but his drinking progresses from occasional relief-drinking to constant relief-drinking. The sudden onset of 'blackouts' marks the beginning of the Prodromal Phase which is typified by a collection of behavioural symptoms including surreptitious drinking, preoccupation with alcohol and the occurrence of guilt feelings. Without any prior discussion of the point, Jellinek writes: 'It goes without saying that even at this stage the only possible modus for this type of drinker is total abstinence.'

The Crucial Phase of alcohol addiction is defined, of course, by the onset of loss of control and we shall need to consider exactly what Jellinek meant by this. Loss of control is a state which occurs during the addict's drinking, which may take hours or weeks for its full development, and lasts until the drinker is too intoxicated or too sick to ingest more alcohol. Obviously, this physical discomfort was not the drinker's original intention and, indeed, the bout may not have been started by any individual need but by a social drink. Furthermore: 'After recovery from intoxication, it is not the "loss of control" – i.e. the physical demand, apparent or real – which leads to a new bout after several days or several weeks; the renewal of drinking is set off by the original psychological conflicts or by a simple social situation which involves drinking.' Thus it is clear that Jellinek (1952), like Alcoholics Anonymous, saw loss of control in terms of an inability to stop once drinking had commenced, and not as a lack of choice over whether or not to start drinking in the first place. The reason why the addicted drinker perversely returns to drinking despite his disastrous experiences of it is that he continues to feel the need to master a will which, although he does not fully realize it, has already been subverted once alcohol has entered the blood stream. The Crucial Phase is succeeded by the Chronic Phase in which alcohol tolerance is reduced, the resistance of the alcoholic breaks down and he becomes entirely incapacitated.

Despite the fact that it was for many years the definitive statement on the course of alcohol addiction, Jellinek's (1952) paper is remarkable also for its omissions. The most immediately relevant of these is of any discussion of the therapeutic requirement of total abstinence. As we have seen, Jellinek merely asserts that abstinence becomes indispensable as early as the Prodromal Phase, but precisely why this should 'go without saying' is nowhere explained. Similarly, the author is strangely silent on the subject of irreversibility – in relation to loss of control or to any other symptom of alcoholism. The only passing reference to the issue is the statement that the ethical deterioration and impairment of thinking characteristic of the Chronic Phase are *not* irreversible. It was as if Jellinek wished to endorse the 'loss of control' element in the AA model, thus absolving alcoholics from personal responsibility for their behaviour, without also subscribing to the irreversibility of the condition.

Ignoring for the moment the all-important differentiating symptom of loss of control, it is essential to note that Jellinek's first conception of alcoholism, incorporating as it does a continuum in the functional use of alcohol for the relief of psychological stress, is fully compatible with the tension-reduction/ reinforcement model which began to be developed shortly after Jellinek's publication (Conger, 1956). Thus, Jellinek's formulation could accurately be described as a learning theory of alcoholism were it not for the crucial component of loss of control. It follows that the justification for a specifically disease conception turns on the empirical validity of this concept; 'loss of control' ceases to be merely a symptom of alcoholism and becomes a hypothesis upon which the entire disease conception depends.

JELLINEK'S SECOND DISEASE CONCEPTION

The background to Jellinek's (1960) second disease conception was heavily influenced by the extensive international experience he had acquired after the publication of his earlier work. Taking note of the considerable differences in the kinds of alcohol-related behaviours identified as problems in various parts of the world, Jellinek concluded: 'By adhering strictly to our American ideas about "alcoholism" and "alcoholics" (created by Alcoholics Anonymous in their own image) and restricting the term to those ideas, we have been continuing to overlook many other problems of alcohol which need urgent attention.' For this reason he proposed the wider operational definition of alcoholism as 'any use of alcoholic beverages that causes any damage to the individual or society or both'. However, because this definition is deliberately broad and vague, there is a distinction between 'alcoholism' and 'alcoholics'; the latter are not identical with those who suffer from alcoholism in the sense defined but are confined instead to persons conforming to the particular species of alcoholism Jellinek intends to describe. Nor is the term alcoholism equivalent to alcoholism as disease; only some of the problems covered by the definition may properly be described as illnesses.

His international experience also influenced Jellinek's new account of the predisposing factors in the development of alcohol addiction. Here he drew attention to evidence of cultural variation in the economic factors affecting alcohol production and consumption, and the differences in drinking patterns and attitudes to drinking among the countries he had visited. Impressed by the fact that the majority of French alcohol addicts did not display pre-alcoholic or other gross psychological vulnerabilities, he reasoned that in societies having a low degree of acceptance of large daily amounts of alcohol those individuals possessing high vulnerability were mainly exposed to the risk of addiction, whereas in societies with an extremely high degree of acceptance of large daily amounts, like France, the presence of any small vulnerability, whether psychological or physical, would suffice.

Jellinek's (1960) book is best known for its Greek letter classification and the five species of alcoholism included in this are as follows:

Alpha alcoholism is said to represent a *purely* psychological and *continual* dependence or reliance upon the effect of alcohol to relieve bodily or emotional pain. There is no pharmacological addiction. Drinking may be undisciplined and may contravene the rules of society but does not lead to loss of control. Some instances may simply be developmental forerunners of alcohol addiction, but in respect of pure alpha alcoholism there are no signs of a progressive process. The alpha alcoholic is clearly equivalent to Jellinek's (1952) 'habitual, symptomatic excessive drinker'.

Beta alcoholism refers to the presence of physical complications from excessive drinking, such as polyneuropathy, gastritis and liver cirrhosis, but without any physical or psychological dependence. In this case, heavy drinking may reflect customs of a particular social group combined with poor nutritional habits. Beta alcoholism may also develop into alcohol addiction but the transition is less likely than with the alpha variety.

Gamma alcoholism is the term used to refer to what Jellinek (1952) called 'alcohol addiction' and is the species he describes as having been moulded in the image of Alcoholics Anonymous. It is characterized by (*i*) acquired increased tissue tolerance to alcohol; (*ii*) adaptive cell metabolism; (*iii*) withdrawal symptoms and craving (i.e. physical dependence), and (*iv*) loss of control. In this species alone there is a definite progression from psychological to physical dependence, accompanied by the behavioural deterioration described in Jellinek (1952). The type of loss of control attributed to gamma alcoholics was termed by Marconi (1959) 'inability to stop'.

Delta alcoholism shows the first three characteristics of gamma alcoholism just listed but instead of 'inability to stop' there is 'inability to abstain'. That is, the ability to control intake on any given occasion remains unaffected but there is no capacity for abstention from alcohol even for a few days without the occurrence of withdrawal symptoms. This species is associated especially with the 'inveterate drinking' found in France and other wine-drinking countries and, hence, there may be little pre-alcoholic psychological vulnerability.

Epsilon alcoholism describes the relatively rare and little known form of periodic alcoholism, previously called dipsomania.

Jellinek emphasizes that, given his broad definition of alcoholism as any drinking that causes any harm, there must be other species which could be delineated, but only the five he describes can possibly come into consideration when the question is asked, whether alcoholism is a disease. Jellinek's answer to this question is that only the gamma and delta species are diseases, the reason being that only they entail physiopathological changes analogous to those in drug addiction. These physiopathological changes, i.e. adaptation of cell metabolism, acquired increased tissue tolerance and withdrawal symptoms, are responsible for bringing about craving and loss of control or inability to abstain. In case his position is not clear, Jellinek states: 'The current majority opinion to which the present writer subscribes . . . is that anomalous forms of the ingestion of narcotics and alcohol, such as drinking with loss of control and physical dependence, are caused by physiopathological processes and constitute diseases.' Thus Jellinek firmly ties in his later disease conception with drug addiction in general and, unlike in his 1952 paper, unequivocally endorses a neurophysiological substrate for addiction and loss of control. With regard to the remaining species, alpha alcoholism may be thought of as a symptom of some underlying disease in the psychopathological sense but is not itself a disease; beta alcoholism results in serious diseases but the excessive drinking itself does not indicate any pathology or dependence; epsilon alcoholism may be a form of physiopathological disease but too little is known about it to be certain.

Jellinek (1960) greatly extends his earlier discussion of loss of control and craving. He states that loss of control does not emerge suddenly but rather progressively in the course of the alcoholic's drinking career and several years after the first intoxication. Moreover, it does not occur every time the alcoholic takes a drink, and here Jellinek introduces an element of indeterminacy into the concept of loss of control which was later expanded by Keller (1972). He also chides other students of alcoholism for mixing up loss of control with 'uncontrolled' or 'undisciplined' drinking; the latter terms should be reserved for the *deliberate* transgression of social rules relating to amount, times, occasions and locales of drinking. Further on in his discussion Jellinek is more specific about the postulated mechanism of loss of control. It is said to occur in gamma alcoholics as a result of minor withdrawal symptoms in the presence of alcohol in the blood stream. Continued drinking is forced on the alcoholic because of the need to abolish these unpleasant symptoms, which include tremors of the fingers and lips, slight twitchings, motor restlessness and sometimes delusions. They are relieved by more alcohol and the drinker achieves some degree of temporary elation, but only for a short period before the withdrawal symptoms recur and further drinking becomes necessary. The dysphoria induced by withdrawal symptoms is aggravated by increasing anxiety which in turn increases the need for more drink. The demand for alcohol, i.e. craving, is of a twofold nature. Firstly, there is the physical demand brought about by the need to allay distressing withdrawal symptoms and, secondly, there is the obsessive belief based on the alcoholic's experience before loss of control became established that continued drinking will eventually provide a reduction of tension. Jellinek then goes on to offer a technical hypothesis, based on 'short range accommodation of nervous tissue', to account for the occurrence of minor withdrawal symptoms during the gamma alcoholic's drinking. We shall not have space to consider this hypothesis in detail.

As in relation to Jellinek's (1952) previous formulation, it should be noted that the sole justification for a specifically disease conception is the notion of loss of control. In the case of gamma alcoholism the physiopathological processes advanced as the basis for pharmacological addiction are identical with those used to explain loss of control and the two concepts are therefore synonymous. A combination of these same processes is invoked to account for the delta alcoholic's 'inability to abstain' and this inability has been conceived of, as we shall see in Chapter 3, as an alternative version of 'loss of control'. Therefore loss of control in one sense or another is the *sine qua non* of Jellinek's (1960) disease conception and without it his model would become a learning theory of alcoholism incorporating individual differences in the tension-reducing effects of alcohol and supplemented by a sociocultural perspective.

There is a further striking similarity between Jellinek's first and second disease conceptions. Nowhere in his book does Jellinek endorse the irreversibility of the disease process. On the contrary, he states that the acquired increase tissue tolerance which is an essential component of addiction, although it may carry over from one drinking occasion to the next, 'may be lost after abstinent periods of long duration'. And, 'physical craving cannot be postulated as the cause of resumption of drinking after a considerable period of abstinence when withdrawal symptoms are no longer present'. Furthermore, although the therapeutic requirement of total abstinence is referred to in his 1952 paper in passing, in the 1960 book there is no mention of it whatever! In the absence of any relevant discussion by Jellinek himself, we can only conclude that there is nothing in Jellinek's own disease conception to suggest the irreversibility of the disease process or the necessity for *permanent* abstinence from the former alcohol addict. It is a considerable irony in view of this conclusion that Jellinek's (1960) masterpiece is sometimes appealed to by advocates of total and lifelong abstinence as the authoritative statement of the disease conception which supports their position.

PSYCHOLOGICAL EXPLANATIONS OF ALCOHOLISM AS A DISEASE

Following Jellinek's (1960) book, his conception of alcoholism has become dominant in medical and psychiatric circles. This is not to say that the complexity and subtlety of Jellinek's thought have been retained, but that his view of alcoholism as a disease characterized by a form of pharmacological addiction based on physiopathological changes, which are caused in turn by prolonged excessive drinking, has been widely adopted. However, submerged beneath this dominant conception there has persisted an alternative tradition associated chiefly with those who practise or recommend intensive psychotherapy for alcoholics. This alternative comprises explanations of alcoholism founded on central concepts such as 'mental illness', 'psychopathology', 'neurosis' and 'personality disorder', which were discussed by Jellinek (1960) under the rubric of 'psychological formulations' of the disease conception. These explanations have the common property that they do not propose any somatic substrate but refer instead to pathology of the mind or psyche as the precipitating cause of abnormal drinking.

Psychological explanations are perhaps most often identified with positions which see alcoholism not as an illness in itself but as the symptom of some underlying psychological illness. Jellinek's alpha type would come into this category but proponents of psychological explanations would extend this type to cover all forms of alcoholism. Jellinek (1960) divided psychological formulations into those which regarded alcoholism as an illness and those which regarded it as a symptom of another illness, but concluded that the former did not achieve any more useful explanation than the symptomatic interpretations. Moore (1968) defended the conception of alcoholism as a mental illness in its own right by insisting that, irrespective of whether remote etiology was biological, psychological or social, 'the final pathway of behaviour results in some type of maladaptation to social living or such internal psychological discomfort that the person is not at rest with himself. Rather than the defective function of an internal organ, defective function in life makes it (alcoholism) a mental illness'. Although relevant to an understanding of psychological disease conceptions, the illness versus symptom debate is not of primary concern here.

Returning to the question of irreversibility, many psychological explanations do subscribe to the permanence of the disease condition (e.g. Lolli, 1952; Fox, 1957). This is because the neurosis or personality disorder giving rise to alcoholism is thought to be intractable. For example, Lolli (1952) states that 'the emotional conflicts underlying his addictive urge to drink are never solved in an alcoholic'. On the other hand, in a discussion of persistent differences of opinion among psychiatrists on the need for abstinence during treatment, Bolman (1965) describes the 'permissive approach' to treatment as one which 'holds that alcoholism should be treated as a character neurosis; the therapist does not take a stand for or against the patient's drinking, but rather attempts to understand its symptomatic meaning'. Bolman has an altogether more optimistic impression of psychotherapeutic intervention than Lolli:

> According to this view, as treatment progresses and the patient is better able to cope with inner and outer stress, one finds that his drinking gradually comes under control. He then may or may not drink in a controlled fashion at the conclusion of successful treatment.

From an entirely different critical stance, Gitlow (1973) has attributed to 'the psychoanalytically inclined' the pernicious and often repeated promise 'to return the alcoholic to social drinking as soon as the cause of his "symptom" has been elucidated'. Clearly, the extent to which alcoholism is regarded as reversible and total abstinence necessary depends on the degree of potential change, either through psychotherapy or increasing maturity, ascribed to the postulated neurotic disturbance. From the present perspective it is interesting that, before a behaviouristic theory of drinking gave birth to controlled drinking treatment methods, the possibility of normal drinking in recovered alcoholics was allowed in some psychological disease conceptions.

THE ALCOHOL DEPENDENCE SYNDROME

During this brief historical survey we have noted a repeated conceptual dichotomy between individuals said to be suffering from the disease of alcoholism and those whose drinking may be both abnormal in quantity and harmful but who are not diseased. It began with the early Alcoholics Anonymous separation of 'real alcoholics' from mere hard drinkers and then ran through Jellinek's (1952) distinction between alcohol addicts and habitual symptomatic excessive drinkers and his (1960) classification of alcoholics into delta and gamma types on the one hand and alpha and beta types on the other. This basic dichotomy has been preserved in the concept of the Alcohol Dependence Syndrome and its distinction from less specific alcohol-related disabilities, although the distinction here is not between individuals but between types of disability caused by alcohol abuse. The syndrome, the development of which is without doubt the most important recent event in the history of disease conceptions of alcoholism, was provisionally described by Edwards and Gross (1976), further described and distinguished from other alcohol-related disabilities in a subsequent WHO publication (Edwards *et al.*, 1977), and canvassed as a useful idea by Edwards (1977). It will be discussed here at some length because of its great importance among recent developments in the alcoholism field. It will also be essential to defend our inclusion of the syndrome in this chapter on disease conceptions of alcoholism.

Edwards and Gross (1976) admit that their delineation of the Alcohol Dependence Syndrome is based more on clinical impression than on substantiated scientific evidence. They also stress that by the term syndrome they mean to imply no more than the concurrence of a set of phenomena. The elements of the syndrome need not always be present, nor be present with the same intensity, and no assumptions need be made about cause or pathological process. The syndrome is described as consisting of seven essential elements: (*i*) narrowing of the drinking repertoire; (*ii*) salience of drink-seeking behaviour; (*iii*) increased tolerance to alcohol; (*iv*) repeated withdrawal symptoms; (*v*) relief or avoidance of withdrawal symptoms by further drinking; (*vi*) subjective awareness of compulsion to drink; and (*vii*) reinstatement of the syndrome after abstinence.

The emphasis in the WHO publication (Edwards *et al.*, 1977) is upon the entire range of alcohol-related disabilities of which the damaging consequences of the Alcohol Dependence Syndrome form only a part. It is vital for society to recognize that not all drinkers showing alcohol-related disabilities are necessarily dependent and medical and social concern should not be restricted to the syndrome. The disabilities of physical, mental and social functioning caused by abnormal drinking are too many and varied to be conveniently classified. Nevertheless, the Alcohol Dependence Syndrome, which incorporates both Jellinek's gamma and delta alcoholism, is the *core* syndrome among alcohol-related disabilities. The syndrome itself is described somewhat differently by Edwards *et al.* and is said to comprise three diagnostic components, viz. altered behavioural state, altered subjective state, and altered psychobiological state, but none of the seven essential elements listed by Edwards and Gross (1976) is missing from the description of these altered states. In Edwards (1977) it is made clear that the syndrome is a psychophysiological disorder; dependence is neither purely physical nor psychological but entails a complex interaction of both. In the same article, Edwards stresses that the syndrome is always environmentally and personally coloured. The presentation of the core syndrome will be very different in the heavy-drinking milieu of France from the dry American state of Utah. Equally, it will show itself in a markedly different form in a person of poor impulse control than in a previously well-integrated personality still responsive to social controls.

The clinical usefulness of the syndrome idea was expounded by Edwards (1977) mainly in terms of a shared model of understanding. Firstly, since the syndrome underlined psychological and social contributions to dependence, it could serve as a rational basis for communication between medical and nonmedical members of a treatment team. Secondly, because it does not lead to 'the sudden imposition by medical fiat of an arbitrary label', it could improve communications between clinician and patient. In addition, a clinical decision as to the degree of dependence reached could become a basis for negotiating a treatment goal. If the syndrome is severe the patient's chances of returning to social drinking are slender and abstinence should usually be recommended; if the syndrome is only minimally developed the likelihood of attaining a social drinking goal should be considered very possible; in the middle ground between these extremes negotiation rather than imposition should still be the rule, but 'the clinician may believe that a conservative approach is generally the most responsible, and that abstinence is normally the safest choice of goal'.

Edwards and Gross (1976) refer to the issue of loss of control in their discussion of the element 'subjective awareness of compulsion to drink'. They state that conventional ways of describing the dependent person's experience are not wholly satisfactory. For example, it is not clear whether reported awareness of loss of control – as when the patient says, 'if I have one or two, I'll go on' – truly describes losing control rather than deciding not to exercise it. Control is best viewed as 'variably and intermittently impaired rather than "lost" '. Similarly, the subjective experience of craving may be influenced by the environment, as when the withdrawing patient in a hospital ward does not report feelings of craving. Cues for craving may include the feeling of intoxication, as well as withdrawal symptoms, affective states and situational stimuli. The key subjective experience of dependence comes close to fulfilling the classic psychiatric conditions for the presence of compulsion, in that 'the desire for a further drink is seen as irrational, the desire is resisted, but the further drink is taken'.

The element of the syndrome which is clearly of greatest relevance to the question of irreversibility is the reinstatement of dependence after a period of abstinence. Edwards and Gross (1976) state that, although patients find abstinence surprisingly easy to maintain, especially in the ward environment where drinking cues are absent, reinstatement of the other elements of the syndrome is typically rapid in the severely dependent person who returns to drinking. Even here there are exceptions, but the time taken for relapse to the previous stage of the dependence syndrome is a function of the previous level of dependence. The fact that 'a syndrome which had taken many years to develop can be fully reinstated within perhaps 72 hours of drinking' is regarded by Edwards and Gross as one of the most puzzling features of the condition. The only experimental evidence directly relevant to this phenomenon appears to be the finding of Kalant *et al*. (1971) that rats given a series of exposures to alcohol later show reinstatement of physical dependence. However, the theoretical implication, stated by Gross (1977), is that rapid reinstatement in cases of previous severe dependence reflects the persistence of long-lasting toxic effects of alcohol, which are also related to the analogous carry-over of functional tolerance. Clearly, the reinstatement phenomenon could provide a solid theoretical justification for the recommendation of abstinence in severely dependent individuals and this possibility will be returned to in Chapter 3.

Apart from research evidence throwing doubt on the proposed undimensionality of the syndrome (see Chick, 1980), it is also subject to certain internal logical difficulties. These arise from the repeated insistence that the syndrome is not all-or-none but refers rather to a continuous variation in syndrome elements. This may be illustrated by a quotation from Edwards (1976):

In any culture where alcohol is an accepted recreational drug, dependence on alcohol is in a statistical sense a normal condition – actuated by a variety of external or internal cues. The graph which would result if distribution of drive state were charted out for a population is conjectural, but it seems possible that toward the right end there would be a long low upper tail, representing the zone where people manifesting the dependence syndrome would be found. The syndrome implies not only a statistically abnormal degree of dependence, but the existence of abnormal drinking cues (drinking to avoid withdrawal symptoms): the intensity of those cues again is not all-or-none.

In this passage the appeal to continuous variation is made on two counts. Firstly, dependence is said to be continuous throughout the population of drinkers and, secondly, a special kind of dependence is posited as being continuous *within* the syndrome. An ambiguity as to which kind of continuity applies to the syndrome idea is apparent at several places in the published work on it. Here is the logical problem. If dependence is continuous in the entire population, there is no sense in describing a specific syndrome, however plastic and subtle it is declared to be. If, on the other hand, an abnormal kind of dependence is continuous only within the segment of the drinking population allocated to the syndrome, then the syndrome *is* all-or-none, being exclusively defined by 'the existence of abnormal drinking cues'. In appealing at the same time to the existence of a continuous distribution of dependence in the drinking population and the reality of a specific core syndrome, the authors of the Alcohol Dependence Syndrome appear to wish to have their cake and eat it too. It seems that a disease entity is being simultaneously rejected and objectified.

This ambiguity is relevant to our opening contention that the Alcohol Dependence Syndrome is a continuation of the dominant tradition in the disease theory of alcoholism. There is considerable equivocation in the writings on the syndrome over whether or not it is to be regarded as a disease. For example, in Edwards *et al.* (1977) we find:

> The decision as to when a syndrome is to be designated a disease is in large measure socially determined and must be congruent with wider cultural interests and habits; the syndrome formulation does not therefore undermine the position of those who have made the disease concept of alcoholism a central tenet of education and health-directed activism.

Similarly, Edwards (1977) writes: 'Whether a syndrome is a disease is largely semantic.' But this is simply not good enough. The designation of a particular form of social deviance as a disease and the labelling of certain persons as suffering from that disease, are not merely semantic issues; they have profound consequences for how society responds to such persons and for how they make sense of their own behaviour. The crucial point is that, whether or not the authors of the syndrome describe it as a disease, it is *in effect* a disease conception. The proof of this assertion is made by referring to Edwards *et al.* when they write that the syndrome 'might be defined simply as a disability marked by impaired capacity to control alcohol intake', and that the leading symptom of the syndrome is 'impaired control over the drug ethyl alcohol'. This centrality of impaired control is pointed out by Shaw (1979), who also demonstrates that the only firm evidence on which the syndrome rests is that pertaining to altered psychobiological state and reviewed by Gross (1977). The evidence for the altered behavioural and subjective states is either tenuous or entirely absent, and no evidence exists relating the increased tolerance and withdrawal phenomena of the altered psychobiological state to the other components. Therefore, the Alcohol Dependence Syndrome is a conception of abnormal drinking based primarily on psychobiological dependence with impaired control as its leading symptom. With the substitution of 'loss of control' for 'impaired control', how different is this from Jellinek's (1960) formulation? Shaw (1979) has argued that the syndrome idea was an attempt to find a particular kind of substitute concept for alcoholism – one which coped with all the critiques of the disease theory, yet retained all its major assumptions and implications.

SUMMARY

It will be recalled that this chapter on disease conceptions of alcoholism was undertaken primarily in order to provide a background for a coherent discussion of controlled drinking in alcoholics, the main subject matter of the book. We are now in a position to summarize the reasons why so many authorities in the field have expressed the view that total and lifelong abstinence is essential and normal or controlled drinking impossible in the true alcoholic. For this purpose it will be convenient to expand slightly on the three major beliefs underlying such a view described by Pattison, Sobell and Sobell (1977):

1. 'For those who believe that alcoholics have a biogenetic defect which makes them react differently to alcohol than nonalcoholics, a logical corollary belief is that the alcoholic will never be able to drink without encountering problems unless scientific research somehow discovers a method of reversing the defect.' This position is mainly associated with Alcoholics Anonymous but has had a profound influence on medical thinking. The alcoholic's pre-existing defect has also been thought of as an intractable personality disorder, although other psychological explanations of alcoholism are more optimistic about the possibility for change in the underlying neurotic disturbance.

2. 'For those who believe that, regardless of possible predisposing factors, alcoholics undergo a permanent physiological change as a result of chronic ingestion of alcohol, resumed drinking is also seen as logically impossible without discovering a means of identifying and reversing the physiological changes which have occurred.' This position is identified with conceptions of alcoholism which view its disease nature primarily in terms of physical dependence on alcohol, although in the most outstanding of these conceptions (Jellinek, 1952; 1960) the irreversibility of neurophysiological changes caused by excessive drinking is not explicitly endorsed. In the Alcohol Dependence Syndrome (Edwards and Gross, 1976) rapid re-instatement of physical dependence is said to occur in severely dependent persons, making abstinence necessary for recovery.

3. 'The belief, which is most represented in traditional notions, that alcoholics are never able to drink again appears to be due to the clinical experience of alcoholics and those in the helping professions who have known or worked with alcoholics.' As Pattison *et al*. suggest, this belief is based, not upon theory or research findings, but upon a received body of 'folk wisdom' in the alcoholism treatment field.

In the next two chapters we propose to review the scientific evidence which is relevant to these beliefs. In the immediately following chapter will be found a review of follow-up studies bearing on the question, whether some alcoholics *do* in fact successfully return to normal drinking. This evidence is most obviously relevant to belief 3 above. The subsequent chapter contains a review of experimental investigations of the related phenomena 'loss of control' and 'craving' and attempts to summarize the evidence which is relevant to the more theoretical content of beliefs 1 and 2 above. Although, as we have noted in the work of Jellinek (1960), the loss of control concept does not in itself necessarily imply the permanence of loss of control, in the way in which the dominant tradition in the disease theory has been received in treatment circles, especially if influenced by AA thinking, and in the way in which the disease theory has been popularized in the media, loss of control *is* regarded as permanent. Moreover, as we have pointed out several times, loss of control is the hallmark of dominant disease conceptions and marks that stage in the alcoholic's drinking career when the disease process sets in. Therefore, while loss of control does not logically imply an irreversible disease process, irreversibility always assumes loss of control.

2 Normal drinking in former alcoholics

One of the main lines of evidence responsible for undermining disease conceptions of alcoholism is the repeated finding that individuals who have been diagnosed as suffering from this disease have been able to return to drinking in a normal, controlled fashion. We intend in this chapter to review this evidence, beginning with the classic paper of D.L. Davies in 1962 and ending with the controversial, so-called Rand Report published in 1976, together with its follow-up report four years later.

Our reasons for conducting this review are twofold. Firstly, there still exist specialists in the alcoholism field who deny the validity of this evidence, chiefly on the ground that the individuals in question were not 'real' alcoholics. We shall therefore devote some attention to this crucial issue, as well as to other prominent criticisms which have been made of the evidence. Secondly, even if it is conceded that the question of normal drinking in former alcoholics is now beyond doubt, as we believe it is, there is still much to be gained from a study of papers reporting the phenomenon. They may shed light on such important further questions as, what is the nature of the control which is re-established, under what conditions is it most likely to develop, and, of most practical significance, what types of client are most likely to benefit from the controlled drinking treatment methods to be described later in the book. Note however that in this chapter we are concerned only with events following treatment directed at total abstinence and not with the results of treatment aimed deliberately at controlled drinking. There may be little difference between the modes of harmfree drinking arrived at by either of these routes, but this can be only a presumption at present. We will also include here evidence relating to the 'spontaneous' resumption of normal drinking in alcohol abusers who have experienced no treatment intervention whatever.

It should also be made clear that the review is not intended to be complete. One of the strongest arguments for the acceptance of resumed normal drinking is precisely that the number of papers in which it is described now precludes an exhaustive survey of all relevant scientific documents. At the latest count, Pattison, Sobell and Sobell (1977) listed seventy-four publications, including studies of controlled drinking treatment, and even this thorough search of the literature missed a few references. We have therefore decided to exclude all redundant findings and also to restrict attention to papers written in English, with the single exception of the important study by de Morsier and Feldman (1952).

Before embarking on the review, a few words about terminology may be in order. There continues to be some debate about what term is to be preferred for the kind of drinking which is at issue in this chapter. The words 'normal', 'controlled', 'social', 'moderate', 'limited', 'attenuated' and 'harm-free' have all been suggested at one time or another for a variety of reasons. We do indeed regard this debate as more than merely semantic since a number of empirical and conceptual issues are raised by it; we shall be discussing these issues later in the book (see p. 147) and will refer to them here only in passing. In the meantime it will be convenient to use the term employed by the authors whose work is being described. In other places we shall follow established custom by using the term 'normal' drinking to designate the consequences of abstinence-directed treatment, reserving 'controlled' drinking for the results of treatment programmes directed specifically to that end. But in this chapter the term 'normal' is not intended to convey any special connotations or theoretical implications. Similarly we have already used the phrase 'resumed normal drinking' as a shorthand way of referring to the phenomenon of normal drinking in ex-alcoholics. We are not unaware, however, that the drinking of many alcoholics has never been normal in quantity or quality and that, strictly speaking, the word 'resumed' is therefore a misnomer in many cases.

THE ORIGINAL CONTROVERSY

DAVIES' (1962) report of normal drinking in recovered alcohol addicts emerged as an unintended consequence of a follow-up study conducted at the Maudsley Hospital, London (Davies, Shepherd and Myers, 1956). A recent interview with Davies (1979) printed in the *British Journal of Addiction* reveals the unanticipated and almost accidental nature of the finding. What interests us here is that this is the hallmark of the anomalous discoveries which are said by Thomas Kuhn (1970) to herald the emergence of a new scientific paradigm. However, we shall deal more fully with this aspect of Davies' finding when we come to consider the wider implications of controlled drinking for the theory of alcoholism in Chapter 8. Here we may note that Davies was not especially interested in alcoholism at the time. Indeed, it is possible to speculate that had it not been for Davies' lack of specialization, which seems to have provided him with a degree of immunity from the therapeutic dogma of total abstinence, he might never have written his seminal paper. Ironically, before being accepted for publication in the *Quarterly Journal of Studies on Alcohol*, the paper was rejected by the *Lancet* as being of insufficient general interest!

In fact, Davies reported only seven male patients showing normal drinking out of a total of ninety-three followed up, but the importance of these seven cases in the history of alcoholism research and theory is out of all proportion to their number. All patients who had been treated for alcohol addiction prior to 1955 had been followed up routinely through outpatient attendances, contact by a social worker and correspondence with relatives. After scrutiny of these follow-up records, those individuals who appeared to show evidence of normal drinking were visited at home, and in some cases at work, and specific enquiries were made, from relatives as well as from the patient himself, about drinking history since discharge. Davies made clear in the title of his article that the patients in question were to be regarded as 'alcohol addicts', as defined by the WHO (1951) committee. In common with all other patients in the series, they showed the cardinal symptom of loss of control. The treatment directed against this addiction was a fairly standard package of disulfiram, discussions with the patient on an individual basis, and social work with relatives and others.

With regard to the duration of normal drinking, the shortest period before follow-up contact was seven years and the longest eleven, so it could hardly be claimed that normal drinking was merely ephemeral. Although not included in the original paper, it emerged later in discussion that all seven patients had achieved a period of complete abstinence, ranging from a few months to a year, before taking up normal drinking. We shall discover that the frequency and significance of these prior periods of abstinence are topics of some interest in this area of research. Davies did not attempt to establish any rigorous criteria for normal drinking but simply reported that his patients tended to take 'at the most three pints of beer each evening . . . and smaller quantities in other cases'. One drank only at Christmas or with meals when on holiday abroad. Interestingly, this patient continued to take disulfiram on business trips, suggesting that even after ten years he felt the need to be on his guard against excessive drinking in certain dangerous situations. However, despite this particular patient's obvious wariness, Davies subsequently described the drinking of all seven as 'comfortable', implying presumably that there was no evidence of craving for larger amounts after a few drinks. The most compelling evidence for the harmfree nature of drinking was the fact that none of the patients had been drunk during the seven to eleven years which had elapsed since discharge from treatment, although Davies did not provide any definition of drunkenness and also did not state to what extent this information was authenticated by collateral accounts. Assuming it to be accurate, this suggests that patients *were* on guard against a possible relapse into abusive drinking since occasional episodes of intoxication must be regarded as part of 'normal', in the sense of typical drinking behaviour. Certainly, if drinking was veritably 'comfortable', one would expect at least one episode of intoxication in the course of seven years or more. Apart from drinking behaviour itself, Davies stated that all patients had improved in terms of employment, family relationships and social adjustment.

In an attempt to delineate factors which might be seen as contributing to control over drinking, Davies noted that four of his sample had followed advice originally given during treatment to change from high-risk alcoholism occupations, such as publican, merchant seaman, crane driver in a liquor warehouse and regular army officer, to those with a lower risk attached to them. In two other cases domestic problems which had been regarded at the time of admission as contributing to the development of addiction had been resolved. However, in both cases, anxiety symptoms had persisted although abnormal drinking had disappeared. More generally, Davies affirmed that nothing had been done which might have been expected to bring about far-reaching personality changes in these patients.

Davies can scarcely have anticipated the reaction to his brief and cautiously worded scientific report. A measure of the interest aroused is that the *Quarterly Journal of Studies on Alcohol* subsequently published an unprecedented seventeen commentaries from alcoholism experts throughout the world. The great majority of these were highly critical. The controversy also found its way into the popular press which added appreciably to the warmth of the debate. The major criticisms may be divided into four types and will be closely examined because they introduce recurring themes in the research literature on resumed normal drinking.

1. Several commentators were adamant that in many years of practice they had never encountered a 'true' alcoholic who had recovered the ability to drink normally. An example of what Selzer (1963) described at the time as an 'almost reflex rejection' is the statement of Williams (1963): 'In many years of clinical experience I have not yet met an alcoholic – a true addict that is – who has regained control and retained it without complete abstinence.' These critics then went on to argue that if the patients observed by Davies had genuinely recovered control over drinking, then they could not have been genuine alcoholics in the first place. Lemere (1963) even went so far as to propose that the inability ever to drink again in a normal, controlled manner should be made a defining requirement of alcoholism; any previously diagnosed alcoholic whose subsequent behaviour ran counter to this rule should be reclassified as, by definition, a pseudo-alcoholic. This attempt to solve the problem by fiat ignored the warning against logical circularity of argument in this context previously issued by Armstrong (1963).

Less illogical were those critics of Davies who stressed his reliance on the WHO definition of alcoholism, which had indeed been subject to a severe analytical mauling by Seeley (1959). For one thing, the definition allowed the inclusion into the category of 'alcoholic' individuals who were best described as habitual excessive drinkers, rather than alcohol addicts as such. It was pointed out that only one of Davies' case histories contained a mention of delirium tremens and even in this case the presence of the symptom was not based on direct observation. Davies had empahsized the feature of loss of control in establishing addiction to alcohol, but Williams

(1963) maintained that this was not enough to warrant the diagnosis in the absence of other components, most importantly the occurrence of withdrawal symptoms. Esser (1963) agreed that loss of control was the crucial defining characteristic of alcohol addiction but insisted that this referred to the inability to stop drinking after the first ingestion of alcohol, rather than the inability to refrain from drinking in the first instance which was more prominent in the case histories presented by Davies. A further line of argument was that the seven patients showed drinking which was symptomatic of some underlying and pre-existent psychological disturbance and should therefore be classified under Jellinek's (1960) scheme as alpha alcoholics, as opposed to the true addicts, i.e. gamma and delta alcoholics; it was not uncommon to find normal drinking in alpha alcoholics after the underlying disturbance had ameliorated but this was hardly a reason, so it was argued, to revise one's basic conception of alcoholism.

Davies replied to these criticisms by pointing out that the WHO definition of alcohol addiction does not demand the presence of withdawal symptoms. 'In practice one feels satisfied that a man is addicted to alcohol when he has tried to break off his use of the drug, which in some way is proving harmful, but has failed' (Davies, 1963). The seven patients showing normal drinking were in no way different in respect of this addiction than the remainder of the sample and evidence of the serious level of the problems caused by alcohol in the treatment sample as a whole might be gathered from the finding of Kessel and Grossman (1961) that 8 per cent had committed suicide within a few years of discharge. As for the claim that the seven had been symptomatic alcohol abusers, Davies replied that this was simply not borne out by the case records. Although the presence of anxiety symptoms in two of the patients has already been noted, Davies had been careful to point out that this had contributed towards the establishment of *addiction*. The most important outcome of this phase of the debate is the conclusion that, whether or not they fitted the WHO definition of alcohol addiction and whether or not this definition is a useful one, the normal drinkers described by Davies were unlikely to have experienced severe withdrawal symptoms.

2. A second sort of criticism was to claim that, although Davies' seven patients may have been genuine alcoholics, they were not genuine normal drinkers. For example, Smith (1963) suggested that, unlike ordinary social drinkers, these patients would have to engage in a great battle with themselves to stop drinking at the end of an evening. We have already noted Davies' reply that drinking in these cases was 'comfortable', but we have also encountered grounds for supposing that some of the normal drinkers felt the need to be on guard against excessive drinking. From a somewhat different point of view, Kjolstad (1963) argued that alcoholics might be able to consume amounts below a certain threshold level without losing control, but

that this was merely 'nibbling' which failed to satisfy them; if they ever exceed their level and began to 'feel' their drink again, they would once more lose control. Thus Kjolstad was suspicious of the normal drinking described by Davies because the amounts reported were too low. A similar idea was later advanced by Glatt (1967). At the other extreme, one sometimes hears it claimed that normal drinking ex-alcoholics are simply concealing the amounts they consume and are in reality still drinking abusively. In the interview with Davies (1979) mentioned above, the interviewer alleged that one of Davies' original seven patients had been well known among local treatment personnel as a notorious liar. Although it is inconceivable that all descriptions of resumed normal drinking ever recorded are based on false information, the problem of underreporting of drinking consumption is a serious one and will crop up again in this chapter.

3. A further somewhat obvious criticism claimed that normal drinking in former alcoholics was simply a prelude to a full relapse. In spite of the fact that the periods of normal drinking had lasted for a minimum of seven years, Tiebout (1963), passing on the views of his alcoholic patients, was able to write: 'Unanimously they say that no matter how long they might be drinking normally again, they could never overcome the fear that their control might slip and that they would be plunged once more into the rat-race of their alcoholism.' This introduces the recurring issue of the stability of resumed normal drinking.

4. The last sort of criticism, sometimes made by the same authors who had denied that the seven patients had been real alcoholics, was to insist that the phenomenon of resumed normal drinking was, in the words of Thimann (1963), 'a freak anomaly of human biochemistry or psychopathology', and therefore of no clinical or theoretical importance. In an excessively literal interpretation of the disease model of alcoholism, Block (1963) and Thimann (1963) employed the identical analogy of spontaneous remission in cases of cancer; although such 'miracle cures' sometimes occur they can have no possible significance for treatment. At this juncture it is relevant to point out an error made by several contributors to the debate. This was to assume that the remaining eighty-six cases in the series were all successes, an assumption which had the effect of reducing the numerical significance of the seven normal drinkers. In fact, at the two-year follow-up reported by Davies, Shepherd and Myers (1956), 31 out of 50 of these discharges had already returned to drinking. Thus, expressed as a proportion of all successfully treated patients, the normal drinkers amount to 17 per cent at the very least, a figure of immediate clinical relevance. The question of the comparative rarity of resumed normal drinking will be another recurrent theme of this review.

In addition to the four types of substantive criticism of the paper, nearly all commentators expressed anxiety lest abstinent former alcoholics should come to hear of the reported findings and take it upon themselves to experiment with alcohol once more to see if they too could drink normally, with probably disastrous consequences. As would be expected, Davies in his reply was most sympathetic to this concern but reminded his readers that in the original article he had written that all patients should be told to aim for total abstinence. Thus Davies had not envisaged at this time, and certainly was not recommending, any change in treatment goal on the basis of his results. He also maintained, quite correctly, that although communications to scientific journals might be reported in the press with unwelcome repercussions, this could never be an argument for suppressing clinical findings. In this connection Selzer (1963) recounted that, when he had reported that confirmed alcoholics could become social drinkers (Selzer and Holloway, 1957), he had been virtually ordered by the body who had provided funding for his research to omit these 'embarrassing' findings.

While on the subject of the work of D.L. Davies, it will be convenient to consider some later evidence collected at the Maudsley Hospital. DAVIES, SCOTT AND MALHERBE (1969) addressed themselves to the criticism that the seven patients previously described had been only mildly addicted or not very severely affected by alcohol. Once more using the WHO definition of alcoholism, these authors observed that only in cases of 'alcoholism proper' were mental complications consequent to excessive alcohol intake said to arise. They than described four patients who all showed the development of a severe mental illness, namely alcoholic psychosis. Three were cases of alcoholic hallucinosis and the remaining illness, which had occurred twenty-seven years in the past, was rediagnosed as a severe episode of delirium tremens. Like the original seven, these four patients all showed evidence of very moderate drinking habits and no current problems caused by alcohol, the longest period of normal drinking being fully twenty-seven years. In three instances a major change in life situation had accompanied the return to normal drinking, an observation which echoed the suggested importance of this factor in Davies' earlier report.

Brief mention may also be made of a further report by DAVIES (1969) in which he described four ex-alcohol addicts encountered on a visit to Finland. These four men were remarkable for having formed a self-help group devoted to resumed normal drinking, which they called the 'Polar Bears', after each had spent from five and a half to fourteen years in total abstinence. They had formulated their ideas without being influenced by Davies' (1962) paper. In order to demonstrate a real independence from alcohol, two of these men had deliberately tried the effect of getting drunk, but had found it to be merely an unrewarding experience they had no desire to repeat. They had not been precipitated into a drinking bout. The other two men were somewhat different in that they became drunk with friends about five or six times a year, again without ever continuing into a bout. However, Davies discusses the possibility that these two individuals were still vulnerable to loss of control over drinking and it would be of great interest to know what subsequently became of them. Davies also speculates in this paper that some resumed normal drinkers, of the type who imbibe nearly every day, are more accurately described as 'stabilized addicts' who remain physically dependent on small but regular amounts of alcohol without disruption to their lives. In order to confirm this hypothesis it would of course be necessary to demonstrate that withdrawal of alcohol caused noticeable discomfort in such persons.

STUDIES BEFORE DAVIES

As Davies (1962) himself made clear, he was not the first to report the phenomenon of normal drinking in former alcoholics. The reason why his paper caused such a fuss when earlier publications had not is probably that he was the first to devote a complete paper to the topic and therefore the first to draw attention to it in the title. It may also be the case, as Reinert and Bowen (1968) have suggested, that the article appeared at a time when the disease model of alcoholism was just about to achieve widespread public acceptance and that the notion of irreversibility was a crucial element in the promotion of the disease concept.

Whatever the reason for their neglect at the time, we now intend to review briefly the more important reports of resumed normal drinking appearing before Davies wrote. At the outset, however, it is necessary to make a distinction between resumed normal drinking as such and the frequently employed outcome category of 'drinking but improved'. For example, in a follow-up study of hospital treatment, Wall and Allen (1944) noticed nineteen patients who were managing better than before treatment but who had carried on drinking. These men were gainfully employed but, in the opinion of the authors, continued to struggle with their drinking problems. This paper has been cited (e.g. Miller and Munoz, 1976) as an early report of resumed normal drinking but, lacking more detailed information, it must be assumed that at least some of these patients continued to show behavioural impairment as a result of drinking. In order for drinking to qualify for consideration as normal, in other words, it is necessary to provide *prima facie* evidence of the absence of impairment. It may nevertheless be true that, in papers where the necessary distinction is not made, many examples of genuine normal drinking are buried in the 'drinking but improved' category.

Perhaps the first report of resumed normal drinking proper may be credited to HARPER AND HICKSON (1951), although it is very unlikely that these authors were aware of the significance of their findings. In a follow-up of eighty-four patients treated at the Crichton Royal Hospital, Dumfries, sixteen were classified as 'much improved' after a minimum of two years. This group included complete abstainers, patients with one relapse only, and also those who 'at the most have consumed only very small quantities of alcohol'. From this description it is safe to assume that these patients were drinking in a harmfree fashion, although the precise number is not given.

A much more important study from the present perspective was reported by DE MORSIER AND FELDMAN (1952) from France. These authors followed up 500 cases treated roughly five years previously with apomorphine and found 76, or 15 per cent, to be drinking socially. The subjects drank an occasional glass of wine or beer with meals and the presumption is that they did so because they feared looking eccentric in the context of pervasive French drinking customs. De Morsier and Feldman surmise that social drinking was possible for these subjects because they had arrived at a clear conception of the noxiousness of alcohol for them.

Employing the unusual method of asking current alcoholic patients for information about their alcoholic relatives, LEMERE (1953) analysed the life histories of 500 deceased alcoholics. He found a group of about 10 per cent who had moderated their drinking to the extent that, at the time of death, it had not been a problem for many years. In the majority of these cases, moderation had been achieved by increasingly long intervals of abstinence between bouts of drinking, but in fourteen cases, 3 per cent of the total sample, 'the amount and the degree of intoxication abated to the point of normal drinking'.

The only detailed single-case study of a normal drinking ex-alcoholic in the literature is provided by SHEA (1954) who reported on a 50-year old lawyer under treatment in psychoanalysis. This man had drunk constantly in enormous quantities over a 20-year period, had been hospitalized four times for acute alcoholism and once for a severe attack of alcohol-induced peripheral neuropathy. However, ten years before seeing Shea, he had stopped drinking entirely, quite independently of any professional assistance, and had maintained total sobriety for five years. He had then decided to drink in moderation, a pattern which he had also successfully maintained for the further five years preceding his contact with the author. He drank on average two bottles of beer or two glasses of wine per day. When on a single occasion he had exceeded these rough limits to the extent of four or five glasses of sherry, he had at once become alarmed and hurried to eat until the effect of the extra dosage had worn off. He never trusted himself to drink spirits.

It is unfortunate that Shea does not describe, or speculate upon, the factors which were influential in persuading his patient to move from abstinence to moderate drinking. Nevertheless, this report contains several interesting features. It is important to note that neither of the changes in drinking behaviour achieved by the patient appear to have had any connection with his extreme neurotic unhappiness, which is vividly described by Shea. The years of abstinence as well as of moderation were years of 'desolation, frustration and spiritual agony', and it was for this reason that he sought Shea's help, not because of any lingering doubts about his drinking. It would seem that, for this patient, radical changes in drinking pattern could occur on the level of habitual behaviour without any changes in personality organization, degree of emotional maturity or, indeed, any other possible target of psychotherapeutic intervention being required or instituted. This is reminiscent of Davies' (1962) remarks about the independence of resumed normal drinking from personality change.

Despite his patient's remarkable achievement in autonomously solving a severe drinking problem in this particular way, Shea saw no reason to revise his conception of alcoholism. He reasoned that recovery from the disease occurs only with the substitution of one obsession for another; the obsession with being drunk is replaced by an obsession with being sober, as in the case of successful membership of Alcoholics Anonymous. He concluded that an analogous obsession was necessary for the occurrence of resumed normal drinking in those very few alcoholics for whom it was possible. The validity of this view is clearly related to the degree to which normal drinking is regarded as 'comfortable' or as requiring constant vigilance by the former alcoholic.

NORVIG AND NIELSON (1956) followed up a series of alcoholics who had received inpatient treatment at a hospital in Copenhagen. Follow-up commenced from about three to five years after discharge and was effected by a staff of social workers, although some patients had personal interviews with the psychiatrist authors. The results are notable for the extremely high proportion of normal drinkers encountered. Of the 114 patients for whom complete information was available, no fewer than half stated that they drank occasionally at social gatherings. This may be compared with the 37 patients who said they were total abstainers. It is also interesting that 16 of the normal drinkers said they continued to use disulfiram from time to time, although unfortunately no information is provided about the circumstances which led to the use of this precaution. As regards drinking behaviour itself, no details of quantity or frequency are given but patients are described as drinking 'not more than is compatible with attention to their work and, in most cases, with preservation of their social status'.

The high proportion of normal drinkers recorded by Norvig and Nielson should be interpreted with caution. Firstly, if account is taken of patients who had died since discharge, those who could not be contacted, and those for whom only partial information was available, the proportion of normal drinkers is reduced significantly. Of the 221 patients in the total sample, normal drinkers amount to 26 per cent. Secondly, it is probable that some of the normal drinkers had a poor outcome in terms of social criteria, since the number of subjects reported as having good or fair outcomes is less than the total previously given for normal drinkers and abstainers combined.

Despite these reservations, it is impossible to dispute Norvig and Nielson's own general conclusion that they had seen alcoholic patients who had been able to revert to moderate drinking without overindulgence and in a resocialized existence. It is also tempting to conjecture why such a large number of normal drinkers was discovered in this follow-up even after allowances have been made for exaggeration. Norvig and Nielson do describe a Danish organization which is said to be similar in some ways to Alcoholics Anonymous, but it is very likely that the abstinence treatment ideology was less influential and pervasive in Denmark at that time than in the United States and, to a lesser extent, Britain. Thus the occurrence of normal drinking following alcoholism may have been a less unexpected eventuality, both to psychiatrists in reflecting upon their outcome results and to patients in making their drinking decisions, as Kendell (1965) has also suggested.

PFEFFER AND BERGER (1957) followed up 169 alcoholics who had been referred by industry to a specially designed programme consisting of out-patient group and individual psychotherapy. Only 60 patients co-operated with follow-up which took place at a minimum of one year after discharge; 48 had been abstinent for at least a year, reflecting the good prognosis of patients with high levels of job stability. An additional seven patients (12 per cent) were classified as 'changed-pattern alcoholics' who 'while continuing to drink, showed notable positive change, in the sense of drinking less or in a less pathological manner'.

The most useful pre-Davies account of resumed normal drinking was provided by SELZER AND HOLLOWAY (1957). These authors describe the patients in their sample specifically as alcohol addicts, who displayed 'uncontrollable craving for alcohol' before entering treatment; follow-up was conducted at a reassuring interval of six years after discharge; and this report is the first, apart from Shea's (1954) single-case study, to include case histories of normal drinking ex-alcoholics. Selzer and Holloway were also the first to use the finding of resumed normal drinking to challenge conventional wisdom in the alcoholism field when they wrote: 'The fact that . . . patients were able to return to social or non-pathological drinking seems to warrant a second look at the long-cherished theory that no alcoholic can ever become a moderate drinker.'

Ninety-eight alcoholics who had received treatment in a state hospital in Michigan, USA during 1948/49 were contacted six years later and interviewed where available by a social worker. Relatives were also interviewed if possible. Adequate data were obtained for eighty-three patients and these constituted the follow-up sample. In the main successful outcome group, 22 per cent of this sample were found to have been abstinent since discharge, but a second successful outcome classification contained sixteen patients (19 per cent) who 'drank small amounts or intermittently, with good adjustment'. These sixteen could be further subdivided into twelve patients who were said to drink smaller amounts than before treatment, and four who drank only somewhat less but at much longer intervals than in the past. It is possible that only the first twelve were genuine normal drinkers although we are assured that all patients in the outcome group made a definitely adequate post-hospital adjustment.

Case histories are given for five patients, including one who drank heavily for three years following discharge but subsequently reduced her intake. Three are described as drinking small quantities of beer, never more than twelve bottles a week, and two were whisky drinkers with a maximum consumption of one pint per week. In two of the five cases there was a period of abstinence of a year or more before drinking was taken up again. We are not told how typical this was among the remaining patients, but it clearly was not universal. One patient attributed his success to having learned how to avoid stressful jobs, while another, who is said to have been highly unusual in this respect, credited the insight he had gained in contacts with professional helpers during treatment. The only major criticism which can be made of this report, with the benefit of hindsight, is that Selzer and Holloway did not use their extensive data to compare pre-treatment characteristics of abstainers and normal drinkers.

Finally in this section, MOORE AND RAMSEUR (1960) followed up 100 male, gamma alcoholic war veterans who had received psychoanalytically oriented psychotherapy in an open-ward setting. Follow-up was conducted an average of three and a half years after discharge, with a range of less than one year to over six years. Twenty-three patients were found to have been drinking less than at admission to hospital, compared with fifteen who were abstinent. No details are given but it is clear that not all of these patients were actually drinking in a completely harmfree fashion. Moore and Ramseur also classified their sample in terms of overall adjustment, including such factors as level of insight, general control of behaviour, marital adjustment, and reduction of symptoms other than abusive drinking. Here we are informed that, of the fourteen most improved patients at follow-up, five were 'well-controlled social drinkers'. In contrast to this finding, six of the fifteen who were abstinent at follow-up were rated as only slightly improved in overall adjustment. This observation introduced for the first time the notion that normal drinking may have certain advantages over total abstinence as a goal of treatment for some individuals and this issue will be returned to in Chapter 4.

CORROBORATIVE EVIDENCE

After the immediate controversy surrounding Davies' (1962) paper had subsided, it was to be expected that other researchers would direct their attention towards the crucially important question of normal drinking in former alcoholics. Indeed, in the next five or six years a handful of articles appeared which thoroughly explored and essentially corroborated the main implications of the original finding.

The first of these papers was that of KENDELL (1965), reporting research which had also been carried out at the Maudsley Hospital. An important difference from Davies' work, however, was that Kendell's subjects had not received any treatment before regaining, or acquiring for the first time, the ability to drink within normal limits. The four persons he described were found among a group of sixty-two men and women who had been referred by their general practitioners or psychiatrists but who had not been admitted as inpatients to the hospital, either because they refused treatment or were considered unsuitable. Neither did they receive any outpatient treatment beyond an initial assessment interview. Each of the four was subsequently seen by Kendell himself for a prolonged interview and in three cases the wives were also seen and detailed histories obtained from them. In the other case the husband of the ex-alcoholic endorsed her account by letter. Thus good collateral evidence was available for self-reports of drinking behaviour.

Kendell's article is of great theoretical importance because it was the first to provide a clear resolution of some of the ambiguities in Davies' paper. In the first place, there can be no doubt that all four subjects had experienced very severe problems through drinking. They had all drunk very large quantities over considerable periods of time and had managed to inflict substantial damage on their lives. More germanely, however, there can also be no doubt that they were true alcohol addicts or, in Jellinek's (1960) terminology, gamma alcoholics. Using the features of gamma alcoholism listed by Jellinek, Kendell pointed out that all four showed a clear history of dependence on alcohol, as witnessed by repeated attempts, and failures, to reduce drinking and by presumptive evidence of increased tissue tolerance for alcohol; they all reported the occurrence of withdrawal symptoms, including visual and auditory hallucinations and early morning drinking; lastly, they all showed unambiguous evidence of loss of control over drinking, in the sense of being unable to stop once they had started. The one individual who gave less than perfect evidence of withdrawal symptoms was the one who gave the clearest account of loss of control. Thus, criticisms which were made of the case histories offered by Davies with regard to lack of definite evidence of pharmacological addiction could not be directed against the cases reported by Kendell.

The quantities currently consumed by Kendell's normal drinkers tended to be very small and were similar in this respect to those reported by Davies' patients. However, one was able to get drunk perhaps twice a year on festive occasions without losing control. This man had been a classic bout drinker who, once started, had gone on to drink for days on end until either he or his money were completely exhausted. We may recall Kjolstad's (1963) argument that alcohol addicts who have become normal drinkers are only able to drink quantities below a certain threshold, because if they were to exceed this threshold they would once more lose control. This may be true of some resumed normal drinkers but the case described by Kendell shows that it was possible for this former gamma alcoholic to become intoxicated very occasionally without losing control over drinking. The duration of normal drinking reported was between three and eight years. Kendell stressed that normal drinking was not done merely to keep up appearances, as was the impression of de Morsier and Feldman (1952), but was actively enjoyed by his informants.

When it came to finding common features among the four cases in the manner in which they had achieved control, Kendell admitted himself frankly puzzled, since each case appeared unique. Nevertheless, each history contained something of interest. The first case was a woman who had never drunk normally since her teens. She first achieved abstinence by attending AA meetings but then joined Jehovah's Witnesses whose teaching apparently is that alcoholism is not a disease but simply a loss of self-control which may be regained with divine help. It seems that the normal drinking here was buttressed by devotion to a religious sect which did not happen to regard abstinence as necessary to a good life. It may be that this woman's avoidance of further excessive drinking was founded on the same kind of emotional commitment and social support as provided by Alcoholics Anonymous, but with the target of normal drinking instead of abstinence.

The second case, the former bout drinker already mentioned, was unusual for displaying a specific aversion to whisky after the disappearance of his drinking bouts. Whisky had been his drink of choice during binges. This phenomenon is also described by Quinn and Henbest (1967) (see p. 45), with the difference that the aversion in Kendell's subject arose naturally without therapeutic intervention. Another interesting feature of this case was that there was no period of abstinence between abusive and normal drinking; rather, the frequency of bouts simply decreased until they eventually disappeared altogether. This lack of a period of abstinence was also shown by another of Kendell's cases who never attempted to stop drinking completely. The chief aid to resumed control here may have been a change of job and a consequent escape from a group of regular drinking cronies. The remaining case showed a feature of great interest. This man had been abstinent for two years while in contact with Alcoholics Anonymous, when he attempted a drink at an office Christmas party. He promptly got drunk, thus confirming all the worst fears which must have been voiced by his AA colleagues about the dangers of attempting to drink socially when one is an alcoholic. Yet this man went on from this, without any further extended period of abstinence, to regain control. In other words, the 'loss of control' evinced by this man when he first attempted to drink within normal limits was not a permanent property of his future drinking behaviour.

To summarize the evidence presented by Kendell, he described four untreated alcoholics, three of whom were undoubtedly and one probably gamma alcoholics or alcohol addicts. Despite frequent failures to control their drinking in the past, all four had managed by various means to achieve a state of normal drinking which had lasted for at least three years. The harmfree nature of this drinking was confirmed by spouses. An estimate of the incidence of resumed normal drinking in untreated alcoholics provided by this research is four out of a total sample of sixty-two and, thus, it would still be possible to argue that it was a comparatively rare occurrence.

Untreated alcoholics were also the focus of an influential paper by BAILEY AND STEWART (1967). The subjects in this study were originally identified as part of a community health survey in New York. In the first phase of the survey conducted in 1960–1, questions concerning difficulties in living associated with drinking were asked of all respondents. Those presumed alcoholics thus identified were re-interviewed during 1963–4 when additional items regarding frequency and quantity of alcohol consumed were included, together with further items comparing past and present drinking and reasons for changes. Of the ninety-one respondents who acknowledged past or current problem-drinking in this second round of interviews, thirteen appeared to be persons with previous drinking problems who were now drinking in a normal manner and a third interview schedule was designed to investigate this putative normal drinking in more detail. At all three stages of Bailey and Stewart's procedure spouses were interviewed at the same time and it was therefore possible to arrive at a good estimate of the validity of each subject's responses. Indeed, subjects were included in the final normal drinking phase of the research only if the spouse agreed in the second interview that problems connected with drinking were no longer present.

A significant advance made in Bailey and Stewart's study of resumed normal drinking was that it was the first to use an objective criterion for moderate consumption. Moreover, in contrast to previous investigations in which the researcher had decided on a *post hoc* basis whether or not a subject's drinking could be described as normal, a method which is obviously open to unconscious bias on the part of the investigator, in Bailey and Stewart's research the rules for normal drinking were set out beforehand, using an adaptation of Mulford and Miller's (1960) quantity–frequency index. To be considered moderate drinkers, subjects had to drink less than twice a week or, if they drank two or more times a week, they had to drink no more than five glasses or three bottles of beer, two drinks containing spirits or three glasses of wine on each drinking occasion.

The thirteen respondents identified in the second round of interviews were eventually narrowed down to six who were judged to be definite cases of normal drinking in former alcoholics, the other seven being eliminated for various reasons. In maintaining that these remaining subjects had been definite cases of alcoholism, Bailey and Stewart appealed to Keller's (1960) much quoted definition of it as 'a chronic disease manifested by repeated implicative drinking so as to cause injury to the drinker's health or to his social or economic functioning'. The case sketches presented all clearly conformed to this definition, being typical chronicles of the tragic consequences of alcohol problems lasting from seven to twenty years. Moreover, all histories contained subjective evidence of loss of control, again defined by Keller as meaning that 'whenever an alcoholic starts to drink it is not certain that he will be able to stop at will'. However, Bailey and Stewart explicitly state that they cannot demonstrate the presence of addiction in the pharmacological sense; in only one case is morning relief drinking mentioned and there are no instances of delirium tremens. In this respect the cases presented by Bailey and Stewart are akin to those of Davies (1962), but unlike those of Kendell (1965) in which pharmacological addiction was conclusively established.

The six cases described include the now familiar mixture of those where normal drinking was preceded by periods of abstinence, varying in these examples from eighteen months to three years, and those in which there was no such hiatus. Normal drinking quantities given are light and, as we have noted, strictly consistent with an objective index of moderate consumption. Two subjects reported getting occasionally 'high', but with no adverse consequences. In one case the respondent continued to perceive herself as vulnerable to abusive drinking, a verdict which was endorsed by her husband. The duration of normal drinking ranged from two and a half to more than twenty years. Five respondents still preferred the same beverage as in their alcoholic pasts, but one had changed from beer to whisky because he feared losing control on beer.

In discussing reasons why control over drinking had been re-established, Bailey and Stewart make the useful distinction between causes and accompaniments of reduced drinking. In all six cases there was a noticeable change in the circumstances under which drinking took place; more precisely, drinking was now done at home or in the homes of friends whereas it had previously taken place in bars. Similarly, all six respondents reported losing contact with former drinking companions and, in the majority of cases, making new friends who were not excessive drinkers. Thus, it is easy to see how aspects of the normal drinkers' social environments encouraged the maintenance of moderate drinking and mitigated against abusive drinking. However, these factors can hardly be claimed to be causes of recovered control since it is clear from these accounts that they followed upon a prior decision to cut down drinking; rather, they were accompaniments or consequences of resumed normal drinking. On the other hand, factors such as the change to a less vulnerable occupation which also occurred in three of Bailey and Stewart's cases, appear to have happened before the attempt at control began and might therefore have had some contributory causative effect. The same is true of the good marriages which seem to have been decisive for a further two subjects. As the authors point out, however, many alcoholics experience changes of job or marital status without this affecting the magnitude of their drinking. Although radical changes in life-style which have been shown to precede recovered control over drinking may well be necessary for resumed drinking to occur in many cases, they are clearly not sufficient conditions for change.

Before leaving Bailey and Stewart's paper it is worth noting that two of their respondents were already elderly before alcoholismic drinking was finally terminated. Both these men described their current reaction to alcohol in a way which implied that they were unable to consume sufficient quantities to get drunk without first feeling weak or stuporous. Drinking appears to have been reduced simply because the object of the exercise, an active state of drunkenness, had become unattainable owing to advancing years. It is likely that these two men were illustrations of the tapering off frequently found in elderly alcoholics and discussed by Drew (1968). They should therefore be regarded as representing a special category of normal drinking in former alcoholics.

Further corroborative evidence for Davies' finding emerged from a study by PATTISON, HEADLEY, GLESER AND GOTTSCHALK (1968) which examined the subject of normal drinking in a methodologically more sophisticated fashion than had been employed in any previous research. Apart from a straightforward attempt to investigate the claim for the existence of resumed normal drinking, Pattison *et al.*'s study was the first to aim at a direct comparison of normal drinkers with successful abstainers. We intend to devote a later section of the present chapter to a comparison of the pre-treatment characteristics of the two outcomes and will therefore postpone a consideration of this aspect of Pattison *et al.*'s results. Moreover, in Chapter 4 we shall present a comparison of various outcome measures between abstainers and normal drinkers in order to answer the question whether, when adjustment is viewed in a wider, multidimensional context, normal drinking appears to sustain as adequate an overall adjustment as abstinence. We shall therefore confine attention here to the direct evidence for resumed normal drinking.

The sample studied was drawn from the population of all alcoholic patients who had been discharged from an outpatient clinic during a certain period in 1962–3 and was confined to 'improved' patients in order to maximize the number of successful abstainers and normal drinkers appearing at follow-up. A minimum of ten therapy sessions was an additional criterion for selection and follow-up was also restricted to patients who had been discharged for at least a year. Excluding those who could not be interviewed for any reason, the final sample consisted of thirty-two male alcoholics.

Drinking behaviour at outcome was assessed by means of a specially devised Drinking Status Scale and, although there are several criticisms which can be made of this scale as presented in Pattison *et al.*'s paper, this method of defining what is to count as normal drinking constitutes in principle a further point of progress in this area. As in Bailey and Stewart's work, the definition of normal drinking here was objective and decided upon before the outcome data were inspected. It improved on Bailey and Stewart's definition by including components of drinking behaviour beyond mere quantity and frequency. Pattison *et al.* also state that a crucial component of what they wish to call normal drinking has been omitted from their scale, presumably because it cannot be operationalized in behavioural terms, namely, the motivation for and meaning of drinking. Whether or not this last point is taken, the concept of normal drinking was usefully widened and enriched in this paper.

More corroborative evidence appearing during the 1960s was supplied by REINERT AND BOWEN (1968). These authors interviewed a sample of 156 alcoholic patients one year after hospital treatment and found four to be social drinkers. This was defined as 'using some form of alcohol more or less regularly in the company of other persons without losing control, getting drunk or having any other of the previously associated problems'. From the case histories provided it is clear that one of these social drinkers had not been an alcohol addict, but in the three other cases problems caused by alcohol were much more serious and there was evidence of loss of control.

The main interest in Reinert and Bowen's paper lies in their discussion of the nature of the drinking engaged in by former alcoholics. In distinguishing between 'normal' drinking and 'controlled' drinking, they write:

> A normal drinker imbibes alcoholic beverages on occasion with the knowledge and complete confidence that well before he gets into any trouble he will have simply lost his appetite for more. In contrast, the controlled drinker has no such feeling of security and has learned from past experience the bottomless pit that may sometimes be opened by the taking of a few drinks. He must be on guard. The controlled drinker must choose carefully and even compulsively the time, the place, and the circumstances of drinking, and he must rigidly limit the amount he drinks.

It was because of the special meanings they wished to attach to the concepts of 'normal' and 'controlled' drinking that Reinert and Bowen chose the neutral term 'social' drinking at the outset of their enquiry. However, their three ex-alcohol addicts were obviously controlled drinkers in Reinert and Bowen's sense since they reported being very careful of the circumstances under which they attempted social drinking. Never drinking alone and always drinking just before or during a meal are examples of the strategies employed by these patients. It is also clear that some other cases described in the literature were also controlled drinkers in this particular sense, for instance the single case discussed by Shea (1954). On the other hand, several instances of moderate drinking have been described in which infrequent episodes of intoxication could occur on special occasions without loss of control being reinstated (e.g. Kendell, 1965; Bailey and Stewart, 1967; Davies, 1969). Perhaps these were examples of normal drinkers proper in terms of Reinert and Bowen's distinction, although it is clearly implied by them that this mode of drinking is never possible for alcoholic addicts. It is unfortunately impossible to reach a more definite conclusion about the proportions of 'controlled' and 'normal' drinkers reported in the literature in the absence of specific information about the ways in which the ex-alcoholic perceives his situation and some estimate of the degree of anxiety he continues to experience when engaged in limited drinking. Phenomenological enquiries could be usefully directed to this end in future.

It is worth remarking here that Reinert and Bowen's distinction is similar to that made by Pattison *et al.* (1968) between those normal drinkers for whom the meaning and function of alcohol use has changed and those for whom it has not. Both sets of authors refer to the work of CAIN (1964) who, in a book which is mainly a polemic against Alcoholics Anonymous, speaks of *recovered* alcoholics as distinct from *arrested* alcoholics. The recovered alcoholic does not drink because he does not want to drink and he experiences no desire to become intoxicated. The arrested alcoholic, on the other hand, has never lost his desire to get drunk and succeeds merely in managing to avoid doing so. It is only the recovered alcoholic who is able to drink normally again, precisely because he has no strong desire to feel the effects of alcohol. The arrested alcoholic, Cain concludes, can never return to normal drinking because his life still revolves around alcohol even though he does not drink. Cain referred in his book to four recovered alcoholics who had regained the ability to drink small quantities of alcohol and who did not wish to feel any differently after having done so. He also suggested that there must be a minimum period of two years 'creative sobriety', that is of total abstinence, before normal drinking could be attempted. Reinert and Bowen also regarded an extended period of abstinence as essential to a subsequent resumption of social drinking.

The fact that they were able to find only three examples of social drinking in ex-alcohol addicts justified Reinert and Bowen in concluding that the phenomenon was a rare event, particularly when compared with the 20 per cent of successfully abstinent patients at one-year follow-up. It should be noted however that this proportion of normal drinkers is one of the lowest recorded in the relevant literature. Reinert and Bowen also commented that, when compared with the average length of heavy, problem, and alcoholismic drinking in the total sample of 156, the social drinkers showed a relatively short interval between the origin of alcohol abuse and the seeking of treatment. They implied in this way that the social drinkers had been cases of early-stage alcoholism.

As a final example of corroborative evidence, the study of RAKKOLAINEN AND TURUNEN (1969) may be cited. In an attempt to replicate Davies' finding, these authors examined the histories of seventy-nine male residents of Turku, Finland who had died during 1962–5 and who had been arrested at least ten times for drunkenness during their lives. The results showed that at the end of their lives six of these men had been controlled drinkers and two had been abstinent, compared with a total of fifty-six who had continued to drink without control. In a further seven cases there had been no possibility of drinking for various reasons. The histories suggested that in only one of the controlled drinking cases could the original abusive drinking be regarded as secondary to some other psychological problem. Thus, controlled drinking was shown to be a more likely outcome than abstinence in this sample of alcoholics, although both were relatively uncommon. It should be emphasized that this was a highly selected sample in terms of low socio-economic status, low social stability and a high degree of delinquency unconnected with drinking. However, compared with the sample as a whole, it appears that the controlled drinkers were more likely to have been married and employed in skilled occupations, once more supporting Davies' (1962) observation of an improved general adaptation among resumed normal drinkers. Apart from this, the authors could discern no distinguishing features between controlled and uncontrolled drinkers. However, all the controlled drinkers had been over forty when control had been resumed and from inspection of the case histories it would seem that several could well have been further illustrations of the normal drinking associated with advancing age and physical debility first commented on in relation to Bailey and Stewart's (1967) paper.

Before concluding this section on corroborative evidence, this will be a convenient place to discuss briefly a study which has been quoted by the National Council on Alcoholism in America as evidence which refutes the existence of resumed normal drinking (see Armor *et al.*, 1978). PITTMAN AND TATE (1969) followed up 255 individuals who had been treated for alcoholism at a detoxification centre. The object of the investigation was to compare an outpatient programme following detoxification with inpatient care only. In spite of the fact that 60 per cent of the experimental and 55 per cent of the control patients reported they were drinking less at follow-up than before admission, Pittman and Tate stated that they had observed

> no patients who had returned to what may be called normal drinking. In many cases what we did find was a moderation of drinking patterns characterized by longer periods of abstinence between drinking bouts and ingestion of small quantities of alcoholic beverages. In no sense, however, should this moderation be construed as normal drinking, since the crucial variable – loss of control – was still a factor in their drinking patterns.

As Sobell (1978a) has pointed out, a serious methodological deficiency of this study is that nowhere do Pittman and Tate attempt to define what they mean by normal drinking, despite the fact that other variables utilized in the research are carefully defined and quantified. Indeed, no figures of any kind relating to drinking behaviour are provided, a curious omission in view of the methodologically sophisticated tone of this paper. In the absence of such data, there is no way of deciding whether the classification of outcomes has been properly conducted, whether the attribution of loss of control has been made on reasonable grounds, and whether the 'smaller quantities' mentioned preclude a normal drinking designation. In any event, it seems unreasonable in this situation to prefer the conclusion of Pittman and Tate to those of other investigators who provide either detailed case studies (Davies, 1962; Kendell, 1965; Reinert and Bowen, 1968; Rakkolainen and Turunen, 1969), objective and predetermined criteria for normal drinking (Pattison *et al.*, 1968), or both (Bailey and Stewart, 1967).

Apart from the study by Pittman and Tate (1969), no other evidence is available which directly disconfirms the existence of normal drinking in former alcoholics. Many follow-up studies have simply ignored the issue, but Pittman and Tate's is the only report to have claimed specifically that resumed normal drinkers were not found and, as we have seen, this evidence is methodologically suspect. The only other kind of argument advanced in denial of the existence of normal drinking ex-alcoholics is based on clinical impression; typically clinicians of many years' standing will simply declare that no such persons exist, as happened in the controversy over Davies' (1962) paper and in the more recent furore following the Rand Report (see pp. 58–64). The problem here is to explain how it is that highly respected clinicians have failed to observe resumed normal drinking when research evidence has been overwhelmingly in its favour. One reason which is often proposed for this discrepancy is that clients who successfully maintain normal drinking are unlikely to keep in contact with clinics in which the goal of total abstinence has been strongly urged upon them. Beyond that, it is also possible that normal drinking outcomes are not registered precisely because such a category does not exist in the observer's conceptual framework. But in the last resort, of course, these sweeping assertions of clinical truth are not capable of being refuted and, therefore, no matter how experienced or distinguished the authority uttering them, they can have no place in serious scientific discourse.

INCIDENTAL FINDINGS

Quite apart from research directly addressed to the topic, a careful reading of the alcoholism literature reveals a not inconsiderable number of papers in which the subject of resumed normal drinking is mentioned in passing, without any detail being entered into. An example is the study of ROBSON, PAULUS AND CLARKE (1965) who followed up 155 patients between 10 and 46 months after first contact with a clinic devoted to the rehabilitation of alcoholics. These authors merely state that 'a surprisingly large number seemed to have managed to control their drinking while not completely abstaining'. Again, DUBOURG (1969), in a follow-up of 76 male patients who had been treated for alcohol dependence with loss of control, found that 'three patients have resumed controlled social drinking and have so far survived for 16, 20 and 26 months without deteriorating'. Two of the 85 wives of alcoholics studied by JAMES AND GOLDMAN (1971) reported that 'their husbands had returned to the SDS (social drinking stage) again after having passed through the SDS, EDS (excessive drinking stage) and ADS (alcoholismic drinking stage)'. And BHAKTA (1971) found that three out of twenty alcoholics whose social anxiety had been treated with desensitization 'were drinking moderately without significant adverse effects on family or work'.

More incidental findings of resumed drinking similar to these could be listed. However, it will be more useful here to confine attention to research reports in which the phenomenon is discussed more fully and which add something to our understanding of it. For example, in a survey by BARCHHA, STEWART AND GUZE (1968) into the prevalence of alcoholism among general hospital ward patients, it was discovered that about one third of all the definite and possible alcoholics identified reported a marked reduction in their consumption for at least a year prior to admission to hospital for various physical illnesses. Perhaps it is not surprising that, among this particular population, the reasons most commonly given for reducing drinking were connected with the patient's physical illness – either the symptoms of the illness prevented or discouraged them from drinking more, the treatment they were receiving was incompatible with heavier drinking, or they heeded medical advice to cut down. Despite the urgent nature of these reasons, many of the patients interviewed by Barchha *et al.* must count as alcoholics who had regained control over drinking.

Easily the most important incidental findings are contained in the work of Donald L. Gerard and his colleagues. The data reported in the first of these papers, GERARD, SAENGER AND WILE (1962), was collected before Davies' (1962) paper appeared but was not included in the section dealing with reports of resumed normal drinking before Davies because it is better considered in conjunction with the more extensive research of Gerard and Saenger (1966).

The purpose of the paper by Gerard *et al.* (1962) was to describe and analyse the overall adjustment of 'the abstinent alcoholic' and this classic research will be discussed more fully in Chapter 4. A total of fifty-five patients were found to have been completely abstinent for at least a year on follow-up at various intervals after treatment at one of five outpatient clinics in Connecticut. Also observed were a further forty-one patients (14 per cent of the follow-up sample) who were 'still using alcohol but no longer with a drinking problem'. Since this paper was published before the interest in normal drinking created by Davies' report had shown itself, no further details of the actual drinking behaviour of this group are supplied, but we are told that the patients had no longer become intoxicated, gone on binges, been arrested, or received medical treatment related to alcoholism for at least a year. No details are given of the degree or kind of alcohol dependence for any of the patients in this research but they had all been diagnosed as alcoholics at a specialist clinic.

The same loose definition of normal or 'controlled' drinking was employed in the later research of GERARD AND SAENGER (1966). This was a larger study than the earlier one and attempted to follow up the patient populations of eight separate outpatient clinics one year after intake. In total, 797 patients were followed up. Regarding successful outcome as acceptable drinking behaviour shown at the time of follow-up and for at least six consecutive months prior to follow-up gave 100 abstinent patients (13 per cent) and 41 normal drinkers (5 per cent).

One of the most interesting of Gerard and Saenger's findings was that the percentages of controlled drinkers observed, and the ratios of controlled drinkers to successful abstainers, varied considerably from clinic to clinic. In the most extreme case, no normal drinkers were found at all, compared with a 12 per cent outcome for abstainers, and at another clinic the ratio of outcomes was twelve abstainers to every one normal drinker. This must be contrasted with the clinic where normal drinkers were twice as numerous as abstainers, 10 per cent compared with 5 per cent. The other clinics gave percentages and ratios intermediate between these two extremes. One possible explanation for this divergence is that patient populations with different characteristics were being sampled, with some more likely to provide normal drinkers than others. However, the usual interpretation of this evidence is that differences in treatment philosophy between the clinic staffs were responsible. Accepting this interpretation for the sake of argument, there is a curious paradox here. It would seem from previous evidence that the achievement of normal drinking is unlikely to have been directly assisted by the treatment the alcoholic has received. The clinics studied by Gerard and Saenger were typical for their time in not offering any form of treatment directed towards controlled drinking. And yet it would appear possible that the number of patients who return successfully to normal drinking is influenced by the treatment orientations of the therapists they have been exposed to. On a speculative basis, we may surmise that this influence works in a negative direction only; that is, where the possibility of normal drinking is ridiculed in treatment, as is likely to be the case in AA-inspired treatment regimes, the patient may come to regard any drinking as a disastrous 'slip' and relapse via the mechanism of the self-fulfilling prophecy. In other words, the patient is taught to construe the issue in black and white terms with no behavioural alternatives intervening between abstinence and alcoholism. Where normal drinking is not directly criticized, as perhaps in the clinics described by Gerard and Saenger which were devoted to a broad, psychotherapeutic approach and which were indeed the ones which produced the higher proportions of normal drinkers, the natural processes of spontaneous recovery which eventuate in resumed normal drinking are permitted to take their course.

It should not be inferred from this that psychotherapy was found to be effective in changing behaviour in this study. For both abstainers and normal drinkers alike, Gerard and Saenger found evidence of behavioural change unaccompanied by emotional change. Thus, alterations in drinking behaviour did not result from greater self-understanding, reduced tension and anxiety or, indeed, any presumed product of a psychotherapeutic relationship. The characteristic psychological defence attributed to the normal drinkers was denial, which was combined with a heavy reliance on 'willpower'. They were said to be typically without insight into motivations for problem-drinking, apart from an occasional recognition of crude precipitating circumstances. Contact with the clinic appeared even less important for the normal drinkers than for the abstainers, since they made significantly fewer visits during the treatment period. This may well have been due to incipient conflict over drinking goals and, in support of this interpretation, the normal drinkers tended to denigrate their contact with the clinic at follow-up.

With regard to factors positively associated with the attainment of successful normal drinking patterns, Gerard and Saenger listed five which were derived from a careful inspection of patient protocols:

1. *Decreasing physical health*. Two cases are described in which, as in the cases reported by Bailey and Stewart (1967), patients were too physically weak as a result of illness to continue drinking abusively.

2. *Major shifts in life situations.* An example is cited in which the restoration of a previous moderate pattern followed upon a move to another city and an improvement in family relationships.

3. *Satisfaction of intense dependency needs.* A case is described in which such satisfaction resulted from a marriage to a 'bossy' woman, accompanied by a radical improvement in drinking habits. It should be noted that dependency needs were also regarded as an important factor in the attainment of abstinence.

4. *Capacity for self-control or constraint based on shifts in cognitive awareness about self and alcohol.* Under this heading a change in drinking behaviour occurred prior to change in life circumstances. The main cognitive change in question was a full recognition that drinking was endangering the fundamentals of adjustment, such as marriage, family and livelihood. Again, this kind of change was not specific to normal drinking in Gerard and Saenger's account.

5. *Multiple influences.* For most of the patients who shifted from uncontrolled to controlled drinking a combination of the above factors was involved.

An occasional source of incidental findings of resumed normal drinking is the reports of various behaviour therapies for alcoholism which began to appear with greater frequency in the literature at just the time when interest in normal drinking had been aroused. The reports of Anant (1968), Quirk (1968), Blake (1965) and Kraft and Al-Issa (1967; 1968) come into this category. Although all the treatment methods used in these studies were aimed at abstinence, there appears to be nothing in the authors' learning theory conception of alcoholism which would preclude normal drinking. Thus, the relatively high frequency of normal drinking outcomes reported in these studies strengthens the observation made in relation to the differences in rates of normal drinking between clinics observed by Gerard and Saenger (1966); when the possibility of normal drinking is not actively opposed in therapy, it tends to occur more often.

An interesting behaviour therapy report from the present perspective is that of QUINN AND HENBEST (1967) who were interested in the phenomenon of failure of generalization following aversion therapy for alcoholism. This occurs when aversive events such as nausea and vomiting have been paired with the patient's drink of preference, but the subsequent aversive reaction is confined to this beverage and has not generalized to other alcoholic drinks which the patient continues to consume. Quinn and Henbest conducted a search for such cases and found ten meeting their specifications. Three of these had become normal drinkers and had changed in each case from whisky, which had been preferred when they were drinking excessively, to beer or stout. This pattern of drinking had lasted for at least four years. There may be some significance in the fact that five of the six individuals whose drinking had not improved had changed from whisky to another spirit or to wine. We have seen previously in the summary of Kendell's (1965) cases that a specific aversion to a beverage associated with abusive drinking may occur spontaneously.

A few more incidental findings will be included in this section because they show features of special interest. For example, in contrast to the studies previously reviewed which were confined to men (e.g. Davies, 1962; Pattison *et al.*, 1968), SCHUCKIT AND WINOKUR (1972) followed up a cohort of female alcoholics two years after treatment in a psychiatric hospital. The forty-five women for whom sufficient information was available were divided into good outcome patients, who had been free of alcohol-related problems for a minimum of twelve months after discharge, and poor outcome patients who had not. Eleven of the twenty-four showing a good outcome had been able to return to social drinking, defined as 'the intake of moderate amounts of alcohol in a social setting without alcohol-related problems'. This relatively large proportion of normal drinkers might suggest that the drinking pattern is more common among women than men and there is also evidence for this from controlled drinking treatment studies (see pp.216–17). It should be borne in mind, however, that not all these women were necessarily dependent on alcohol.

Another research project reporting a high proportion of normal drinkers was the very thorough follow-up study of POKORNEY, MILLER AND CLEVELAND (1968). Of eighty-eight alcoholics interviewed one year after discharge from hospital, twenty (23 per cent) were drinking in a mild, social way. This was confirmed by spouses or some other collateral source. The number of normal drinkers may be compared with the only marginally higher figure of twenty-two (25 per cent) for abstainers. These similar proportions are all the more remarkable in view of the treatment regime of intensive group psychotherapy in which 'the position of the ward therapist is that life-long abstinence is a necessity in the rehabilitation of alcoholics'. The patients in this study are described as typical of alcoholics who seek treatment.

Although there is a disappointing lack of attention to normal drinking in Pokorney *et al.*'s report, one interesting finding which did emerge was that the normal drinking pattern appeared much more stable during the follow-up interval than the abstinence pattern. At one month after discharge, fully 67 per cent of patients were abstinent, but this had dropped to 25 per cent at one year. By contrast, 17 per cent were drinking normally after one month and this actually increased to 23 per cent at one-year follow-up. It is also of some interest that the rate at which patients took up normal drinking was approximately equal to the rate at which they relapsed; both events were much more likely to occur in the first month following treatment than thereafter. Thus, this study provides no support for the postulation of an extended period of abstinence before normal drinking can successfully be resumed.

A highly selected sample was studied by GOODWIN, CRANE AND GUZE (1971) who followed up a cohort of ninety-three diagnosed alcoholics eight years after their release from prison where they had served sentences for various felonies. This type of alcoholic would be conventionally regarded as having a particularly poor prognosis. Nevertheless, even though only two had ever received treatment for a drinking problem, thirty-eight of these men were found to be in remission at follow-up, including seven who were abstaining altogether and seventeen who were 'moderate' drinkers in that they drank no less than once a month and no oftener than several times a week, rarely becoming intoxicated. These drinking practices had been maintained for at least two years. A further eight men continued to get drunk about once a week, typically on Saturday nights, but had experienced no drink-related problems for two years or more. This was also true of another six who had switched from whisky to beer, despite the fact that they still drank almost daily and sometimes excessively. The respondents' own reports, together with a retrospective analysis of events since leaving prison, indicated that increased control over drinking was responsible for an improvement in social adjustment and a reduction in arrests, rather than the other way around. There was also a strong suggestion in the data that increased age favoured the instigation of moderate drinking habits. Although in terms of symptoms the alcoholics in this research can be positively identified as gamma alcoholics, the high proportion of normal drinkers compared with abstainers raises the possibility that criminal alcoholics are more likely to reject abstinence as a solution to their drinking problems than other alcoholics.

A high proportion of patients showing 'good adjustment with drinking' (32 per cent) was also found by FITZGERALD, PASEWARK AND CLARK (1971) in a follow-up of 117 alcoholics treated by an inpatient programme. This may be compared with 34 per cent who showed 'good adjustment without drinking'. This study is also important for its relatively long and uniform follow-up interval of four years. The authors conclude that 'complete abstinence is not essential to satisfactory post-treatment adjustment'.

Finally in this review of incidental findings of resumed normal drinking, VAN DIJK AND VAN DIJK-KOFFEMAN (1973) made the useful distinction between 'sporadic' and 'frequent' moderate drinkers in their study of treated alcohol addicts in Holland. At follow-up two to five years after treatment, sixteen patients (8 per cent) were found to be sporadic moderate drinkers, with only four frequent moderate drinkers. Any drunkenness was excluded by the definition of moderate drinking employed. The lower number showing a 'frequent' drinking pattern is a similar finding to that of KISH AND HERMANN (1971) who discovered 18.5 per cent of 173 treated alcoholics to be engaged in 'occasional drinking' of a harmfree nature at one year follow-up, compared with 7.5 per cent who were harmfree regular drinkers. Distinctions such as these illustrate a more refined approach to the analysis of normal drinking in former alcoholics.

COMPARISONS OF NORMAL DRINKERS AND ABSTAINERS

After the corroboration of Davies' original finding during the 1960s, it was natural that researchers should devote their efforts to questions which flowed from an acceptance of the existence of resumed normal drinking. Also at this time the first reports of behaviour therapies specifically aimed at controlled drinking began to appear, with ostensibly encouraging results (e.g. Lovibond and Caddy, 1970). Therefore, the question which immediately invited attention was, what kinds of clients of treatment programmes are best suited to these new methods and what kinds of alcoholics are better advised to stick with traditional, abstinence-oriented treatment methods. In this section we shall consider the research which has attempted to answer this question by looking for differences between groups of individuals who have successfully reached one or the other of the two outcomes after participating in the same treatment programme. The variables which are most obviously relevant to the problem of future allocation are pre-treatment characteristics, but any variables which bear on this matter will be taken into account. It should be recalled that this chapter is confined to the results of abstinence-oriented treatment and therefore any properties of normal drinkers which are demonstrated will be only indirectly relevant to decisions about controlled drinking programmes.

Early studies which attempted to differentiate between abstainers and normal drinkers on the basis of clinical impression (e.g. Kendell, 1965; Reinert and Bowen, 1968) met with little success. Employing more quantitative methods, Pattison *et al.* (1968) found no differences in age, race, employment status, type of vocation, living arrangements, attitude towards treatment at the time of intake, or expressed motivation for drinking or abstinence. Gerard and Saenger (1966) reported that normal drinkers tended to be younger and to have experienced a shorter duration of drinking problem than abstainers, without either of these differences reaching statistical significance.

The first major comparison between the two outcome groups was undertaken by ORFORD, OPPENHEIMER AND EDWARDS (1976). The data for the comparison were taken from a two-year follow-up of 100 married male alcoholics given either intensive outpatient treatment or a single advice session (see Orford and Edwards, 1977). Controlled drinking in this study was defined by a conjunction of the patient's own report and that of his wife, both of whom were asked to make judgements about drinking behaviour in each of the fifty-two weeks which preceded follow-up interview. Although this must have placed a severe strain on the informants' memories, the principle of making criteria for controlled drinking depend on an implicit agreement between alcoholic and spouse must make for more valid categorization. Eight men were found who stated that they had never exceeded 200 grammes of alcohol (about ten pints of beer, ten doubles of spirits or the equivalent) on any single day during the last year and whose wives also stated that drinking had been acceptable to them. In two other instances wives reported a single week's unacceptable drinking but here drinking was said by the husband never to have exceeded 100 grammes in a day. The ten normal drinkers defined in this way should be compared with the total of only three who met similar criteria at one year follow-up, and this serves to support Kendell's (1965) comment that an extended period of follow-up after treatment may be necessary before all potential normal drinkers come to light. The first-year patterns of the ten second-year normal drinkers showed that six had drunk in a fashion acceptable to their wives directly after first contact with the treatment service and only two had demonstrated clear periods of abstinence before normal drinking ensued, a month in one case and twelve months in the other. Frequencies of drinking varied considerably among these men but one drank every day and several others relatively often. The abstinent group, categorized along similar lines, comprised eleven men, and a further five in the good outcome group could not be classified as either controlled drinkers or abstainers because of disagreement over details of drinking between husband and wife.

TABLE 2.1
Significant differences between abstainers and controlled drinkers

	Frequency of subjects	
	Abstainers	Controlled Drinkers
4 + / symptoms	8	2
3 − / symptoms	3	8
Gamma alcoholism	6	0
Non-gamma alcoholism	5	10
Unconfident about abstaining	8	2
Confident about abstaining	2	7
Intensive treatment	9	3
Brief counselling	2	7

Source: Orford, Oppenheimer and Edwards (1976).

Contrary to Gerard and Saenger's tentative finding, Orford *et al.* found that age and duration of problem did not discriminate between the two groups. The variables which were found to distinguish between normal drinkers and abstainers are displayed in Table 2.1. All these differences are significant at the 5 per cent level of confidence. As will be seen, controlled drinkers were likely to have endorsed fewer 'symptoms' on a seven-item scale concerning early morning drinking, morning tremor, morning nausea, loss of control over amount drunk, passing out when drunk, secret drinking, and hallucinations when drinking. In view of this, it is not surprising that the abstainers were more likely to have been diagnosed as gamma alcoholics since some of the above items are definitive of this type of alcoholism. It will be observed from Table 2.1 that none of the normal drinkers had been diagnosed as a gamma alcoholic, the most common alternative being alpha alcoholic, where dependence is said to be psychological rather than physical. An unexpected difference is that successful abstainers tended not to be confident about abstaining at the time of intake whereas most normal drinkers *were* confident about their ability to abstain. This judgement was made after the client, whether intensively or minimally treated, had been strongly advised to abstain completely from alcohol and the difference observed presumably reflects the greater confidence of individuals with a less serious drinking problem in their ability to achieve a goal which has just been suggested to them. The remaining difference between the groups, that normal drinkers were more likely to have received a single counselling session and abstainers the intensive treatment, is also confounded with the other predictor variables.

The most important general finding to emerge from this comparison is clearly that the normal drinkers had the less 'serious' drinking problems at intake, as shown by their lower average symptom scores and by the fact that they were not diagnosed as gamma alcoholics. What lessons do the authors wish to draw from this finding? First of all they suggest that controlled drinking may be relatively easier to achieve when the major symptoms of physical dependency have not been experienced, or have been experienced but less severely. This inference is unexceptional. However, Orford *et al.* go on to write: 'Depending upon how alcoholism is defined, there could even be some truth in the charge that alcoholics who have returned to controlled drinking were not real alcoholics in the first place.' This statement is seriously misleading and is precisely the kind of pronouncement which might be seized upon by those with irrational prejudices against controlled drinking treatments. The implication presumably is that, if alcoholism is defined as *gamma* alcoholism, then the research has discovered that normal drinkers were not 'real' alcoholics but 'habitual symptomatic excessive drinkers'. Now, the controversy which followed Davies' report concerned the truth or falsity of a proposition of the kind 'all swans are white', or more pertinently, 'no swan is black'. According to Popper (1959), a universal proposition can only be falsified, it cannot be verified. Thus the affirmation that no gamma alcoholic, or alcohol addict, can become a normal drinker needs only one contrary observation to refute it. It so happens that, as we have seen, there have been many such observations, including the reports of Kendell (1965) that normal drinkers previously showed severe withdrawal symptomatology and of Davies *et al.* (1969) that they showed alcoholic psychoses. On the other hand, no conceivable amount of evidence of the kind offered by Orford *et al.*, to the effect that among a group of normal drinkers no gamma alcoholics were found, can ever *confirm* the assertion that gamma alcoholics cannot become normal drinkers; positive instances may be found in another study employing different methods, carried out in a different place and investigating different kinds of alcoholics. Indeed, there are grounds for supposing that the design of this study minimized the chances of normal drinking in former gamma alcoholics from being observed. Given that normal drinking is relatively easy for alpha alcoholics to achieve, it is no doubt very difficult for gamma alcoholics. But not only did these patients receive advice to abstain from alcohol and *not* attempt controlled drinking, but many of them were given only a single counselling interview. It may be that many gamma alcoholics need intensive treatment aimed at controlled drinking before it is possible for them. Certainly, the work of Sobell and Sobell (1978*b*), to be reviewed in Chapter 6, shows that a high number of gamma alcoholics who are allowed to choose controlled drinking can benefit from the appropriate treatment methods. There is also some evidence from Polich *et al.* (1980) that married alcoholics like those studied here are more likely to be successful in pursuing abstinence than normal drinking, whereas for unmarried alcoholics the reverse is true. Even if this were not the case, however, all Orford *et al.* have shown is that when a sample of resumed normal drinkers is examined, many of them will have been alcoholics of a less serious variety; their results do nothing to contradict previous findings that it is *possible* for gamma alcoholics to become normal drinkers. Moreover, given the limitations of their sample, the results have a restricted relevance to the question of the proportion of gamma alcoholics who can become normal drinkers, either unaided or with therapeutic assistance. We have devoted some space to this argument because of its crucial importance in the debate about the limits of controlled drinking treatment methods.

BROMET AND MOOS (1979) studied a total of 429 patients at five different treatment settings for alcoholics. Data were collected at intake and at six to eight months after discharge. For the purpose of comparison, the total sample was divided into the two groups of 262 mainly lower-class, residentially mobile and unmarried patients who had been treated in a Salvation Army, public hospital-based, or halfway-house programme (the so-called 'low-bottom group') and 167 mainly middle-class to upper-class, residentially stable patients who had been treated by an aversion conditioning or milieu-oriented programme (the so-called 'high-bottom group'). Among the low-bottom group, 38 patients (15 per cent) were found to be abstainers at follow-up and 58 (22 per cent) were defined as moderate drinkers. In the high-bottom group, 77 (46 per cent) were abstaining and 48 (29 per cent) were moderate drinkers. The relatively high percentages of normal drinkers recorded here, compared with some other studies, may well have been due to the rather generous criteria for moderate drinking used by Bromet and Moos. Patients were called moderate drinkers if they were not abstinent, had not been rehospitalized for alcoholism during the follow-up period, and described their drinking during the previous month as 'never drank', 'special occasions only', or 'social drinking'. The lack of a collateral source of information about drinking means that some of those describing their drinking as 'social' would almost certainly have been regarded as drinking in an excessive manner from a more objective viewpoint. Three sets of variables were measured – sociodemographic and premorbid psychosocial and drinking factors, treatment experiences during the follow-up period, and post-hospital psychosocial and drinking factors.

It will have been noted that this research involved an impressively large sample and was carried out with an admirable thoroughness. Unfortunately it is flawed by the fact that the authors do not guard against the danger of spuriously significant results from multiple comparisons. When a large number of statistical tests is being employed, some are bound to appear significant on the basis of chance alone. In this instance, altogether 158 variables were compared between the two groups and, at the conventional 5 per cent level of confidence, this would result in no fewer than eight differences spuriously significant by chance. Since there is no means of deciding which of Bromet and Moos' reported differences between groups reflect a real, underlying difference and which do not, it is necessary to discard all findings which do not exceed the more conservative confidence level of 1 per cent significance. Thirteen significant differences are discarded by this rule.

Having decimated Bromet and Moos' results in this way, we are left with five significant differences between groups at the 1 per cent level. In the low-bottom group more of the abstainers reported no arrests during the year preceding treatment than did the normal drinkers (63 per cent vs. 40 per cent) and abstainers reported lower consumption levels before intake. On an item asking patients to rate their drinking problem at follow-up, 68 per cent of the abstainers rated it as 'no problem', compared with 33 per cent of the normal drinkers. In the high-bottom group there was a significant tendency for abstainers to live near more bars than the normal drinkers and, as in the low-bottom group, abstainers were more likely at follow-up to rate their drinking as 'no problem' than normal drinkers (79 per cent vs. 56 per cent).

Bromet and Moos conclude from their study that 'few meaningful differences exist between abstaining and moderate drinking alcoholics'. Having reduced the differences observed still further, we must agree with this conclusion. In particular, there was no evidence from this study that the normal drinkers had any less serious drinking problems before treatment than the abstainers. Indeed, in the case of two relevant findings the difference which emerged was in the opposite direction, with abstainers in the low-bottom group having had lower consumption levels and fewer arrests in the year preceding intake. However, it must be emphasized that, from their paper, there is no evidence that Bromet and Moos actually recorded the presence of alcoholism symptoms, as opposed to general psychiatric symptoms, at admission. The fact that fewer normal drinkers than abstainers rated their drinking as 'no problem' at follow-up may reflect a continuing anxiety about drinking on the part of some, but may also be a consequence of the over-generous definition of moderate drinking commented on above.

A well designed and executed comparison of normal drinkers and abstainers was carried out by SMART (1978) whose sample was even larger than that of Bromet and Moos. 1091 male and female alcoholics were followed up one year after discharge from one of seven treatment facilities in Ontario. Those 66 clients (6.1 per cent) who were classified as 'true social drinkers' had experienced no benders in the follow-up period, had scores on an alcoholic involvement scale which were below the mean recorded for general population social drinkers in previous research, had an average daily consumption less than or equal to five drinks, and had not been intoxicated during the last 99 drinking occasions. A further group of 82 quasi-social drinkers (7.5 per cent) was described who met all but the last of the above criteria. 143 abstinent clients (13.1 per cent) were also observed. Smart remarks that these figures indicate true social drinking to be unusual in treated alcoholics. However, it seems too conservative a view of normal or social drinking to exclude the quasi-social drinkers who apparently had no problems due to drinking and whose only imperfection was to become intoxicated at least once out of 99 drinking episodes. If the quasi-social drinkers are included, social drinkers are in fact more numerous than abstinent clients.

A further commendable feature of Smart's method was that he advanced specific hypotheses before collecting his data. These were that at intake the social drinkers would: (*a*) be younger; (*b*) have lower alcohol consumption, and (*c*) have lower scores (i.e. show better functioning) on scales measuring alcoholic involvement, problems due to drinking, isolation, physical health, marital stability, social stability, motivation for treatment, attitudes towards abstinence, and patient satisfaction. Data were analysed in a way which took proper account of the multiple comparisons being made. In summarizing his results, Smart writes:

As expected, true social drinkers (and quasi-social drinkers) had significantly lower alcohol consumption rates, fewer problems due to drinking, and less alcoholic involvement at intake than those remaining nonsocial drinkers or who became abstinent. Relative to those remaining nonsocial drinkers, the true social drinkers were significantly older, had higher marital and social stability, were more satisfied with themselves, and had better attitudes towards achieving abstinence. True social drinkers also had significantly higher motivation for treatment than quasi-social drinkers; however, contrary to predictions regarding physical health or isolation from beneficial interests and others, the true social drinkers did not differ from other groups.

This evidence clearly supports the conclusion of Orford *et al.* (1976) that normal drinkers tend to have been less 'serious' alcoholics than abstainers. However, the same comments which were made in relation to Orford *et al.*'s conclusions (see p. 50) are also relevant here. The evidence shows that the majority of normal drinkers discovered at follow-up have less serious drinking problems at intake, not that it is impossible for those with serious problems to become normal drinkers. Although in Smart's data there existed significant differences between group means on the relevant variables, there is likely to have been some overlap between group scores and, therefore, a few normal drinkers who had as high levels of consumption and as numerous problems due to drinking as the majority of the abstainers.

In the summary of Smart's paper it is stated that 'those who become social drinkers are those who are less serious alcoholics with more social and other supports'. This gives a false impression. The differences found in marital and social stability were differences between social drinkers and nonsocial drinkers, or in more conventional terminology, those who relapsed. There were no significant differences on these variables between social drinkers and abstainers. Thus, for the normal drinkers, the imputed characteristic of higher social stability is not at all of the same kind as the characteristic of less serious drinking problems, and to link them together as in the summary just quoted can only lead to confusion. Indeed, the difference in social stability found here may simply reflect the fact that this variable is one of the most consistent predictors of favourable outcome in the research literature (see Gibbs and Flanagan, 1977).

The hunt for distinguishing common characteristics of normal drinkers following treatment was also the aim of LEVINSON (1977). This author followed up 115 patients five years after inpatient treatment and discovered eleven controlled drinkers. Two had resumed drinking immediately after discharge from hospital and the remainder had had initial periods of abstinence ranging in duration from three to twenty-four months, with an average of ten months. Five had experienced major changes in their lives of the kind described by Davies (1962) and five had clearly discernible built-in controls on drinking such as a family highly vigilant for signs of alcohol abuse.

When compared with other patients in the cohort on a variety of physical, social and psychological test variables, only one significant difference was observed; a higher proportion of the controlled drinkers were married at intake. Levinson also remarks on the interesting trend for all the controlled drinkers in the work force to be employed in full-time jobs. Unfortunately, since Levinson's comparisons were made with the entire follow-up sample, including all the patients who had relapsed, these features may, once more, simply reflect the fact that marriage and full-time employment are favourable prognostic indicators.

In one of the longest follow-ups on record, HYMAN (1976) traced a group of alcoholics fifteen years after discharge from a treatment centre in New Jersey. Of twenty living, ambulatory, locatable subjects who did not appear deteriorated, five were drinking daily without problems, five were complete abstainers, two more were mainly abstainers who occasionally went on binges, and seven were unimproved problem-drinkers. Hyman then examined the pre-treatment characteristics of these former patients from records. The complete abstainers presented histories of legal problems, often involving violence, were mostly unmarried and not in regular employment. By comparison the moderate drinkers showed a relatively low level of social deviance before treatment; they tended to be married, in regular work, unaggressive and had few problems with the law. This difference was not merely a matter of socio-economic status, since both groups consisted of blue-collar workers without college education. The continuing problem drinkers showed yet a third pattern, resembling the moderate drinkers with respect to regular employment and the complete abstainers with respect to trouble with the law and belligerence.

ANDERSON AND RAY (1977) followed up 110 male alcoholics one year after an intensive group therapy programme in which the primary emphasis was said to be on realistic self-management skills. Perhaps because of this emphasis they found the surprisingly high proportion of 44 per cent 'non-destructive drinkers', defined as those who would fall into Emrick's (1974) category of drinking but never to excess during the follow-up period. A further 38 per cent had abstained totally since discharge and 18 per cent had relapsed. In a comparison of the outcome groups, it transpired that the non-destructive drinkers were somewhat older than the abstainers, with a mean of 49 compared to 47 years. Although we are not told whether this or any other difference was statistically significant, this finding appears to contradict the commonly held assumption that normal drinkers tend to be younger than abstainers. When drinking behaviour before admission was examined, abstainers showed the greatest number of days abstinent the year prior to treatment, with non-destructive drinkers coming in between abstainers and relapsers in this respect. In the same way that successful controlled drinkers may be alcholics with more experience of control in their drinking histories, as Orford (1973) has suggested, it may also be the case that many successful abstainers are those who are more accustomed to abstinence.

SPONTANEOUS REMISSION

We have seen that important evidence of normal drinking in former alcoholics has come from research dealing with untreated alcoholics. Kendell (1965) looked at individuals who had been referred for treatment but who, for one reason or another, had received none; Lemere (1953) studied the life histories of deceased alcoholics from interviews with surviving relatives; and Bailey and Stewart (1967) discovered their resumed normal drinkers among respondents in a community health survey. To use the medical term, these papers were concerned with cases of spontaneous remission from alcoholism. In this section we shall consider briefly more evidence of this kind from household surveys of the general population.

A considerable body of relevant information has been amassed by Cahalan and his associates at the Social Research Group, University of California, Berkeley (e.g. Cahalan, 1970; Cahalan and Room, 1974; Clark and Cahalan, 1976). Beginning from the 'problem-drinking' perspective rather than the traditional disease model of alcoholism, this research has greatly increased our knowledge of the course of drinking problems over time when studied in the natural environment, rather than in the clinic setting. We shall not be able to describe the results of this research in any detail, but suffice it to say that one of the principal general findings is of a much greater changeability in drinking behaviour than the traditional view might lead us to expect. In particular, fluctuations from problem-drinking to non-problem-drinking, both into and out of problem-drinking status, are much more common than had previously been supposed; the notion of alcoholism as an inevitable and irreversible progression of more and more serious problems is seriously challenged by this evidence. Another consistent finding is that the major correlates of changes in drinking-problem status are environmental and role factors, such as financial ability to buy drink, opportunities and time for drinking, and increased family responsibilities, rather than psychological and emotional factors such as anxiety, tension and guilt.

One recent community survey will be described more fully because it provides an opportunity for a direct comparison of former alcoholics who had received treatment in the past with those who had not. Also, respondents identified as alcoholics in this survey were so labelled on the basis that, if they had been interviewed as psychiatric outpatients at the time of interview, they would have been diagnosed as suffering from the disease of alcoholism. Thus there is less possibility here of arguing that the spontaneous remitters discovered by the survey were qualitatively distinct from a clinic-based population. SAUNDERS AND KERSHAW (1979) sampled some 3500 persons in the Clydebank area of Scotland and singled out for personal interview those who gave affirmative answers to the question, 'do you think that you drank too much in the past?'. Of the 115 completed interviews, 16 (14 per cent) were classified as 'questionnaire errors', 37 (32 per cent) as 'episodic over-consumers' who had not harmed themselves through drinking, 41 (36 per cent) as past 'problem-drinkers' who reported that their alcohol intake had been excessive and had been associated with problems recognized by them-selves or their families, and 19 (17 per cent) as 'definitely alcoholics' who gave evidence of being physically dependent on alcohol at some stage in their lives. The 'definitely alcoholic' group also had to reach a certain score on the shortened version of the Michigan Alcoholism Screening Test (Pokorney *et al.*, 1972) and to be confirmed as clinically diagnosable alcoholics by both authors independently. Two further positive respondents were considered to have continuing drinking problems.

All interviewees were asked to provide a maximum of three major reasons for remission. The most prominent reasons given by the definitely alcoholic group were marriage and job-change; only seven out of nineteen of these informants reported that treatment had been influential in their recovery and, even here, successful treatment coincided with changes in life circum-stances in five of these examples, previous treatment having proved unavail-ing. Marriage and job-change, together with physical ill-health, were also the most commonly given reasons among the problem-drinker group and, interestingly, roughly the same picture emerged from the episodic over-consumers, whom the authors suggest may be regarded as a normal control group. This tendency towards uniformity in ascribed reasons for changes in drinking habits between the three groups implies that the determinants of alcoholismic and problem-drinking are continuous with those which affect ordinary drinking behaviour. Moreover, the salience of life-circumstance variables in these results is in essential agreement with the findings of Cahalan and his colleagues mentioned above.

Saunders and Kershaw also looked for possible differences between pre-viously treated and untreated definite alcoholics. The most immediately relevant difference was that eleven out of the twelve cases in the 'no-treatment' group reported being current, regular and trouble-free drinkers, whereas in the group of seven treated individuals only one was a regular drinker, the rest being teetotallers. This may have been due to a differential exposure to the abstinence treatment orientation or to a further significant difference between the groups in the duration of drinking problems, the treatment group experiencing a greater need for abstinence on account of the greater chronicity of their problems.

THE RAND REPORT

The background to what has become known in alcoholism circles as the 'Rand Report' is as follows. In response to a growing concern over the extent of alcoholism in the United States, the government founded in the early 1970s the National Institute on Alcoholism and Alcohol Abuse (NIAAA) whose remit was 'to develop and conduct comprehensive health, education, training, research, and planning programmes for the prevention and treatment of alcohol abusers and alcoholics'. As part of this remit, the NIAAA established a network of Alcoholism Treatment Centres (ATCs) throughout the country and also provided for the continuous monitoring of their treatment efficacy. The Rand Corporation eventually assumed responsibility for the collation and analysis of all data pertaining to outcome of treatment given by the ATCs, as well as data from several commissioned population surveys. The Rand Report was the first summary of this research effort (Armor, Polich and Stambul, 1976).

As with Davies' paper fourteen years earlier, it was the findings in respect of resumed normal drinking which caused the furious controversy over the report. Shortly after its release the National Council on Alcoholism (NCA), a body whose view of alcoholism is very similar to that of Alcoholics Anonymous, convened a press conference at which a procession of alcoholism experts were paraded to denounce the finding of resumed normal drinking and condemn the report in its entirety. It was called dangerous, unscientific and the motives of its compilers were impugned; there was even a suggestion that its publication should have been suppressed. This extraordinarily hostile reaction, together with the report itself and the replies of the authors to their critics, may now be consulted in a single volume (Armor *et al.*, 1978) where it will be seen that many of the criticisms were irrational in the extreme. Nevertheless, as a result of this adverse publicity, it became common in the alcoholism treatment and research community to hear it said, even by people who had never actually read it, that the report was unsound and could safely be ignored. This is a wholly false characterization; although like any other research it has its imperfections, many of which are recognized and acknowledged by the authors, there can be no doubt that the Rand Report is a careful, accurate and in many ways impressive scientific publication.

What is even more remarkable about the controversy over the Rand Report is that, as has been amply documented in this chapter, the main conclusions regarding normal drinking were far from being original. As perhaps the most reasonable of the report's early critics, Emrick and Stilson

(1977), pointed out, 'what is new about the Rand findings is not the findings *per se* but rather the heated controversy about them at the level of the media.' In any event, the Rand Report is concerned with much more than the subject of normal drinking in ex-alcoholics and, indeed, some other of its findings, particularly those relating to the effectiveness of treatment in general (see Hodgson, 1979), are of at least equal scientific interest.

The two samples of alcholics studied in the report were drawn from forty-four ATCs across the United States. Female alcoholics and clients referred by the courts for driving while intoxicated were excluded at the outset on the grounds of evidence showing that they constituted separate populations from male alcoholics in general in terms of drinking behaviour. Roughly one third of all clients treated at the ATCs were followed up about six months after intake as part of the routine monitoring system. This resulted in 2339 male alcoholics for the six-month follow-up sample, representing 21 per cent of the relevant intake. Comparison of intake information between the sample and the entire population revealed no major differences on the variables measured. For the purposes of a more extended follow-up, an additional sample was formed from eight selected ATCs using a special team of interviewers and employing the same data collection sheets used at intake and six-month follow-up. For this 18-month follow-up the response rate was 52 per cent, amounting to 597 male alcoholics. 225 of the 18-month sample had also been interviewed at six months.

Before describing any results, we shall need to consider first the criteria for normal drinking used in the report. All clients so defined met the following four demands: (*i*) a mean daily consumption over the month prior to follow-up of less than three ounces of absolute alcohol (roughly equivalent to three and a half pints of beer); (*ii*) typical quantities on drinking days of less than five ounces of absolute alcohol (about six pints of beer or a bottle and a half of wine); (*iii*) no report of tremor in the last month; (*iv*) no serious symptoms of alcoholism reported in the last month. In the last criterion, the presence of serious symptoms was defined as frequent episodes of three or more of the following: blackouts, missing work due to drink, morning drinking, missing meals, being drunk. Frequent meant three or more episodes in the last month in the cases of blackouts and missing work, and five or more episodes for the other symptoms. The consumption limits used were arrived at from inspection of population drinking frequencies from a national survey described earlier in the report. The separate emphasis on tremor was justified by the fact that this was the only item in the data collection procedure which referred to an aspect of the alcohol withdrawal syndrome, so that special attention could be paid to physical dependence on alcohol. Apart from the 'normal drinking' category, three other outcome categories were employed: long-term abstention, defined as six months prior to follow-up with no drinking at all; short-term abstention, defined as no drinking in the past thirty days but some drinking in the previous five months prior to follow-up; and nonremission, i.e. all clients who did not fit into the above categories.

At six-month follow-up, 68 per cent of the sample were in remission, divided into 18 per cent six-month abstainers, 38 per cent one-month abstainers and 12 per cent normal drinkers. It is of some interest that the averages of the consumption figures reported by the normal drinkers were considerably below the defining thresholds; the average mean daily consumption was 0.5 ounces (about a single whisky), the average typical quantity was 1.9 ounces (just over two pints of beer), and the average number of drinking days in the month was seven. Thus, if the permissible consumption levels are regarded as high, it should be borne in mind that few normal drinking clients actually approached these limits. At 18-months follow-up, the total percentage in remission was nearly identical to the six-month follow-up at 67 per cent. However, the percentages for outcome categories had changed somewhat: six-month abstention, 24 per cent; one-month abstention, 21 per cent; normal drinking, 22 per cent. The main effect of these changes is clearly a redistribution of nearly half the short-term abstainers at six months to either the long-term abstention or normal drinking categories at 18-months, implying that short-term abstention is a relatively unstable outcome. It will have been noted that, whereas the percentage of normal drinkers was lower than that for long-term abstainers at six months, the figures for eighteen months are nearly equal, again supporting Kendell's (1965) observation that the proportion of normal drinkers found is likely to increase as follow-up interval increases. The average consumption figures for the normal drinkers are slightly higher than at six months, but still low. Only three respondents reported a mean daily consumption of over two ounces and only five a typical drinking day consumption of over four ounces.

Although the proportion of normal drinkers observed increased at the 18-month follow-up, it is still possible that individual normal drinking clients were more likely to relapse than abstainers. Armor *et al*. addressed themselves to this question, whether normal drinking was simply a temporary stage for the alcoholic on his way back to full relapse, by inspecting outcome for those clients who were included in both follow-up samples. Relapse here was defined as a change in outcome from a remission status at six months to nonremission at eighteen months. The important figures from this analysis for immediate purposes are that 13 per cent of normal drinkers at six months showed relapse, compared to 17 per cent of six-month abstainers. Thus, in this analysis, not only is there no evidence that normal drinkers are more likely to relapse than abstainers, but normal drinking actually appears to be the more stable outcome, although the difference is not large and may not be statistically significant. Also noteworthy is the fact that only 10 per cent of this sample showed long-term abstention at both six and eighteen months, so that, if stable long-term abstention were seen as the sole standard of treatment success, relatively few clients would have attained it.

Armor *et al.* were also aware of the argument that alcoholics who achieve normal drinking were not real alcoholics to begin with, or at least had less serious drinking problems caused by alcohol. To investigate this hypothesis, they divided the follow-up samples into definite alcoholics, in the sense of being physically addicted to alcohol, and clients with less serious symptoms at intake, who were alcohol abusers but who may not have been physically addicted as such. A client was considered definitely alcoholic at intake if in the past thirty days he met *any* of the following criteria: (*i*) drinking more than twelve ounces of absolute alcohol on typical drinking days (about a bottle of whisky); (*ii*) experiencing episodes of tremors; and (*iii*) falling into the category of 'serious symptoms' as defined in the rules for normal drinking given above.

A reanalysis of the data on the basis of this distinction gave figures for definite alcoholics at six-month follow-up of 15 per cent six-month abstainers and 10 per cent normal drinkers. These figures are not greatly different from those for the entire follow-up sample because most clients at intake were classified as definite alcoholics. The corresponding figures for the less definitely involved clients were 27 per cent for six-months abstainers and 18 per cent for normal drinkers. Thus, for both groups normal drinking was less likely than long-term abstention at six months. However, this was not true for the 18-month follow-up when 28 per cent of the less serious symptoms group were long-term abstainers and no less than 36 per cent were normal drinkers. In the definitely alcoholic group, 25 per cent were six-month abstainers at the 18-month follow-up and 16 per cent were normal drinkers. Thus for this group normal drinking is less likely than long-term abstention, although it is not by any means uncommon. Armor *et al.* note that the greater overall remission rate at eighteen months for the less impaired group is almost entirely accounted for by a higher proportion of normal drinkers; that is to say, the better prognosis for the less severely impaired clients is due largely to the fact that they are more likely to achieve normal drinking.

Other relevant findings of the report were concerned with the various influences of treatment on rates of normal drinking at follow-up. As a method of examining the effectiveness of treatment, Armor *et al.* were able to form two groups of untreated clients, a single contact group consisting of men who made only one visit to the treatment centre and subsequently received no further treatment, and a pre-intake group who received minimal services, usually detoxification, but who then left and never resumed contact. These two groups were compared with two groups of treated clients, those who received low amounts and those who received high amounts of treatment. The immediate conclusion from this comparison was of higher remission rates for the treated clients, especially those who had received high amounts of treatment.

However, this difference in remission at 18-months was accounted for entirely by differential rates in the abstinent categories. For example, only 11 per cent of the single contact group and 15 per cent of the pre-intake group were six-month abstainers at follow-up, compared with 22 per cent and 26 per cent respectively for the low and high amounts of treatment groups. This must be contrasted with the figures for normal drinkers which were 29 per cent of the single contact group, 27 per cent of the pre-intake group, 20 per cent of the low treatment group and 26 per cent of the high treatment group. It might be inferred from these figures that treatment actually reduced the proportions of normal drinkers observed, although the relatively small differences would probably not justify such a conclusion. But it would be fair to conclude, what commonsense suggests, that treatment directed at abstinence has little or no consistent effect on the reinstatement of normal drinking. As with Gerard and Saenger's (1966) results however, the last statement needs to be qualified by the observation that differences between proportions of normal drinkers did exist between various treatment centres. Among the eight treatment centres for which results at eighteen months were available was one which produced 22 per cent long-term abstainers compared with 46 per cent normal drinkers, and another giving 29 per cent for long-term abstainers compared with 14 per cent normal drinkers. Again, it looks possible that the orientation of the counsellors the alcoholic comes in contact with has an effect on the probability of normal drinking. This effect is independent of treatment setting, however, since the proportions of normal drinkers coming from hospital, intermediate or out-patient settings, or combinations of these settings, were highly similar if the overall remission rates are taken into account. It should be noted in passing that the intermediate, halfway-house and hostel-type treatment setting, which tended to cater for the most disadvantaged and unstable alcoholics, produced 12 per cent normal drinkers at eighteen months compared with 15 per cent long-term abstainers.

A remaining finding which should be mentioned was that the likelihood of normal drinking was strongly affected by evidence of affiliation to Alcoholics Anonymous. Indeed, among a group of clients who had received no ATC treatment, or a low amount of it, and who had attended AA meetings regularly in the year before 18-month follow-up, there were no normal drinkers observed at all. However, in the group which had the same lack of contact with ATCs but no AA attendance, 31 per cent were normal drinkers and 16 per cent long-term abstainers. A similar order of difference was shown between the two groups of clients who had received high amounts of treatment at ATCs; regular AA attenders gave 10 per cent normal drinkers and non-AA attenders 41 per cent. Although the effect of AA attendance was to increase overall remission rates for the low-ATC contact group, as might be expected, it had no such effect on the group receiving a high amount of treatment at ATCs. In the latter case, the influence of AA attendance was merely to increase the relative proportion showing long-term abstention as compared with normal drinking. In more general terms, the fact that AA affiliation appears as such a powerful predictor of remission category supports the suggestion that differences in rates of normal drinking are determined by clients' initial decisions to aim for normal drinking or for abstinence, rather than any differences in their capacities to achieve their goal once this has been decided upon.

Before concluding this summary of the original Rand Report an interesting study by HINGSON, SCOTCH AND GOLDMAN (1977) may briefly be described. As with Davies' (1962) paper, a large part of the hostility generated by the report derived from the claim that alcoholics would come to hear of the findings of resumed normal drinking and attempt it themselves, with possibly tragic consequences. With an admirable dedication to empirical methods, Hingson *et al.* attempted to put this claim to the test by interviewing: (*i*) 244 persons receiving treatment for alcohol-related problems; (*ii*) 62 professionals involved in alcoholism treatment; (*iii*) a random telephone sample of 174 persons; and (*iv*) a sample of 44 homeless men. Only four patients reported that they had attempted to drink normally as a result of the report and in each case there were grounds for believing that personal factors were more important. Five of the professionals indicated that they had changed their treatment procedures because of the report, but in four of these cases this amounted to no more than discussing it with patients. Only one professional stated that the report had made her more tolerant of patients who drank occasionally. The impact in the general population was even less pronounced; only one person in the telephone sample said she had been influenced. None of the homeless men claimed to have been influenced by the report despite the fact that most of them were aware of it. Obviously, there are problems in evaluating the impact of the Rand Report in this way, but this study certainly provides no evidence to support the view that large numbers of lives were adversely affected by it. Other more valid criticisms of the original Rand Report will be mentioned in the next section.

THE FOUR-YEAR FOLLOW-UP

The controversial issues emerging from the original Rand Report (Armor *et al.*, 1976) were vigorously pursued in a follow-up study of the same treatment population conducted four years after admission (Polich, Armor and Braiker, 1980) and we shall attempt to determine here the extent to which the conclusions of the first report need to be modified in the light of this later information. Three samples were studied: (*i*) all clients interviewed at 18 months (n = 593); (*ii*) a 35 per cent random sample of clients selected at 18 months but not interviewed for various reasons (n = 165); and (*iii*) a 75 per cent random sample of clients who had had a single contact with an ATC and who were interviewed at 18 months (n = 164). As before, female clients and those referred from the courts for driving while intoxicated were excluded in order to provide homogeneous samples of individuals studied.

In the four-year follow-up great efforts were made to correct the major faults and answer the most prominent and justified criticisms of the first survey, in the following ways:

1. The follow-up did not rely exclusively on the self-reports of clients. All those seen were given a breathalyser test immediately after interview but were not forewarned that they would be asked to take it. Additionally, some subjects were re-interviewed one or two weeks later when a further breathalyser test was given, again without their prior knowledge. As well as BAC readings, one third of the clients in sample (*i*) above were asked to name a collateral source of information who was also interviewed in order to provide a check on the accuracy of the respondent's answers. Co-operation was enlisted throughout these procedures by payments to respondents. It may briefly be mentioned here that data relevant to both types of validity measure, BAC readings and collateral interviews, resulted in no compelling reasons for a reclassification of drinking status at follow-up. This classification was found to be fairly robust against the effects of under-reporting of consumption and of symptoms and adverse consequences of excessive drinking.

2. In the first report only 60 per cent of the intended sample were successfully located and interviewed and this was made the ground for several criticisms of the Rand Report. In the four-year follow-up, considerable time and money was expended in an effort to interview as many selected clients as possible. This eventuated in an overall completion rate of 85 per cent, obviously a far more satisfactory figure. Moreover, a comparison of the 85 per cent interviewed with the 15 per cent not interviewed revealed no significant differences on intake characteristics. Polich *et al.* were also able to comment on the general effects of nonresponse by estimating the degree of error which would have been caused had they taken less pains to locate respondents and stopped their completion rate at various lower levels. They found that, even under the most extreme assumptions, completion rates from 60 to 70 per cent would result in a maximum error of 5 per cent for allocation to drinking status category, with the extrapolation that at 85 per cent completion rate the error would be 2 per cent at most. The conclusion is

that the earlier results were unlikely to have been seriously distorted by nonresponse bias and the four-year follow-up results definitely not distorted. In any event, it is difficult to see how the criticism of a low completion rate, although crucially relevant to an evaluation of treatment effectiveness (see Hodgson, 1979), could affect the relative rates and probabilities of relapse of normal drinking and abstinence.

3. It could be claimed that the 18-month period used in the original report was a misleadingly short follow-up interval. Although aggregate patterns of remission are known to be fairly stable after one year (Gerard and Saenger, 1959), individual outcomes may fluctuate considerably after this and such a possibility is clearly relevant to an assessment of the relative stability of abstinence and normal drinking outcomes. The four-year follow-up obviously corrected for this potential deficiency.

4. We have seen that the original report used a restricted 'window', the thirty days previous to interview, for the collection of detailed information on drinking behaviour. This led to the outcome category 'short-term abstention', defined as those individuals who had been abstinent for the last month but had drunk during the previous five months, and this was included as a remission category. However, it was also shown that short-term abstention was a highly unstable drinking status, an observation which was amply confirmed by the four-year data, and it was therefore possible that the inclusion of short-term abstainers among remissions artificially enlarged overall remission rates. In the four-year follow-up clients were asked about the thirty days *before the last drink,* which could have occurred at any time during the six months before interview. Also, with respect to the normal drinking category, it was established in all cases whether the thirty days nonproblem-drinking before the last drink was representative of the entire six-month period, thus making a direct comparison with long-term abstention over six months more reasonable.

5. The criticism of the 1976 report most immediately relevant to present concerns was the charge of overgenerous criteria for a definition of normal drinking (see, e.g. Emrick and Stilson, 1977; Blume, 1977; Orford, 1978). In particular, it so happened that a client could report the frequent occurrence during the last month of two serious symptoms and still be designated a normal drinker. Interestingly, Polich *et al.* (1980) were themselves able to show the invalidity of this criterion by demonstrating that clients at eighteen months showing *any* dependence symptoms were far more likely to have relapsed or died by four years than those showing none. For this reason the four-year classification excluded from the nonproblem-drinking category all persons showing at least *one* of the following dependence symptoms: tremors, morning drinking, loss of control, blackouts, missing meals,

and continuous drinking over twelve hours or more. However, the same increased risk of relapse did not apply to consumption levels. Higher consumption normal drinkers at eighteen months were no more likely to have relapsed by four years than lower consumption normal drinkers, given that neither reported any dependence symptoms. On these grounds, relatively high consumption *without* symptoms was allocated to the nonproblem-drinking category.

Turning now to the substantive results of the four-year follow-up, we shall consider first the basic data regarding drinking status among survivors. (Nearly 15 per cent of subjects had died during the four years since admission.) Altogether 28 per cent of those interviewed had totally abstained during the six months before interview. However, it should be noted that one quarter of these had drunk during the six months before that and only 7 per cent of the total sample had been consistently abstinent during the complete four-year period since admission, emphasizing again the comparative rarity of continuous abstention following treatment. Eighteen per cent of the sample were classified as nonproblem-drinkers under the new, stricter criteria. These included 8 per cent low-quantity consumers who reported typical quantities of less than two ounces of ethanol on drinking days and no days over three ounces during the thirty days before the last drink. Also included were 10 per cent high-quantity consumers who exceeded the above limits but never drank more than five ounces on any of the thirty days and, it must again be stressed, had not experienced any symptoms or other adverse consequences of drinking during this period. The remaining 54 per cent were classified as problem-drinkers, divided into 6 per cent who had experienced adverse consequences such as trouble with law enforcement agencies or interference with health, work or interpersonal relationships, 12 per cent who had experienced dependence symptoms and 36 per cent who had experienced both.

It will have been noted that the rate of 18 per cent for nonproblem-drinkers at four years is less than the 22 per cent rate recorded at eighteen months. However, virtually all this decrease is due to the stricter criteria employed on the second occasion and thus the extension of the follow-up period to four years does not result in any meaningful decrement to the overall normal drinking rate. Moreover, the normal drinkers at four years are more directly comparable with the 28 per cent six-month abstainers because for only a very few of them was the one-month 'window' on drinking behaviour unrepresentative of the full six months before interview. Only 2 per cent of all low-quantity consumers and 7 per cent of high-quantity consumers reported any occurrence of any dependence symptoms over the six-month period. By contrast, 33 per cent of subjects reporting adverse consequences without symptoms for the 30-day window admitted to at least one symptom over six months. If the nonproblem-drinkers showing any dependence symptoms during the six months are excluded, the overall nonproblem-drinking rate would fall by less than 1 per cent. A further important analysis is concerned with the severity of alcohol problems shown at admission to treatment by four-year nonproblem-drinkers and abstainers. The data showed that 45 per cent of clients who were drinking at admission but without symptoms were classified as nonproblem-drinkers at four years, compared with 21 per cent classified as abstainers. Among those showing from one to ten dependence symptoms in the 30 days before admission, 30 per cent were nonproblem-drinkers and 27 per cent abstainers at four years. Finally, for those with eleven or more symptoms at admission, only 12 per cent were nonproblem-drinkers but 30 per cent were abstainers. Thus it is by no means true that nonproblem-drinkers at four years were *confined* to those showing less serious problems at admission. On the other hand, the proportion of nonproblem-drinkers relative to abstainers was shown to decrease as a function of increasing levels of dependence symptoms.

A major difference between the original and the follow-up reports consists in a sharp decrease in the total percentage of clients in remission, from 67 per cent at eighteen months to 46 per cent at four years. It is essential to understand that this decrease is almost entirely accounted for by the change in definitions for remission categories between the two surveys. When the same definitions are applied to the two sets of data, a nearly identical picture emerges. We have seen that one change in definition involved stricter criteria for nonproblem-drinking, which in the four-year classification now required a complete absence of dependence symptoms during the thirty days before the last drink. But by far the most important change, accounting for most of the drop in reported overall remission rates, was the elimination from the four-year remission scheme of the 'short-term abstention' drinking status. Short-term abstainers at eighteen months had a much poorer prognosis than long-term abstainers at eighteen months – for example, an alcohol-related death rate of 9 per cent in the former compared with only 1 per cent in the latter. With regard to the stability of short-term abstention, only 35 per cent of those so classified at eighteen months were long-term abstainers at four years and the majority of the remainder had relapsed. If the older categories had been applied to the four-year data, fully 84 per cent of those who would have been classified as short-term abstainers, i.e. those who had abstained for thirty days before interview, reported dependence symptoms or adverse consequences during the preceding six months. On all these grounds the retention of short-term abstention as a remission category was clearly unjustified. There are two ways of explaining the large differences in prognosis and stability between long-term and short-term abstention. On the one hand, short-term abstainers could constitute a quite separate group from the long-term abstainers. Although no differences were found between the two groups in terms of characteristics measured at intake and no differences between the eighteen-month short-term abstainers who became long-term abstainers at four years and those who did not, it is possible that the short-term group as distinguished by unmeasured variables such as motivation to stop drinking or personality factors. On the other hand, it is equally plausible to suggest that short-term abstention is an early, high-risk phase of long-term abstention, a phase which all abstainers have to pass through with a relatively poor prognosis before they reach the more favourable prognosis of long-term abstention. These alternative explanations for the differences observed are highly relevant to the inter-pretation of the relapse data from the four-year report and will be returned to below.

As with the earlier survey, an important part of Polich *et al.*'s (1980) report is concerned with the analysis of relapse and, in particular, with the differential stability of various drinking statuses. It will be recalled that a crucial finding of the 1976 report was that there was no significant difference in the rate of relapse between six and eighteen months follow-up for normal drinkers and long-term abstainers. The basic relapse data for the four-year follow-up are shown in Table 2.2 which includes two indices of relapse, relapse rates among survivors and percentages of alcohol-related deaths. The crucial point about Table 2.2 is that, while the superiority of long-term abstention over short-term abstention is statistically significant, the differ-ences between long-term abstention and nonproblem-drinking are not. Thus, contrary to what has been reported in the media, this analysis provides no evidence that normal drinking is associated with a poorer prognosis than long-term abstention. Further, although it cannot be denied that long-term abstention gave the lowest relapse rates, even this conclusion is complicated by the high relapse rate of the short-term abstainers. As was argued above, a plausible explanation for the differences in prognosis between long-term and short-term abstention, an explanation which has not so far encountered any invalidating evidence, is that the latter is simply an early, high-risk phase of the former. Assuming this to be the case for the sake of argument, then it would appear that the *initial* attainment of normal drinking does not have a higher risk of relapse attached to it than the *initial* attainment of abstinence and may even be superior in this respect. Moreover, the classification of normal drinking at eighteen months was made on the basis of only thirty days' successful nonproblem-drinking, whereas long-term abstention re-quired six months' successful avoidance of alcohol. There is no way of knowing whether relapse rates for normal drinkers who had achieved six months' nonproblem-drinking behaviour would have been equally favour-able to the rates for six-month abstainers, but this is a distinct possibility. At the same time, it would seem fairer to compare one-month nonproblem-drinkers at eighteen months with *all* abstainers and not merely those of the long-term variety. If this were done, normal drinking would certainly not have a higher associated relapse rate than abstention.

TABLE 2.2

Two measures of relapse at four-year follow-up

Status at 18 months	Relapses at 4 years	
	Among survivors	Alcohol related deaths
Long-term abstainers	30%	1%
Short-term abstainers	53%	9%
Nonproblem-drinkers	41%	3%

Source: Polich, Armor and Braiker (1980) (adapted).

As well as the basic relapse data, Polich *et al*. also report a very useful analysis of the differential risk factors attached to abstinence and normal drinking when background variables measured at intake are taken into consideration. A regression analysis was used to generate estimates of the extent to which the background variables of level of dependence symptoms, socio-economic status, marital status, employment status, age, race and prior treatment were associated with higher or lower relapse rates at four years when either long-term abstention or nonproblem-drinking had been adopted at eighteen months. The clearest single predictor was an absence of dependence symptoms at admission, in which case relapse was more likely if abstinence had been adopted. The next most important predictors were unemployment at admission and age over forty, both of which favoured abstinence. Following these came the presence of low levels of dependence symptoms as opposed to high levels, which again favoured normal drinking. The importance of this particular observation is that severity of dependence appears to be a less efficient predictor of the differential risks associated with abstinence and normal drinking than age and unemployment and this evidence argues against the exclusive emphasis on severity of dependence in some discussions of the appropriateness of controlled drinking treatments. Marriage was also a significant predictor with unmarried individuals more likely to do well if they were normal drinkers. Socio-economic status, race and prior treatment did not yield significant predictions of differential risk factors.

To enrich this analysis, Polich *et al*. report several very interesting interactions between background variables and especially between level of dependence symptoms at admission, age and marital status. The expected relapse rates derived from the regression analysis for nonproblem-drinking and for at least one month's abstention at eighteen months may be compared for each cell of these interactions in Table 2.3. There it will be seen that, although a high level of dependence generally favours the abstinence outcome, there is an exception to this rule. Young, unmarried, highly dependent individuals were more likely to relapse if they chose abstinence than if they chose normal drinking. The reverse of this situation is true of the older, married, highly dependent men among whom there was a much poorer prognosis for normal drinking. Equally, while a low level of dependence generally favours normal drinking, older, married, low-dependence individuals were *more* likely to relapse if they adopted this solution to their problem. The largest proportional difference in relapse rates of all occurs among the young, unmarried low-dependence group and here relapse is nearly ten times more likely with abstention than with normal drinking. It is interesting to speculate on the reasons for the importance of age and marriage in these figures. It could be that younger unmarried men are more likely to succeed with normal drinking because they receive no social support for abstinence or because intense pressures are directed against this alternative in their social settings. On the other hand, married men may not only receive more support for abstinence but may actually be criticized by their wives for any drinking. While these speculations could be empirically investigated, the most arresting immediate conclusion from this analysis is that severity of dependence is not the be-all and end-all in determining the prognosis for normal drinking. Polich *et al.* warn that their results are not intended as bearing on choice of treatment for alcohol abusers but these differential relapse rates have some clear implications for selection and recommendation of treatment goals.

It was noted above that 46 per cent of the total sample were in remission at the four-year follow-up point, comprising 28 per cent abstaining and 18 per cent engaging in nonproblem-drinking. It should be recognized, however, that many of these remissions had been of relatively short duration. Combining the results of the eighteen-month and the four-year follow-ups, only 13 per cent of the relevant sample were classified as long-term at both points and only 9 per cent were nonproblem-drinkers on both occasions. Thus altogether 28 per cent were in remission at both follow-up points, including 6 per cent who had switched from one remission category to the other. Compared with the percentages of total numbers in remission at each point, the 28 per cent figure again emphasizes the high degree of variability in drinking outcomes following treatment.

Finally, Polich *et al.* found some evidence suggestive of the efficacy of treatment in that the difference in total percentage in remission between the high amount of treatment and the contact-only groups was statistically significant at the 0.1 per cent level of confidence. But it cannot be directly concluded from this that treatment was effective in increasing the proportion of remissions because these groups were not randomly assigned to treatment conditions. With regard to the relationship between treatment and nonproblem-drinking, the main effect of increasing amounts of treatment was to increase the proportion of successful abstainers observed at follow-up, while having relatively little effect on the numbers of nonproblem-drinkers. This supports the similar 1976 finding and is not surprising in view of the abstinence-directed nature of the treatment offered. As an incidental observation, there was evidence that those who attended AA regularly at eighteen months were no more likely to be in remission at four years than non-attenders, but no conclusions about the effects of AA affiliation can be drawn from this because of the possibility of self-selection. However, the 1976 finding was again confirmed that AA affiliates were much more likely to become abstainers and non-affiliates normal drinkers.

We cannot conclude this description of the Rand four-year follow-up results without remarking on the distortion they were subject to in the media coverage of Polich *et al.*'s (1980) report. A fine example of this is an article appearing in the *International Herald Tribune* dated 25 January, 1980 by Lois Timnick. The article is headed: 'Study Says Alcoholics Can't Learn to Drink'; and subheaded: 'Reverses Findings of 4 Years Ago'. The article proceeds to quote Loran Archer, executive assistant to the director of the NIAAA, to the effect that 'those who were dependent on alcohol cannot go

TABLE 2.3

Predicted relapse rates for all abstainers versus nonproblem-drinkers at 18 months

| Background characteristics | % relapsing at 4 years | | | |
| | Age under 40 at admission | | Age over 40 at admission | |
	Abstainers	Nonproblem-drinkers	Abstainers	Nonproblem-drinkers
High dependence symptoms				
Married	12	17	14	50
Unmarried	21	7	24	28
Low dependence symptoms				
Married	16	7	19	28
Unmarried	29	3	32	13

Source: Polich, Armor and Braiker (1980).

back to normal drinking'. The preceding pages will have shown precisely how unjustified such conclusions are and this article points up the extreme irrationality which continues to pervade public discussions of the issue of normal drinking in former alcoholics.

CONCLUSIONS

As a device for summarizing much of the material in this chapter, we may revert to the four criticisms which were made of Davies' claim to have observed normal drinking in former alcoholics and which were listed at the beginning of the chapter. Although in their original form these criticisms may quickly be rejected as being without foundation, it so happens that they each raise an issue which has been encountered as a recurrent theme throughout this review. These are the issues of 1. the nature of the drinking problems previously experienced by resumed normal drinkers; 2. the nature of the normal drinking engaged in; 3. the stability of the normal drinking outcome relative to total abstinence, and 4. the rate at which normal drinking occurs.

1. The contention that persons with previous drinking problems who have recovered the ability to drink normally were not 'real' alcoholics in the first place has been shown to be false. What is usually meant by this statement is that resumed normal drinkers have not been alcohol addicts (WHO, 1951) or gamma alcoholics (Jellinek, 1960). But abundant evidence has been presented to demonstrate that, whichever of these two definitions is preferred and whatever precisely is intended by 'loss of control', such alcoholics have been able to succeed in regaining control over drinking. Moreover, if the criteria for 'real' alcoholism are raised still further to admit only those showing signs of severe physical dependence, the evidence of Kendell (1965) and Davies *et al.*, (1969) in particular is that normal drinking is not thereby excluded. At present, there is no evidence of an upper limit to severity of alcohol dependence which would absolutely preclude the possibility of recovered control. There is evidence that the event becomes increasingly rare at higher levels of severity of dependence (Polich *et al.*, 1980).

Recently, Orford *et al.*, (1976) and Smart (1978) have shown that, if a group of resumed normal drinkers is compared with a group of abstainers, the former will tend to have had less serious drinking problems than the latter, although this was not the finding of Bromet and Moos (1979). In any event, there appears to have been some confusion in the literature between statements about what types of alcoholic often *do* and what types *can* become resumed normal drinkers. The preponderance of the less serious alcoholics among normal drinkers is probably due to the fact that the attainment of normal drinking is easier for these individuals than for the more seriously involved; but to repeat, there is no proof that it ever becomes impossible in principle.

2. Although the possibility of under-reporting in self-reports of normal drinking is a proper methodological concern, enough studies have been conducted using collateral sources of information about drinking behaviour (Davies, 1962; Kendell, 1965; Bailey and Stewart, 1967; Orford *et al.*, 1976; Polich *et al.*, 1980) to guarantee the validity of reports of resumed normal drinking. The reliable classification of drinking behaviour in this context was advanced considerably by the introduction of objective and predetermined criteria for normal drinking by Bailey and Stewart (1967). The available evidence suggests that the majority of normal drinkers consume only small amounts of alcohol in a drinking session, as described originally by Davies (1962) and supported by Armor *et al*. (1978), but those drinking somewhat higher amounts should not be excluded from the normal drinking classification because the evidence is (Polich *et al., 1980) that such amounts, in the absence of dependence symptoms, are not predictive of future problems. Some studies have described cases in which control over drinking is maintained only by continuing vigilance (Reinert and Bowen, 1968) or obsessional preoccupation with normal drinking (Shea, 1954). Similarly, some authors have maintained that a change in the meaning of drinking is necessary before a true normal drinking pattern can be achieved (Cain, 1964; Pattison *et al.*, 1968). Against this, other studies have found resumed normal drinking to be 'comfortable' (Davies, 1962) or to include occasional episodes of intoxication without loss of control or other adverse consequences (Kendell, 1965; Bailey and Stewart, 1967; Davies, 1969; Goodwin *et al.*, 1971). Further research, including studies using phenomenological methods, is needed to clarify these discrepant depictions. The observation by Orford *et al.* (1976) of a range of frequencies of drinking is compatible with the findings of Kish and Herman (1971) and van Dijk and van Dijk-Koffeman (1973) that occasional drinking is more frequently found than regular drinking. A further difference in emphasis is whether normal drinking is engaged in merely for the sake of appearances (de Morsier and Feldman, 1952) or whether it is actively enjoyed by former alcoholics (Kendell, 1965). No doubt Sobell (1978*a*) is correct in arguing for the existence of a number of distinct nonabstinent outcomes.

3. The preliminary evidence from Davies' (1962) study that normal drinking can be maintained over an extended period of time without relapse has been confirmed many times. Individual cases described in the literature have included two in which the duration of normal drinking has exceeded twenty years (Bailey and Stewart, 1967; Davies *et al.*, 1969) and follow-up studies have found sizeable proportions of former alcoholics who have maintained control for periods up to four (Fitzgerald *et al.*, 1971), six (Selzer and

Holloway, 1957) and eight (Goodwin *et al.*, 1971) years. Two investigations have described normal drinking up to the time of death (Lemere, 1953; Rakkolainen and Turunen, 1969). Other research has found normal drinking to be a stable outcome, at least as stable as total abstinence (Pokorney *et al.*, 1968; Armor *et al.*, 1978). The latest available evidence has shown that nonproblem-drinking produces slightly higher rates of relapse up to four years after treatment than long-term abstinence, but this difference was not statistically significant. Moreover, the issue of the relative risks of the two outcomes is complicated by the possibility of an early, high-risk phase of abstinence with generally poor prognosis. Severity of dependence is by no means the only major determinant of relative relapse rates; age, marriage and employment are at least equally important. For example, it was found by Polich *et al.* (1980) that severely dependent, young, unmarried men had a lower rate of relapse with nonproblem-drinking than with total abstinence.

4. The description of normal drinking in former alcoholics as a rare event can no longer be justified by the evidence. Although one study has estimated the rate at under 3 per cent of a sample of alcoholics (Reinert and Bowen, 1968), other findings have ranged up to 32 per cent (Fitzgerald *et al.*, 1971) and 44 per cent (Anderson and Ray, 1977). Compared with abstainers, normal drinkers have been found to constitute substantial minorities in several studies (e.g. Gerard *et al.*, 1962; Pokorney *et al.*, 1968; Schuckit and Winokur, 1972) and to be in a majority by others (e.g. Norvig and Nielsen, 1956; Moore and Ramseur, 1960; Rakkolainen and Turunen, 1969; Goodwin *et al.*, 1971). These differences in rate will undoubtedly be affected by the way in which normal drinking is defined and a consensus between researchers in this respect is therefore desirable. It is probable that rate is also partly determined by the type of alcoholic from which the research sample is drawn. There is some evidence to suggest that higher rates of normal drinking may be found among alcoholics with less serious drinking problems (Orford *et al.*, 1976; Smart, 1978), women alcoholics (Schuckit and Winokur, 1972) and criminal alcoholics (Goodwin, Crane and Guze, 1971), but more systematic investigation of such differences is needed. Rates of normal drinking have also been shown to decrease with affiliation to Alcoholics Anonymous (Armor *et al.*, 1978; Polich *et al.*, 1980) and to vary considerably from one treatment centre to another (Gerard and Saenger, 1966; Armor *et al.*, 1978), although type of treatment setting appears to have no consistent effect. The possibility that cultural factors may play a part in determining rates of normal drinking is suggested by the work of de Morsier and Feldman (1952) and Norvig and Nielsen (1956). Kendell's (1965) suggestion that the proportion of normal drinkers observed increases as length of follow-up interval increases has been supported by the findings of Orford *et al.* (1976) and Armor *et al.* (1978), but there may well

be a limit on the duration of this increase (Polich *et al.*, 1980). Given the variation in rates reported and the effect of proposed influences upon these rates, there is no reason to believe that the estimated range of 5 to 15 per cent for normal drinking advanced by Pattison (1976*a*) is inaccurate. It should be emphasized that this estimate refers to a proportion of all alcoholics sampled and not merely of treatment successes.

In addition to the above, the following conclusions also appear justified:

A.   The change in life situation involving an improved general adaptation first mentioned by Davies (1962) as a correlate of resumed normal drinking has been observed by several other authors (Gerard and Saenger, 1966; Davies *et al.*, 1969; Rakkolainen and Turunen, 1969; Levinson, 1977). Looked at in more detail, such alterations in life-style often entail moves to less vulnerable occupations (Selzer and Holloway, 1957; Kendell, 1965; Bailey and Stewart, 1967; Saunders and Kershaw, 1979) and marriages (Bailey and Stewart, 1967; Quirk, 1968; Saunders and Kershaw, 1979). Environmental factors such as financial ability to purchase drink, opportunities and time for drinking, location of drinking, and the formation of non-drinking friendships are more important than psychological and emotional factors as correlates of changes in drinking-problem status (Kendell, 1965; Bailey and Stewart, 1967; Cahalan, 1970; Saunders and Kershaw, 1979). However, it is often not clear whether such environmental changes are to be regarded as causes, accompaniments or consequences of reduced consumption. Moreover, even if environmental changes are seen as necessary for the resumption of normal drinking in some alcoholics, they cannot be sufficient conditions of it since other alcoholics experience these changes without controlling their drinking.

B.   A special case of resumed normal drinking is the tapering off of consumption observed in elderly alcoholics by Bailey and Stewart (1967), Rakkolainen and Turunen (1969) and Goodwin *et al.*, (1971) and discussed by Drew (1968). A related phenomenon may be the reduction in consumption after physical illness commented upon by Gerard and Saenger (1966), Barchha *et al.*, (1968) and Saunders and Kershaw (1979).

C.   There is no evidence from the literature that personality changes of the kind typically sought in psychotherapy are necessary to the reinstatement of control over drinking. The studies of Shea (1954), Davies (1962) and Gerard and Saenger (1966) suggest that stable patterns of normal drinking may be acquired on the level of habitual behaviour alone without, for example, increased insight into motivation for drinking abusively. This is not to say, however, that subjective changes in the meaning of drinking as suggested by Pattison *et al.* (1968) may not be helpful in the successful maintenance of stable drinking patterns.

D.   There is conflicting evidence in regard to the frequency with which periods of abstinence, varying in duration from a few months to several years, precede the onset of normal drinking. In some studies this has been found to be the universal, or almost universal, pattern (Shea, 1954; Davies, 1962; 1969; Cain, 1964; Reinert and Bowen, 1968; Levinson, 1977); in others the sample is about evenly divided between those who show a prior period of abstinence and those who do not (Selzer and Holloway, 1957; Kendell, 1965; Bailey and Stewart, 1967); in yet other studies prior abstainers were in a small minority (Pokorney *et al.*, 1968; Orford *et al.*, 1976). No research has yet explored the possibility of consistent differences between the alcoholics who adopt these two paths to resumed normal drinking. A simple hypothesis is that a period of abstinence becomes more necessary as severity of dependence increases.

E.   An event which occurs sufficiently often to be of interest is the change in preferred beverage which sometimes accompanies resumed normal drinking and which occurs either naturally (Kendell, 1965; Bailey and Stewart, 1967; Goodwin *et al.*, 1971) or as an unintended consequence of behavioural aversion therapy (Quinn and Henbest, 1967). The change is usually from whisky or some other spirits to beer or stout, but one case has been recorded where the switch was from beer to whisky (Bailey and Stewart, 1967).

F.   There has been a suggestion in the literature that normal drinkers are younger than abstainers (Gerard and Saenger, 1966), but this has not been replicated by Pattison *et al.* (1968), Orford *et al.* (1976), or Anderson and Ray (1977). Polich *et al.* (1980) found that younger normal drinkers were more likely to be successful than older normal drinkers. Similarly, some researchers have found previous alcohol problems to be of a shorter duration among normal drinkers than abstainers (Gerard and Saenger, 1966; Reinert and Bowen, 1969; Saunders and Kershaw, 1979) but this was not confirmed by Orford *et al.* (1976). Various other differences between normal drinkers and abstainers have been described by Orford *et al.* (1976), Hyman (1976), Anderson and Ray (1977), Smart (1978), Bromet and Moos (1979) and Saunders and Kershaw (1979).

G.   Resumed normal drinking can arise spontaneously without any treatment intervention. There is no good evidence that treatment directed at total abstinence has any consistent effect on rates of normal drinking one way or the other. However, findings that relative proportions of normal drinkers vary widely from one treatment centre to another (Gerard and Saenger, 1966; Armor *et al.*, 1978) have been interpreted as showing that the treatment philosophies espoused by the therapists the client has come into contact with can influence the probability that normal drinking will be taken up. It is possible to speculate that when normal drinking is actively discouraged in treatment lower rates will be discovered. Certainly, attendance at AA meetings has been shown to reduce the likelihood of resumed normal drinking (Anderson and Ray, 1977; Armor *et al.*, 1978; Polich *et al.*, 1980).

3   Loss of control and craving

It was made clear in the opening chapter that 'loss of control' was the hallmark of dominant disease conceptions of alcoholism, the concept which ensured the specifically disease status of these conceptions. As Keller (1972) puts it, loss of control is pathognomic of the disease. We saw that loss of control corresponded to the impairment of the will central to the early nineteenth-century medical view of habitual drunkenness and, in Jellinek's (1952) rediscovered disease conception, was a disease condition *per se* which marked the stage of the excessive drinker's career when the addictive process began. We also saw that the centrality of the concept has been retained in modified form in the most recent expression of the disease view of alcoholism, the Alcohol Dependence Syndrome. In the sociopolitical context of the disease theory, some kind of notion of loss of control over drinking behaviour is essential for the attempt to absolve the alcoholic from legal and moral responsibility for his actions, since it implies, by definition, that his deviant drinking behaviour is no longer within the realm of personal choice. Finally, in terms of more immediate considerations, loss of control is the theoretical foundation upon which claims for the irreversibility of the disease alcoholism have been based and therefore provides the conceptual underpinning of the therapeutic requirement of total and lifelong abstinence.

Having covered the most influential of the early accounts of loss of control in Chapter 1, it now becomes necessary to make an important distinction between the use of the concept as an *explanation* and as a *description* of alcoholismic drinking. There is no doubt that in all disease conceptions loss of control is employed as an explanation of the alcoholic's behaviour, but in many of these conceptions such a use cannot be justified because it perpetrates the logical error of circularity of explanation. In those conceptions where the concept is not supported by theoretical relationships with other variables, the existence of loss of control can be inferred only from the behaviour the concept has been designed in the first place to explain (cf. Maisto and Scheft, 1977). To make the same point another way, a preliminary requirement for any scientific explanation is that it attempts to specify the conditions under which the phenomena to be explained will occur. But with an unsupported concept of loss of control it is only possible to specify these conditions *after* the behaviour has occurred and it therefore has no power to reduce our uncertainty about the nature of the behavioural phenomenon in question. In other words, although this use of loss of control is purported to be an explanation of the alcoholic's drinking behaviour, it has no explanatory value and is merely descriptive. The question then arises whether the description is accurate and can be corroborated by empirical evidence.

In order to qualify as a scientific explanation, then, the concept of loss of control must be related to specific hypothesized mechanisms which account for the behavioural phenomenon. The AA view that loss of control is a manifestation of an allergy to alcohol could conceivably qualify in this way if only it could be expressed in a precise and testable manner. Jellinek's (1960) short-range accommodation hypothesis certainly qualifies because testable propositions may be deduced from it. To provide one other example, Marconi (1970) hypothesized that when the gamma alcoholic takes a drink after a period of abstinence, ethanol acts as a direct stimulant on two central neuronal circuits, one regulating the desire for alcohol and located in the hypothalamus and the other regulating the appearance of anxiety and displeasure and located in the dorsomedial thalamic nuclei. As a test of this hypothesis Marconi surgically coagulated the thalamic nuclei in three alcoholic subjects. The results of this treatment were inconclusive but in one case it was suspected that the wrong part of the brain had been coagulated 'owing to technical mistake'. Two subjects showed clinical signs of an organic brain reaction lasting up to at least three years following the operation.

It will have been noted that the above hypotheses are all of a physiological or at least psychobiological type. However, it is possible to construct an explanation for loss of control which is purely psychological in nature, in the sense that it does not refer to any impairment of neurophysiological functioning. For example, Storm and Smart (1965) have proposed a dissociation hypothesis based on the law of stimulus generalization deficit. The important point here is that this learning theory conception of loss of control is specifically stated by its authors not to imply irreversible phenomena. In general we may say that psychological or learning explanations of loss of control do not propose an irreversible basis, and, while it is not the case that physiological explanations do invariably propose irreversibility, the converse of this statement *is* true; the postulation of irreversibility is confined to physiological explanations.

With regard to craving, Isbell (1955) postulated the existence of two kinds – physical or *nonsymbolic* craving which is manifested by withdrawal symptoms and the most important effect of which is to make drinking bouts even more protracted and continuous, and *symbolic* craving which applies to the initial abuse of alcohol and to relapse after abstinence and which is psychological in origin, being due to a combination of cultural and psychiatric factors. Isbell's (1955) two types of craving imply two distinct etiologies. These were both formally recognized by a WHO committee (Jellinek *et al.*, 1955), as well as a third possible type of etiology. Craving, or the alternative terms employed in the literature to describe the same phenomenon, had been used to explain drinking arising from (*a*) a psychological need; (*b*) the physical need to relieve withdrawal symptoms, and (*c*) a physical need which originates in physiopathological conditions involving metabolism, endocrine functions, etc., and existing in the alcoholic before he starts on his drinking career or developing in the course of it. Etiological theories classifiable under the last heading were reviewed by MacLeod (1955). Among the best known of the many theories in this class are Williams' (1948) 'genetotrophic' theory in which inherited patterns of metabolic abnormalities cause increased requirements for vitamins obtainable in alcohol, Smith's (1949) theory in which a constellation of dysfunctions in endocrine glandular activity creates a demand for alcohol, and MacLeod's own theory involving an interaction between alcohol and brain systems responsible for the production of acetylcholine. Despite the fact that none of these theoretical formulations has ever been confirmed by experimental evidence, the search for a single biochemical substrate for craving continues to be a major preoccupation of researchers into alcoholism.

The remarks which were made earlier (p. 78) about the circularity of unsupported conceptions of loss of control also apply to craving. Where the existence of craving is simply inferred from abnormal drinking behaviour, without reference to observable underlying variables, the concept is clearly tautologous and in this case has no descriptive content either (cf. Mello, 1972). On the other hand, if craving is seen as a subjective experience qualitatively different from normal mental states which is effective in causing abnormal drinking, then such a concept is not circular in principle. However, the only possible information upon which statements about such craving may be directly based are the introspective reports of alcoholics, and the methodological problems inherent in the use of private reports of experience in scientific enquiry, as opposed to clinical practice, are of course enormous. Later in this chapter we shall encounter various attempted solutions to these methodological problems in the ways in which craving and loss of control have been operationally defined for research purposes.

LABORATORY STUDIES OF INTOXICATION IN ALCOHOLICS

Up to the early 1960s the evidence on which formulations of loss of control and craving had been based were the clinical observations of psychiatrists and other professional helpers and the historical reports of their experiences given by recovered alcoholics themselves. Thus the ultimate source of this evidence was, in both cases, the retrospective accounts of past or present alcoholics made when sober. However well-intentioned and devoted to accuracy, such accounts are obviously suspect for scientific purposes, owing, for example, to alcohol-induced amnesias, to the general fallibility of human memory, the possibility of conscious or unconscious anticipation of the interviewer's expectations and the influence of theoretical constructions of alcoholism to which the alcoholic individual or the interviewer may have subscribed. The main point is that no systematic observations of alcoholics' drinking behaviour had been made under controlled conditions and subject to elementary objective criteria for the collection of scientific data. This gap in the legitimate data base for an understanding of alcoholism was filled by a programme of research carried out in the 1960s at the National Institute of Mental Health, Maryland, USA under the direction of J.H. Mendelson, and this section will be given over to a selective review of the pioneering work of this laboratory. A concomitant innovation made by Mendelson's team was the introduction of the principle of giving alcohol to alcoholics for research purposes, thus effecting a necessary infringement of a taboo which had previously existed on such a procedure. For the first time in the history of the study of alcoholism, theory and hypothesis were forced to confront objective and systematic observations of alcoholics' actual drinking behaviour. Of the many important experiments conducted by Mendelson and his colleagues, we shall consider here only those which have an obvious bearing on the notions of loss of control and craving. All these experiments employed a similar basic design and used similar criteria for the selection of subjects and these may be consulted in Mello (1972).

The design of all the experiments we shall be reviewing was based on the principles of operant methodology as set out by Skinner (1953). It is important to note that this behaviourist methodology is not at all interested in arriving at generalized statements regarding differences in average measures between groups of individuals, as is generally the aim in conventional psychological research. Rather, the purpose is to determine the environmental correlates of designated behavioural responses in the individual case. This is done by manipulating the environmental consequences, or contingencies, attached to designated responses and by observing the ensuing changes in the frequency and patterning of those responses. It should also be pointed out that the underlying goal implicit in this use of operant methodology is the identification of variables which contribute to the maintenance of abusive drinking in alcoholics, rather than the attempt to discover etiological factors.

The first experiment to employ operant methodology in this fashion was that of MELLO AND MENDELSON (1965). In this experiment two alcoholic subjects had free access to an operant conditioning apparatus at any time during the day or night over periods of 11 and 14 days respectively. Subjects could choose whether to work for a single shot of whisky or for the money equivalent by turning an appropriate switch. When the glass containing whisky was removed, the whole apparatus was shut off for ten minutes. The response required to earn whisky or money was pressing a translucent key which changed colour according to a complex and random sequence of schedules of reinforcement.

The immediately apparent finding of this experiment was that both sub-jects continued to drink steadily during the experimental period, with no extended intervals of abstinence except when drinking was disrupted by gastritis. Despite the fact that their performance at the apparatus was highly inefficient, subjects were able to maintain high levels of blood alcohol concentration ranging between 150 and 250 mg/100 ml, with peaks at 300 to 350 mg/100 ml. In order to achieve this, they needed to spend on average about two hours per day at the machine and tended to work in short sessions of between 10 and 25 minutes' duration. It further appeared that, in order to stabilize these high BACs, both subjects learned to work in progressively shorter sessions and increasingly more at night. Both preferred to work for alcohol directly than for money to spend later. Although it might seem that the ten-minute shut-down after removal of the glass was an incentive to accumulate alcohol before drinking, this did not in fact occur; the two men worked for small amounts, consumed them slowly and then returned to the task. At the end of the experiment these alcoholics both experienced severe withdrawal symptoms involving in one case frightening delusions of the operant instrument. During intoxication, they had complained that the task required of them was monotonous and dehumanizing.

Chiefly in order to replace the key-pressing task with one more attractive to subjects, MENDELSON AND MELLO (1966) devised a further experiment along the same lines as that described above. Here, however, the required task involved a driving machine similar to those found in amusement arcades. The two subjects taking part could earn points by keeping a model car on a simulated road and by responding quickly to commands from the machine. Alcohol or money was dispensed after subjects had amassed a designated number of points. Access to the machine was limited to alternate hours of the day and night, but subjects were allowed to participate for an unlimited number of days.

The central finding of this second experiment was similar to that of the first, in that the two subjects drank in a manner which served to maintain a stable BAC, ranging between 150 and 250 mg/100 ml in one case and 200 to 300 mg/100 ml in the other. They did not become grossly intoxicated and, indeed, displayed only mild intoxication with alteration to mood but without marked impairment to speech or motor functions. Owing to their high tolerance, these subjects were able to work efficiently at the driving task with blood alcohol levels which would produce a definite impairment in normal individuals. The shift towards working and drinking more at night found in the previous experiment was also observed here. An interesting incidental finding was that, when one subject opted out of the experiment after fourteen days because of gastritis, the other alcoholic elected to stop two days later, complaining that he missed his drinking companion. Thus, although this man had been identified as being physically dependent on the substance alcohol, the relatively easy availability of the drug was not sufficient in itself to maintain his drinking. And although he must have become aware that his drinking would shortly have to stop, this subject made no attempt gradually to reduce his drinking; as with his former companion, the abrupt cessation of drinking resulted in the appearance of the withdrawal syndrome.

Although we have seen that drinking in the above experiments seems to have been motivated by the attempt to maintain high and constant BACs, the actual patterns of drinking shown by subjects were highly variable and can be assumed to have been influenced by several interacting factors. In later research, therefore, the Mendelson team became less interested in studying spontaneous drinking patterns as such and more concerned with assessing the relative contributions of specifiable factors which might affect drinking in alcoholics. In MELLO, McNAMEE AND MENDELSON (1968) the main emphasis was upon the cost of alcohol, cost being defined in the laboratory situation as the amount of work required to acquire alcohol. The task was a vigilance procedure in which the subject had to press a key within half a second of the random and intermittent appearance of a stimulus light in order to make a correct response. Two groups of subjects were used. In the first group of six, an alcohol or money reinforcement was provided upon completion of sixteen consecutive correct responses, whereas in the second group of the same size reinforcement was contingent on the completion of thirty-two consecutive correct responses. The basic finding was that subjects in the first group showed average BACs roughly twice as high as those in the second group. In other words, the amount of alcohol consumed, inferred from blood alcohol level, was a predictable function of the degree of effort required to earn it.

Other relevant observations from this experiment were that there appeared to be a definite limit to the amount of time subjects were prepared to devote to alcohol acquisition, there was a tendency for subjects in both groups to work for moderate amounts of alcohol, and that subjects neither hoarded alcohol nor consumed it as soon as it became available. All these observations again suggest the continuing presence of some kind of control over drinking behaviour in these alcoholic men. The length of this particular experiment was seven days and all subjects expressed considerable anxiety at the prospect of withdrawal symptoms upon the removal of alcohol. Despite these anxieties, however, only four reduced their drinking towards the end of the experiment in the attempt to avoid withdrawal symptoms and three actually increased their intake on the final day. Nevertheless, the four who did attempt to 'taper-off' exhibited a further interesting form of control over drinking.

The aim of the experiment reported by MELLO AND MENDELSON (1972) was to observe the drinking patterns of alcoholics over a longer period than had previously been used. Four subjects were studied for thirty days and another four for sixty-two days. The task used in this experiment consisted simply in pressing a pushbutton on an individual box one thousand times in order to earn a reinforcement in the form of a poker chip. The chips could subsequently be used to purchase a single ounce of whisky or one cigarette. This task was so simple that it could not be impaired by alcohol intoxication and could be performed while watching television, eating or talking. Under these conditions, all eight subjects showed a very clear and surprising dissociation between drinking and work periods. Typically, they would work during periods of abstinence of one or two days' duration until they had earned enough tokens to drink for two or three days. The cycle would then begin again. During the abstinent working periods subjects frequently displayed withdrawal signs, ranging from mild to moderate in severity and associated with rapid falls in blood alcohol level. However, it is important to note that, despite the occurrence of these partial withdrawal phenomena, subjects did not immediately start drinking to abolish them even though alcohol was available, but generally preferred to continue working to amass more tokens.

A somewhat different pattern of drinking was shown by a further group of eighteen subjects in the Mello and Mendelson (1972) experiment who were allowed completely free access to alcohol over periods of time from twelve to fifteen days. These subjects also showed some evidence of a cyclical pattern of drinking, but the range of blood alcohol levels within individual subjects over time was much narrower than in the work-contingent condition and no intervals of abstinence were observed. It is reasonable to assume that the work-contingent situation more closely resembles that of the real world and the more marked cyclical variations shown in this experimental condition may be taken to represent the bout drinking so often found in alcoholics in the natural environment. However, the evidence suggests that these cycles do not occur because alcoholics are reluctantly forced to adopt them by external constraints or because they are prevented for whatever reason from continuing to drink, as a loss of control formulation might suggest. The present interpretation is supported by perhaps the most striking observation from the free-access experimental condition. This is that, despite the absence of any kind of limitation on the volume of alcohol subjects were permitted to drink, none of the eighteen subjects drank all the alcohol available and tokens which could have been exchanged for large quantities of drink were handed back at the end of the experiment!

Let us try to summarize the most important implications of the experiments reviewed in this section for the concepts of loss of control and craving. Firstly and most obviously, none of the subjects studied, who all conformed to the standard criteria for the presence of pharmacological dependence on alcohol, attempted in a situation where they could determine the volume and pattern of their own drinking to drink themselves into a state of unconsciousness or collapse. This is not to claim that these men had never engaged in such drinking behaviour in the natural environment, but it is to claim that, to put it in the most conservative manner possible, the compulsion to continue drinking to severe intoxication does not predictably occur in alcoholics. Secondly, no subject studied chose to drink all the alcohol available to him, even when no effort was required to obtain it. Thirdly, these alcoholic subjects demonstrated positive sources of control over their drinking, in that (i) they drank to maintain high but roughly constant BACs during shorter drinking periods; (ii) they did not drink continuously but spontaneously initiated and terminated drinking sessions over a longer experimental period; (iii) they tended to work for and drink moderate amounts of alcohol and did not consume it as soon as it became available; (iv) some subjects chose to taper-off their drinking in order to avoid or reduce withdrawal symptoms following the termination of the experiment, and (v) subjects chose to work over one- or two-day periods to accumulate alcohol rather than drink to abolish partial withdrawal symptoms. All these observations are inconsistent with the concept of loss of control in the sense of an inability to stop once drinking has commenced, and with the related concept of craving in the sense of an uncontrollable urge to consume more and more alcohol during a drinking session.

One remaining piece of evidence from these experiments which goes against the traditional position deserves separate consideration. This is the finding that the amount of alcohol consumed by alcoholics in a free choice laboratory situation was a function of the cost of alcohol, measured by the degree of effort required to obtain it. The importance of this observation is that it most clearly shows alcoholic drinking to be an *operant* behaviour, that is to say, one which is shaped and maintained by its environmental consequences. In the next section we shall encounter examples of other ways in which the drinking of alcoholics may be properly regarded as operant behaviour, contingent in these examples on the occurrence of other classes of reinforcer. This is not to deny, of course, that the particular reinforcement contingencies applying to the drinking behaviour of individual alcoholics will show differences from those applying to nonalcoholics; this is self-evident from the fact of markedly different drinking practices. But what these findings do clearly demonstrate is that alcoholics' drinking behaviour is subject to the same *kind* of laws which can be shown to describe normal drinking behaviour, or indeed, goal-directed behaviour of any kind. More specifically, drinking is partly a function of the cost of alcohol in both cases. It will be readily appreciated that this is an entirely separate conception of alcoholic behaviour from that offered by a disease perspective which proposes a sharp distinction, in its use of concepts like loss of control and craving, between abnormal and normal drinking behaviour, and assumes that the former obeys a qualitatively different set of laws from the latter.

OTHER EXPERIMENTAL INVESTIGATIONS OF ALCOHOLICS' DRINKING BEHAVIOUR

Following the precedent set by Mendelson's team of giving alcohol to alcoholics for research purposes, there have appeared a large number of reports of experimental investigations of alcoholics' drinking behaviour based on the operant paradigm. All these studies have demonstrated, in various ways, that within a laboratory or hospital inpatient setting the drinking of chronic alcoholics is a function of environmental contingencies. Pattison, Sobell and Sobell (1977) listed fifty-eight such reports, including those of Mendelson and his co-workers, and it will clearly be impossible to describe them all here. Instead, we shall concentrate on the work of three separate research teams, all reporting in the early 1970s and all based in the United States.

The first research team of interest is one centred at the Johns Hopkins University, Baltimore. As in Mello, McNamee and Mendelson (1968), the focus of the first reported experiment by COHEN, LIEBSON, FAILLACE AND SPEERS (1971) was upon cost factors in alcoholic drinking. Unlike the earlier experiment, however, the target behaviour used in this experiment was abstinence and the broad aim could be described as an attempt to determine what reinforcement contingencies were necessary to 'buy' abstinence from alcoholics. This was done by examining the subtle interactions between cost factors and two other important variables, a priming dose of alcohol and a delay in reinforcement. Subjects were four male chronic alcoholics who had all lost jobs and been hospitalized for alcoholism in the past. Other selection criteria and the living arrangements for subjects were similar to those employed by the Mendelson group.

Subjects were allowed to purchase a relatively large amount of alcohol every third day of the experiment. On subsequent days each was offered a certain amount of money to abstain for an entire day. If the subject did not abstain the incentive was increased for the next occasion, but if he abstained, it was decreased. Subjects were not told how payments for abstinence were calculated. The results showed that abstinence could be bought from each subject for a varying amount of money ranging from seven to twenty dollars. The two subjects who required the largest amounts to abstain requested to be discharged from the programme and did not contribute further to the results.

The first experimental manipulation was concerned with delay in reinforcement. The two remaining subjects were offered the same amount for which they had previously abstained but this time payment was delayed for periods ranging from three to twenty-one days. Again, payment was increased if the subject drank but in this condition delay in reinforcement was increased if he abstained. The results showed that delay in reinforcement disrupted abstinence, in that with a delay of three days in one case and fourteen in the other the previously successful incentive was insufficient to procure abstinence. However, an increase in payment was effective in reinstating abstinence, so that, for example, one subject was able to tolerate a twenty-one-day delay for a payment of twenty dollars. Essentially the same results were produced by the administration of a priming dose of alcohol on the morning of the day on which payment for abstinence was offered. A varying amount of alcohol disrupted abstinence for each subject, but increasing the magnitude of monetary reinforcement re-established it. The results for the priming dose condition are shown in Figure 3.1.

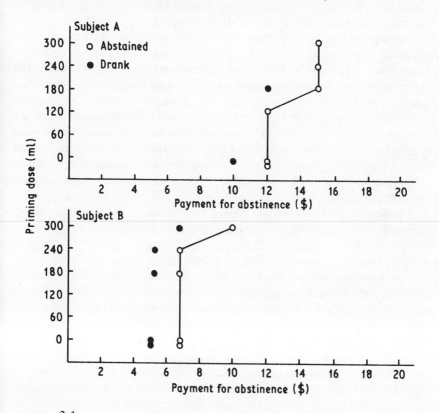

FIGURE 3.1
Relationships for two subjects between amount of priming dose, magnitude of reinforcement and reinstatement of abstinence (see text). (From Cohen, Liebson, Faillace and Speers, 1971).

Perhaps the greatest significance of this ingenious experiment is that it suggests how belief in the notion of loss of control could have arisen. It is consistent with this notion, for example, that having consumed a certain amount of alcohol chronic alcoholics will reject abstinence even though it has reinforcing consequences and even though they might have accepted it when initially sober. The very important point demonstrated by Cohen *et al.*, however, is that drinking could be brought under control once more by providing a sufficiently large positive reinforcement, showing that any first impression of uncontrolled drinking would be an illusion. Delay in reinforcement is also highly relevant to the issue of loss of control, since it may be assumed that the positive reinforcing consequences of abstinence for the alcoholic in the real world are usually more remote than the immediate reinforcement expected from drinking. But it was nevertheless shown that alcoholics will tolerate a relatively long delay in reinforcement given that the incentive for abstinence is sufficiently inviting.

Cost factors, both in the form of physical effort needed to obtain drink and of actual cost in money tokens, were also the object of attention for BIGELOW AND LIEBSON (1972). In their first experiment, these authors made the dispensing of a drink contingent on a fixed ratio of lever-pulling responses, ranging on different days of a free-access situation from 100 to 5000 responses per drink. The results showed simply that the amount of work done and the number of drinks consumed were a direct function of the ratio in effect on a given day. At a ratio of 3000 responses per drink, neither of two subjects chose to abstain, but drinking was considerably moderated as compared with lower ratio conditions. At a ratio of 5000, both subjects chose to abstain totally on occasional days. In a second experiment, the use of a progressive price schedule meant that the cost of a drink in tokens previously supplied by the experimenters rose if the subject drank more than two drinks in a single hour. All four alcoholics used as subjects showed an increased temporal spacing of drinking under these conditions. Note that in this second experiment drinking was modified by the relatively remote consequence of a reduction in the total number of drinks which could be consumed within a day. Note also that two aspects of drinking were brought under environmental control in these experiments, amount consumed and frequency of drinking. The bald conclusion stated by the authors is that 'alcoholic drinking is not an uncontrollable process, but is modifiable by environmental contingencies'.

A different class of reinforcer was investigated by COHEN, LIEBSON AND FAILLACE (1972). In this experiment the provision of an enriched or an impoverished environment was made contingent on the occurrence of moderate drinking. Subjects were five healthy, male alcoholics who had manifested withdrawal symptoms on admission to the hospital and would have been classified as gamma alcoholics. They were kept in the experiment by means of a money incentive which could only be obtained at the end of it. Subjects were given the option to drink up to ten ounces of 95 per cent proof ethanol free of charge on weekdays for five consecutive weeks. In the contingent condition which was in operation during the first, third and fifth weeks, subjects were given an enriched environment if they drank less than five ounces of alcohol in a day. This enriched environment consisted of the opportunity to work in the hospital laundry for payment, the use of a private telephone and a recreation room which included TV, a pool table and other games, the chance to engage nursing staff in games and to participate in daily group therapy sessions, a regular diet, a bedside chair and reading materials in the subject's room, and access to visitors. If the subject exceeded the five ounce limit, he was put in an impoverished environment in which all the above privileges were removed, he had to stay in his room and was given pureed food. Furthermore, all alcohol was taken away for a day following that of the excessive drinking. There was a fine for breaking any of the rules of the experiment. In the second and fourth weeks a non-contingent condition was in operation and moderate drinking was not differentially reinforced. The subject had an impoverished environment no matter how much he drank. The design of the experiment permitted a comparison of amount drunk between contingent and non-contingent weeks for each subject.

The result showed that all five subjects drank less during the contingent weeks than during the non-contingent weeks. This difference was statistically significant at the 1 per cent level of confidence. It is interesting to note that subjects adopted various ways of remaining in an enriched environment, with some drinking up to the prescribed limit from the start of the experiment and others beginning with abstinence and gradually approaching the limit. These individual differences notwithstanding, these results demonstrate clearly that alcoholics' drinking behaviour may be moderated by the occurrence of a reinforcer which has obvious relevance to drinking in the natural environment.

A possible objection to the above experiment is that the greater drinking observed during the non-contingent condition was not a result of the absence of contingencies as such but of the aversive nature of the impoverished environment in which the subjects were required to live. It could possibly be argued that excessive drinking was a kind of protest on the part of subjects who were forced to live in unpleasant circumstances no matter how they behaved. This interpretation was put to the test by COHEN, LIEBSON, FAILLACE AND ALLEN (1971). These investigators established moderate drinking in five alcoholics by the same method as described above. They then employed four of the same subjects in a further experiment in which the non-contingent condition involved not an impoverished but an enriched environment. Subjects were placed in an enriched environment no matter how much they drank. The results showed the same difference between drinking in contingent and non-contingent weeks at an even higher level of statistical significance.

A further objection to the design of these experiments is that alcoholic subjects may have chosen moderation over excessive drinking because they were prevented from going on a binge for several days, which may have been their preferred way of being drunk. It will be recalled that if subjects in the Cohen *et al.* (1972) experiment were given an impoverished environment following excessive drinking, alcohol was completely withdrawn for the following day. In addition, drinking was only permitted on weekdays. As a simple test of this alternative interpretation, COHEN, LIEBSON AND FAILLACE (1973) used the same basic design as in the two experiments described above but gave their three subjects continuous access to 24 ounces of ethanol every day for seventeen to twenty days. This experiment yielded the same result as the others and the alternative explanation may therefore be discounted.

The relationship between drinking behaviour and another type of re-inforcer was examined by BIGELOW, LIEBSON AND GRIFFITHS (1974). Ten chronic alcoholic volunteers were able to drink on request from twelve to twenty-four drinks per day. However, the immediate consequence of taking a drink was a brief period of 'time-out' from positive reinforcement. In other words, if subjects took a drink they were placed in a situation of physical and social isolation for ten or fifteen minutes. The only activities allowed during time-out, which was spent in a small isolation booth on the ward, were drinking and smoking. Drinking behaviour in the experimental condition was compared with baseline observations made when contingent isolation was not in effect and, in the case of six subjects, with a reversal condition following the experimental condition when the contingency was once more abandoned.

The results of this experiment were that drinking was suppressed to roughly half its baseline level in seven out of ten subjects. In the baseline, subjects had consumed over 90 per cent of the alcohol available but in the experimental condition this was reduced to an average of about 50 per cent. In the reversal, drinking once again returned to over 90 per cent of the quantity available, showing that contingent isolation was the effective behaviour modifier. Subjects showed some variation in the degree of suppression demonstrated but the majority were close to the average effect. The significance of these results is that they show the social and recreational activities associated with drinking to be important sources of reinforcement in the maintenance of drinking behaviour, in many alcoholics as well as in normal drinkers. This is contrary to a traditional view of alcoholic drinking as being a relatively automatic and mechanical activity unresponsive to social situations.

Social factors in alcoholic drinking represented one focus of enquiry for a group of investigators based at Boston City Hospital and some of the output from this laboratory will be briefly described. NATHAN*et al.* (1970) reported a behavioural analysis of twelve male, gamma alcoholics who were given the opportunity to convert reinforcement points earned by disrupting a photocell beam into alcohol. In each of three studies a drinking period was preceded by a pre-drinking period in which subjects could accumulate reinforcement points to be spent later and was followed by a post-drinking withdrawal period. The main experimental manipulation was to divide each of the above periods into alternate socialization and isolation conditions lasting for three days. In the socialization condition subjects had access to all parts of the ward, while in the isolation condition they were confined to their bedrooms where the operant apparatus was located. Several kinds of data were gathered during these experiments – operant data from a fixed-ratio schedule, observations of behaviour on the ward recorded by staff, data on emotional state derived from a mood adjective checklist, and various physiological measures.

The interpretation of results from these experiments bearing on the effects of social interaction is at first equivocal. If conclusions had been based solely on anecdotal material, that is, upon nursing notes and interview data, subjects' behaviour would have conformed to the stereotype of the alcoholic as social isolate for whom the intoxicating effects of alcohol have become the overriding preoccupation. Certainly, these subjects appeared to prefer to be by themselves than to be with their fellows, even during scheduled periods of socialization. On the other hand, the more objective data from operant records, BAC readings and checklist ratings demonstrated that all subjects to some extent and several subjects to a great extent showed differential behavioural responses to socialization and isolation. For example, five subjects worked for and drank less alcohol during isolation than during socialization conditions and eight rated themselves as more anxious and depressed during isolation. This combination of findings may serve to explain how the impression of a correlation between alcoholism and social isolation could have come about, while at the same time revealing that under a closer and more objective analysis alcoholic drinking continues for the most part to be responsive to social circumstances.

A novel feature of an experiment reported by NATHAN AND O'BRIEN (1971) was that it was the first to compare the patterning and effects of prolonged drinking in alcoholics and nonalcoholic subjects. Previous research (e.g. Cutter, Schwaab and Nathan, 1970) had restricted such a comparison to the effects of short-term drinking. The design of the Nathan and O'Brien study was similar to that used by Nathan *et al.* (1970) and described above. Four male alcoholics were studied, all conforming to criteria for the presence of chronic alcoholism of the skid-row variety. They were compared with four volunteers matched for age and socio-economic status whose drinking had been observed in the natural environment and found to be harmfree. Although they were regular drinkers and inhabited the same skid-row neighbourhoods as the alcoholics, they appeared not to have suffered any adverse consequences from drinking. During the drinking period of the experiment all subjects had free access to the operant apparatus and unlimited opportunity to buy drink with reinforcement points earned.

The first somewhat surprising result of this experiment was that both groups reached the same high blood alcohol levels early in the drinking period. The differences were that the alcoholics maintained these high levels over a three- to five-day spree and returned to them more often later in the experiment. Thus it was the duration of high BACs rather than the level itself which discriminated initially between the drinking of the two groups, suggesting that therapeutic efforts might be usefully directed towards shortening the duration of excessive drinking in alcoholics as well as lowering the amount consumed. Previous findings with respect to dysphoric mood changes in alcoholics during drinking (e.g. McNamee *et al.*, 1968) were confirmed here. During the drinking period alcoholics became significantly more depressed, less active and showed more psychopathology as measured by a psychiatric rating scale than did the nonalcoholics. Moreover, in this experiment it was found that, compared with the liveliness and conviviality of the nonalcoholics' behaviour, the alcoholics could be described as social isolates before, during and after drinking, preferring to spend more time drinking alone in their rooms than at the communal bar and generally avoiding social interaction with other subjects. Nathan and O'Brien conclude that social isolation acts as a cue for excessive drinking in alcoholics.

At first sight this last finding seems at variance with the conclusions of Nathan *et al.* (1970) mentioned above and also with evidence from other research centres. For example, Bigelow (1973) found that alcoholics engaged in social interaction significantly more often when drinking than when not drinking and when drinking were more likely to prefer an opportunity to socialize over small amounts of money. Bridell and Nathan (1975) have suggested that this apparent discrepancy in results may be due to the relatively large amounts of alcohol consumed in the Nathan and O'Brien study and that, although moderate amounts may facilitate social interaction in alcoholics as in normal drinkers, larger amounts have the reverse effect, again as in other drinkers. It may also be the case that the artificial drinking environment and the fact that subjects were presumably strangers to each other influenced Nathan and O'Brien's results. Certainly, evidence from Mendelson's laboratory strongly suggests that the alcoholic drinking of dyadic pairs, such as father–son and brothers, is subject to discernible rules of conduct and provides the opportunity to adopt interpersonal roles which are not psychologically available during sobriety. STEINGLASS, WEINER AND

MENDELSON (1971), for example, showed that interpersonal roles between two alcoholic brothers were more clearly defined when one was intoxicated. They rarely became drunk together but alternated between a passive supportive role when sober and a more assertive behaviour pattern when drunk. The partner who happened to be sober at the time combined criticism of the other's drinking with assistance in getting him more to drink. Clinical experience indicates that the same kind of patterning is often found in alcoholic marriages. On a larger scale, Rubington (1968) has conducted a detailed analysis of the subtle and complex social structure of a skid-row bottle gang and the experimental study of such a group has been carried out by Mendelson, Mello and Soloman (1968). Finaly, Goldman *et al.* (1973) observed the drinking behaviour and decision-making of a group of four alcoholics in the same laboratory setting as used in the experiments described above and concluded that the drinking pattern of each individual was heavily influenced by norms established in the group as a whole.

The third and last research group to be considered was based at Thomas Jefferson University, Philadelphia and headed by Edward Gottheil. The work of this group is somewhat different from the material we have covered so far in this section in that it is not based on the operant conditioning paradigm and involves a combination of investigative research with treatment for alcoholism. However, since all research data are derived from the drinking behaviour of alcoholics observed under controlled conditions, the conclusions from this research are highly relevant to the issues of loss of control and craving.

The treatment and research design common to these investigations is termed the Fixed Interval Drinking Decisions programme (FIDD) and has been described by GOTTHEIL, CORBETT, GRASBERGER AND CORNELISON (1971; 1972). Patients studied were groups of seven to ten male alcoholic veterans aged between twenty-five and fifty and without psychosis or serious medical or neurological disease. The great majority had previously been hospitalized for alcoholism. Each group took part in a six-week treatment cycle consisting of a one-week pre-drinking phase when alcohol was not available and initial assessments were carried out, a four-week drinking phase when alcohol was once more removed, when assessments were repeated and clinical decisions taken as to future offers of treatment for individual patients. During the drinking phase patients could elect to drink nought, one or two ounces of 40 per cent ethanol, with or without water, each hour from 9 a.m. to 9 p.m. on weekdays. Thus there were thirteen decision points for each patient daily with a maximum possible intake of 26 ounces. BAC readings were taken four times daily and an upper limit was set at 250 mg/100 ml, although no patient exceeded this level. If the patient decided to drink he simply went to the ward station at the appropriate time, requested a drink from nursing staff and drank it there. No task performance was required to obtain a drink. Numerous measures of behaviour, emotional state and self-perception were taken during the experiment. In addition to the research activity, the programme included a variety of treatment modalities, including group and individual psychotherapy, marital casework, occupational and recreational therapy and Alcoholics Anonymous meetings. Therapeutic attention was also directed to feelings, behaviour and beliefs associated with drinking decisions, without staff approval or disapproval of individual decisions.

The first quantitative results from the FIDD programme were reported by GOTTHEIL, MURPHY, SKOLODA AND CORBETT (1972). These authors also set out to test three hypotheses selected from the literature on loss of control and craving:

(*a*) alcoholic patients will not be able to resist drinking available alcohol while on a closed ward in the presence of others who are drinking;

(*b*) once they have started drinking, they will be unable to stop; and

(*c*) they will regularly and consistently elect to drink at every available opportunity.

The results of these investigations unequivocally disconfirmed all three hypotheses. Nine out of twenty-five patients (36 per cent) did not drink at all during the treatment cycle; a further nine began drinking but stopped before the final week; three men drank sporadically throughout the programme and only four drank heavily and consistently. It will be noted that these drinking patterns are markedly different from those observed by the Mendelson, Cohen and Nathan groups described earlier, since in the latter experiments no subjects were found to abstain completely when alcohol was available. There are two possible reasons for this. Firstly, the limitations on drinking imposed in the FIDD programme, that is, drinking only every hour and an upper BAC limit, meant that the observed drinking was not only remote from alcoholics' customary patterns but may actually have proved aversive, an impression supported by the subjective reports of a few patients. Secondly, the programme was presented primarily as a treatment regime; patients entered the programme in the anticipation of help for their problem, and may therefore have been more likely to adopt a patient role rather than a role as experimental subject from whom drinking was expected. However this may be, these considerations do not affect the main conclusion with respect to a disconfirmation of the loss of control account of alcoholic drinking, both in the 'inability to stop' and the 'inability to abstain' senses. Moreover, the fact that roughly a third of the patients abstained entirely refutes any hypothesis of craving resulting from primary physical dependence without previous ingestion of alcohol. As Jellinek (1960) pointed out, this sort of hypothesis has great difficulty with clinical observations suggesting that inpatient alcoholics are not preoccupied with and do not crave for alcohol. The results of Gottheil *et al.* (1972) show this to be true when alcohol is freely available to be drunk and even though others on the ward are drinking heavily.

Gottheil and his colleagues were also able to examine the relationship between drinking patterns observed during the FIDD programme and a follow-up outcome classification six months later. Contrary to expectations, SKOLODA *et al.* (1975) in a follow-up of one hundred patients found that programme abstainers tended to fare better following treatment than either moderate or heavy drinkers who did not differ from one another in outcome. However, a considerable number of patients who had drunk on the programme did appear to have benefited from treatment to some extent and a small subgroup of five individuals was noted who had consumed very limited quantities and whose outcome appeared to parallel that of the typical nondrinker. These impressions were confirmed in a larger follow-up of 249 patients by Alterman, Gottheil and Thornton (1978) who showed that controlled or moderate programme drinkers had much better outcomes than those who had not exercised as great a degree of control over drinking.

PRIMING DOSE EXPERIMENTS

The evidence presented in the last two sections of this chapter appears to demonstrate that the concept of loss of control, as depicted in the earlier literature, has little value as a description of alcoholics' drinking behaviour. When given the opportunity to determine the amount and patterning of their own drinking in a laboratory situation, alcoholics do not drink mechanically to extreme degrees of intoxication and do not drink all the alcohol available to them. They do not show inability to stop drinking. Moreover, circumstances can be easily arranged whereby it is possible to elicit abstinence or moderation from alcoholics and under other circumstances they will abstain spontaneously in the presence of alcohol. They do not typically show inability to abstain. This being the case, it might be thought that there is no sense in pursuing the question of the validity of loss of control and craving as explanations of alcoholics' drinking behaviour, on the grounds that, quite simply, there is nothing to explain. However, it might still be possible to argue that, all the results of laboratory investigations notwithstanding, alcoholics in the natural environment are distinguished from other drinkers because they cannot usually start drinking without continuing to intoxication. The very fact that they persist in excessive drinking despite its obviously injurious consequences for their health and economic and social welfare, this argument might add, is evidence in itself that they have lost control over drinking. While such an argument would be extremely vague and would come close to the assertion that alcoholics are persons who drink more than others, let us temporarily put aside such objections in the interests of this discussion. More seriously, loss of control was synonymous in Jellinek's (1952) disease conception with pharmacological addiction and in Edwards and Gross' (1976) Alcohol Dependence Syndrome impaired control is central to psycho-physiological dependence. Given that, despite the evidence reviewed, alcoholics continue to be regarded as dependent on alcohol in a way in which normal drinkers are not, it could be claimed that loss of control retains potential explanatory value. It might also be claimed that the concept of loss of control has empirical and clinical utility in distinguishing one kind of deviant drinker from another (Stein, Niles and Ludwig, 1968).

Accepting then that loss of control and craving might still have something to offer as explanations, it will be recalled (p. 78) that these concepts can avoid circularity only if tied to some underlying set of hypothetical constructs. The question then arises whether the excessive drinking denoted by loss of control and craving is best explained on a physiological or on a psychological basis. This question may be answered by determining whether it is the bodily effects of alcohol itself which predict subsequent drinking behaviour and the experience of craving in alcoholics or whether other variables unconnected with the physical impact of alcohol provide better predictions. This is the central aim of most of the experiments to be reviewed in this section. They have in common that a priming dose of alcohol is used to study subsequent behaviour and experience.

We begin, however, with an experiment which did not distinguish between physiological and psychological determinants of drinking but which is presented by its authors as supportive evidence for a traditional, physiologically-based conception of loss of control. MARCONI, FINK AND MOYA (1967) gave thirteen alcoholics the opportunity to consume a 20 per cent solution of ethanol in a quantity related to the subject's body weight. A bottle and glass were placed on a table at which the subject and two observers were seated. The subject was told that he could drink freely in the manner and quantity he chose and that his only obligation was to begin drinking. This last instruction justifies the inclusion of this study in the category of priming dose experiments, since it is the effect of the required first drink on subsequent drinking behaviour which is of interest. The thirteen subjects were divided into seven diagnosed as intermittent alcoholics with inability to stop (gamma alcoholics) and six inveterate alcoholics with inability to abstain (delta alcoholics). The results were that the intermittent alcoholics drank a significantly greater quantity of alcohol than the inveterate types, both in terms of absolute quantities and in proportion to body weight. There was no overlap on these measures between the groups.

Despite the clear-cut results of this simple experiment, it is subject to several damaging criticisms. Firstly, Lloyd and Salzberg (1975) have calculated that the three gamma alcoholics who drank all the alcohol available could only have attained a maximum BAC of 65 mg/100 ml, while the BACs of the other four gammas must have been less than this. Such BACs do not even approach moderate intoxication, expecially in alcoholics with a high degree of tolerance. Secondly, as implied above, four of the intermittent group did not drink all the alcohol available; in other words, they *stopped* drinking when they could have continued. Under these circumstances it is difficult to agree with the authors' claim to have demonstrated 'inability to stop'. Finally, even accepting the validity of the clinical distinction between gamma and delta alcoholics and accepting also that gammas drank more than deltas, there is no indication from this evidence of *why* they did so, since, as we have said, physiological and psychological factors leading to further drinking were not distinguished.

The possibility that psychological factors may have contributed to Marconi *et al.*'s results arises from the obvious fact that subjects were aware they were drinking alcohol and may therefore have behaved according to their differential *expectations* of the effects of alcohol. The reverse of this situation, in which subjects were not aware that they were being given a priming dose of alcohol, was studied in a much-quoted experiment by MERRY (1966). In this experiment nine inpatients diagnosed as gamma alcoholics with loss of control were given one fluid ounce of vodka disguised in orange juice and presented to subjects as a vitamin drink at breakfast. Pilot work had established that the presence of vodka in the mixture was impossible to detect. In the control condition a similar proportion of water replaced vodka in the mixture. Subjects acted as their own controls and were given either mixture in two-day sequences over sixteen days. During the late morning of each day of the experiment subjects were asked to record any degree of craving experienced on a simple five-point scale (no craving, slight, moderate, strong, very strong craving) by nursing staff who were unaware of the purpose of the experiment and of the fact that alcohol was being secretly administered to patients. The results showed no difference in average craving scores between the alcoholic and the nonalcoholic mixtures. There was also no significant difference in the number of occasions when *any* craving was experienced; indeed, there were slightly more such occasions following the nonalcoholic mixture.

As might be expected, Merry interprets these results as refuting the hypothesis that small quantities of alcohol trigger off a biochemical abnormality leading to craving in gamma alcoholics. He reports becoming interested in this topic after observing that his relapsed patients had usually omitted to take their prescribed disulfiram (Antabuse) two or three days before they embarked on a binge, suggesting the existence of a 'mental set' to drink preceding the first ingestion. Consequently, 'psychological and environmental factors . . . play a part more or less important in the "loss of control" reaction'. Unfortunately this conclusion is somewhat vitiated by an additional observation reported by Merry. On the final day of the experiment he increased the dosage of vodka in the mixture to two fluid ounces and obtained significantly higher craving scores. He concludes from this, rather strangely, that 'there is no doubt that two fl. oz. of vodka taken under the experimental conditions described would have a strong disinhibiting effect and would allow a good opportunity for the emergence of psychological tendencies to relapse'. However, it is equally parsimonious to conclude that a higher quantity of alcohol was required to trigger the putative biochemical reaction. These alternative explanations of the additional finding are complicated because we cannot be sure that the presence of two ounces of vodka was undetectable. Despite the deserved amount of attention attracted by this pioneering experiment, it can also be criticized for employing a relatively crude measure of craving without established reliability and validity. As we shall discover, this problem was taken up by later investigators.

Before proceeding to experiments which have elaborated on the basic design used by Merry (1966), it will be convenient to mention briefly two other studies which may be classified in the priming dose category. PAREDES, LUDWIG, HASSENFELD AND CORNELISON (1969) gave 66 alcoholics a three- or four-ounce dose of vodka before interviewing them with audiovisual recording. The main object of these investigators was to examine the effects of audiovisual feedback on alcoholics' self-image, but as an incidental part of their findings they were able to comment on the validity of conventional notions of craving. Only three of their subjects mentioned craving for alcohol after having ingested the experimental drink and none of seventeen subjects followed up on an outpatient basis appears to have gone on a binge after the experimental session was over. The authors conclude that the social setting and significance of drinking might be critical in the induction of craving.

In a most ingenious experiment, CUTTER, SCHWAAB AND NATHAN (1970) employed psychological decision theory in an attempt to devise an adequate operational definition of craving in terms of the 'utility' of alcohol. Although we shall not have space to describe this experiment in detail, we may note that alcoholics who had been given a priming dose of alcohol did not work more efficiently or more quickly in order to earn further alcohol than non-primed alcoholics, primed nonalcoholics and subjects who were given no alcohol incentive for work. It is possible to criticize the operational measure of craving used in this experiment because of its remoteness from relevant experiences and drinking behaviour, but the results nevertheless provide *prima facie* evidence against the predictive value of the concept of craving.

We turn now to the most important material in this section, a series of experiments elaborating on the basic design of Merry's (1966) priming dose experiment but adding the crucial element of a separation of physiological and psychological determinants of craving and subsequent drinking behaviour. ENGLE AND WILLIAMS (1972) studied a sample of forty male and female hospitalized alcoholics whose histories all showed an inability to control drinking. Ten subjects were randomly allotted to each of four groups. Groups 1 and 2 were administered as standard medication a strongly flavoured 'vitamin mixture' at 7 a.m. on the fifth morning of their stay in the hospital. In the case of Group 2 the mixture contained one ounce of 100 per cent proof vodka without the subjects' being aware of this. Groups 3 and 4 were also given a mixture at the same time but were informed that it contained alcohol. In the case of Group 3 this was true, but in the case of Group 4 it was not. The staff member giving the drinks did not know which mixtures subjects had received. Forty minutes after subjects had drunk the mixture they were presented with a questionnarie within which, disguised among items relating to desire for food and to feelings of tension, was a scale which rated desire for alcohol from four to one (almost uncontrollable desire for drink – very strong desire – slight desire – no desire). The same questionnaire had been given on the previous day of hospitalization in order to familiarize subjects with the procedure and to provide a comparison with data recorded on the drinking day, and was also given later on the fifth day after sufficient time had elapsed for the intoxicating effects of alcohol to have been eliminated. In addition, as a behavioural measure of craving, subjects were told that if they experienced a 'stronger than usual urge or desire for drink', they could obtain one by approaching the nursing staff before noon of the same day. It will be readily appreciated how the above design enabled the experimenters to assess independently the influence of the chemical effects of alcohol on the organism and the role of expectancy in determining subsequent feelings and behaviour.

Group means for craving scores on the drinking days were as follows: Group 1 = 1.3; Group 2 = 1.0; Group 3 = 1.7; Group 4 = 1.5. The only significant difference between these means was that between Groups 2 and 3, that is, between the two groups who had been given alcohol. The group who had not been informed of this (Group 2) had the lowest mean score, and the group who had been so informed (Group 3) had the highest mean craving score. Only one subject requested alcohol to counteract a strong desire for drink and this subject came from Group 4, in which subjects had received the nonalcoholic mixture but had been told they were drinking alcohol. Engle and Williams interpret these results as showing that an alcoholic's desire for alcohol increases when he has been informed he has drunk alcohol, whether in fact he has or not. The results therefore support a psychological interpretation of craving and provide no evidence for a physiological relationship between the effects of and reported desire for alcohol.

It must be pointed out that Engle and Williams' interpretation is not perfectly consistent with their own data. Under the hypothesis that the 'expectancy' due to instructional set was the main determinant of later craving, *both* groups who had been told they were drinking alcohol should have had higher mean scores than *both* groups who were not told. In particular, Group 4, who received no alcohol but were informed to the contrary, should have higher scores than Group 1 who were correctly told they were drinking a nonalcoholic mixture, but this difference was not significant in Engle and Williams' analysis. Unfortunately, these authors employed an unnecessarily weak statistical test of the 'expectancy' hypothesis by using a simple one-way analysis of variance rather than a two-way analysis which would have statistically separated out the variance due to instructional set from that due to the beverage-content variable. A further criticism of Engle and Williams' interpretation is that they cite no evidence to establish the validity of their 'desire for alcohol' measure. They write that they recorded this measure on two occasions other than the crucial forty minutes after the drinking test but report no data for these other administrations. It would of course be essential for an expectancy interpretation of the results that the effect of instructions was confined to the post-drinking test and did not also show itself in craving scores measured the day before.

Both these problems of interpretation were addressed by MAISTO, LAUERMAN AND ADESSO (1977), who had available to them for statistical reanalysis a more extensive report of this same experiment prepared by Williams (1970). These authors replaced the original one-way analysis with a two-by-two design and also included scores from the three repetitions of the craving questionnaire in their analysis of variance. They found no main effect or interaction due to the beverage-content variable, showing again that the physiological reaction to alcohol was not predictive of craving. Although the main effect due to instructions did not quite reach statistical significance, there was a significant interaction between instructions and repeated craving questionnaire administrations. This interaction was caused by the fact that there was no effect of instructions on the first administration of the questionnaire on the day before drinking, but on the second administration forty minutes after drinking, subjects from both groups told they were drinking alcohol scored higher than subjects told they were not, exactly as the expectancy hypothesis would predict. Moreover, there was a significant increasing trend in craving scores for subjects in the expectancy groups lasting until the third questionnaire administration later on the fifth day, but no such trend in the other two groups. This suggests that the desire for alcohol induced by expectation of its effects lasts for some time after the consumption of the first drink and is even stronger support for the expectancy hypothesis since the third measure was taken at a time when the physiological reaction to alcohol could not have been present in the group who did actually receive it. We may conclude that Maisto *et al.*'s reanalysis places Engle and Williams' earlier interpretation of their results on a much sounder statistical and logical footing.

MARLATT, DEMMING AND REID (1973) used the same kind of design as Engle and Williams (1972). Subjects were given either a mixture of one part 80 per cent proof vodka to five parts tonic water alone, and were either informed that they were drinking alcohol or that they were drinking tonic water. This resulted in four conditions: told vodka—given vodka; told vodka—given tonic; told tonic—given vodka; told tonic—given tonic. There are, however, important differences between the two experiments. Firstly, the thirty-two alcoholics studied by Marlatt *et al.*, despite meeting strict criteria for the presence of long-standing alcohol-related disabilities, were not hospitalized or seeking treatment and were not made aware that they had been asked to volunteer on the basis of being classified as alcoholics. Secondly, this experiment also studied a sample of thirty-two social drinkers without drink-related problems who were divided among the four conditions in the same way as the alcoholics. Thirdly, the dependent measures used here were directed more to loss of control as such rather than to subjective feelings of craving. Subjects were informed that they were taking part in a 'taste-rating' task, the object of which was to discover whether they could discriminate between three allegedly different brands of vodka or tonic, as appropriate. Twenty minutes after receiving a priming dose consistent with their experimental condition, subjects seen individually were told that they could drink as much as they liked of the beverage in front of them in order to arrive at a decision and were then left alone for fifteen minutes. During this period they were secretly observed by one of the experimenters who was blind as to which condition they were in and who counted the number of sips taken during the fifteen-minute drinking period. Thus, as well as total amount consumed, dependent measures included sip rate, amount consumed per sip (total amount divided by number of sips) and a postexperimental estimate of BAC based on amount consumed and subject's body weight. As a check on the success of the beverage deception, subjects were also asked to rate the percentage alcohol content of the mixture they had been drinking at the end of the experiment.

Results for total amount consumed by subjects are shown in Table 3.1 Cursory inspection of this table suggests that alcoholics drank at a higher level than social drinkers and that, apart from this, the main determinant of amount consumed was instructional set. Both these impressions are confirmed by statistical analysis which in this case is in no need of correction. Alcoholics drank significantly more than social drinkers and subjects told they were drinking alcohol drank significantly more than subjects told they were drinking tonic water. There was no interaction between these two variables, so the expectancy effect can be assumed to have applied equally to both kinds of drinker. There was no main effect due to beverage content or any interaction involving this variable. Indeed, it will be seen from Table 3.1 that mean consumption tended to be very similar within each instructional set, suggesting that the actual presence of alcohol had a negligible influence on subjects' drinking behaviour. An analysis of variance applied to amount consumed per sip produced the same significant results. Alcoholics consumed more per sip than social drinkers but the expectation of drinking alcohol gave higher amounts per sip in both types of drinker.

TABLE 3.1
Group means for total amount of alcohol consumed (in fluid ounces)

Beverage condition	Alcoholics		Social drinkers		Condition mean
	Told tonic	Told alcohol	Told tonic	Told alcohol	
Given tonic	10·94	23·87	9·31	14·62	14·69
Given alcohol	10·25	22·13	5·94	14·44	13·19
Condition mean	10·60	23·00	7·63	14·53	

Source: Marlatt, Demming and Reid (1973)

Marlatt *et al.* conclude that their findings provide strong support for the role of cognitive factors in the determination of loss of control drinking. They are careful to point out, however, that they have demonstrated only 'an experimental analogue' of loss of control and that their experimental design also placed limitations on the duration and extent of drinking. Experimental evidence for the importance of cognitive factors in alcoholic drinking must be supported by observations of alcoholics in the natural drinking environment. Despite these qualifications, the significance of this experiment is that it corroborates the earlier findings of Engle and Williams (1972). After Maisto *et al.*'s (1977) reanalysis of Williams' data, the two experiments yielded essentially similar results with respect to a confirmation of the expectancy hypothesis but did so with markedly different dependent variables. While Marlatt *et al.* used a variety of behavioural measures of drinking, they did not attempt to assess subjective feelings of craving directly. Engle and Williams measured craving but their behavioural measure was unsatisfactory for their purposes. Thus, as Maisto *et al.* emphasize, the two experiments complement each other nicely. It should also be borne in mind that these two experiments sampled very different populations of alcoholics, those engaged in treatment in one case and those actively drinking and not seeking treatment in the other. That the two experiments should have resulted in the same conclusions under these varying circumstances increases confidence in the validity of the main finding.

Maisto *et al.* also speculate as to the specific process underlying the relationship between expectancy and consumption. They postulate that this is best seen as 'a placebo effect', by which the effects of a beverage consumed are interpreted as analogous with those of alcohol. However, the relevance of such a placebo effect to real-life drinking is obviously very limited. The more important point about these experiments is the implication that drinking behaviour conventionally described as loss of control is mediated by cognitive processes and not by a physico-chemical reaction to ethanol. But as Maisto *et al.* again point out, it would be premature to reject completely a physiological explanation of loss of control on the evidence of these experiments, since to do so would be equivalent to 'proving the null hypothesis'. That is to say, the only legitimate conclusion which may be drawn is that the two experiments provide no evidence for the existence of a physiological basis for loss of control, *not* that they provide positive evidence that it does not exist. It may be, for example, that such a basis would be demonstrated in a more sensitive experimental design than employed in the experiments described above.

A claim for such increased experimental sensitivity could be made on behalf of two experiments carried out by Ray Hodgson and his colleagues at the Addiction Research Unit, Institute of Psychiatry, London. There are two principal design features on which this claim might be based. Firstly, these experiments employed a more adequate operational measure of craving than had been used in the past and, secondly, they distinguished between levels of severity of alcohol dependence, as recommended by Edwards and Gross (1976). It might also be claimed that this research was founded on a more sophisticated conceptualization of craving than had been arrived at by previous investigators. Contrary to the opinion of Mello (1972), Hodgson, Rankin and Stockwell (1979) insist that craving is not a redundant concept in the study of alcoholism. The radical behaviourist regards craving in the same way that he regards other subjective states, as unobservable epiphenomena whose presence or absence can only be assessed through their effects on behaviour and which are therefore redundant in the scientific explanation of human behaviour. However, drawing on his earlier research in the field of fear and anxiety, Hodgson argues that craving, like fear, can be usefully viewed as a complex system of interrelated responses involving subjective, physiological, behavioural and biochemical components, and that to omit any of these components is to distort the nature of the phenomenon which is to be explained.

The main measure of craving employed by this research team was 'speed of drinking' and Rankin, Hodgson and Stockwell (1979) provide some evidence of the validity of this measure in a comparison of two drinking situations which can reasonably be supposed to correspond to high and low craving conditions. This study also provided some support for Hodgson's multidimensional conception of craving. In a free choice drinking situation, speed of drinking was also found to distinguish between alcoholics rated as moderately and as severely dependent on alcohol by Rankin, Hodgson and Stockwell (1980). The problem of an adequate operational measure of craving has also been interestingly explored by Funderburk and Allen (1977).

The first priming dose experiment by this group of researchers is that reported by HODGSON, RANKIN AND STOCKWELL (1979). As stated above, one of the objects of this experiment was to examine the possible differential effects of a priming dose on alcoholics with varying levels of dependence. Twenty alcoholics were used as subjects, eleven classified as severely and nine as moderately dependent according to criteria taken from Edwards and Gross (1976). In one of their experimental conditions Hodgson *et al.* used a higher priming dose of alcohol than had been used in any previous investigation. In the high dose condition subjects were given 150 ml of 40 vol. per cent vodka, equivalent to about three doubles; in the low dose condition they were given 15 ml vodka; and there was also a no-dose condition. It is important to note that this experiment involved no deception; subjects were fully informed of the dose they were about to receive. Each subject acted as his own control, with the three conditions being given on different days separated by at least one day of abstinence. All had been abstinent for at least ten days prior to the first day of testing in order to eliminate severe withdrawal symptoms. Craving tests took place three hours after consuming the morning primer and measures consisted of a five-point rating scale for 'desire for a drink', pulse rate, blood alcohol level, a speed of drinking test which measured the time taken to consume the first of five drinks available to the subject, and the total amount consumed.

The results showed that, ignoring priming dose conditions, severely dependent subjects reported a significantly greater desire for a drink, consumed more alcohol during the craving test and drank the first drink faster than moderately dependent subjects. Ignoring severity of dependence, the only significant difference to emerge between priming dose conditions was a higher pulse rate after the high dose than after the other two priming conditions. However, the main result of interest from this experiment is an interaction between the two variables, priming dose conditions and severity of dependence. The severely dependent subjects consumed their first drink quicker in the high dose condition than in the other two conditions but this trend was reversed in the moderately dependent group, so that the interaction between high vs. low/no-dose conditions and severe vs. moderate dependence was statistically significant (p <0.01). To make this interaction clearer, nine out of eleven severely dependent subjects drank faster after the high-dose primer compared with their individual mean for the low- and no-dose primers, whereas only one out of nine moderately dependent alcoholics showed this direction of difference.

Hodgson *et al.* emphasize that had they not measured severity of dependence the demonstrated effect of the high priming dose would not have been shown in their results and that they would have appeared to have come up with negative results of the same kind as Engle and Williams (1972) and Marlatt *et al.* (1973). However, the distinction between severely and moderately dependent individuals raises a problem of interpretation for this experiment. This consists in the fact that the moderately dependent group were on average *slower* to consume the first drink after the high-dose primer than after the low- and no-dose primers, and that this undoubtedly made a major contribution to the discovery of the reported statistical interaction. This is not to deny that the severely dependent group drank faster in the high-dose conditions, but no data are reported for this group in isolation and it may be that the straight difference between priming conditions for severely dependent subjects was not statistically significant. There is surely no rationale from a craving hypothesis which would predict a slowing down of drinking for moderately dependent alcoholics given higher priming doses, but, whatever the reasons for this curious event may have been, they are not discussed by the authors. A further difficulty concerns the absence of any significant priming effect on the subjective measure of craving used. Against this, Hodgson *et al.* argue that subjects found this rating difficult to make, they showed little variability across occasions on which they did so and that one subject reported being surprised how much he wanted a drink once he had started. The unobtrusive behavioural measure of speed of drinking is therefore superior to the subjective rating of craving. Additionally, there was a low but statistically significant correlation between the subjective and the behavioural measures of craving. Despite these arguments, the lack of a subjective accompaniment to the behaviourally demonstrated priming effect is somewhat disturbing, especially in view of the authors' insistence on a multidimensional view of craving.

Leaving these problems of interpretation aside, it might be concluded from the above results that a high dose of alcohol is needed to stimulate craving and subsequent loss of control over drinking behaviour, and that this was the reason why previous experiments have failed to demonstrate it – the priming doses used were too small. This would be consistent with Glatt's (1967) suggestion of an individual threshold for each alcoholic above which loss of control is induced and below which it is not. Such a point of view would also account for Merry's (1966) finding of significantly higher reported craving when he doubled the surreptitious dose of alcohol given. But this would be an erroneous conclusion, as Hodgson *et al.* would doubtless agree. They do not claim that the presence of craving in severely dependent alcoholics would always eventuate in uncontrolled drinking. After all, there is plenty of evidence that even large quantities of alcohol do not necessarily trigger alcohol-seeking behaviour in alcoholics. For example, PAREDES, HOOD, SEYMOUR AND GOLLOB (1973) gave relatively large amounts of alcohol, enough to maintain BACs of roughly 140 mg/100 ml, over a two-day period to 30 men conforming to traditional criteria for gamma alcoholism. Despite the fact that they were completely free to leave the hospital at any time they wished, 27 of these men stayed on to complete a therapy programme under conditions of total abstinence. The stated belief of most of these patients that once they had started drinking they would be unable to stop was shown to them to be without foundation. Similarly, in one sense the research of the Gottheil group (see pp. 93–5) can be seen as a kind of priming dose experiment on a large scale, since a substantial proportion of their patients drank heavily during the first three weeks of a therapy programme but stopped spontaneously before the end. Again, in the studies of prolonged drinking by Mello and Mendelson (1972), it was found that alcoholics frequently remained abstinent for a whole day, despite clearly observable withdrawal symptoms, in order to accumulate alcohol for the next binge. Finally, we have seen from the experiment of Cohen *et al.* (1971) that a priming dose of alcohol can disrupt abstinence, in the sense that a higher monetary reward is required to buy it. However, the essential conclusion from this experiment is that the alcoholic drinking thus primed continued to be responsive to environmental contingencies. It would be instructive to repeat Cohen *et al.*'s experiment using the severe/moderate dependence distinction regarded as so important by Hodgson *et al.* The prediction would be that a relatively greater increased incentive would be needed to reinstate abstinence in the severely dependent subjects than in the moderately dependent, but that, nevertheless, control over drinking could be introduced. Thus the findings of Hodgson *et al.* (1979), even if accepted without demur, should not be interpreted as providing support for conventional notions of loss of control.

It will not have been missed that, as in the study by Marconi *et al.* (1967), the experiment just described did not distinguish between physiological and psychological determinants of craving, since all subjects were informed correctly of the amount of alcohol they were drinking. Thus it would still be possible to maintain that the greater degree of craving in severely dependent alcoholics after a high priming dose was due to their differential expectations of the effects of alcohol. This central issue was returned to in a further experiment by STOCKEWELL, HODGSON AND RANKIN (1980) which was based on essentially the same design as used by Marlatt *et al.* (1973), with the difference that social drinkers were not included. Stockwell *et al.* also found certain faults in the Marlatt experimental design which they attempted to rectify in their own. They point out, firstly, that the beverages used in the taste-rating task were the same as those given in the priming dose condition, so that subjects given tonic water were tested on tonic water and subjects given vodka and tonic were tested on that. Generally speaking, a procedure in which the dependent variable is measured under different conditions in different groups is clearly inadmissible. Secondly, they suggest that, owing chiefly to the inclusion of the alleged taste-rating task, the circumstances under which drinking was done departed radically from those of drinking in the natural environment. Consequently, Stockwell *et al.* gave their subjects a fairly accurate description of the purposes of the experiment so as to ensure that their attention was not distracted from their internal state, they thoroughly familiarized subjects with the experimental situation and, to emphasize the *mislabelling* rather than the ignoring of interoceptive cues, they provided feedback to subjects on blood alcohol level which was false where necessary. Finally, of course, severe and moderate levels of dependence were distinguished in this experiment.

Subjects were twenty alcoholic inpatients who were free from withdrawal symptoms and from medication, ten being classified as severely and ten as moderately dependent under the usual criteria. Each group contained one female. Subjects acted as their own controls for the four conditions (given soft-drink—told soft drink; given alcohol—told soft drink; given soft drink—told alcohol; given alcohol—told alcohol) and, as before, order of presentation was balanced between subjects. The amount of alcohol given was 60 ml of 40 vol. per cent vodka, equivalent to just over one double. Various subjective and physiological measurements were taken at intervals after the priming dose but the most crucial dependent variable was the speed of drinking the first of two standard vodka and tonics shortly over one hour after the priming dose. At the end of the experiment subjects were debriefed and were asked certain questions which served as a check on the effectiveness of the deception manipulation.

The results of this study are complex owing to the large number of dependent variables measured. In brief, however, it was clear that the two groups of alcoholics studied differed markedly in expected directions. Over all conditions, the severely dependent subjects evinced a higher 'drive to consume alcohol' and more 'difficulty in resisting available alcohol'; they consumed the test drinks faster and rated them more positively than the moderately dependent subjects. Among the severely dependent group there existed significant correlations between behavioural, subjective and physiological measures of craving, thus supporting the adequacy of speed of drinking as a measure of the hypothesized motivational state. However, such significant intercorrelations did not emerge in the moderately dependent group, a finding which casts some doubt on speed of drinking as a valid measure of craving for these subjects. The most crucial result was that the severely dependent individuals consumed their first drink significantly faster in both 'given alcohol' conditions than in both 'given soft drink' conditions, whereas the moderately dependent subjects drank significantly faster in the 'told alcohol' than in the 'told soft drink' conditions. It should be noted, though, that in the severely dependent group the *belief* that they had consumed alcohol was associated with elevations in subjective desire to drink and hand tremor when measured fifteen minutes after the priming dose, but that one hour later their speed of drinking was *only* significantly influenced by the actual alcohol content of the priming dose. Although there are certain statistical criticisms which can be made of the data analysis reported by Stockwell *et al.*, they probably do not affect the main conclusion that in severely dependent alcoholics behaviourally measured craving was *primarily* determined by alcohol content while in moderately dependent alcoholics it was *primarily* determined by instructional set. Stockwell *et al.* state that the implications of their experiment for an understanding of loss of control over drinking are that neither cognitive nor physiological factors exclusively determine the phenomenon, but that physiologically mediated processes appear to assume greater importance in individuals with a severe degree of dependence on alcohol while cognitive influences are operative both for severely and for less dependent alcoholics.

Unless disconfirmed by subsequent research, the above evidence must be accepted as having revived the possibility of a physiologically-based craving in severely dependent alcoholics, a craving which is mediated by the direct effects of alcohol on the organism and not by 'expectancy' or some other cognitive mechanism. However, two essential riders to this statement should be borne in mind. The first is that Stockwell *et al.*'s results by no means rule out the important contribution of cognitive factors to the forms which alcoholic drinking takes, as suggested in the experimental analogues of Engle and Williams (1972) and Marlatt *et al.* (1973). Secondly, a physiologically-based craving of the kind demonstrated would be predicted, it is true, by a disease theory of alcoholism but, as Hodgson *et al.* (1979) emphasize, it is equally consistent with a learning theory approach. The crucial difference in craving between severely and moderately dependent individuals in the learning theory view would not, of course, be explained by the postulation of any greater degree of biochemical malfunction in the former, but by the differential reinforcement histories attaching to the two levels of dependence. In particular, the definition of severe dependence by which the groups used in the above experiments were divided makes clear that the severely dependent alcoholic has engaged in repeated and frequent consumption of alcohol in order to escape or avoid withdrawal symptoms. The manner in which this reinforcement history leads to the presence of craving will be described in detail later in this chapter, but here it should be noted that the consequences of the disease and the learning interpretations of craving are very different. What has been learned can, in principle, be unlearned, so that in the learning theory view craving, whether physiologically or psychologically determined, need not be an irreversible phenomenon.

CONCEPTUAL REVISIONS

Largely as a result of the evidence we have so far considered in this chapter, the traditional concept of loss of control has been subject to certain revisions made by two prominent authorities, Glatt in the UK and Keller in the USA, who wish to retain a disease view of alcoholism. The major purpose of these revisions has been to take account of some of the experimental evidence reviewed above, and of other criticisms of the disease theory, while at the same time attempting to prove that such evidence does not radically affect the theoretical justification for total abstinence. As might be expected, the outcome studies documenting the existence of normal drinking in former alcoholics, which were reviewed in Chapter 2, have also been instrumental in forcing these conceptual revisions.

The first revision of this sort was made by Glatt (1967) and consisted primarily in a response to the earlier evidence of resumed normal drinking. Glatt's major proposal is the existence of a threshold blood alcohol concentration above which loss of control sets in. A few alcohol addicts might be able to remain below the critical threshold – for example, following a process of emotional maturation and increasing insight or, occasionally, a reduction in the social pressure to drink – but this will not affect the appearance of loss of control should the threshold be exceeded. As we commented earlier (p. 105), the postulation of such a threshold might be made to account for the negative results of some priming dose experiments, such as that of Merry (1966), but the evidence of the Mendelson, Cohen and Gottheil research teams shows that alcohol addicts who have reached very high blood alcohol levels are able under appropriate circumstances to moderate their drinking or abstain altogether.

In a later paper Glatt (1976) concedes that 'the hypothesis of an irreversible, metabolic change as the basis of loss of control (in all types of alcoholism) certainly seems untenable'. Nevertheless, the concept of loss of control is defended on the basis of a multidimensional conception of alcoholism involving pharmacological, physiological, psychological and sociocultural factors. Unfortunately, however, Glatt nowhere attempts to define loss of control and, although he mentions several social and psychological 'factors' which may prevent it from emerging, fails to address the task of specifying under what conditions it *will* be produced. And although physiological reactions to alcohol are not regarded as irreversible, Glatt does not tell us how his revised conception of loss of control results in his continued insistence on total abstinence as the only safe solution for the alcohol addict.

The most influential revision to be considered in this section is that by Keller (1972) who begins by reiterating his conviction that loss of control is pathognomic of alcoholism; without loss of control, there is no alcoholism. However, his main purpose in this essay is to criticize Jellinek's (1952) early formulation of loss of control, a formulation which he believes to rest on a fundamental error and to have engendered great confusion. It will be recalled that Jellinek used the concept exclusively to refer to the alcoholic's inability to control the quantity consumed once he has started to drink. But although he has lost the ability to stop, the alcoholic can still control whether he will drink on any given occasion or not. Now, claims Keller, this version of loss of control was obviously influenced by Alcoholics Anonymous sloganizing, but these slogans were intended only as a means to a useful and practical policy; they were not intended to be taken too literally. Most AAs will admit privately that they were able to have one or two drinks on certain occasions without going on to drink more, before the inevitable occasion arose when they were unable to stop. For this reason, the experimental results reported by, for example, Mendelson and Mello (1966) and Merry (1966) are not surprising. These experiments do not prove loss of control to be a myth because they were directed towards an erroneous chain-reaction conception of loss of control which Keller now completely repudiates. Indeed, Keller goes as far as to say that if the inability to stop version of loss of control were truly the basis for the disease conception of alcoholism, then the US Supreme Court, in the famous Powell case (see Fingarette, 1970), would have been justified in their majority decision to reject the disease conception. As reformulated by Keller, the notion of loss of control during drinking *should* be taken to mean that if an alcoholic takes a drink, *he can never be sure* that he will be able to stop before he loses control and starts on a bout. Keller then asserts that it was this unpredictability of alcoholic drinking which Jellinek (1952) originally intended to convey.

Having rejected loss of control during drinking as the foundation of the disease conception of alcoholism, Keller then states what this foundation should rightfully be. It is the inability of the alcoholic to choose consistently whether or not the *first* drink is taken. It is, in other words, an impairment to just that area of choice which Jellinek believed the alcoholic retained. For Keller, the inability to choose whether or not to start drinking 'is precisely the nature and the essence of the addiction'. Borrowing from learning theory, Keller goes on to propose a view of loss of control centred on the notion of a conditioned drinking response elicited by environmental stimuli. The concept of stimulus generalization is also used to account for the spread of addictive conditioning, leading to a growing frequency of bouts or a pattern of continuous inebriation. Furthermore, the idea that a particular blood alcohol level may serve as a conditional stimulus for further drinking allows Keller to embrace within his revised conception of loss of control drinking behaviour during a bout as well as the initiation of it. Nevertheless it is the onset of drinking which has become primary in Keller's account. It must also be made clear that the inability to choose whether to start drinking is, like the inability to choose to stop drinking, *inconsistently* present in the alcoholic, so that, apparently, the alcoholic can sometimes be in complete control of his drinking.

There are, of course, very great problems with Keller's use of learning theory to buttress his revised conception of loss of control. He wishes to defend the disease conception of alcoholism in the classic manner by pointing to a sense in which the alcoholic's drinking is outside the realm of personal choice, or at least not consistently within it. He does this by arguing that the alcoholic's initiation of drinking is 'conditioned'. The implication is that the drinking of nonalcoholics is not 'conditioned', being unimpaired by a reduction of control. This is surely a misuse of learning theory which would insist that *all* drinking, and not merely the drinking of alcoholics, was learned behaviour and subject to conditioning processes. Thus, in his appeal to learning theory in an ultimate defence of a disease conception of alcoholism, Keller is hoist by his own petard. Another problem concerns the addition of the element of unpredictability to the traditional notion of loss of control. This unpredictability applies, as we have seen, both to the inability to choose whether or not to start drinking and to the inability to stop once it has started. The difficulty here is that this proposition is completely untestable. The only deductions which may be drawn from it are that sometimes alcoholics drink and sometimes they do not, and that sometimes they get drunk and sometimes they do not. There is no way such deductions could ever be made the subject of empirical enquiry and, hence, no way they could ever be disconfirmed.

Despite these enormous difficulties, Keller's (1972) essay was a highly influential document in the development of the disease theory of alcoholism. It marked a turning away from the emphasis on loss of control during the alcoholic's drinking, a version of loss of control which found it impossible to accommodate the experimental evidence reviewed earlier in this chapter, towards a new emphasis on the alcoholic's decision to start drinking in the first place.

THE SUBCLINICAL CONDITIONED WITHDRAWAL SYNDROME

The classical conditioning approach to the resumption of drinking roughly sketched by Keller (1972) was refined and elaborated in the work of Arnold M. Ludwig and his colleagues at the University of Kentucky. A major difference with Keller's views, however, is that, while paying the same degree of attention to the determinants of the first drink, Ludwig's starting-point was the alcoholic's subjective experience of craving after a period of abstinence, a craving which was hypothesized to mediate between environmental conditioned stimuli and the resumption of drinking. In more general terms, the 1970s witnessed a considerable revival of interest in the concept of craving, as opposed to that of loss of control, one end-product of which was the work of the Hodgson research team described above (pp. 103–8). A questionnaire study by Hore (1974) also illustrates the same shift in research attention. There can be little doubt that, in historical terms, this renewed interest in craving after abstinence resulted from the failure of the notion of loss of control during drinking to satisfactorily explain much of the experimental evidence collected in the 1960s.

The first study of craving by LUDWIG (1972) was based on questionnaire data. 176 male alcoholics who had received inpatient treatment were followed up and asked, among other things, to give a reason why they had 'fallen off the wagon', if indeed they had done so. Only the first occasion on which the patient had relapsed and his primary reason for this relapse were taken into account. The reasons supplied by 161 patients were classified by Ludwig as follows: (1) psychological distress = 25%; (2) family problems = 13%; (3) effect or pleasure = 11%; (4) sociability = 10%; (5) curiosity = 7%; (6) employment problems = 5%; (7) other reasons = 9%; (8) craving or need to drink = 1%; (9) no specified reason = 19%. The two reasons classified under the craving category were 'not enough willpower to resist' and 'just felt I had to'. Ludwig remarks that 'surprisingly, only the smallest percentage of patients . . . offer reasons akin to the subjective feeling of craving as the cause of their relapse', and therefore concludes that these findings 'do not support the traditional clinical explanation of craving as a primary determinant'.

A further questionnaire survey was reported by LUDWIG AND STARK (1974) but on this occasion alcoholics were asked directly about their experiences of craving, as in the Hore (1974) study. Sixty male alcoholic inpatients were given a Drinking and Craving Questionnarie (DCQ) in which they responded to a series of questions on a 4-point scale. The basic result from the DCQ is that 78 per cent said they had experienced craving, although it is not made absolutely clear how this figure was arrived at. However, it would appear that the main evidence for the importance of craving in the experience of alcoholics was derived from items which referred to ongoing drinking behaviour and not from items concerned with periods of abstinence. Seen in this light it is difficult to agree with the authors' own conclusion that 'regardless of the particular symbolism alcoholics employ to describe the experience of craving, the common denominator of this experience is that it provides them with an acceptable excuse to *resume* or continue drinking' (italics added).

Despite the lack of any clear justification from the self-reports of alcoholics themselves, LUDWIG AND WIKLER (1974) proceeded to make the concept of craving the cornerstone of a theoretical model of alcoholic appetitive behaviour. The model was based on the earlier work of Wikler in the field of opiate addiction (e.g. Wikler, 1971) and is centred on the notion of the 'subclinical conditioned withdrawal syndrome'. According to this general theory, concomitantly with the development of physical dependence on a drug, withdrawal phenomena become classically conditioned to certain stimuli, such as the physical environment in which the drug is taken, the presence of drug-using associates and induced emotional states, through a process of repeated temporal contiguity between these stimuli and the unconditional withdrawal symptoms. Moreover, drug-seeking behaviour is also reinforced by the reduction of withdrawal symptoms following self-administration of the drug in a process of operant conditioning. Following detoxification and discharge of the patient to the home environment, exposure to the same or similar stimuli now evoke conditioned withdrawal phenomena, leading to drug-seeking behaviour and relapse. The theory is supported by evidence that, in rats, a selected opiate withdrawal sign can be experimentally conditioned to a physical environment and can persist for many months after withdrawal of the opiate. With specific regard to alcoholism, Ludwig and Wikler write:

> If we apply a similar thesis to alcoholism, we should expect that craving and other withdrawal phenomena would become conditioned through prior alcohol withdrawal experiences. The more frequent and severe the prior withdrawal experiences, the greater the predisposition to conditioned withdrawal symptoms with consequent desire for relief (i.e. 'craving') through drink. Moreover, just as there are gradations of severity of alcohol withdrawal symptoms, ranging from hangover and tremulousness to full-blown seizures and delirium tremens, craving could also be expected to vary in degree. While the experience of craving provides an alcoholic with the necessary cognitive symbolism for goal-directed, appetitive behaviour (i.e. the negative reinforcement provided by alcohol), there is no cogent reason (as with anger, hunger or sexual urge) why this subjective desire for alcohol should be directly acted upon or expressed in overt behaviour. We would regard craving, then, as a necessary but not sufficient condition for relapse or loss of control.

Having described the origins of the subclinical conditioned withdrawal syndrome, Ludwig and Wikler go on to discuss in more detail the range of stimuli by which the syndrome can be evoked. Interoceptive conditioning would arise after the ingestion of a sufficient amount of alcohol and could also be induced by any physiological state resembling the alcohol withdrawal syndrome. Exteroceptive conditioning, on the other hand,

> would pertain to a variety of situations associated with prior heavy drinking or with the uncomfortable psychological effects of prior withdrawal experiences. A conditioned withdrawal syndrome, generally subclinical in nature, with associated craving might result, therefore, whenever the alcoholic passed a bar or was in the presence of other people drinking or encountered cues relevant to previous drinking practices.

At this point, it is far from obvious how the hypothesized conditioning is thought to spread from situations associated with withdrawal phenomena to those involving merely heavy drinking and other stimuli associated with drinking. Ludwig and Wikler also state that, since various types of emotional dysphoria or physical discomfort represent major features of the alcohol withdrawal syndrome, any combination of these factors, however induced, might also evoke craving. They add later that the necessary preconditions for the appearance of craving include the presence of a subclinical conditioned withdrawal syndrome *or* a state of neurophysiological arousal.

A further part of the model is concerned with the conditions under which alcoholics will consciously interpret their feelings as craving and translate these feelings into alcohol-acquisition behaviour. Situational variables play a major role in this, since 'in the presence of drinking companions, in a bar or at a social gathering, or in the solitary confines of a hotel room, an alcoholic may experience an overwhelming desire for alcohol; in a psychiatric treatment unit, at an Alcoholics Anonymous meeting, or in an experimental setting, the same alcoholic will report no craving'. A failure to appreciate the importance of mental set and setting has misled other investigators, such as Marlatt *et al.* (1973), into concluding that they have failed to demonstrate craving and loss of control. (This seems a strange charge for Ludwig and Wikler to make since it is precisely because these investigators *do* appreciate the importance of cognitive variables that they were led to devise the experiment and obtain the results they did.) Another crucial determinant for the expression of craving in the model is the individual alcoholic's *capacity* for symbolization and accurate symbolization. In other words, alcoholics employ a variety of cognitive labels to interpret similar visceral states, labels which are highly modifiable by external situational or internal cognitive factors. It is this which explains the inconsistent results obtained when alcoholics are asked about their drinking experiences.

Ludwig and Wikler's (1974) central idea of the subclinical conditioned withdrawal syndrome is attractive in its simplicity. However, it must be recognized that the larger theoretical model as presented extends far beyond this simple basis in ways which are far less satisfactory. For example, we have seen that the original stimulus conditions associated with the syndrome were extended from those involving withdrawal phenomena to those involving heavy drinking. Moreover, the necessary conditions for the experience of craving are extended from the presence of the conditioned withdrawal syndrome itself to any state of physiological arousal and this in turn can be induced by, among other things, 'arguments with spouses, employment difficulties and loneliness' (Ludwig *et al.*, 1974). In this way, no account of relapse which, at first sight, might seem better explained in sociopsychological terms need be an embarrassment to the theory, since the all-encompassing construct of arousal state can be introduced to accommodate it.

Finally, the cognitive labelling element of the theory, the extreme plasticity postulated for the interpretation of 'visceral states', means that if an alcoholic describes his return to drink without reference to any experience of craving for alcohol, he can quite simply be assumed to be mistaken. In conclusion, it is impossible to imagine *any* account of relapse after a period of abstinence which *could not* be explained by Ludwig and Wikler's theoretical model.

Despite the inherent unfalsifiability of the complete model, LUDWIG, WIKLER AND STARK (1974) attempted to put certain aspects of their theory to experimental test. This experiment could have been included in the section on priming dose studies but, because of its direct links with the theorizing of Ludwig and Wikler (1974), it is more convenient to describe it here. Twenty-four detoxified male alcoholics were assigned in equal numbers to either an experimental, label group (L) or a control, non-label group (NL). The L subjects received their preferred alcoholic beverage plus mixer whereas the NL subjects received a comparable amount of alcohol in a standard artificially sweetened mixer. Also, a quart of the subject's preferred beverage was within easy reach and view throughout the L session, whereas a quart of water was in the same location during the NL sessions. Work expended for alcohol enabled both L and NL subjects to drink a corresponding amount of their preferred beverage at the end of each session. Within each of the two groups each subject also participated in three dose conditions in which the amount of alcohol given was disguised. The placebo condition (P) consisted of 5 ml of 100 per cent ethyl alcohol floated on top of ten ounces of mixer. The high dose condition (Hi) corresponded to the equivalent of 1.2 ml/kg of body weight of 100 per cent alcohol dissolved with mixer to make a quantity of ten fluid ounces. In the low condition (Lo) the amount of alcohol was 0.6 ml/kg of body weight. The administration of each dose condition was separated by at least two days and the order of presentation was randomized. Dependent variables were subjective, behavioural, physiological and neurophysiological and were measured at baseline and at 20, 80, 140 and 200 minutes after the priming dose. Subjective ratings of craving were obtained from a 'craving meter' with a scale ranging from 0 to 100. Behavioural measures were derived from two five-minute work periods presented in random order, one in which 15 presses of a button dispensed 0.7 ml of 100 per cent proof alcohol and the other in which 15 presses earned one cent. The alcohol-dispensing task was assumed by the authors to be a measure of loss of control despite the fact that alcohol could only be consumed at the end of the session. Physiological measures included heart rate, respiratory rate, evoked skin potential, tremor and blood pressure, while various neurophysiological measures were obtained from an electroencephalograph. All subjects were informed that the object of the experiment was 'to learn more about alcoholism through the administration of sedative, stimulant and alcohol-like drugs', any of which might be given during any of the three scheduled sessions.

In this experimental situation, Ludwig *et al.* made the following predictions from their theory:

1.   A low dose of alcohol, compared to a high dose, should produce greater craving and alcohol-acquisition behaviour. This is because the low dose is assumed to act as an appetiser stimulating craving, whereas the higher dose is assumed to suppress it to some extent.

2.   Compared to an inappropriate (NL) drinking situation, an appropriate (L) situation conducive to natural cognitive-labelling should produce greater craving and alcohol-acquisition behaviour.

3.   The conditions and situations above producing greater craving and alcohol-acquisition behaviour should be associated with a number of physiological effects attributed to the alcohol-withdrawal syndrome or related states of CNS-ANS arousal.

4.   Most important, the maximum expression of craving should be elicited by the *combination* of appropriate interoceptive (Lo) and exteroceptive (L) situations.

Before proceeding to the results of the experiment, two technical problems concerned with the method of statistical analysis employed by Ludwig *et al.* should be mentioned. Firstly, the design of the experiment confounded between-subject and within-subject effects since one independent variable, the labelling variable, employed different subjects in each group while the other, the dose variable, used the same subjects in each condition. In these circumstances it is not sufficient to use the standard nonparametric test of significance for separate comparisons, as Ludwig and Wikler have done, since this cannot independently assess the contribution to the variance made by between-subject and within-subject factors. Secondly, the authors state that, because of the small number of subjects used, they decided to accept the 10 per cent level of confidence as the criterion for statistical significance. Such an increase over conventionally accepted levels for the risk of Type 1 errors, that is, of rejecting the null hypothesis when it is in fact true, would not normally be regarded as acceptable. These statistical problems cloud any interpretation of the results which might be offered.

Even accepting the results reported by Ludwig *et al.* at face value, these do not generally confirm the predictions from theory given above. In regard to prediction 1, the highest level of craving measured 20 minutes after the priming drink came from the placebo, 'label' condition. It is true that the low-dose group under the appropriate labelling conditions showed somewhat higher levels of craving in later assessment periods, but at no time was there any significant difference, even by the generous criterion used, between this group and the high-dose 'label' condition. A similar state of affairs applied to the alcohol acquisition measure; in no comparison was there any significant difference between the Lo/L condition and the Hi/L condition, as would be demanded by prediction 1. Thus, the experiment provided no evidence in support of this prediction. For the same reasons, prediction 4, which entailed a maximal expression of craving in the Lo/L condition, was also not supported by the results. In relation to the physiological and neurophysiological variables covered by prediction 3, the many kinds of measure reported are confusing but none of them clearly supports the hypothesis. The only prediction which was confirmed was prediction 3. Across all dose conditions, the 'label' group recorded significantly higher levels of craving and alcohol acquisition behaviour than the non-label group. However, in the absence of any confirmation of the other predictions, this finding is best explained by the potent effects of cognitive expectancy factors, without resort to any appetizing contribution of low doses of alcohol. In the light of these findings, it is little short of astonishing that Ludwig *et al.* should have commenced their discussion of results with the statement: 'In general, the results of this study support the hypothesis advanced pertaining to determinants of craving and alcohol-seeking.' It should also be recalled that the findings of Hodgson *et al.* (1979) appear to be in direct contradiction to predictions 1, 3 and 4 above with respect to the relative effects on craving of high and low priming doses of alcohol.

Although their initial emphasis was upon craving for alcohol after a period of abstinence, Ludwig and Wikler (1974) also discuss the implications of their theory for the concept of loss of control. They reject, first of all, the idea that loss of control implies 'that alcoholics have no volitional power at all to control the amount and frequency of drinking or that they turn into servo-mechanisms guided solely by the desire to obtain mental oblivion through alcohol'. Rather, from Ludwig and Wikler's viewpoint, all that loss of control denotes is the relative inability to regulate alcohol consumption. Loss of control is the behavioural state initiated by craving and characterized by activities indicative of this relative inability; it need not eventuate in gross intoxication or stupor. Loss of control may even take the form of total abstinence, when the alcoholic has accepted the belief that he cannot handle alcohol normally. In more specific terms, the authors state that social drinkers rely primarily on both exteroceptive and interoceptive sources of information to regulate their drinking. For example, exteroceptive cues relate to counting the number of drinks consumed, setting limits on total amount and drinking at socially specified times or in appropriate social contexts. Interoceptive cues might include the relative state of perceived intoxication, the degree of speech and motor impairment and so forth. To the extent that drinkers 'do not or cannot' attend to such sources of feedback information, they can be regarded as demonstrating loss of control. Therefore, Ludwig and Wikler's hypothesis of loss of control is that the 'regulatory dysfunction in alcoholics is related to a relative deficit in ability to respond to such feedback'.

This hypothesis was put to experimental test by LUDWIG, BENDFELDT, WIKLER AND CAIN (1978). The object of this study was to evaluate the comparative ability of alcoholics and social drinkers to maintain their blood alcohol levels within a predetermined range by relying predominantly on interoceptive cues experienced during a previous training session. Forty detoxified, male alcoholics and twenty control subjects were studied, matched as far as possible on relevant variables. The subjects were informed that the study was designed to 'evaluate whether people with drinking problems could learn to drink socially'. In the initial training session, subjects were brought into a laboratory and given the equivalent of 0.65 ml/kg of body weight of their preferred beverage combined with a mixer and were told to pay particular attention to the way they felt internally. A BAC reading 45 minutes after the ingestion of the dose was taken to mark the 'socially desirable drinking range', spanning 10 mg/100 ml, for each individual subject. During the course of the next two and a half hours subjects were accurately informed of BAC readings every 15 minutes and were then administered the equivalent of 0.05 ml of 95 per cent proof ethanol disguised in a mixer. The training session was followed on consecutive days by two experimental sessions. Subjects were told that their task was to maintain their blood alcohol level within the previously designated range. They were instructed to recall how they felt during the training session when their BAC was within the required range and to rely solely on these internal cues as a basis for deciding whether or not to accept drinks at each of ten decision points spaced 15 minutes apart. A priming dose containing the same amount of alcohol as that given in the training session was followed 45 minutes later by the first maintenance dose which, unknown to subjects, contained twice as much alcohol as the maintenance doses used in the training session. Thus a roughly stable BAC would result if the subject accepted drinks at alternate 15-minute intervals. Finally, in contrast to the training session, subjects were given false BAC feedback. In one experimental session they were given overfeedback to the extent of 10 mg/100 ml at each of the ten decision points, and in the other underfeedback session their BACs were underestimated by the same extent. Because subjects were unaware of these manipulations, the false feedback put them in a position of choosing between internal and external cues as the basis for their drinking decisions. Dependent variables included mean BAC, the number of drinks taken during experimental sessions, the average deviation from the designated BAC range, interoceptive errors of commission (i.e. accepting a drink with a BAC above the designated range) and interoceptive errors of omission (i.e. refusing a drink with a BAC below the designated range).

The results showed that alcoholics accepted significantly more drinks and attained significantly higher mean blood alcohol levels over both experimental sessions compared to controls. With respect to deviations from the individually designated BAC range, alcoholics tended to be above the range and social drinkers tended to be below the range, and there was no significant difference between the groups in terms of *absolute* deviation scores. However, when the sign of the deviation was considered, whether positive or negative, alcoholics showed significantly higher values than controls. Thus, these results do not demonstrate that alcoholics showed less regulatory capacity *overall* than social drinkers, but merely that their deviations from the designated range were in a different direction from those of the controls. The results for errors of commission and omission, adjusted for the effects of age and weight, are given in Table 3.2. As might be expected from the fact that they accepted more drinks than social drinkers, alcoholics made a significantly greater number of errors of commission averaged across both feedback conditions. However, they did not make more errors of omission than the controls, suggesting again that it cannot be a *general* lack of regulative ability which is being tapped. It is also worth noting from Table 3.2 that, comparing errors between overfeedback and underfeedback conditions within groups, the direction of difference would be expected, with one exception, by assuming that subjects were responsive to the type of false information being given them. In other words, there are more errors of commission under conditions of underfeedback and more errors of omission under overfeedback. The exception to this is the controls in the underfeedback condition and this might be explained by saying that the social drinkers, unlike the alcoholics, did not wish to ingest more alcohol when their BACs were already high. Be that as it may, the results displayed in Table 3.2 do not show that alcoholics make more interoceptive errors of all kinds, but merely that they are more likely to accept drinks inappropriate to the task requirement. As a last part of the results, Ludwig *et al.* calculated for each subject the slope function giving the best fit to the progression of BACs from the beginning to the end of the experimental session. Loss of control was operationally defined as a line slope significantly greater than zero. The results showed that 50 per cent of the alcoholics gave such a slope in one or both experimental sessions whereas only 5 per cent of control subjects did so. As with the finding of Marconi *et al.* (1967) however, this is a very tame sort of loss of control which is being demonstrated since the highest mean BAC at the end of the sessions was less than 80 mg/100 ml, i.e. less than the legal driving limit in Britain. All this sophisticated statistical analysis proves is that alcoholics' BACs tended to rise during the experimental period and this in turn reduces to the established fact that they drank more alcohol.

As with the experiment reported by Ludwig *et al.*, (1974), it is very

TABLE 3.2
Mean values for interoceptive errors

Type of error	Underfeedback	Overfeedback	
Commission			
Alcoholics	4·4	3·1	} p <0·05
Controls	1·9	2·0	
		NS	
Omission			
Alcoholics	0·4	1·4	} NS
Controls	0·7	1·1	
		p <0·05	

Source: Ludwig, Bendfeldt, Wikler and Cain (1978).

difficult to agree with the authors' own conclusion that 'all results are generally supportive of the theory that alcoholics as a group possess a relative inability to modulate ethanol consumption on the basis of their interoceptive cues'. The hypothesis as stated by the authors must be interpreted as predicting that alcoholics would show deviations and make mistakes in *both* directions, that is, their lack of ability to regulate would eventuate in overconsumption *and* underconsumption. If this had indeed been demonstrated, it would have been a surprising and impressive finding. As it stands, however, any putative lack of regulation which has been shown is in one direction only, that of above average deviations from the stipulated range and a greater number of occasions when drinks were accepted inappropriately to the task requirement. To explain this, all we need to assume is that alcoholics were less interested in the stated object of the experiment, and more interested in consuming alcohol, than the controls. Even without this assumption, all this curious experiment seems to have shown is that alcoholics drink more than social drinkers. This is precisely the problem to be explained but Ludwig *et al*. (1978) have not given us an explanation of it, merely a somewhat weak and redundant demonstration.

We have seen that there is no evidence to support Ludwig and Wikler's (1974) particular hypothesis of loss of control. There is also very little evidence to support the same authors' larger and less precise theoretical model of craving. Nevertheless, the notion of a subclinical conditioned withdrawal syndrome, if restricted to the conditioning of withdrawal symptoms, does appear to have some merit. As described by Rankin and Hodgson (1977) this form of conditioning would apply simply to the repeated consumption of alcohol in order to relieve or avoid withdrawal symptoms in severely dependent individuals, thus leading to a strengthening of the compulsion to drink, i.e. craving, through operant and classical conditioning. Minimal withdrawal symptoms, for example tremor, or the learned expectation of withdrawal symptoms, become discriminative stimuli for further drinking. This view of craving as a learned compulsion based on conditioned withdrawal symptoms is supported by the findings of Hore (1974) and led to relatively successful predictions in the experiments of Hodgson *et al.* (1979) and Stockwell *et al.* (1980). As Hodgson *et al.* (1979) emphasize, however, this approach to craving by no means implies a symptom of an irreversible disease. On the contrary, it leads naturally to the assumption that, since craving is a learned compulsion, it can be unlearned, or extinguished. As an illustration of this possibility, Hodgson and Rankin (1976) report a case study in which, as part of his treatment, an alcoholic was given four vodkas which it had previously been established would lead to a very strong craving for more drink in this individual. The therapists then supported the patient while he resisted further drinking. As a result of this cue exposure, craving diminished over time, as assessed by subjective measures, during the treatment session. It also diminished at an increasing rate across sessions, so that by the end of the twelfth cue exposure treatment session no craving was present after the consumption of four vodkas. Apart from the reduction of craving by behaviour therapy, it may also be deduced from this simple model that craving may naturally extinguish after a certain period of abstinence if the alcoholic encounters cues previously associated with withdrawal phenomena without engaging in avoidance behaviour. In any event, it is likely in our view that craving conceived in this way has far more to do with the maintenance of excessive drinking than with the return to drink after abstinence.

THE CONTINUED UTILITY OF 'LOSS OF CONTROL' AND 'CRAVING'

To end this chapter, we will consider the utility of retaining the concepts of loss of control and craving for a scientific understanding of alcoholism. This will also serve as a summary of some of the main conclusions which may be drawn from the evidence reviewed, especially with regard to the extent to which, and the form in which, loss of control and craving increase our knowledge of the processes determining alcoholics' drinking behaviour. One of the major criteria by which the continued utility of the concepts must be judged is their present ability to provide, as they have done in the past, a theoretical justification for the abstinence requirement in treatment. Because of their increasing bifurcation in the literature, the two concepts will be taken separately, beginning with loss of control. The distinction made earlier between loss of control as a description and as an explanation of alcoholismic drinking will also be employed.

The first version of loss of control which must be evaluated is the most primitive one, the version we have called for convenience the 'one drink, one drunk' hypothesis. This states that as soon as any alcohol enters the alcoholic's blood stream a chain-reaction occurs in which the alcoholic will continue to ingest more and more until he is prevented from drinking further by unconsciousness or stupor, running out of money, arrest and incarceration, or some other forcible removal of access to alcohol. In other words, the alcoholic shows an *inability to stop* drinking. This description of the alcoholic's drinking behaviour has been massively contradicted by the evidence collected in Mendelson's laboratory and reviewed earlier in this chapter. When allowed to determine the volume and pattern of their own drinking, alcoholics do *not* drink to oblivion but *do* clearly demonstrate positive sources of control over drinking behaviour. In assessing the implications of this evidence it should be remembered that this primitive version of loss of control is not a straw man. Owing to its advocacy by Alcoholics Anonymous and its early endorsement by the most prestigious authority the world of alcoholism studies has known (Jellinek, 1952), it continues to exert a profound influence on thinking and practice in the field and, especially, on the way alcoholism is presented to the general public. This influence persists despite the fact that a mechanical conception of loss of control has been disavowed even by the most ardent defenders of the disease perspective on alcoholism (Keller, 1972; Glatt, 1976; Ludwig and Wikler, 1974). It is high time this particular ghost were laid finally and unreservedly to rest.

In rejecting a chain-reaction type of loss of control, it is not being denied, of course, that alcoholics never drink until they pass out or get arrested etc.; some frequently do and this is one of the most damaging and perplexing aspects of their behaviour. The point is, however, that this extreme drunkenness cannot be accounted for on the basis of some internally located inability to stop since it has been shown that on other occasions they are able to stop. This evidence also makes extremely dubious the traditional distinction, again endorsed by Jellinek, between real alcoholics who cannot choose to stop and mere excessive drinkers who *wilfully* exceed culturally prescribed limits. This is not to say that alcoholics do choose to get drunk and are therefore responsible for their behaviour. These terms are irrelevant to the present discussion. The submission is that the drinking behaviour of alcoholics drifts between ostensible control and lack of control in the same essential manner as the drinking of others who sometimes get drunk. Neither can the mechanical conception be saved by appealing to a blood alcohol threshold for the onset of loss of control (Glatt, 1967). Mendelson's evidence (e.g. Mendelson and Mello, 1966) shows that after the ingestion of one drink, a few drinks, or many drinks, alcoholics do not necessarily lose control over drinking. The evidence reviewed also refutes the alternative version of loss of control which states that alcoholics, or a particular variety of them, suffer from an inability to abstain. Cohen *et al.* (1971) demonstrated that abstinence could be bought from alcoholics with a sufficient incentive, even when they had received a large priming dose, and the work of the Gottheil team (e.g. Gottheil *et al.*, 1972) showed that some alcoholics will spontaneously revert to abstinence when alcohol is freely available in a treatment programme.

For many years, the twin notions of inability to stop and inability to abstain have formed the pivot on which the demand for total abstinence in alcoholics has been based; if they wish to arrest their disease of alcoholism, alcoholics must never touch alcohol again because, if they did so, they would either be unable to stop drinking or once more be incapable of abstaining for any length of time. In view of the evidence presented in this chapter, it is clear that the abstinence requirement can no longer rely on such a simplistic and misleading conception of loss of control.

We have seen that one important response to the evidence from experimental studies of intoxication in alcoholics has been a watering down of the concept of loss of control, principally by Keller (1972), to include an element of unpredictability or indeterminacy. In this revised formulation, the alcoholic has not lost control, but can never be sure once he starts drinking that he will be able to stop. This added indeterminacy was incorporated, as explained in Chapter 1, into Edwards and Gross' (1976) Alcohol Dependence Syndrome in the form of a control, not lost, but 'variably and intermittently impaired'. Ludwig and Wikler (1974) also speak of a *relative* inability to regulate ethanol consumption. What are we to make of this relative or impaired control as a description of the alcoholic's drinking behaviour? At the risk of repetition, we must first of all insist that such a conception of impaired control does not qualify as a scientific proposition because, by the epistemological canons currently accepted by the majority of scientists (Popper, 1959), it is not *falsifiable*. The reason it is not falsifiable is that it cannot specify the conditions under which uncontrolled drinking will occur and the conditions under which it will not. For the purposes of scientific discourse, therefore, it is strictly meaningless. A second, closely related and equally embarrassing question for this notion of impaired control is, to what extent does such a conception tell us any more than that alcoholics drink more, that is, more often or in larger quantities, than other drinkers. In what particular way, in other words, does it achieve more than a restatement of the original problem to be solved? We believe the answers to these questions to be, to no extent and in no way. The error of believing that it does say more than this can be economically illustrated by quoting from Ludwig and Wikler (1974) who write: 'The very fact that they [alcoholics] choose to drink so much, even though they do not have to [*sic*], argues in favour of some sort of internal regulatory dysfunction or excessive, non-environmentally derived need.' One is bound to ask what kind of reasoning this is. The fact that alcoholics drink so much argues for nothing in itself, except that this is precisely the fact which needs to be explained.

So far it has been concluded that the mechanical conception of loss of control is descriptively inaccurate and that the revised concept of impaired control is untestable, or at least has not yet been cast into an adequately testable form. We are left with the basic observations that alcoholics drink more often and/or drink larger amounts and/or get drunk more often than nonalcoholics. Since this behaviour appears to be doing them harm, we assume that in some way they must be dependent on alcohol. These fundamental facts of alcoholism do require an explanation, and some of the explanations which have been advanced to account for loss of control or impaired control might be relevant. It is not impossible that a few alcoholics, probably a very few, are born with a predisposition to react abnormally to alcohol, owing to genetic (Goodwin *et al.*, 1974) or intrauterine causal factors (Jones and Smith, 1973). This abnormal susceptibility would presumably be irreversible so that, when diagnosed, further drinking in such individuals would be contra-indicated. It is also possible that excessive and prolonged ingestion of alcohol produces irreversible brain damage in some chronic alcoholics with the result that their ability to regulate alcohol consumption is seriously impaired. Both of these instances would qualify as specific disease entities and would justify the recommendation of total abstinence.

But it is highly unlikely that the great majority of persons diagnosed as alcoholics would fall into the above categories. By far the most outstanding explanation of impaired control over drinking is that advanced by Jellinek (1960) and based on the need to continue drinking in order to abolish unpleasant minimal withdrawal symptoms. In this conception, loss or impairment of control is equated with addiction or physical dependence. None of the evidence reviewed in this chapter refutes the existence of such relief drinking and, in our view, it is impossible seriously to deny the role of addictive mechanisms in alcoholic behaviour. However, there are distinct grounds for believing that the importance of physical dependence has been overestimated in traditional disease conceptions. One of the most interesting observations of Mello and Mendelson (1972) was that alcoholics preferred to continue working to amass tokens rather than drink immediately to abolish partial withdrawal symptoms. Thus, whether the occurrence of minimal withdrawal symptoms leads to uncontrolled drinking would appear to depend on prevailing circumstances. Moreover, the evidence from priming dose experiments, while not excluding the influence of some physiological interaction of alcohol with the organism, is in agreement on the significant contribution of expectancy factors. When unpacked, the notion of expectancy refers to the way in which drinking behaviour is a function of the situation in which it occurs and, in another sense, to the social and interpersonal drinking roles available to the alcoholic. The research of Nathan and his colleagues (e.g. Nathan *et al.*, 1970; Goldman *et al.*, 1973) reveals the involvement of social processes in the patterning of alcoholic drinking. More generally, the work of McAndrew and Edgerton (1969) has alerted us to the profound influence of cultural prescriptions on drinking behaviour of all kinds. Such considerations have been summarized by Room (1972*b*) who points out that traditionally the 'glue' which holds a drug user to a repeated pattern of behaviour has been exclusively thought of as being a property of the individual. Rather, Room suggests, drug dependence may be located at any one of five general analytical levels: the physiological, the psychological, the level of interaction in face-to-face groups, the level of subculture and social worlds, and the cultural level. Dependence seated at one level may cause dependence at another and the extinction of dependence at only one level will not necessarily cause the behaviour to disappear. Relating alcohol dependence to drug dependence in general, there is an increasing tendency among social scientists to view dependence, not as a purely physiologically determined phenomenon, but as learned behaviour intimately linked with symbolic definitions of his situation made by the drug abuser himself, which are in turn derived from cultural norms and definitions of drug dependence (Coleman, 1976).

Our criticisms of disease theory conceptions of impaired control should not be taken to mean that we regard the wider issue of control as being dead or irrelevant. Naive disease conceptions of alcoholism made the mistake of dichotomizing drinking behaviour into that of alcoholics which was completely or periodically constrained by loss of control and that of non-alcoholics which was entirely voluntary. In our view, it would be an error of equal magnitude to go to the other extreme and assume that both alcoholics and normal drinkers are free to drink as they wish and choose to drink the way they do. The alcoholic who is drinking too much for his own good and *complains* that he is doing so has clearly, in some sense, lost control over his drinking. It appears that he wishes to drink differently but, again in some sense, feels *unable* to do so. These truisms mean that the problem of control over drinking behaviour cannot be brushed aside and, indeed, that it remains central to an understanding of harmful drinking. The essential point is, however, that there are more satisfactory ways of explaining this apparently diminished control than by arbitrarily assuming the presence of some pre-existent physiological or biochemical abnormality or some other mysterious disease process located inside the individual, the evidence for which is nonexistent. For example, Storm and Cutler (1975) defined loss of control simply as drinking more, and becoming more intoxicated, than one had intended. Defined in this way, loss of control is obviously an event experienced by many drinkers, those who are in some sense pathological and those who are not, and applying to many levels of consumption. Storm and

Cutler then give a useful semantic analysis of the conditions which might affect the occurrence of loss of control in this sense, only one of these conditions being the effect of alcohol in the system as a result of previous drinks. As another example, Bacon (1973) has provided a purely sociological account of the process of addiction to alcohol and of loss of control. As the developing alcoholic reduces the number and variety of his social activities, he changes membership to social groups which are more tolerant of his drinking and which exercise less control over him. His drinking behaviour therefore appears out of control to persons and institutions which define such behaviour as intolerable.

The main point we wish to make is that the issue of impaired control in alcoholics may be profitably explored in psychological, sociopsychological or broad sociological terms and need not be confined to physiological or other internal events. The important implications of these alternative explanations are that none of them rests on a strict separation of alcoholics from nonalcoholics and that none of them would entail any suggestion of an irreversible process.

We turn now to what is perhaps the most important single conclusion to be drawn from the evidence reviewed in this chapter. This is the experimental demonstration that alcoholic drinking behaviour is *operant* behaviour. This means simply that the amount and patterning of alcoholic drinking is shaped by the environmental consequences of that drinking. In the research of the Mendelson, Cohen and Nathan groups we encountered a variety of reinforcing events which were shown to be effective in modifying alcoholic drinking and we did not meet with an example where no form of control could be exerted. Ludwig and Wikler (1974) consider this evidence and conclude that, because the alcoholics taking part in these studies typically reached high blood alcohol concentrations, they were 'manifestly demonstrating a relative inability to control, regulate or modulate their ethanol intake'. Moreover, Ludwig and Wikler claim, 'it is fallacious to assume that, because the drinking behaviour of alcoholics can be modified by experimental manipulations of environmental reinforcement contingencies . . . the behaviour is not primarily influenced by neurophysiological mechanisms or internal drives'. However, this is to miss completely a crucial point. Since operant behaviour is modifiable behaviour, there is no justification for making qualitative distinction between the drinking of alcoholics and nonalcoholics. Whether or not alcoholic behaviour is 'primarily influenced by neurophysiological mechanisms or internal drives', and there is no convincing reason to suppose that it is, this is irrelevant to the demonstrated fact that alcoholic drinking is subject to the same kind of environmental contingencies and modifiable according to the same kind of principles as all drinking behaviour. One does not have to be a radical behaviourist, and to believe that reference to internal states has no place in scientific discourse, to realize the profound significance of this. If alcoholic drinking is modifiable in the same essential way as normal drinking then there is no sense in describing a specific disease of alcoholism and no sense in searching for the roots of a general and irreversible loss of control in the alcoholic. In consequence, the main theoretical foundation of the abstinence requirement in treatment is radically undermined.

Compared with loss of control, the traditional notion of craving seems to have fared rather better in the light of experimental evidence. This is not to say that the pre-existent physical need originating in a metabolic or endocrine disorder which was recognized by the WHO (Jellinek *et al.*, 1955) committee has received any empirical support; it has not. However, there is no reason to doubt the existence of what Isbell (1955) called 'nonsymbolic craving' and which is equivalent to an awareness of unpleasant minimal withdrawal symptoms during a drinking bout, provided it is remembered that this dysphoric experience does not inevitably lead to uncontrolled drinking. The most significant recent development in the conceptualization of craving is the description of conditioned withdrawal offered by Hodgson *et al.* (1979) and, given that the additional paraphernalia of the subclinical conditioned withdrawal syndrome is discarded, by Ludwig and Wikler (1974). Our only cavil with Hodgson *et al.*'s multidimensional conception of craving is when they write that it is 'a system of interrelated responses involving subjective, physiological, behavioural and *biochemical* components' (italics added). We accept the evidence for the contribution of the first three of these components but are at a loss to appreciate the evidence for the contribution of biochemical factors. As with minimal withdrawal symptoms during drinking, the presence of conditioned withdrawal does not mean that uncontrolled drinking will necessarily ensue. Of most importance for this conception, however, is the fact that craving is subject to extinction and has been made the target of therapeutic extinction procedures by Hodgson and Rankin (1976). Even so, it is likely that the contribution of this somewhat mechanical conditioning model to the treatment of alcoholism will become more limited as knowledge in the field progresses. To take an example from an area with a much older history of learning theory applications, the treatment of phobias has moved a long way from reliance on simple deconditioning procedures into the realms of 'perceived self-efficacy' (Bandura, 1978). It is probable that the role of cognitive processes will become increasingly recognized in the behavioural modification of craving.

It was concluded that the contribution of physical dependence to the maintenance of excessive drinking may have been exaggerated in the traditional disease perspective. There are also grounds for believing that the presence of physical dependence may be one of the least significant factors in alcoholism treatment, as Shulman (1979) has suggested. This is because the more serious consequences of alcoholism occur through a repetitive return to drinking after extended periods of abstinence, especially those occurring after treatment. In Shulman's view, relapse following treatment is not a function of physical but rather of psychological dependence, a view with which Jellinek (1960) would have agreed. Indeed, there is an accumulating body of evidence, reviewed by Marlatt (1978), that environmental and situational factors, together with the cognitive and emotional reactions which accompany them, are the most important determinants of the relapse process. Nevertheless, it is still possible to argue that previous excessive drinking has produced long-lasting neurophysiological changes which make relapse more likely if further drinking is attempted. This is clearly the implication of the reinstatement element in the Alcohol Dependence Syndrome summarized in Chapter 1. However, there are several very important research questions to be answered here. Firstly, is the clinical impression of reinstatement and its relationship to previous severity of dependence supported by empirical studies of relapsed alcoholics? Secondly, does the rapidity of reinstatement, if confirmed, decrease with the passage of time since the last drink and, if so, when does the psychobiological response return to normal? According to Gross (1977), the only available data on the reversibility of long-term effects of alcohol exposure in severely dependent persons are studies of reduction in slow-wave sleep (e.g. Wagman and Allen, 1975) and these studies show that 'the slow-wave sleep of most of these individuals tended to recover, although it may have taken several months to do so' (Gross, 1977). Thirdly, what quantities of alcohol are necessary for reinstatement to occur and is there a cut-off below which drinking would not result in renewed physical dependence? Finally, and probably of most importance, what is the relative contribution to the relapse process of neurophysiological and sociopsychological factors? These questions are not being asked here in order to press for a recommendation of controlled drinking in severely dependent persons; such a recommendation could only be based on the empirical evidence relating to the success or otherwise of their attempts at control (see Chapter 2 and 6). Rather, these research questions are posed in the hope of reaching a greater understanding of the postulated reinstatement phenomenon and of investigating a much-needed theoretical foundation for the abstinence requirement.

SUMMARY

As we have repeatedly pointed out, loss of control and craving, conceived of as irreversible properties of the alcoholic's drinking behaviour, have formed the traditional justification for the requirement of total abstinence in the treatment of alcoholism. The general conclusion from the evidence reviewed in this chapter is that this justification is no longer possible. The concept of loss of control is either descriptively inaccurate, explanatorily tautologous and scientifically meaningless, or translatable into terms which are not specific to alcoholics and which do not imply an irreversible process. In the restricted sense of physical dependence based on withdrawal symptoms, loss of control may have a limited role in the maintenance of abusive drinking but psychological, social and cultural factors are also important. The concept of craving has phenomenological validity as a short-hand description of the alcoholic's experience of minor withdrawal symptoms while drinking and the conditioned association of such withdrawal after short periods of abstinence. However, in both physiological and conditioned senses, craving is clearly reversible. Relapse after drinking following an extended period of abstinence is more likely to be explained by a socio-psychological model with behavioural and cognitive referents. For all these reasons, 'loss of control' and 'craving' can no longer constitute a sound theoretical underpinning for the therapeutic requirement of total and life-long abstinence. This is not to say that a theoretical rationale for permanent abstention will never be found, but merely that it does not exist at present.

4 Possible advantages of a controlled drinking treatment goal

The evidence reviewed in the last two chapters shows that total and lifelong abstinence is not always necessary as a solution to the alcoholic's problems. The theoretical underpinning of the abstinence requirement in the related concepts of loss of control and craving has been shown, to say the very least, to be in need of considerable modification. And it has also been established that some alcoholics, either spontaneously or in actual defiance of the professional advice they have probably received, have been able to achieve stable patterns of normal, harmfree drinking. All this evidence clearly suggests the possibility of substituting controlled drinking for abstinence as a treatment goal for some alcoholics, and further invites the question of what increase in the proportion of successful normal drinking outcomes could be expected if this were done.

Chapters 5, 6 and 7 of this book are devoted to controlled drinking treatments. They will describe the conceptual bases of controlled drinking treatment methods in modern psychological theory, the evidence presently available for the effectiveness of these methods, and the practical problems which arise in implementing them. Before proceeding to these matters, however, it will be worthwhile to pause and consider what potential advantages might accrue from a controlled drinking goal in comparison with total abstinence. There is a body of research and opinion which is relevant to this issue and which can be discussed in advance of a consideration of the treatment methods themselves. Our discussion of the potential advantages of controlled drinking will begin with the implied converse, the possible disadvantages of the total abstinence treatment goal.

ABSTINENCE IN CONTEMPORARY SOCIETY

In Chapter 1 we traced the organizational form adopted by Alcoholics Anonymous back to its origins in the nineteenth-century Temperance Movement. We saw that this enormously powerful social movement enthusiastically adopted total abstinence from alcohol as its recommended solution to the habitual drunkard's predicament. In the nineteenth-century context, urging someone to become abstinent was to make a much more realistic demand of him than it is now. Large numbers of the population were abstinent and they included some of the most influential and prestigious members of the community. The recovered drunkard had shining examples of sobriety to emulate and could expect to receive considerable encouragement and praise for his new resolve. Moreover, the Temperance Movement was but an overt expression of a larger and more fundamental set of moral values in European and American society, commonly known as the Protestant ethic (Weber, 1930). This ethic endorsed the virtues of hard work and sobriety, the postponement of immediate gratification in the interests of long-term achievement, ascetic self-discipline and independence from others. Success in life was presumed to be a sign of the exercise of these moral qualities. In this way, abstinence from alcohol found a ready place in an integrated and familiar set of social values and the reformed drunkard had available to him a ready-made identity with which to equip his new life.

But things have changed. The demise of the Temperance Movement in the twentieth century is bound up with the decline of organized religion in general. The work ethic and the rigid adherence to moral values it implied have been largely replaced in Western industrial societies by an increasing preoccupation with consumption, leisure and interpersonal relationships, a preoccupation summarized by Riesman (1950) in his concept of the 'other-directed man'. The place of abstinence in this twentieth-century value-system has been put by Gusfield (1963) in the following terms:

> For the 'other-directed' man neither the intolerance nor the seriousness of the abstainer is acceptable. Nor is the intense rebelliousness and social isolation of the hard drinker acceptable. Analysis of American alcohol consumption is consistent with this. The contemporary American is less likely than his nineteenth-century ancestor to be either a total abstainer or a hard drinker. Moderation is his drinking watchword. One must get along with others and liquor has proven to be a necessary and effective facilitator to sociability. It relaxes reserve and permits fellowship at the same time that it displays the drinker's tolerance for some moral lapse in himself and others.

Certainly, there is evidence that total abstinence is an increasingly rare event in Western industrial society. Cahalan and Cisin (1968), reporting on a nationwide survey of American drinking practices in 1964/65, found that 32 per cent of respondents drank less than once a year or not at all. This comprised 23 per cent of men and 40 per cent of women interviewed. A comparison with earlier American surveys by Riley and Marden (1947) and Mulford (1964) indicated that the proportion of drinkers in the population was increasing, especially among women. Cahalan and Cisin conclude that drinking is typical behaviour and both total abstinence and heavy drinking atypical. The prevalence of drinking varied directly with the status of the individual in society, with the higher status groups providing the greater proportions of drinkers. As well as being more likely in men than in women, drinking was also more likely in younger persons across all status levels. Apart from age and sex, whether a person drank at all was primarily associated with sociological variables, such as urban residence, race, religion and national identity, rather than with personality variables. For example, those living in large suburbs (13 per cent), Catholics (17 per cent) and respondents of Italian origin (9 per cent) had the lowest rates of abstention. In a survey carried out in Scotland in 1972, Dight (1976) found only 5 per cent of men and 12 per cent of women to be nondrinkers, with 74 per cent and 46 per cent of men and women respectively being regular drinkers. Whether the differences from Cahalan and Cisin's figures are due to national variations or to the passage of time or to both is, of course, impossible to determine. A later Scottish survey of the Clydebank area by Saunders and Kershaw (1978) produced somewhat higher proportions of nondrinkers than Dight – 9 per cent of males and 26 per cent of females. However, the same trend was observed for regular drinking to be under-taken largely by young, adult males and to diminish after about the age of thirty-five.

Dight (1976) also provided evidence that older attitudes of disapproval towards drinking have waned considerably. Ninety-three per cent of men and 87 per cent of women agreed with the statement that 'there is nothing wrong in having a few drinks'; 3 per cent of men and 8 per cent of women disagreed, the remainder being undecided. There was also less disapproval than might be expected of occasional drunkenness. A majority of men (56 per cent) but not of women (39 per cent) agreed with the sentiment: 'It does some people good to get drunk once in a while.' While we know of no evidence from general population surveys directly relevant to the extent of disapproval or unfavourable attitudes towards total abstinence, a study by Windham and Preston (1967) has an indirect bearing on the matter. These authors looked at the relationship between amount of alcohol consumption among Mississippi high school students and a sociometric index of popular-ity for the same subjects. Under the age of fifteen, this relationship was negative, with higher consumption individuals tending to be less popular. But an important finding was that over the age of fifteen the direction of the relationship reversed, higher consumption being positively associated with greater popularity. Such a finding clearly suggests the presence of inter-personal incentives and rewards for alcohol consumption and informal sanctions for avoidance of alcohol in the older age-group. Similarly Maddox (1964) found that the heaviest drinkers in a student group showed more closeness and integration with the group than lighter drinkers. Abstainers showed the least degree of integration and abstinence was likely to lead to social constriction. It would be interesting to conduct similar studies with adult samples.

More directly relevant to the question of attitudes to abstinence are the findings of Davies and Stacey (1972) who conducted a survey of adolescents in Glasgow. They found that nondrinking teenagers were perceived as very low on a factor described chiefly by 'toughness' and 'rebelliousness'. The implication was that a strong incentive to drink among adolescents was the attempt to avoid appearing 'weak' or 'cissy'. Nondrinkers were also seen as low on another factor concerned with attractiveness to the opposite sex and general popularity, although not so low in this respect as heavy drinkers. Although this evidence concerns attitudes to drinking and abstinence among adolescents, it is very unlikely that such attitudes are confined to this group. Heather (1979) has proposed that the attitudes in question form part of a nexus of subterranean values (see Matza and Sykes, 1961) which are attached to the pursuit of leisure goals and which permeate the social order. Drinking becomes attractive because of its function in releasing the expression of these subterranean values, which are associated at the same time with attitudes of suspicion and even hostility towards those who choose to remain abstinent. It must be recognized, however, that both the relative extent of drinking and abstinence and the degree of approval/disapproval shown towards them are closely related to age, sex, social status and other sociological variables.

THE ABSTINENT ALCOHOLIC

Against this background of the general problems which may be met by the abstinent individual in our society, let us now consider what special problems may be encountered by the person whose abstinence is a solution to previous alcohol abuse. Because of its employment in the older literature (e.g. Gerard *et al.*, 1962), we have used the traditional, AA-derived term 'the abstinent alcoholic' to describe such a person.

Scattered through the earlier literature are occasional comments and empirical observations on the quality of life experienced by the abstinent alcoholic. For example, WELLMAN (1955) found that during the first half year of abstinence his patients were plagued by irritability, depression, insomnia, fatigue, restlessness, a sense of aloneness and distractibility. During the second six months the symptom of fatigue became dominant and showed itself in patients' reports that they could not do as much work as when they were drinking or handle interpersonal and emotional problems without undue tiredness. The reasons for this fatigue, whether the continuing after-effects of organic sequelae of excessive drinking or the sociopsychological consequences of abstinence, are not made clear.

Despite the unquestioning acceptance of therapeutic abstinence by most early investigators, HAYMAN (1955) reported that many psychiatrists in southern California felt that improved marital, occupational and social adjustments may be greater gains than abstinence. One outstanding difficulty identified with the abstinence goal was that the patient might need a lifelong treatment regime.

Perhaps the first systematic study of the abstinent alcoholic was reported by FLAHERTY, McGUIRE AND GATSKI (1955) in a paper entitled, 'The psychodynamics of the "dry drunk" '. Flaherty *et al.* had heard the expression 'the dry drunk' being used by nondrinking, former alcoholics and enquired as to its meaning. They were informed that it referred to a period of emotional and physical tension similar to those experienced during excessive drinking. In order to investigate this phenomenon more fully, they sent 111 questionnaires to members of a local AA group and received replies from 37 men and 15 women with an average age of 49 years. They found that the dry drunk, as described by their respondents, corresponded in many ways to the syndrome delineated by Wellman (1955) with the difference that it was reported to be present in episodic form long after one year's abstinence and to occur irregularly but with diminishing intensity as the duration of sobriety lengthened. Also, Flaherty *et al.* concluded that manifestations of depression were more prominent than physical fatigue as such. As well as tiredness, nervousness and irritability, their respondents frequently mentioned mental and emotional confusion, despondency, self-pity, and resentment and frustration because of the inability to drink. The duration of the dry drunk ranged from one hour to four months, and such was the intensity of depression during these periods that nineteen respondents reported having entertained suicidal thoughts, twelve having actually planned it. With regard to precipitants, the most common response referred to the individual's 'inner life'. The most frequently mentioned source of prevention or ameliorization of the dry drunk among these AA members was contact with other members of the fellowship.

In a comparative study of different treatment methods, WALLERSTEIN (1956) found that the therapeutic administration of Antabuse produced the highest rates of abstinence. He also noted that for some patients the abstinence enforced by Antabuse could have disastrous results for personality organization. This was especially true for two groups of patients, those whose primary diagnosis was depressive reaction and those diagnosed as borderline schizophrenic. There was a tendency for enforced abstinence to release more florid symptoms in both these groups.

There have been several outcome studies of abstinence-oriented treatment which show that there is no necessary correspondence between the attainment of the treatment goal and overall improvement in life functioning. To mention but two of these studies, THOMAS *et al.* (1959) found that, although only 35 per cent of patients in treatment had achieved total abstinence, 51 per cent could be considered improved in terms of family and social adjustment, 45 per cent in occupational adjustment and 39 per cent in physical status; WILBY AND JONES (1962) were surprised to discover that, while rates of abstinence increased between follow-ups at 18 and 24 months after treatment, rates of overall improvement decreased during this interval.

Such considerations in the area of treatment outcome led BRUUN (1963) to distinguish between being 'cured', defined as abstinence or nondeviant drinking, and being 'changed' after treatment, defined purely in terms of social and psychological variables. Bruun suggested that in evaluating the effects of treatment, drinking behaviour should be considered quite separately from other indicators of improvement. In confirmation of such a view, GILLIS AND KEET (1969) reported that 58 per cent of their patients showed notable improvement in life adjustment although they were still drinking. They also noted that the extent of pathological drinking in these individuals was reduced from 70 per cent to 20 per cent of drinking episodes.

The classic study of the abstinent alcoholic was reported by GERARD, SAENGER AND WILE (1962). These authors followed up and interviewed 50 treated alcoholics who had been totally abstinent for at least one year, with a range of up to 19 years. The first thing to note is that in the external, public aspects of their lives, these patients had undoubtedly benefited to a major extent. Compared with those who had continued to drink, the abstinent group looked and felt healthier and had better overt relationships with their families. Their employment records were also considerably improved. Among all patients who were employed at admission to treatment, the abstinent ones were much more likely to have maintained employment in the interval, and, among those unemployed at intake, abstinent ex-patients were much more likely to have found employment. In general, then, the outward structure of their lives seemed more normal and socially desirable in comparison with nonabstinent ex-patients and with themselves before they stopped drinking. However, Gerard *et al.* were also interested in the patient's inner life, with the quality of his personal relationships and his psychiatric status. They found they were able to classify their 50 abstinent alcoholics into four ideal types; some of those interviewed were fully representative of a type, while others displayed additional characteristics of another type. The four types were as follows:

1. *The overtly disturbed.* This was the largest subgroup, comprising 27 of the 50 interviewees. The authors describe them thus:

These ex-patients suffer with tension to a degree which concerns them; and/or they are angry, dissatisfied, or resentful, projecting aggressive attitudes or ideas into their environment; and/or they are driven by anxiety so that they are restless, unable to relax, seeking to distract or sedate themselves from their conflicts by spending inordinate amounts of time at work or social activities of a community nature; and/or they are overtly psychiatrically ill, displaying disturbances of mood, thought and behaviour to a psychotic degree.

Case histories are given to illustrate these psychological abnormalities.

2.   *The inconspicuously inadequate*. Twelve patients were classified in this subgroup which contained those 'whose total functioning is characterized by meagreness of their involvement with life and living'. A typical case history is presented of an individual who 'is abstinent at the price of surrender or resignation to a remarkably limited life. We would speculate that his drinking had been motivated by an attempt to support action and relatedness, to find meaning and strength etc. Without alcohol, he has shrunk back to the nest.'

3.   *Alcoholics Anonymous successes*. This subgroup consisted of six ex-patients. Although many in the two previous subgroups had attended AA meetings, they had not made a successful adjustment to the fellowship, unlike those in this category. These six individuals were said to have acquired a sense of purpose and value in life through their AA membership. Nearly their entire social lives centred around AA and it was evident that they were now as dependent on AA as they had previously been on alcohol. This transfer of dependence is, of course, in no way antithetical to the aims of the fellowship. Apart from the advantages and disadvantages of almost total dependence on AA, what Gerard *et al.* find regrettable is that so few of the abstinent ex-patients studied could enter into the fellowship in this manner, even though most were dedicated members or had at least been exposed to AA meetings.

4.   *Independent successes*. The smallest subgroup containing only five individuals comprised those who had achieved a state of self-respecting independence, of personal growth and of self-realization. They were not overtly disturbed, they were alive and interesting as human beings, and their efforts at self-realization were independently and not institutionally supported.

What is surprising about Gerard *et al.*'s analysis is the low proportion of abstinent alcoholics who could be described as having made any kind of successful overall adjustment to their new lives, i.e. the 22 per cent in subgroups 3 and 4. From their psychiatric point of view, the authors remind us that alcoholism is notoriously difficult to modify and that the loss of a symptom may be as threatening to the person's total life situation, or even more so, as the maintenance of the symptom may be harmful to health and social adjustment.

In summarizing the available evidence relating to the quality of life under abstinence, PATTISON (1966) arrived at the following conclusions: 1. Abstinence as a necessary condition for successful treatment is an over-statement. It is a prescription which should be used judiciously. 2. Abstinence as a criterion of successful treatment is misleading. It may be maintained at the expense of total life functioning, as in some Alcoholics

Anonymous abstainers. Abstinence may also be followed by personality deterioration.

Apart from evidence that abstinence does not always lead to overall improvement in life functioning, there are also grounds for suspecting that the social and psychological consequences of abstinence pose certain problems which may contribute to relapse. In a repertory grid investigation of psychological changes occurring during group therapy, HEATHER, EDWARDS AND HORE (1975) found a major dimension of change to involve perceived respectability and self-respect, as might be expected in view of the alcoholic's presumed awareness of his deviant behaviour. On relating psychological change to outcome, these authors found that relapse was significantly more likely under two circumstances – when patients had experienced a large degree of recovery in self-respect and feelings of respectability and when they had actually shown a decrease on these dimensions during therapy. Patients who had sustained abstinence at follow-up tended to be those who had shown only modest recovery of self-respect and who can therefore be presumed to have been able to tolerate some degree of self-attributed social deviance. To interpret this finding, Heather *et al.* hypothesized that the abstinent alcoholic's situation was that of 'the marginal deviant', defined as 'one who has been excluded from the conventional world and at the same time has been denied admission and certification into a deviant subculture' (Rubington and Weinberg, 1968). In other words, the condition of abstinence excludes the individual both from the conventional world in which social drinking is normative behaviour and from the alcoholic subculture. The task faced by the abstinent alcoholic is one of tolerating the discomfort engendered by this situation of exclusion. One obvious means of achieving this is by successful affiliation with Alcoholics Anonymous and, indeed, it may be one of the most important functions of AA to counter the psychological problems arising from marginal deviance by putting recovering alcoholics in touch with others in a similar position, in the context of a deviant but not unrespectable subculture. As we have seen, however, many alcoholics are not able to identify with AA and others who maintain contact are not able to make a successful affiliation.

Evidence that the social role of the abstainer is psychologically alien from the majority of alcoholics comes from a study by RICHARD AND BURLEY (1978). These authors gave 20 hospitalized alcoholics a form of the semantic differential in which they were asked to rate the concepts of 'total abstainer', 'controlled drinker' and 'myself' on a collection of evaluative dimensions. The results showed that the psychological distance between 'myself' and 'total abstainer' was significantly greater than that between 'myself' and 'controlled drinker'. Richard and Burley speculate that when some alcoholics are asked to adopt the role of the total abstainer, which is not generally in accord with their self-concept, they will incur the problem of role-conflict, the consequences of which are said to include anxiety, withdrawal, illness and inefficiency. If this analysis is valid, relapse could be expected as part of the attempt to resolve role-conflict.

A different approach to the same issue begins with the idea that the traditional 'one drink – one drunk' maxim popularized by Alcoholics Anonymous may act as a form of self-fulfilling prophecy (Schaeffer, 1971; Sobell *et al.*, 1972). In other words, if the abstinent alcoholic takes a single drink, for whatever reasons, he may construe himself as having immediately lost control over drinking and proceed to act on that assumption by getting properly drunk. The implication is also that he is using his endorsement of the AA maxim as an excuse for returning to a secretly desired state of drunkenness. In vernacular terms, the alcoholic may tell himself that 'he may as well be hanged for a sheep as for a lamb'. MARLATT (1978) has phrased this hypothetical psychological event in more technical language in his concept of 'the abstinence violation effect' (AVE). This effect applies to any consummatory behaviour, such as smoking and overeating, and is postulated to occur under the conditions (*i*) that the individual is personally committed to an extended or indefinite period of abstinence from engaging in a specific behaviour, and (*ii*) that the behaviour occurs during this period of voluntary abstinence. The intensity of the AVE is said to vary as a function of several factors, including the degree of effort expended to maintain abstinence, the length of the abstinence period and the value of the behaviour to the individual concerned. More fundamentally, the AVE is characterized by two key cognitive elements – (*a*) a cognitive dissonance effect (Festinger, 1957) in which the occurrence of the restricted behaviour is dissonant with the self-image of abstinence and which produces a state of conflict which would popularly be described as guilt, and (*b*) a personal attribution effect (Kelley, 1967) in which the individual attributes the occurrence of the prohibited behaviour to internal weakness or personal failure rather than to situational or environmental causative influences. From the point of view of cognitive dissonance theory, continued drinking following the violation of the abstinence rule is effective in reducing feelings of dissonance or guilt and the alcoholic is able to modify his self-image to conform to his behaviour by, possibly, construing himself as a helpless victim of a disease process. Clearly, the existence, precise nature and functions of the abstinence violation effect have not as yet been supported by sufficient empirical evidence but form part of a hypothetical model of relapse from abstinence which appears eminently researchable.

A COMPARISON OF OUTCOMES

Some of the evidence reviewed in the preceding section showed that there may be special problems attached to the abstinence treatment goal and that abstinence does not necessarily lead to fulfilment in aspects of life divorced from drinking. However, it would obviously be scientifically improper to pass any judgements on the abstinence treatment goal without first comparing it with the normal drinking outcome in terms of measures of psychosocial adjustment. Fortunately, some evidence exists which enables this comparison to be made. In considering this evidence it should again be borne in mind that in this chapter we are concerned only with normal drinking spontaneously arrived at or following treatment directed at abstinence, and not with the results of controlled drinking treatments as such. Before proceeding to the evidence a general point may be made. This is that we have been technically guilty of an error in referring to abstinence and controlled drinking as treatment *goals*. Properly speaking, the goal of all treatment is an enhancement of the patient's or client's quality of life and an increase in his or her general satisfaction with existence. Modifications of drinking behaviour of whatever kind should be seen solely as *means* towards this end; they are not themselves the *ends* of therapy. This point has been consistently and articulately made over the years by Mansell Pattison (1966, 1976*a; b*).

It may be recalled from Chapter 2 (p. 32) that Moore and Ramseur (1960) were the first to suggest that some resumed normal drinkers might have a better outcome in terms of overall adjustment than some total abstainers. Five of fourteen patients found to be most improved on psychosocial variables at follow-up were 'well-controlled social drinkers' and six of fifteen who were abstinent were only 'slightly improved' on these variables. However, the most important early comparison of normal drinkers and abstainers was included in the paper on the abstinent alcoholic by GERARD, SAENGER AND WILE (1962). The findings of a comparison between 55 abstainers and 41 nonproblem-drinkers are shown in Table 4.1 taken from the later commentary by Gerard and Saenger (1966). It will be seen that on four measures of adjustment – health, medical treatment, problems at work and relationship with spouse – the percentage of the abstinent group displaying a good adjustment was higher than in the normal drinking group, without the difference being large enough to reach an acceptable level of statistical significance. However, on two variables the abstinent group was statistically superior. Fifteen per cent of the normal drinkers were deemed to be alienated from their families at follow-up compared with only 2 per cent in the abstinent group, which may reflect continuing anxieties on the family's part concerning the patient's drinking. More highly statistically significant was the difference in the percentages judged to be at the lower end of a scale of social participation; patients at the lower end of this scale could be characterized as 'socially isolated, as having solitary activities only, or at best having casual and sporadic relationships with friends and family'. The abstinent group contained a substantially smaller proportion of such patients than did the normal drinking group. The only adjustment measure to show no difference between the two groups was the important one of occupational mobility. Note that this was the only variable which, since it entailed a simultaneous comparison of occupational status at intake and at follow-up, did not allow the possibility that the abstinent group were already superior on the measure of adjustment at intake.

TABLE 4.1
Percentages of abstainers and normal drinkers showing good adjustment on seven measures at follow-up

Measure of adjustment	% of abstinent patients	% of normal drinking patients	Level of statistical significance
1. Unconditionally good health reported by patient	62	51	–
2. No medical treatment in last year	69	56	–
3. No downward occupational mobility between intake and follow-up	81	81	–
4. No problems getting along at work	67	56	–
5. Not alienated from family at follow-up	98	85	5%
6. Good or fair relationship with spouse at follow-up	66	50	–
7. Not at lower end of a scale of social participation	73	44	0·1%

Source: Gerard and Saenger (1966) (adapted).

A possible interpretation of the apparent superiority in general adjustment of the abstinent patients in this study is to refer to the fact mentioned in Chapter 2 (p. 43) that specific criteria for normal drinking were not used by Gerard *et al.* Thus, although the gross consequences of alcohol abuse, such as medical treatment and arrest, were avoided by the 'normal' drinkers under the definition used in this study, they could have continued to use alcohol in what would be regarded by most observers as an excessive manner. In short, some of these patients could have been, in Pattison's (1976*a*) term, 'attentuated drinkers' – those who show improvement but who continue to drink abnormally. If so, this would account for the relative deficits in some measures of adjustment shown by the nonabstinent comparison group in this study.

As we have seen, the same loose definition of normal drinking was used by Gerard and Saenger (1966) who also measured outcome on five nondrinking variables. The comparison of 100 abstinent and 41 normal drinking patients at one year follow-up resulted in higher percentages of good outcome among the abstinent patients on all five measures: health status, 60 per cent vs. 49 per cent; social stability, 64 per cent vs. 51 per cent; interpersonal relationships, 60 per cent vs. 51 per cent; work adjustment, 55 per cent vs. 54 per cent; work status, 59 per cent vs. 49 per cent. However, none of these differences is statistically significant and there is therefore no firm evidence that they represent a real superiority of the abstinent outcome on these variables. Also, the differences tend to be smaller than those reported by Gerard *et al.* (1962). The higher percentages on all five measures are certainly suggestive of superiority but, again, Gerard and Saenger's method of defining controlled drinking may have resulted in a misleading impression being given by these data.

Further comparative evidence comes from the study of PATTISON, HEADLEY, GLESER AND GOTTSCHALK (1968). In line with Pattison's (1966) arguments for judging outcome on the basis of a variety of areas of adjustment, rather than simply on drinking behaviour alone, Pattison *et al.* borrowed separate scales for measuring physical health, interpersonal relationships and vocational health from Gerard and Saenger (1966) and added another scale to measure mental health. The results of the comparison between eleven abstainers, eleven normal drinkers and ten pathological drinkers showed that, generally speaking, the normal drinkers were no worse off than the abstainers at follow-up one year or more after treatment. All three outcome groups, including the pathological drinkers, demonstrated some improvement over intake scores on the four health scales used but, whereas the three groups showed no differences with each other on the physical health scale, the abstainers and normal drinkers showed an equal and relatively greater improvement compared with the pathological drinkers on vocational and interpersonal health. Only on the measure of mental health did the abstainers obtain lower and thus healthier scores than the normal drinkers, but the authors suggest that this was due to the inclusion among the eleven normal drinkers of three individuals who, in the opinion of the interviewing psychiatrist, were not true normal drinkers because, although not drinking in larger quantities than the others, they had not changed their motivation for drinking but were merely 'controlling their impulses'. When these were excluded, mental health scores did not differ statistically between abstainers and normal drinkers.

A later study by PATTISON, COE AND RHODES (1969) employed a similar methodology to investigate differences between three types of treatment facility. Of interest here is the finding that, over all categories of outcome, changes in drinking scores and changes in various health measures were by no means perfectly correlated. Abstinent patients tended to show the greatest improvements, but even the patients classified as 'unsuccessful drinkers' showed a marked improvement in interpersonal relationships, almost as much as the abstainers. Another outcome subgroup comprised those patients considered to be treatment successes who were drinking in a limited way. These persons' average improvement in other areas of life functioning was intermediate between that of the abstainers and the unsuccessful drinkers. The authors stress, however, that this group is not to be confused with the normal drinkers described, for example, by Pattison (1966) because they had not changed their pattern of drinking but were engaging in a controlled effort to avoid more pathological drinking. The restrictions on the improvement shown by these limited drinkers are reminiscent of the slight inferiority in outcome measures among Gerard *et al.*'s (1962) and Gerard and Saenger's (1966) controlled drinkers and reinforces the suggestion that many of the latter may have been limited or attenuated drinkers in Pattison's sense. When Pattison *et al.* (1969) considered the true normal drinkers in their sample they found improvement in general functioning almost identical with that of the abstinent group.

The most extensive recent comparison of relevance to this section is that undertaken by POLICH, ARMOR AND BRAIKER (1980) as part of the four-year follow-up of the original Rand Report. These authors compared abstainers and nonproblem-drinkers on a great variety of variables, including measures of social adjustment, psychiatric symptoms, psychological traits and overall life satisfaction. The main conclusion is that there were no consistent and meaningful differences between abstainers and nonproblem-drinkers on these variables. On the measures of social adjustment, high quantity nonproblem-drinkers were at least equal to the two abstention categories (i.e. six-month and one-year abstainers) but, curiously, low-quantity nonproblem-drinkers gave slightly lower rates for marriage and full-time employment. A somewhat higher percentage of high-quantity nonproblem-drinkers reported experiencing depression and tension or stress 'all or most of the time', but this did not apply to anxiety. With regard to 'lack of enjoyment' of daily experience, the shorter-term abstainers were worse off. Somewhat more abstainers than nonproblem-drinkers said that they were very satisfied with their lives, but this was balanced by the greater percentage of abstainers who complained of being dissatisfied. The four psychological traits measured again demonstrated no consistent differences between remission categories. Long-term abstainers give the highest percentage of those qualifying as emotionally stable, but the lowest percentage of those classified as autonomous.

To summarize the evidence reviewed in this section, research has generally failed to demonstrate any consistent differences in nondrinking outcome measures of improvement between total abstainers and normal drinkers. Earlier studies which suggested that some small differences may exist (Gerard *et al.*, 1962; Gerard and Saenger, 1966) are subject to methodological difficulties and are especially prone to the criticism that some of the 'normal' drinkers studied may have been limited or attentuated drinkers (Pattison *et al.*, 1969). Certainly the most recent and most extensive study of treatment outcome in the literature (Polich *et al.*, 1980) has failed to show any differences on a variety of measures of social and psychological adjustment. In view of the comments made earlier in the chapter on the potential disadvantages of the abstinence treatment goal, it should be made clear that there is obviously no evidence from these comparisons that the normal drinking outcome is superior to abstinence in terms of overall life functioning.

THE REQUIREMENT OF ABSTINENCE IN TREATMENT

One consequence of the abstinence treatment goal is that abstinence is usually seen as essential during the patient's treatment. Such a condition for treatment might also have certain advantages and disadvantages which could be discussed. For example, the need for abstinence as a requisite for the psychotherapy of alcoholism was the focus of a debate between Moore (1962) and Krystal (1962). Also from a psychotherapeutic point of view, Bolman (1965), in a careful review of the relevant literature, pointed out the need to distinguish between alcoholics whose improvement, seen in terms of desirable intrapsychic change, was contingent on abstinence, those in whom continued but controlled drinking was necessary for improvement to occur, and those for whom improvement was independent of either abstinence or controlled drinking.

The best known discussion of the abstinence requirement in treatment is that of CANTER (1968). The main emphasis of this discussion is on the absurdity of forbidding the manifestation of the specific 'symptom' of the alcoholic's 'disease' in the treatment environment. Alternatively, in learning-theory terms, the point is that a behaviour cannot be modified or extinguished which is not allowed to occur in the first place. Canter reports that, in his experience, astonishingly few alcoholics drink during their stay in hospital, despite having ample opportunities to do so. Yet, an equally astonishing number of treated alcoholics return to drinking within a brief period of discharge. Canter interviewed twenty-five patients, eleven men and fourteen women, who had spent from three to eight months in hospital and who had relapsed within forty-eight hours of leaving. The results indicated that almost 100 per cent denied any experience of craving for alcohol during the period of hospitalization and expressed the belief that they were cured of their alcoholism because they had not wanted or even thought about a drink during their stay as inpatients. As a result few had made any plans for dealing with subsequent craving after discharge since they could not believe that such craving would reappear. On readmission these patients tended to be puzzled by their failure, resentful, rationalizing, again full of vows and promises to do better next time, but dubious of the advantages of rehospitalization because they were sure that they had finally 'learned their lesson'. Canter concludes that this curious *volte face* can be explained by assuming that, on admission, the patient joins a particular kind of society, one of whose major values is not drinking, as contrasted to the society he has temporarily left where drinking is a definite value and where high status, approval and a sense of power are immediate rewards of drinking. Canter continues:

> The treatment problem in this situation became a very contradictory and difficult one. Literally, the patient was being 'treated' for a condition which did not exist in his experience in any meaningful way at the time. The often-observed resistance of alcoholic patients to psychological explanations of their difficulties and to psychotherapy of conventional kinds may be regarded as the normal response of a person who is being told he feels bad when in actuality he is aware of no such discomfort. To get the patient to plan for a contingency (a craving or impulse to drink at some future time) in the face of a present and complete disinterest in drinking which extends over the impressive and convincing period of time of his hospitalization is asking quite a bit of individuals who are notoriously considered to be motivated primarily by their feelings of the moment.

Canter concludes that drinking behaviour must be the central focus of concern in treatment, and it must be not only allowed but encouraged to appear in the treatment situation so that the associated emotions and motivations could be understood and new learning patterns developed. He thus advocates a treatment milieu which incorporates as much of the 'natural' drinking world of the alcoholic as possible and where techniques can be applied to provide different consequences to the drinking experience than would normally occur.

Contrary to the opinion of Moore (1962), it is possible to argue that the inculcation of slight to moderate levels of intoxication is a useful adjunct to the exploration of the patient's perceptions and feelings in the here and now and thus an important aid to the induction of psychotherapeutic change. Psychotherapy under these circumstances is less likely to encounter the obstacles of intellectualization, denial of reality and dissociation from the drinking event than when the patient is sober. Such at any rate, is the view of Feinstein and Tamerin (1972). We have seen in the preceding chapter that the use of alcohol in therapy has been systematically explored by Gottheil and his colleagues in Philadelphia with results certainly no worse, and perhaps better, than conventional abstinence regimes (see, e.g., Gottheil *et al.*, 1972). Narrol (1967) makes the point that by observing a patient respond adaptively to the presence of alcohol it may be possible to make a much more informed and accurate evaluation of his ability to face the outside world. Over and above the employment of alcohol in inpatient and/or psychotherapeutic programmes, however, the main potential advantage of continued drinking in treatment attaches to outpatient behaviour therapy. For example, to anticipate one of the conclusions from Chapter 6 of this book, regulated drinking practice, in which the patient's actual drinking behaviour is supervised and modified by the therapist, has been shown to be an effective ingredient of some controlled drinking treatment programmes. Finally, a study by Faillace, Flamer, Imber and Ward (1972) showed that giving alcohol to alcoholics in treatment does not have detrimental effects; indeed, patients given alcohol fared at least as well, if not better, than a control group who did not receive it.

OTHER POTENTIAL ADVANTAGES

There are two related arguments which must be included in any discussion of the possible advantages of a controlled drinking treatment goal, arguments which do not rely so much on empirical evidence as on commonsense reasoning. The first concerns the suggestion (e.g. Brunner-Orne, 1963; Reinert, 1968) that the reason many alcoholics continue to deny that drinking is a problem is because of their reluctance to face a life of permanent abstinence, which they have gathered is the only course open to them in treatment. Similarly, it is not unreasonable to suppose that the abstinence treatment goal deters many alcoholics from seeking treatment (Drewery, 1974). Certainly we know that AA have not been successful in attracting alcoholics earlier in the course of their drinking problems (Robinson, 1979) and, again, it is reasonable to conclude that the requirement of abstinence is responsible for this. While we know that alcoholism is not the irreversible and progressive condition it was once though to be, it is obvious that many problem-drinkers do deteriorate to chronic and self-destructive alcoholism. The commonsense suggestion, then, is that by including controlled drinking in the treatment possibilities available to problem-drinkers, many would be persuaded to attend for treatment earlier in the course of their problem, when their drinking behaviour was still more amenable to change, before rock-bottom had been reached, and before irreparable damage to health and family welfare had been done.

The related proposition is that if and when relatively less serious problem-drinkers *do* seek treatment they are likely to be confronted with a wholly unrealistic demand for total abstinence. As Sobell (1978a) points out, there is little participation in Alcoholics Anonymous by persons under the age of thirty (Leach and Norris, 1977), yet the highest incidence of drinking problems among males occurs in their late twenties (Cahalan and Room, 1974). And it is precisely among young males that abstinence is the most deviant and probably the most unsatisfying role. Moreover, Polich *et al.* (1980) showed that abstinence was much more likely to lead to relapse in young, single males. Unfortunately there are few easily identifiable and accessible treatment services in existence whose aims are attuned to the needs of drinkers with minimal problems and this is clearly a major deficiency in the effort to prevent more serious alcohol problems from developing. As the Sobells have repeatedly stressed in their writings (e.g. Sobell and Sobell, 1974; 1975; Sobell, 1978*a*; *b*), this constitutes a very good reason, among others, for *legitimizing* controlled drinking as a treatment goal for suitable alcohol abusers. Such legitimization would also help to protect the person with previous drinking problems who continues to drink in a controlled fashion from hostility and stigma derived from a rigid adherence to traditional conceptions of alcoholism.

THE RANGE OF NONABSTINENT TREATMENT GOALS

At various places in this book, we have referred to the need to distinguish true 'normal' or 'nonproblem' drinking following alcohol dependence from forms of drinking which may be an improvement over previous alcohol abuse but which nevertheless continue to attract adverse consequences. However, there is no reason why a consideration of the possible advantages of a controlled drinking treatment goal should be confined to normal drinking as such. In a series of papers, PATTISON (1976 *a; b; c*) has proposed a typology of nonabstinent treatment goals, as follows:

Attenuated drinking. This concept begins from the observations of Ludwig *et al.* (1970), Mayer and Myerson (1971), Gillis and Keet (1967) and many others that a continuation of problem-drinking after treatment may nevertheless entail significant improvements in overall life functioning. This in turn relates to Pattison's continued insistence that drinking outcome and psychosocial adjustment should be considered independently (see also Belasco, 1971). This accumulating evidence suggests that the goal of modification or attenuation of serious drinking problems be regarded as an acceptable treatment goal, if combined with improvement in other areas of adjustment. It is clearly not an ideal goal, but it may be sufficient to enable the alcoholic to recover some degree of successful life functioning. On the other hand, if we ignore these facts, says Pattison, and fail to see that degrees of improvement are realistic treatment goals, we may miss the opportunity to foster improvement and to make the alcoholic realize what limited gains he may have made.

Controlled drinking. This is defined by the establishment of control over the drinking situation, the frequency of drinking or the amount of alcohol consumed in a session. However, it does not imply that the meaning or functional use of alcohol has been changed or that basic conflicts and impulses have been resolved. The alcoholic has learned to control his drinking within limits that are not dysfunctional but improvements in other areas of adjustment do not necessarily follow suit.

Normal drinking. In contrast to controlled drinking, and also to abstinence in former alcoholics, the definition of normal drinking contains the rule that a change in the symbolic meaning of drinking has taken place. Pattison (1976a) states that most of the reports of normal drinking in alcoholics, which were reviewed in Chapter 2, do not contain enough information to allow a decision as to whether or not the meaning and functional use of alcohol has changed in these cases. In this sense very few alcoholics *return* to normal drinking since their drinking has always been to some extent pathological, even before they showed overt problems. Moreover, according to Pattison, much American social drinking is actually psychopathological since it is instrumental drinking, i.e. designed to achieve an effect. The majority of drinkers control what is essentially alcoholic drinking.

In our view, Pattison's distinction between normal and controlled drinking is of dubious value. We agree with Sobell (1978a) that many persons who have suffered no identifiable drinking problems are very conscious of their drinking, will have suffered occasional and relatively minor adverse consequences from it, and will therefore pay attention to the kinds of circumstances where adverse consequences are likely to occur. By Pattison's definition, many of these problem-free alcohol users would be 'controlled drinkers', but this should not be taken to mean that there is anything psychopathological about their use of alcohol. Alcohol is a drug which has both beneficial and harmful effects; anyone who uses it as an integral part of social existence puts himself or herself at risk of incurring the latter and, moreover, becomes aware of such risks and the conditions attaching to them as part of his learning history. The difficulty with Pattison's idealized conception of 'normal' drinking is that it may encourage the pursuit of an unobtainable and indeed, unnecessary perfection in nonabstinent treatment goals. In this book we have used the terms 'normal' and 'controlled' drinking somewhat arbitrarily to refer to drinking behaviour arrived at respectively with and without deliberate treatment intervention to that end. However, we concur with Pattison's opinion that the term 'social drinking' should be abandoned, since excessive and abusive drinking is just as likely to involve the company of others as not. While we appreciate the advantages of using neutral, purely descriptive terms like 'nonproblem' or 'harmfree' drinking, these terms also ignore the fact that the drinking of few people in our society is *entirely* free of adverse consequences.

The chief value of Pattison's typology for present purposes is the introduction of the concept of 'attenuated drinking'. The possibility that a limited but valuable degree of improvement may be a proper and worthwhile treatment objective has been obscured by an exclusive emphasis on abstinence. Attenuated drinking may well be the deliberate choice of treatment goal if there is reason to suspect that an individual will never seriously attempt abstinence and if his life-circumstances are such that a strict control over drinking will clearly be unattainable. As Pattison observes, part of the reason for the low correlation between drinking status and overall adjustment is that the low-bottom or skid-row alcoholic has such major dysfunctions as part of his total life-style that there is little potential for large improvements in adjustment even if sober. There is thus a strong case for giving precedence in treatment to modest gains in social, interpersonal, vocational and physical adjustment over radical changes in drinking behaviour.

It may be superfluous to mention that a great deal of discussion and debate in the literature has centred on the relative merits and demerits of abstinence and controlled drinking as treatment goals in alcoholism. Views in favour of retaining an exclusive emphasis on abstinence may be consulted in Davis (1976), Fox (1976), Nagy (1978), and Seixas (1978), while arguments in favour of including controlled drinking in the treatment objectives offered to alcoholics may be found in Evans (1973), Freed (1973), Sobell and Sobell (1974; 1975), Drewery (1974) and Pomerleau *et al.* (1976). An extension of the debate from alcohol abuse to substance abuse in general has been made by Carrol (1980).

CONCLUSIONS

In the light of the evidence and opinion in this chapter, the possible advantages of a controlled drinking treatment goal may be summarized as follows:

1. In contemporary industrialized society the adoption of total abstinence from alcohol is to occupy a deviant role which may attract problems of psychosocial adjustment. The degree of this deviance will depend on the abstinent individual's position on a number of sociological variables so that, at one extreme, the young, adult male who abstains will exhibit the highest degree of deviance and consequent problems in social living.

2. There is evidence that 'the abstinent alcoholic' may be subject to periodic episodes of fatigue and depression (Wellman, 1955; Flaherty *et al.*, 1955) and that enforced abstinence may have disastrous results for the personality organization of some individuals (Wallerstein, 1956). Many abstinent alcoholics have been shown to be either overtly disturbed, inconspicuously inadequate or dependent on Alcoholics Anonymous, while few

could be described as independent successes (Gerard *et al.*, 1962). The studies on which this evidence is based did not compare abstainers with normal drinking ex-alcoholics.

3. There is only a low correlation between the attainment of abstinence and overall improvement in life functioning (Thomas *et al.*, 1959; Wilby and Jones, 1962; Pattison, 1976*a*; *b*; *c*) and, at the same time, continued drinking after treatment has been shown to be associated with notable improvement in life functioning in some patients (Gillis and Keet, 1969; Mayer and Myerson, 1971; Pattison, 1976*a*; *b*; *c*).

4. There are grounds for speculating that the condition of abstinence *per se* introduces problems of a psychological or sociopsychological nature which make relapse more likely (Heather *et al.*, 1975; Marlatt, 1978; Richard and Burley, 1978).

5. Early evidence that abstainers were slightly superior on average to normal drinkers on measures of psychosocial adjustment following treatment (Gerard *et al.*, 1962; Gerard and Saenger, 1966) is subject to methodological criticisms. Later and more extensive evidence (Polich *et al.*, 1980) has failed to reveal any meaningful differences between the two outcomes.

6. It has been argued that the requirement of abstinence during treatment hampers attempts to change alcoholics' drinking behaviour (Canter, 1968). Giving alcohol to alcoholics may have certain advantages in treatment (Narrol, 1967; Feinstein and Tamerin, 1972) and has been shown not to have detrimental effects (Faillace *et al.*, 1972).

7. It is reasonable to suppose that many alcoholics will be deterred from entering treatment until their problem has reached serious stages by the abstinence requirement (Drewery, 1974) and that the introduction of controlled drinking treatments for some alcoholics might improve this situation. A related point is that very few identifiable and accessible treatment services exist for individuals with less serious drinking problems. The controlled drinking goal should be publicly legitimized as soon as possible (Sobell, 1978*a*).

8. Attenuated drinking may be a realistic and worthwhile treatment objective for alcoholics who there are grounds for assuming will never be abstinent or able to control their drinking within strict limits. Treatment services for socially deteriorated alcoholics might give precedence to an improvement in total life-functioning over an exclusive emphasis on radical changes in drinking behaviour (Pattison, 1976*a*; *b*; *c*).

5 Controlled drinking treatments: origins and methods

Kurume University, Japan, was the site of the first recorded treatment for alcoholism aimed at moderation rather than abstinence. During the late 1950s and early 1960s, a group of medical researchers (e.g. Mukasa and Arikawa, 1968; Mukasa *et al.*, 1964), faced with the very low rate of abstinence among treated alcoholics, developed a treatment using the drug cyanamide, known in this country as Abstem. This is a drug similar to Antabuse, in that it produces unpleasant allergic reactions when taken with alcohol.

Although it is difficult to understand from these badly translated papers exactly what procedures were carried out, it appears that daily doses of this drug were administered at individually determined levels sufficiently low that adverse reactions did not occur until a certain quantity of alcohol – usually the equivalent of just over one pint of beer – had been consumed. The extraordinarily high success rates reported by these authors are explained partly by the use in the majority of cases of their so-called 'Special Method', whereby cyanamide was secretly administered by the patient's family to the patient through his food!

Lazarus (1965) was another therapist who found it necessary to eschew the goal of abstinence. Some six months after the beginning of an abstinence-oriented behavioural programme, one of his patients admitted that he had drunk two brandies on one occasion, without feeling any craving or experiencing loss of control. Instead of urging the man to resist such temptation, the therapist encouraged this moderate drinking. He used hypnosis to instil the suggestion that the man would experience violent nausea and abdominal cramps if he drank more than two measures of spirits or two glasses of wine or beer. Fourteen months later this man was still a successful social drinker.

In both of these studies it was the unavoidable reality of alcoholics drinking moderately despite abstinence-oriented treatment which prompted the new approach. It is against the background of this pioneering work that the development of controlled drinking treatment over the last two decades will be described, and as this development has been based largely on psychological theories and techniques, these must first be outlined.

Before we go on to describe psychological models of alcoholism upon which controlled drinking treatments are based, let it be made clear that we do not believe that they provide an adequate explanation for all the phenomena coming under the rubric of 'alcoholism'. One cannot deny the fact of alcohol-related brain damage, for instance (e.g. Lishman, Ron and Acker, 1979), though exactly how this relates to alcoholic behaviour is a complex issue which we will discuss in detail later (pp. 226–30). There may even be as yet undiscovered biochemical processes which are implicated in craving and loss of control. But what we do assert is that psychological theory leads logically to a variety of treatments whereas an explanation based upon an unspecified disease process has no such implications, except that the alcoholic should never touch alcohol. Such an explanation does not provide any satisfactory theoretical framework on which to base treatment for maintaining abstinence – hence the recourse of many medical facilities to the methods of Alcoholics Anonymous, and to a form of common-sense cajoling and persuasion which has been observed to occur in medically-oriented treatment settings (see Davies, P. 1979).

PSYCHOLOGICAL PRINCIPLES

There are a variety of psychological theories which have been applied to alcoholism and some of these have yet to be integrated into a coherent system. No unified theory exists, and different psychological processes are applicable to different facets of alcoholic behaviour. Classical conditioning theory, for instance, is useful for explaining craving, while cognitive theory provides useful and interesting accounts of relapse (Marlatt, 1978). Our intention in this chapter is to illustrate briefly some of these theoretical models and to describe some of the treatments derived from them. However, psychological processes can be placed on a continuum which ranges from simple 'low-level' phenomena such as classical conditioning at one extreme to highly complex cognitive processes at the other. The thread running through all of these is *learning*, that is, the principle that behaviour, thought and experience are learned through the interaction of the person with his environment. Learning includes the acquisition of simple repetitive motor responses as well as of complex and abstract concepts and it is likely that most kinds of learning are involved in alcoholic behaviour. In Table 5.1 below, a number of psychological processes are listed in order of some approximate measure of complexity, beginning with the least complex. Alongside each is an example of possible applications of the phenomenon in the interpretation of alcoholic behaviour, together with some interventions which follow from this conceptualization.

CLASSICAL CONDITIONING

The paradigm of classical conditioning refers to the way in which previously neutral stimuli can come to evoke responses which are normally only produced by 'unconditioned' stimuli. For instance, Watson and Raynor (1920) showed how a boy became frightened of a white rat after a loud noise had been made on several occasions when he was exposed to the animal. In this case the loud noise was the unconditioned stimulus, the white rat was the conditioned stimulus, and the response was fear. The phenomenon of *generalization* refers to the way in which stimuli similar to the conditioned stimulus can come to evoke the conditioned response even though they have never been paired with the unconditioned stimulus; in the above example of 'little Albert', the way in which the child came to show fear of a white rat is an example of this process.

TABLE 5.1
Some examples of the applications of psychological processes to alcoholic behaviour

Psychological process	Examples of its application to alcoholic behaviour	Examples of psychological treatments following from this analysis
Classical conditioning	Craving elicited by stimuli previously associated with drinking.	Electrical aversion, Chemical aversion, Cue exposure
Operant conditioning	(*i*) Reduction of withdrawal symptoms by further drinking ('Relief drinking'). (*ii*) Warmth, companionship and pleasant surroundings present while drinking alcohol but absent when not drinking. (*iii*) Stomach pain following alcohol ingestion resulting in a reduction in drinking.	Contingency management, Avoidance conditioning
Skilled behaviour	(*i*) Inability to drink slowly. (*ii*) Inability to refuse drinks. (*iii*) Inability to occupy leisure time enjoyably other than by drinking.	Regulated drinking practice, BAC discrimination training, Social skills training
Self-control	(*i*) Absence of accurate self-monitoring of alcohol intake. (*ii*) Failure to recognize situations where heavy drinking is likely. (*iii*) Absence of a set of 'working rules' governing drinking behaviour.	Self-management training, including: Self-monitoring; Stimulus control; Rule setting; Self-reward; Self-punishment.

TABLE 5.1 *continued*

Psychological process	Examples of its application to alcoholic behaviour	Examples of psychological treatments following from this analysis
	(*iv*) Absence of system of 'self-rewards' for non-drinking and moderate drinking.	
Cognitive learning	(*i*) Disorganized and unconstructive cognitive responses to stress in the form of such self-statements as 'I give up' or 'My life is a mess'. (*ii*) Expectation of loss of control following small intake of alcohol. (*iii*) Attribution of a slip following a decision to abstain to personal weakness. (*iv*) Belief that a large intake of alcohol produces beneficial personality changes.	Problem solving skills training, Self-instructional training, Rational-emotive therapy, Cognitive therapy, Anxiety-management training

The phenomenon of 'craving', to take one aspect of alcoholism, has been explained using this paradigm (e.g. Ludwig, Wikler and Stark, 1974). Craving usually refers to the strong desire for alcohol felt by an alcoholic which he often finds difficult to resist (see Chapter 3). Along with this subjective experience, certain physiological changes (e.g. increased pulse, sweating) and certain behaviours such as gulping down drinks may appear (see 'Operant Conditioning' below). Theorists have suggested that craving can be triggered in alcoholics by a drop in the blood alcohol concentration (BAC) below a certain level (e.g. Jellinek, 1960). As this topic is too large for detailed consideration here, we will give one illustrative example.

It is probable that most drinkers experience some discomfort when their BAC-level begins to fall some time after a drinking session has ended. For most normal drinkers this happens while they are asleep since most drinking takes place in the evening. For those who have drunk earlier in the day, the reduction in the pleasant effects of alcohol as the BAC levels wane can lead to a desire to drink more in order to restore a pleasant intoxicated state, and this desire in some cases may be interpreted as craving by the individual. Let us take the hypothetical case of a commuting office worker who sometimes drinks quite a lot of alcohol after work, before arriving home at about 9 p.m. Let us assume that the timing of his drinking and his metabolism are such that his BAC level also usually begins to wane at about 9 p.m. It may be that he then goes to his local pub to alleviate these feelings. What might happen is that by classical conditioning, through association with the drop in BAC, the event of returning home may come to elicit similar sensations to those produced by a drop in BAC, even when no alcohol has been consumed. This is illustrated schematically in Figure 5.1 below.

Stage 1　　　　　　UNCONDITIONED STIMULUS ⟶ RESPONSE
　　　　　　　　　　　　(Waning BAC)　　　　　　　　　　(Discomfort,
　　　　　　　　　　　　　　　　　　　　　　　　　　　　irritability
　　　　　　　　　　　　　　　　　　　　　　　　　　　　craving)

Stage 2　　　　There is a 'pairing' on several occasions of an
　　　　　　　UNCONDITIONED STIMULUS with a　NEUTRAL
　　　　　　　　　　　　　　　　　　　　　　　　　　STIMULUS
　　　　　　　　　　　　(Waning BAC)　　　　　　　　　(Returning
　　　　　　　　　　　　　　　　　　　　　　　　　　home)

Stage 3　　　The neutral stimulus then becomes a conditioned stimulus:
　　　　　　　　CONDITIONED STIMULUS ⟶ RESPONSE
　　　　　　　　　　(Returning home)　　　　　　　　(Discomfort,
　　　　　　　　　　　　　　　　　　　　　　　　　irritability
　　　　　　　　　　　　　　　　　　　　　　　　　craving)

FIGURE 5.1
A hypothetical example of the development of conditioned craving

This is just one example of how craving can become conditioned to hitherto neutral events or stimuli. It is possible for craving to become classically conditioned to many other stimuli including the sight and smell of alcohol, the presence of particular people or even certain mood states. As drinking may be more likely when craving is experienced (see 'Operant Conditioning' below) the more stimuli there are to which craving is conditioned, the more frequent drinking is likely to be. Ludwig, Wikler and Stark (1974) have discussed this in more detail than is possible here.

A number of treatments follow from this model, all aimed at extinguishing the craving response to the conditioned stimuli which elicit it. *Electrical aversion therapy* aims, by pairing the sight, smell and taste of alcohol with electric shock, to substitute responses such as anxiety and fear for the response of wanting to drink. While this may hold up theoretically, in practice the technique has not been found to be effective, as several studies and reviews have shown (e.g. Davidson, 1974; Caddy and Lovibond, 1976; Hedberg and Campbell, 1974; Elkins, 1975). Slightly more evidence exists for the effectiveness of *chemical aversion therapy,* at least among clients of high social class (e.g. Wiens, Montague, Manaugh and English, 1976). Why this should be so is unclear, though it does seem likely that the effects of the chemical agents are more traumatic and unpleasant than those of the electric shocks and produce taste aversions relatively easily.

Cue exposure is based partially on the mechanism of *extinction* which refers to the waning of a response to a conditioned stimulus as the latter is repeatedly presented on its own without the unconditioned stimulus. For instance, to take the first example in this section, if the office worker were to return home many times not having drunk anything, the response of craving should theoretically cease to be elicited by this event.

Cue exposure has not yet been widely used and has not been used in any controlled drinking trials. The cues to which a patient should be exposed will depend upon an analysis of which stimuli appear to elicit drinking or craving responses; these may range from external cues such as the presence of a particular person to internal cues such as alcohol withdrawal symptoms. Rankin and Hodgson (1977) described an individual case study where an alcoholic was given four vodkas which, after a few hours, resulted in his showing minimal withdrawal symptoms. He was given this amount each day for six days and each time the therapist ensured that the man did not drink any more alcohol. Over this period the patient's desire for a drink fell from a very high level to a very low level and this could be explained in terms of extinction. However, cue exposure may also operate through such mechanisms as attitude change; it is possible for instance that the alcoholic who successfully resists the temptation to drink in the presence of alcohol may have his sense of personal competence enhanced; he may also be forced to engage in coping mechanisms which will be of use to him in future high-risk situations.

In *covert sensitization treatment* verbally guided imagery of alcohol and drinking scenes is associated with imagined unpleasant feelings such as nausea and vomiting. The rationale for this treatment is similar to that of chemical aversion therapy, the goal being to develop a conditioned aversion to alcohol. How effective this is remains to be seen, as the findings of controlled studies have so far been equivocal (e.g. Hedberg and Cambell, 1974; Maletzky, 1974; Piorkowsky and Mann, 1975).

OPERANT CONDITIONING

The words *reinforcement* and *reward* are central to operant conditioning theory and their meanings overlap considerably. A positive reinforcer is some event, privilege or object which increases the probability of occurrence of the behaviour which it follows and upon which it is *contingent*. What is reinforcing for one person may not be reinforcing for another: hence one must not assume that events generally held to be pleasurable are indeed reinforcing for a particular individual – this must be determined empirically. Negative reinforcers are any events whose contingent withdrawal increases the probability of the preceding responses. Usually these are considered to be unpleasant events, though again this must be empirically verified.

In simple terms, the central tenet of operant conditioning theory is that behaviour is influenced by the events which follow it. This notion of contingency is useful when trying to understand alcohol problems. One of the most common features of alcoholism is relief drinking, where alcohol is taken to reduce the withdrawal symptoms arising from the previous drinking session. In this case, one of the consequences of drinking is a reduction or elimination of an unpleasant state; the act of drinking is thus reinforced and becomes more likely. The act of drinking under normal circumstances is also strongly reinforced due to the tranquillizing properties of alcohol. Feelings of relaxation and anxiety-reduction are pleasant for most people and, as they are often induced by drinking, drinking is reinforced and becomes more likely. This may be one of the main reasons why drinking is as ubiquitous and difficult to control as it is.

The notion that behaviour is controlled by its consequences appears to lose credibility, however, when one considers one of the most striking features of alcoholic behaviour, namely its apparently self-destructive course: jobs are lost, wives and husbands leave home, faces are cut, limbs are broken and hangovers regularly plague the drinker. These observations apparently fly in the face of the principles of learning just described; if behaviour is governed by its consequences, should not such problem-drinking cease? The answer to this lies in a central principle of conditioning; it is the consequence which follows the response most closely which will have the strongest effect on that response. For example, if a short-term effect of drinking is relaxation and reduction of anxiety, and a relatively long-term effect is marital friction, it is the former which is probably going to have the strongest influence on drinking, because of its immediacy. Similarly, if a short-term consequence of drunkenness is the approval of friends, say in the case of a young offender, but the long-term effects are fines and sentences from the court, it is again the former which is more likely to influence the response.

This model is of course an over-simplification. For example, there is still a good deal of controversy over the issue of whether alcohol does actually reduce tension and anxiety among alcoholics. In fact, some studies have reported that self-reported anxiety and tension actually *increase* during drinking among chronic alcoholics (e.g. McNamee *et al.*, 1968). Hodgson, Stockwell and Rankin (1979) suggest that although drinking coincides with unpleasant feelings, stopping drinking might result in anxiety, so that the *relative* effect of drinking is favourable compared with that of ceasing to drink. However, it is outside the scope of this chapter to review these issues in detail and several excellent papers have dealt with them already (Hodgson, Stockwell and Rankin, 1979; Cappell and Herman, 1972). What emerges from the operant conditioning model is the relatively unfamiliar notion that an alcoholic's drinking may be at least partly under the control of circumstances in his immediate environment. This runs contrary to the long tradition of seeking causes for alcoholism, whether biochemical or psychological, 'inside' the alcoholic.

This model has many implications for treatment, all of which include in some form the systematic design of the alcoholic's environment, or *contingency management* as it is often known. In some cases this has consisted simply of praising the alcoholic for drinking in a controlled way in a laboratory setting (e.g. Czypionka and Demel, 1976). Less naively, others have tried to engineer almost the entire natural environment of the alcoholic (Hunt and Azrin, 1973). *Avoidance conditioning* is an example of laboratory intervention which is based on the principle that if an unpleasant event such as an electric shock can be avoided by behaving in a certain way, then this avoidance behaviour becomes strengthened. In this vein, many controlled drinking studies have created laboratory programmes where the subject can avoid electric shocks by following certain rules.

An example of the use of avoidance conditioning is given by Sobell and Sobell (1973) in which patients drank at a bar situated in the hospital. Staff acted as bar personnel and patients had electrodes attached to one hand. Those on a controlled regime received one-second shocks on half the occasions when they did one of the following things:

– ordered a straight drink (other than beer or wine);
– took a sip larger than one-sixth (spirits) or one-twelfth (beer) of the drink's total volume;
– ordered a drink within twenty minutes of last ordering a drink;
– ordered any more than three drinks in all.

Patients on a non-drinking programme received a one-second shock for ordering any drink, then continuous shock from the time they touched the drink to the time they released it. As in the controlled drinker's case, they were shocked on only half of those occasions. There is however some doubt about exactly how such procedures affect drinking behaviour. Sobell and Sobell (1973) themselves pointed out how few of their subjects were ever actually shocked during the avoidance conditioning trials. In fact, most very quickly learned the rules which they were expected to obey and acted accordingly. One implication of this is that simple verbal instructions may be as effective in changing drinking behaviour as a complex 'conditioning' programme.

Several other researchers have tried to engineer alcoholics' environments such that pleasant consequences consistently follow either abstinent periods or periods of reduced drinking. For example, the studies which were carried out by Cohen and her colleagues in Baltimore (e.g. Cohen, Liebson, Faillace and Speers, 1971), and which were described in detail in Chapter 3, showed clearly how the drinking of alcoholics is responsive to environmental contingencies. Both moderate drinking and abstinence could be achieved by most of the alcoholics studied, given sufficient reinforcement.

An obvious comment on such inpatient operant studies is that, while behaviour may be changed in a closed environment, maintaining that change in the uncontrollable environment of the real world may not be possible; this is the perennial problem of generalization. However, subsequent research has shown that it is possible to alter the contingencies operating in the natural environment of the alcoholic such that his drinking is considerably curtailed (e.g. Miller, Hersen, Eisler and Watts, 1974; Hunt and Azrin, 1973).

The research discussed above has considered mainly chronic alcoholics in institutions, or under circumstances where the therapists had the resources to engineer their environment to a considerable extent. This is partly because behavioural principles can best be demonstrated where the researchers have control over the reinforcers in a person's life. However, these studies also illustrate a fundamental fact which will clarify our understanding of the more complicated outpatient studies, i.e.: *to make a person stop, or cut down his drinking, you must make it worth his while.* In other words, you must ensure that his life is more satisfying while not abusing alcohol than it is while he is abusing it. For people with few satisfactions in sober life, considerable time and money is required to create such satisfactions for them. This apparently obvious fact is not reflected in traditional approaches to alcohol abuse. Too often drinking is rewarded by admission to a warm and comfortable hospital while sobriety can lead to the alcoholic being ignored by treatment services and left to a lonely and unfulfilling life.

While contingency management is easier to implement when the therapist has control over substantial reinforcements in the alcoholic's life, it is quite possible to use the method on a routine outpatient basis with minimal resources. In particular, marital relationships can be adjusted such that nondrinking or controlled drinking are consistently rewarded and abusive drinking non-rewarded. As marriage itself and the quality of marriage are extremely important determinants of outcome in alcoholism (e.g. Armor *et al.,* 1978; Orford and Edwards, 1977), interventions which successfully modify marital relationships may well be effective when applied to alcohol problems. *Behavioural contracting* is one way of attempting to 'engineer' the natural environment of the alcoholic, and this has been used with the spouses of alcoholic clients (e.g. Hedberg and Cambell, 1974) as well as with friends and employers (e.g. Hunt and Azrin, 1973).

SKILLED BEHAVIOUR

Trying to change behaviour by systematically altering a person's environment assumes that he has the skills to carry out the new behaviour. For instance, simply trying to make a chronic alcoholic stop drinking completely is unlikely to be successful if he has no skills for occupying his time in other ways than drinking. If he cannot read, not only is leisure through reading impossible, but applying for jobs will be extremely difficult. Other skills, such as making conversation, refusing drinks effectively or applying for a job, for example, may also be absent and hence contribute to alcohol problems. The notion that some aspects of alcoholism are attributable to skill deficiencies and that the appropriate intervention for these should be didactic in style runs counter to most traditional medically-based conceptions of 'treatment'.

Argyle (1967) was one of the first to apply a skills model to interpersonal behaviour in general and by analysing the components of such behaviour, like posture, eye-contact and voice quality, he laid a basis for identifying individual behavioural deficiencies for which remedial training programmes could be designed. Therapeutic applications of this model in the field of alcoholism have ranged from teaching clients to drink slowly to training them in how to assert themselves. Common to these diverse procedures is a training or teaching philosophy in which the target skills are broken down into a number of component tasks and clients are given corrective feedback about their performance on these intermediate tasks.

Regulated drinking practice is commonly used in controlled drinking programmes. It is frequently integrated with avoidance conditioning procedures such as that used by Sobell and Sobell (1973) but, as we discussed earlier, there is evidence that the training and instruction elements of the procedure are more important than any conditioning factors (p. 157 above). These methods have been based largely on the findings of two studies which found differences in drinking behaviour between alcoholics and normal drinkers (Sobell, Schaeffer and Mills, 1972; Williams and Brown, 1974). Both found that alcoholics tended to drink faster, take larger sips and order unmixed rather than mixed drinks. Several programmes have thus attempted to change these behaviours (e.g. Sobell and Sobell, 1973; Vogler, Weissbach and Compton, 1977*a*). In outpatient settings where regulated practice may not be possible, simple instructions may suffice for non-serious problem drinkers.

While, as will be shown later, there is some evidence that some form of regulated drinking practice may be an effective component of treatment, over-emphasis on the minutiae of drinking must be avoided. This is especially so in the light of one finding that, in Scotland at least, alcoholics do not drink their beer or whisky any differently from nonalcoholics, when observed in a natural setting (Saunders and Richard, 1978). This highlights both the dangers of generalizing from a laboratory setting to real life, and from one culture to another.

BAC discrimination training is another method closely identified with controlled drinking treatments. It was founded on the assumption that alcoholics could be helped to drink less if they could be trained to recognize their
blood-alcohol concentration on the basis of internal sensations. Typically,
alcohol was given, the BAC measured, and the subject asked to notice the
bodily sensations which occurred at different BAC levels. Eventually, it was
hoped, the subject would be able to accurately assess his BAC purely on the
basis of internal sensations, without any feedback from a breathalyser. In
several studies, (e.g. Lovibond and Caddy, 1970) avoidance conditioning
was combined with BAC discrimination training, such that shocks were
given when the BACs exceeded a certain level. While these methods seemed
initially promising, it transpired in subsequent experiments that the use of
internal cues to estimate BAC was, at best, no better than the use of more
simple external ones such as the amount drunk (e.g. Huber *et al.*, 1976) and,
at worst, actually *less* effective, especially with chronic alcoholics (e.g.
Lansky *et al.*, 1978). We do not intend to review this work thoroughly as this
has been done by several other authors (e.g. Nathan, 1978; Miller and
Hester, 1980). The evidence from these reviews, and others, is that not only
is internally-based BAC training likely to be less effective with alcoholics,
but that it is unnecessarily costly and complicated.

A more simple form of BAC training based on *external* cues would appear
to be equally effective. Advertisements warning against drinking and driving
often include elementary BAC training when they provide tables plotting
BACs against number of drinks. More sophisticated procedures include
body-weight and the length of the drinking session in the calculations as
these are known to affect BACs; clients are supplied with tables (e.g. Miller
and Munoz, 1976) or simple calculators (e.g. Compton and Vogler, 1974) to
enable them to predict their BACs.

Social skills training and *assertive training* are based on a skills model of
interpersonal behaviour and their application to alcoholism is based on the
assumption that interpersonal difficulties exacerbate drinking problems.
One interpersonal problem commonly associated with alcoholism is lack of
assertion. For example, Eisler *et al.* (1975) found that the less assertively an
alcoholic behaved, the more alcohol he consumed in a laboratory drinking
experiment. Thus assertive training programmes have tried to teach
alcoholics to be able to express appropriate feelings, both positive and
negative, towards others in their presence.

Social skills training may be appropriate for only a small number of
alcoholics and problem-drinkers. Whether or not this treatment is applied
must depend on a comprehensive analysis of which problems are contributing to drinking. If the person does not seem to have difficulties in
the mechanics of social intercourse, then this training would obviously be
inappropriate. However, there is scope for social skills training specifically

for refusing drinks (e.g. Foy, Miller, Eisler and O'Toole, 1976), coping with round-buying (e.g. Robertson, Manknell and Heather, 1980) and other directly drink-related social behaviours, for most alcoholics.

In so far as some alcoholics and problem-drinkers consume alcohol in order to relieve tension (see p. 156), teaching alternative ways of relieving this tension may be useful. *Relaxation training* is a procedure in which an individual learns to gain conscious control over the level of tension in various muscle-groups in his body. As craving may include an element of tension (Litman, 1974), relaxation training may be useful for those alcoholics who experience craving in this way.

Many treatment regimes also include some form of *alternatives training,* where clients are trained in skills with which to occupy the time they previously spent drinking. This can range from simple counselling about sports and hobbies, to teaching them how to apply for jobs. There is considerable overlap here with social skills training, and clearly the two go hand-in-hand.

SELF-CONTROL PRINCIPLES

This loosely-bound set of principles straddles the boundary between behaviourist and cognitive theories and it is arguable whether they have any independent theoretical status. Their application is so widespread in controlled drinking programmes, however, that they merit separate consideration.

Operant and classical conditioning theories are based on the assumption that the forces shaping a person's life lie primarily in the external environment. In the last decade, the view that man shapes his environment as much as the environment shapes him has become increasingly accepted, and behavioural principles have been adapted to this view (e.g. Bandura, 1977; Thoresen and Mahoney, 1974). Simply stated, a major premise of self-control theories is that an individual can organize his environment to make certain behaviours more likely. Thus, for instance, he can reward himself for doing something which is not intrinsically rewarding, he can arrange for tempting stimuli to be made inaccessible, or he can even punish himself for transgressing predetermined rules (see Thoresen and Mahoney, 1974).

A broad term for a variety of self-control strategies is *self-management training* and the basic process in any such procedure is *self-monitoring*. In order to be able to change a particular habit an individual must first become aware of it. As memory is fallible, self-monitoring usually requires that highly detailed records be kept by the client. In the case of drinking behaviour, the alcoholic may be required to note down how many sips he takes from each drink (e.g. Miller and Munoz, 1976), though more commonly he will be required to log each day exactly what he has drunk. It is often the case that individuals do not realize how much they are drinking until they keep such records. Sanchez-Craig (1980) has found that drinking levels elicited in this way correspond far more accurately to liver-enzyme measures of consumption than does information elicited through normal interviewing procedures. Such self-monitoring usually reveals some pattern in the individual's drinking. Particular times, places or persons may be found to be associated with heavy drinking and others with moderate drinking. Determining the antecedents of particular forms of drinking in this way is a form of *functional analysis.*

Stimulus control procedures follow logically from a functional analysis. The client is helped to organize his environment such that he avoids those circumstances, or stimuli, which have tended in the past to be associated with heavy drinking and is helped to confine his drinking to those circumstances which in the past have been associated with moderate drinking. In some cases the presence of a spouse constitutes a 'safe' stimulus, while in others complex combinations of mood-states and environmental events may be a prerequisite for safe drinking. Common examples of 'danger' stimuli are the presence of certain companions, particular drinking settings and stressful events such as marital arguments. Stimulus control techniques have been used most extensively in the treatment of obesity. Stunkard (1972), for example, described how obese clients can be counselled to restrict eating to very limited situations and times (e.g. at a particular table in the kitchen) so as to reduce the number of cues associated with eating. Richards (1975), among many others, has used similar techniques to help the development of study skills by, for instance, arranging that studying is restricted to particular times and places.

As can be seen in these examples of the application of stimulus-control procedures, it is often necessary not only to avoid drinking in the presence of certain stimuli, but also to specify and plan courses of action when such stimuli are inadvertently encountered. For instance, it is seldom possible for a person to completely avoid periods of mild depression. If this is a cue for heavy drinking for a given individual, he must be helped to develop a strategy for coping with these feelings other than by drinking. While some form of more sophisticated intervention may be necessary, often the formulation of specific behavioural plans will suffice. Such *rule setting* is an important part of controlled drinking treatments, and such rules can be incorporated into behavioural contracts. In any case, it is desirable to have them written down for or by the client to make it more likely that he remembers them.

Bandura (1977) has proposed that two principal cognitive processes mediate intentional control of behaviour. These are the ability to represent future consequences in thought and the setting of goals against which one evaluates one's own performance. Bandura argues that intermediate, short-term sub-goals, when explicitly defined, can strongly mobilize effort and effectively direct action. Bandura and Simon (1977) have shown that in the treatment of overeating, asking clients to reduce their weekly intake of food by 10 per cent was far less effective than asking them to reduce by 10 per cent their intake during each of four periods per day. As Hodgson (1980) has pointed out, this is an experimental test of the AA principle 'one day at a time', except that the day is further subdivided. Similarly detailed planning of behaviour from day to day and even from hour to hour in the treatment of drinking problems can be a useful component in self-management pro-grammes which can easily be incorporated into behavioural contracts (e.g. Miller, 1972).

More general rules are also useful. Miller and Munoz (1976) recommend the negotiation of two 'drinking limits' with clients, one the maximum to be drunk on any one occasion and the other the maximum average daily or weekly consumption. In some cases the type of drink may also be specified, where it appears from the functional analysis that certain types of drink are associated with heavy drinking. Rules such as 'I shall never drink at home' may also be set, again depending upon the functional analysis. Sobell and Sobell (1973) gave each patient a Do's and Don'ts card upon which such individualized rules were written, and clients were instructed to keep the card with them at all times.

Self-reward and *self-punishment* are two other types of self-control procedures in which the client applies operant conditioning principles to his own behaviour. Frederiksen and Miller (1976), among others, have applied self-reinforcement principles to alcoholics, while Wilson, Leaf and Nathan (1975) have used self-punishment techniques in which alcoholics gave themselves electric shocks following the consumption of alcohol.

COGNITIVE LEARNING THEORIES

For a large part of this century, psychologists investigating learning pro-cesses tended to concentrate on how animals learned new behaviour; thus the classical conditioning theories of Pavlov (1927) and the operant con-ditioning theories of Skinner (1953) were based mainly on the behaviour of infra-humans. While both of these theories are extremely useful for explaining some aspects of human behaviour, they omit the hugely import-ant areas of thought and language and how these mediate learning. In recent years a number of loose theoretical models of cognitive learning have been developed which have examined the relationship between cognitive learning and problematic behaviours, emotions and thoughts.

The importance of cognitive learning to alcohol problems is apparent in many areas. Several studies have shown that many of the effects of alcohol on behaviour can be determined by the *expectations* of what these effects should be, independent of any pharmacological effects (see Chapter 3). Pliner and Cappell (1974), for instance, showed that the physiological effects of alcohol on individuals were interpreted differently depending upon whether the person was drinking alone or in a group. Solitary drinkers interpreted the pharmacological state more in terms of physical symptoms, while group drinkers interpreted a similar state in terms of changes in mood. Sexual behaviour in relation to alcohol consumption was examined by Briddell *et al*. (1979), who showed that normal males demonstrated an increased sexual response to deviant, sadistic sexual stimuli when they *believed* that they had drunk alcohol, irrespective of whether they had actually drunk it or not. As was mentioned in Chapter 3, McAndrew and Edgerton (1970) have argued convincingly on the basis of anthropological evidence that cultural norms and expectations are far more important determinants of drunken behaviour than are any pharmacological effects and have shown that far from being a general disinhibitor, alcohol in some societies can lead to more inhibited, taciturn behaviour.

Cognitive learning theories and the derived therapies are obviously of central importance to alcohol problems. Mahoney and Arnkoff (1978) have identified at least ten distinct cognitive therapeutic models but it is outside the scope of this chapter to deal with them in detail. As an example of one such therapy, *problem-solving skills training* (D'Zurilla and Goldfried, 1971), stands out in that it was one of the constituents of a remarkably successful controlled drinking treatment trial (Sobell and Sobell, 1976). This is a procedure with similarities to those used in some other controlled drinking programmes, such as the self-regulation training used by Caddy and Lovibond (1976).

The first element of this training is the development by the individual of an *orientation* or *set* to formulate his troubles as a set of potentially solvable problems rather than as a hopeless mess. This is done by training clients to recognize problems as such when they arise, to suppress the tendency to act impulsively and to accept problems as an inescapable fact of life. *Problem definition* is the second stage of the procedure, and the central element is *specificity;* the client must be precise and specific about the various problems which he faces. 'My life is a mess' is unacceptable; 'I have difficulty in getting to know people socially' is more acceptable. Thirdly comes the stage of *generation of alternative courses of action*. In the face of an awesome list of apparently intractable problems, this can be the most difficult stage. Solutions to unemployment, loneliness and hardship, for instance, are not easy to find, but 'brainstorming' may be of some help. 'Brainstorming' is where two or more people suggest solutions to a particular problem, with the rules that quantity is preferable to quality, criticism of the ideas suggested is suspended and ideas can be colourful, ridiculous and irrelevant. Indeed such 'free wheeling' is encouraged and the various ideas are combined, improved and elaborated upon. Following the elimination of the more impractical solutions, a number of possible alternatives may emerge. Some form of *decision-making* is then required. While one alternative may clearly emerge as the optimal course of action, sometimes difficult decisions must be made. For instance, the decision by an alcoholic whether or not to leave a job where there is pressure to drink would be in most cases a difficult one. In this case, formal methods do exist for making decisions in a systematic fashion (e.g. Mai, 1975) though these will not be discussed here. The stage of *verification* is the final one in problem-solving skills training. This requires the client to anticipate, rehearse and try out the action required to implement a decision. Often some social skills training is included, where for instance a person rehearses how he will tell his companions that he no longer wants to drink with them. In other cases the verification stage may simply involve the detailed anticipation and planning of events in the person's life, followed by a de-briefing after these schedules are implemented.

Many other forms of cognitive therapy are of great potential relevance to alcohol problems. Meichenbaum's (1977) *self-instructional training* is a technique by which clients are trained to rehearse internal monologues by which to regulate their behaviour. Such use of self-talk may well be useful with alcoholics to help them regulate their drinking and cope with craving. Indeed, it has been shown that recovered alcoholics already use such strategies as mentally rehearsing past distress caused by drinking and recalling the benefits of abstinence (Litman, Eiser, Rawson and Oppenheim, 1977).

Beck's (1976) *cognitive therapy* and Ellis's (1962) *rational-emotive therapy* both attempt in slightly different ways to detect maladaptive thought patterns, help the client recognize their harmful impact, and to replace them with more adaptive patterns of thought. Both use didactic procedures to induce more logical and helpful ways of thinking in the client and there are many similarities to the methods by which problem-solving skills training is carried out. The application of such procedures to counteract the hypothetical abstinence-violation effect described by Marlatt (1978) is obvious.

Videotape self-confrontation of drunken behaviour is a technique commonly used in controlled drinking treatment studies. It appears however to have little coherent theoretical rationale and we include it in this section on the assumption that it attempts to alter the attitudes of the alcoholic towards his drinking. Among the rationales given for this treatment are: (*i*) it is stress-inducing for sober alcoholics and seemed to increase their professed motivation to change their drinking behaviour (Schaeffer *et al.*, 1971); (*ii*) it serves to demonstrate various problems (e.g. aggressive behaviour) to the client (Sobell and Sobell, 1973); (*iii*) the therapist can gain useful personal information from the client while he is drunk (Baker *et al.*, 1975); (*iv*) drinking behaviour can be studied in detail so that appropriate intervention can be designed (Baker *et al.*, 1975).

No evidence exists that this treatment is in itself effective (Baker *et al.*, 1975; Bailey and Sowder, 1970) and there is even evidence to suggest that it can be harmful (Schaeffer, Sobell and Mills, 1971; Paredes *et al.*, 1969). Although it has been included in successful controlled drinking programmes (Vogler *et al.*, 1975; Sobell and Sobell, 1976), the studies we have just mentioned stongly suggest that it was not an effective component of these treatment packages, though there is a possibility that it is useful in inter-action with particular treatment methods.

CONTROLLED DRINKING BY OTHER METHODS

Behavioural or cognitive treatments are not the only methods by which alcoholics can come to control their drinking, and controlled drinking as a goal must be separated conceptually from the treatment methods which have predominantly been used to attain it. Davies (1969) for instance, has described how four Finnish alcoholics formed themselves in to a self-help group ('The Polar Bears') with the help of which they succeeded in control-ling their drinking (see p. 27). This group abjured the repeated discussions about drink and drinking which are a feature of meetings of Alcoholics Anonymous and directed their discussions instead to more general life problems. The development of 'Drinkwatchers' (Winters, 1978), a self-help organization aiming at moderate drinking, is another example of non-specialist effort towards controlled drinking. Popham and Schmidt (1976) have also shown how traditional group therapy methods can be successful in helping alcoholics control their drinking and we shall describe their work in more detail in the next chapter.

Some psychotherapists, most notably those of the transactional analysis school (e.g. Steiner, 1971), have also eschewed medical conceptions of alcoholism and in so doing have allowed that controlled drinking is a viable goal of treatment. Whether their methods are more effective than those of informal self-help groups remains to be seen.

Those alcoholics who recover by controlling their drinking without any professional or group support (see Saunders and Kershaw, 1979) must not be forgotten. As Armor *et al.* (1978), Orford and Edwards (1977) and many others have pointed out, one of the main determinants of improvement in alcoholics is the occurrence of intrapsychic changes through which they come to a decision to either reduce or stop their drinking. This decision-making process has been discussed in detail by Orford and Edwards but exactly which changes take place is still unknown. Once such processes are understood it may be possible to develop methods by which to facilitate the natural decision-making process. Given that such life events as marriage, job-change and ill-health have also been shown to be important natural determinants of remission from alcoholism (e.g. Saunders and Kershaw,

1979; Orford and Edwards, 1977), and that reinforcement theory would also predict that these would have significant effects upon drinking (p. 158 above), some integration of decision-making and reinforcement models of alcoholism appears possible. Future research may produce a coherent psychological theory which incorporates the other psychological processes which have been shown to have important implications for the understanding and treatment of alcoholism.

In the next chapter we will review controlled drinking treatment studies which have used some of the treatment methods briefly described here. As a particular method may be known by several different names, we will translate these into the terminology used in this chapter.

6 Controlled drinking treatments: the evidence

We wish in this chapter to rectify a fundamental fault apparent in all reviews of controlled drinking treatment which we have read (e.g. Lloyd and Salzberg, 1975; Miller, 1976; Miller and Hester, 1980). This is that they pay insufficient regard to the severity of alcohol problems of the clients treated in the various studies, and base their conclusions about the general effectiveness of treatment upon studies which are dealing with widely differing populations of alcoholics. It is our contention that the population of clients receiving treatment in controlled drinking programmes fall into two quite distinct groups. While these differ from each other on a number of measures, it is how they are recruited for treatment which is the most immediately apparent difference. In this review of 26 studies of controlled drinking treatments, of the 26 client groups, ten had been recruited mainly through media advertisements and two mainly from the courts. The remaining fourteen were drawn mainly from existing populations of alcoholism-clinic inpatients, outpatients or other psychiatric or medical services.

Before we go on to provide further evidence for this distinction, the work of Room (1977) is important in providing a background to the argument. As Room points out, several epidemiologists (e.g. Edwards, Chandler, Hensman and Peto, 1972; Cahalan and Room, 1974; Mulford and Wilson, 1966) have found in community surveys large numbers of problem-drinkers who have never had contact with established alcoholism treatment services. However such problem-drinkers differ from clinic alcoholics in that they show less severe problems and show more 'disjunctive' responses on various drinking history measures; i.e. they do not exhibit a coherent collection of 'symptoms', whereas the response of clinic alcoholics to a range of questions about alcohol use and alcohol problems tends to cluster together. Room cited evidence to show that it was only about one per cent of the male adult population who exhibited social problems related to drinking as severe as those exhibited by clinic alcoholics. This is in contrast to about 20 per cent of the adult population who could be construed at any one time as being at substantial risk for developing a drinking problem.

It is possible that therapists who recruit clients by advertisement or by compulsory court referral are tapping the population of problem-drinkers hitherto only identified in community surveys and that these differ in many ways from the clients typically seen at alcoholism clinics. If this is so, then our case for dividing the controlled drinking studies into two groups is clearly made. Table 6.1 sets out some of the characteristics of the clients in each study. The research reviewed does not include single-case studies and studies where no attempt was made to generalize behaviour changes outside of a ward setting.

TABLE 6.1

Controlled drinking studies: sources of referral and client characteristics

Author	Source of recruitment for research	Hospitalizations for alcoholism	Evidence of withdrawal symptoms	Mean daily alcohol consumption (in pints of beer equivalent)
Lovibond and Caddy (1970)	Media recruitment	Most had been hospitalized on numerous occasions	?	6·7
Caddy and Lovibond (1976)	Medical referrals Media recruitment	Most had been hospitalized several times	?	?
Mills *et al.* (1971)	Inpatient alcoholism clinic	A mean of six previous institutionalizations	All had shown some symptoms	?
Baker *et al.* (1975)	Ditto	(Currently hospitalized)	'All had experienced withdrawal symptoms'	?
Vogler, Compton and Weissbach (1975)	Ditto	Ditto	?	6·8
Vogler, Weissbach and Compton (1977*a*)	Outpatient alcoholism clinic	A mean of 0·19 previous hospitalizations for alcoholism	?	7·2
Popham and Schmidt (1976)	Outpatient alcoholism clinic	?	?	?
Ewing and Rouse (1976)	Referred by psychiatrists	?	All had suffered 'physiological symptoms' for a mean of 9·6 years	14·0

TABLE 6.1 *continued*

Author	Source of recruitment for research	Hospitalizations for alcoholism	Evidence of withdrawal symptoms	Mean daily alcohol consumption (in pints of beer equivalent)
Czypionka and Demel (1976)	Psychiatric clinic	(currently hospitalized)	Half described as 'gamma' and half as 'chronic', alcoholics	?
Sobell and Sobell (1973)	Inpatient alcoholism clinic	A mean of 2 prior hospitalizations for alcoholism	52%:tremors 20%:black- outs or convulsions 27·5%:DTs or hallucinations	?
Yates (1979)	Inpatient alcoholism facility	A mean of 2·5 previous admissions to hospital for alcoholism	A mean of 1·6 incidences of DTs in the last 3 months	?
Lewis (1979)	Inpatient alcoholism clinic	(Currently hospitalized)	?	?
Maxwell *et al.* (1974)	Inpatient alcoholism clinic	(Currently hospitalized)	?	?
Hedberg & Cambell (1974)	Unspecified	?	?	?
Lovibond (1975)	Court	?	?	3·5
Vogler, Weisbach, Compton and Martin (1977)	Court; Media	?	?	3·5
Miller (1978)	Media; Courts	?	?	3·5
Miller, Gribsov and Mortell (1979)	Mainly Media	?	?	5·0

TABLE 6.1 *continued*

Author	Source of recruitment for research	Hospitalizations for alcoholism	Evidence of withdrawal symptoms	Mean daily alcohol consumption (in pints of beer equivalent)
Miller, Taylor and West (1979)	Mainly Media	?	?	4·0
Taylor and Miller (1979)	Mainly Media	?	?	5·1
Miller, Pechacek and Hamburg (1979)	Mainly Media	?	?	4·0
Alden (1980) 1. 2. 3.	Media; Health agencies	?	(Those showing 'signs of addiction' excluded)	3·5
Pomerleau *et al.* (1978)	Medical referrals; Media	?	?	5·3
Sanchez-Craig (1980)	Media; Outpatient alcoholism clinic	?	?	?

It is clear from the table that the clients recruited mainly through the media or the courts differ from those attending clinics in more ways than the source of referral. Firstly, with one exception (Lovibond and Caddy, 1970), only one set of subjects in the former group of studies had been hospitalized for alcoholism while clients in at least eleven of the latter studies had been so hospitalized. Secondly, six of the latter group reported clients having suffered alcohol withdrawal symptoms whereas none of the former group of studies reported this. Thirdly, the mean daily consumption rate of the second group (4.4 pints of beer equivalent) was much lower than average consumption levels of clinic alcoholics surveyed elsewhere (e.g. Armor *et al.*, 1978).

Michigan Alcoholism Screen Test (MAST) scores were available for four of the media or court-recruited groups of clients. These ranged from a mean of 13.7 to a mean of 19.4. Although Selzer (1971) classified those scoring more than five on this test as 'alcoholic', clearly it would identify most community-survey-identified 'problem-drinkers' as alcoholic also. For instance, someone who has been arrested once for driving while intoxicated, who has once been in a fight while drunk and who has quarrelled with his wife while drinking would qualify as an alcoholic. Clearly this level of problems bears little relation to the multifarious problems suffered by clinic alcoholics (Room, 1977). Indeed, some of the media and court-referred groups would not even be categorized as heavy drinkers by the criteria used in at least one community survey (Dight, 1976).

On the above evidence, there are clear grounds for a division of the studies. We make no assumptions about the theoretical nature of this difference but it is possible that 'severity of dependence' might be one of the differentiating features along with other social and psychological factors. As Orford and Edwards (1977) and Armor *et al.* (1978) have found that severity of dependence is a major predictor of both good versus bad and controlled versus abstinent outcomes, the possibility that the two populations of clients might differ along this dimension further strengthens the validity of the distinction and the necessity for evaluating the two sets of studies separately. For convenience we will, following Room (1977), categorize client groups into problem-drinkers and clinic alcoholics. While this is done primarily according to the source of referral, there are a few anomalies which must be considered.

Lovibond and Caddy (1970) recruited most of their clients through the media. However they state that most of their clients had previously been hospitalized for alcoholism and for this reason we have included this group under the 'clinic alcoholic' heading. Pomerleau *et al.* (1978) recruited a proportion of their clients through medical referrals as well as through the media. However, as no previous hospitalizations or evidence of withdrawal symptoms are reported, this group is included under the 'problem-drinker' heading. Hedberg and Cambell's (1974) clients were referred to them from unspecified sources. As no mention is made of media recruitment, we will include them in the absence of contradictory information under the 'clinic alcoholic' heading.

Having thus classified the 26 studies into 14 which deal with clinic alcoholics and 12 which deal with problem-drinkers, we will attempt to answer some important questions about the effectiveness of controlled drinking treatments.

1. Are any controlled drinking treatments effective?
2. Are some more effective than others?
3. Are controlled drinking treatments more effective than abstinence-oriented treatments?
4. Does the therapeutic goal have any influence on the type of therapeutic outcome, or is this determined by extra-therapeutic factors?

Before reviewing the studies in order to try to answer these questions, we must consider in some detail some of the methodological problems in conducting alcoholism treatment studies in order that the subsequent studies can be critically and consistently assessed.

ALLOCATION TO TREATMENT GROUPS

If two kinds of treatment are to be compared, random allocation to treatment groups is essential. Researchers who simply try to match their groups on important characteristics such as age, sex and occupational status weaken their design, simply because it is not yet known which variables are responsible for most of the outcome variance in alcoholism treatment (Armor *et al.*, 1978). At the very least, random allocation minimizes the chance that the groups are not matched on important variables.

There are however major difficulties in random allocation, which we will discuss in more detail when discussing individual studies. Firstly, there is evidence that clients who are led to expect a particular treatment, but are then denied it as a result of allocation, experience negative feelings of rejection which may actually make their problems worse (e.g. Kissin, Platz and Su, 1970). Secondly, once random allocation has occurred, it may transpire that the groups differ significantly on some measure which is known to influence outcome, such as social stability or pre-treatment alcohol intake. Any differences in outcome which emerge between treatment groups are therefore confounded by these pre-treatment variables.

TREATMENT

A clear distinction must be made between the specific procedures of a particular treatment method and its general, hope-inspiring placebo effects. Too often, a control group receives a treatment in which the therapist does not have much confidence. In such a case any positive findings could be attributable to non-specific factors rather than to a particular treatment method. What must be borne in mind in these cases, however, is the paucity of positive findings in the alcoholism treatment literature. Any positive finding in an otherwise methodologically adequate outcome study must warrant serious consideration. It is by no means inconceivable, for instance, that certain treatment methods potentiate non-specific factors such as staff enthusiasm and expectancy of success. In other words, so-called placebo effects deserve as much study and analysis as treatment methods; indeed it may not be useful to separate them conceptually in the usual way.

Drop-outs

It is well established that alcoholics who cannot be traced following treatment tend to have a poorer outcome than those who are traced (e.g. Polich,

Armor and Braiker, 1980; Moos and Bliss, 1978). Some have argued that studies with low follow-up rates should be regarded as invalid but this argument is justified only where the authors attempt to make some statement about *absolute* success rates. In studies where two treatments are compared, provided the two groups have similar drop-out rates, no matter how large, valid conclusions about the *relative* effectiveness of the treatments can be made, as long as the characteristics of those who remain in the two groups remain similar. In addition, Polich *et al.* (1980) have shown that follow-up rates of upwards of 60 per cent produced results which are fairly representative of the results of the untraced subjects, and that conclusions about success rates are not substantially changed by follow-up rates greater than these.

Length of follow-up

At six months following the end of treatment for alcoholism, the majority of clients who will eventually relapse will already have done so (e.g. Armor *et al.*, 1978; Orford and Edwards, 1977) and this may be regarded as an absolute minimum acceptable length of follow up for outcome studies. Evidence from Orford and Edwards (1977), Gerard and Saenger (1966) and Armor *et al.* (1978) suggests that more controlled drinkers emerge between one and three years following treatment than in the first year. This implies that controlled drinking treatment studies require longer follow-up periods than are generally used in abstinence treatments, though with a few exceptions (e.g. Caddy *et al.*, 1978), this has not been the case.

Measure of outcome

It is only in recent years that abstinence has ceased to be regarded as the sole criterion for successful outcome following alcoholism treatment (Pattison, Sobell and Sobell, 1977), though there is a danger that the authors of modern controlled drinking programmes might fall into a similar trap in the form of a blinkered preoccupation with how much the alcoholic drinks. It was Gerard and Saenger (1966) who first pointed out that abstinence or controlled drinking bore no necessary relationship to improved psychosocial adjustment, and as a result much subsequent research has attempted to measure changes in psychological, marital, vocational, and social and physical well-being as well as changes in drinking behaviour (e.g. Pattison, 1976*a*). Sobell and Sobell (1978*b*) further developed such measurement into a sophisticated system which relied as much as possible upon objective information such as police, hospital and employment records. 'Softer' sources of information about these related areas collected through interviews or questionnaires given to friends or relatives should be strengthened through the use of reliable and valid instruments (e.g. Marlatt, 1976). Unfortunately such information is often collected using unstandardized procedures of unknown reliability or validity if it is collected at all, and in most of the studies reviewed in this chapter, drinking behaviour is the major outcome criterion.

That alcoholics never tell the truth about their drinking has become a received wisdom in the alcoholism treatment world and some research suggests that under certain circumstances they do not (e.g. Summers, 1970). This has caused researchers to turn increasingly to collaterals, especially wives or husbands, in order to assess the drinking of the alcoholic (e.g. Caddy and Lovibond, 1976). Unfortunately, several studies seem to suggest that collaterals can be as unreliable as the alcoholic is purported to be, in reporting his drinking (e.g. Guze, Tuason, Stewart and Picken, 1963; Wilkins, 1974) though several later studies have shown that on certain measures, collateral reports correspond well with self-reports (McCrady, Paoling and Longabaugh, 1978; Miller, Crawford and Taylor, 1979; Morse and Swenson, 1975). Miller (1978) has attempted to overcome such difficulties by differentially weighting self-reported information which is not contradicted by collateral reports and information which is contradicted by the reports of significant others. Such systematic attempts to integrate collateral and self-reports remain however the exception rather than the rule.

Given the difficulties of asking collaterals to report precise quantities drunk by clients, most outcome studies have had to rely heavily on self-report data and some recent work by the Sobells shows that in doing so, unreliable measurement does not necessarily result. Sobell, Maisto, Sobell and Cooper (1979) asked patients about their daily drinking disposition over the 360 days prior to admission. Daily drinking disposition reports required the patients to estimate on how many days they were abstinent, on how many they drank less than about 3.5 pints of beer or the equivalent, on how many they drank more than this, and on how many they were incarcerated. The reliability over six weeks ranged from 0.79 to 0.98. A crucial feature of the interviews was the use of a blank calendar covering the period to be reconstructed, in which clients filled in anchor days such as holidays and birthdays and with this aid to memory, drinking patterns could be reconstructed.

Sobell and Sobell (1978a) also showed that when asked about hard information such as arrests and hospitalizations, alcoholics gave relatively truthful answers in spite of the fact that they were not aware that these could be checked by the researchers against official records. It can be concluded that properly standardized procedures can elicit relatively reliable and valid self-reports from alcoholics, though it is important that the assessors be blind to the treatment conditions. Collateral reports must be equally rigorously treated, though such rigour is not common in the outcome literature. The use of liver-function tests, official records and even breathalyser readings may be useful adjuncts to these measures.

Assuming that reliable valid information has been obtained, the question arises of how significant any differences between groups actually are, since statistical significance does not imply clinical significance. For example, a treatment group may show a post-treatment consumption of alcohol which is lower than that of the control group, but if this is an average of one half of a bottle of whisky per day, the treatment is clearly clinically ineffective, even though statistically it may be superior to the control treatment. Some composite measure of drinking and drinking consequences is necessary if a realistic assessment of moderate drinking is to be made. For instance, mean daily consumption of alcohol is, by itself, unsatisfactory as a measure of harmfree drinking. Some estimate of the distribution of drinking is desirable to counter the possibility that large quantities are being drunk over short periods. Similarly, an estimate of the consequences of drinking is required to counter the possibility that a client with a very low tolerance for alcohol is actually suffering problems from taking quite moderate amounts of alcohol. We will discuss more fully the issue of what constitutes a satisfactory definition of controlled drinking in our conclusions, though in many studies the only data available is that of mean daily consumption.

The research

We will now deal in some detail with each of the controlled drinking treatment outcome studies encountered in our search of the literature. As stated earlier, we do attempt to be exhaustive but have excluded single-case studies and work where no attempt was made to measure generalization from an institutional to the natural environment. We will deal first of all with those studies dealing with what we have termed 'clinic alcoholics'.

CLINIC ALCOHOLICS

LOVIBOND AND CADDY (1970) carried out the first attempt to evaluate systematically the effectiveness of controlled drinking treatment. From its inception this research diverged from most previous outcome studies, in that the authors recruited most of their clients through the media, including television, though a small but unspecified number of the 35 males and 9 females were referred by medical practitioners. Although they are described as having a history of alcoholism extending on average over ten years, it is not specified what is meant by alcoholism. However the fact that most had previously been hospitalized for alcoholism suggests that their problems were not trivial. On average they had been drinking the equivalent of about 6.5 pints of beer daily. Of the 44 clients, 13 were randomly selected for the control treatment but 8 of these did not return after the first or second treatment session, compared with only two from the experimental group.

The experimental treatment consisted of a combination of BAC discrimination training and avoidance conditioning. In addition, a family member was present whenever possible and the importance of his or her supporting role was emphasized. Some self-control advice was also given but this was not described in detail: '. . . the general therapeutic goal is to assist the subject to regain self-respect by exerting the self-control necessary to maintain a pattern of moderate social drinking'.

Outcome was measured through self-reports of daily alcohol intake, but while information on drinking was also collected from a family member, or other informant, it is not reported how much of this information was available, how discrepant it was from the self-reports, or how these discrepancies were resolved. Follow-up was from 16 to 60 weeks, though the distribution of follow-up over this range is not clear. At follow-up, 21 out of the 28 treatment subjects who had not dropped out were considered as 'complete successes', in that they rarely reported drinking to a BAC level exceeding 70 mg/100 ml.

Two striking aspects of this study are the extremely high success rate for the experimental group, and the total inadequacy of the control group. Indeed, the authors could have saved themselves the trouble of reporting what information they did include about the control group. Only five out of thirteen received more than two treatment sessions, and no follow-up data is available for them. This study is therefore not an adequate test of the effectiveness of controlled drinking treatments. However, one cannot ignore the 67 per cent success rate for the treatment group, which is much higher than most reviews of alcoholism treatments have found (e.g. Costello, 1975). A number of points cast doubt on the generalizability of this result. Firstly, although most of the subjects were reported to have been hospitalized for alcoholism, their pre-treatment consumption levels were low compared to those of many clinic alcoholics (see Armor *et al.*, 1978). Secondly, they were recruited through media advertisements and hence were likely to have been quite highly motivated. Finally, while self-reported consumption has been shown to be more reliable than was thought (see p. 175 above), one must assume in the absence of contradictory information that the experimenters themselves collected this information, with the resulting risk of biased findings.

In summary, this study, in common with most pioneering work, is illustrative rather than indicative, and these treatments could not be advocated for alcoholics on the basis of this study alone.

CADDY AND LOVIBOND (1976) attempted to isolate the effective components of their treatment in a second study and, while this appears at first glance to be a replication, it includes a form of self-management training not mentioned in their 1970 article.

Of 49 males and 11 females ranging in age from 21 to 69, 31 were psychiatric referrals, 6 were medical referrals and 23 were self-referrals.

Information about history of alcoholism was no less vague than that given in the previous study and no data about how much they had been drinking was available. However, the fact that most had been hospitalized several times for alcoholism again suggests that they had relatively serious problems. Each of the 60 patients was randomly allocated to one of three groups, and all received BAC discrimination training. The first group received avoidance conditioning while the second received avoidance conditioning plus 'self-regulation treatment' which consisted of stimulus control training, self-reinforcement procedures, regulated drinking practice and general exhortation towards a belief that their behaviour was ultimately their own responsibility and potentially under their control. The third group received only self-regulation training in addition to the ubiquitous BAC discrimination training.

Outcome was measured in a similar way to that used in the previous study. However assistants who were blind to treatment group membership followed up an unspecified number of patients and reviewed the follow-up data on all subjects in order to allocate them to one of the three outcome categories. Follow-up information was available on all patients at six-months follow-up, but only on 62 per cent at twelve months. Statistical significance tests were carried out on the six-month information only, though the authors do not make this clear in the text. The authors conclude that the treatment consisting of self-regulation and aversive conditioning together was more effective than self-regulation alone. However this is only true at six-months follow-up. At twelve-months follow-up ten of the first group, and nine of the latter group were considered either as complete successes or moderately improved. Only five of those receiving aversion treatment alone were considered complete successes. The authors draw rather dubious conclusions from these results. They refer to the 'overall greater effectiveness of the aversion plus self-regulation group' but, while they showed that this group did better than the other two groups *combined*, they did not show that it did better than the self-regulation group alone. In fact, it is clear from the twelve-month data that there would be no such significant difference. Only by combining the poor results of the aversion group with those of the self-regulation group could they come to these conclusions.

The only possible conclusion from this research is that aversion treatment alone is an ineffective form of treatment, compared with aversion and self-regulation together. However, this study does provide a little evidence for the differential effectiveness of particular treatments, a finding which is rare in the alcoholism treatment literature (Emrick, 1975).

Patton State Hospital, California was another centre for some of the early work on controlled drinking. This research reported in MILLS, SOBELL AND SCHAEFFER (1971) and in SCHAEFFER (1972) was a precursor to the subsequent work by Sobell and Sobell and, like this later research, did not baulk at tackling the problems of more chronic alcoholics. Thirteen male inpatients at the hospital who had volunteered for the study were selected on the basis of showing no current physical illness, satisfactory liver function, no current medication, no membership of any other alcoholism programme, no other drug addiction, and no consumption of alcohol for a minimum of two weeks before the start of the study. They were on average 47 years of age, had had a mean of about six previous admissions to various institutions for alcoholism and had all shown some form of withdrawal symptoms, from tremor to delirium tremens. Ten out of thirteen men treated by an avoidance conditioning procedure were located twelve months later. The control group consisted of thirteen men who had also volunteered for the study but the criteria by which they were rejected for the experimental group are not given. Indeed no details of any kind are given about them so that we cannot tell if they were a comparable group, and they presumably received routine inpatient treatment.

Twelve-month follow-up was carried out by a social worker who had been involved in the treatment, and we are not told whether a reliable procedure was used to elicit follow-up information. 'Complete agreement' was reported between family or friends who were interviewed, and the patients themselves. Outcome was categorized as 'abstinent', 'controlled drinking', and 'excessive drinking' where controlled drinking was defined as the consumption of less than about 3.5 pints of beer on a given day, and less than 5.5 pints on any two consecutive days. Categorization was carried out according to the 'majority' status of various periods for which information was available. In other words, if in a two-week period a man was abstinent for ten days, but drinking for four, he was classified as 'abstinent' for that period. Theoretically, over twelve months, a man who was drinking in a controlled way for 183 days, but excessively for 182 days, would be classified as a 'controlled drinker'. By these definitions, at twelve-month follow-up three out of the ten contacted were abstinent, and four were drinking in a controlled way. Two of the control group were abstinent, but none was drinking in a controlled way. These differences were statistically significant.

The fact that the assessor of outcome was also closely involved in the experiment makes these data subject to bias. Also, the classification of outcome according to 'majority status' makes conclusions about the numbers who were actually controlling their drinking subject to considerable doubt. Finally, the fact that we are given no comparative data on the control group means that we do not know whether they were adequate for such a purpose. In conclusion, this study provides little evidence about the effectiveness of controlled drinking treatment.

A further piece of research from Patton State Hospital was carried out by BAKER, UDIN AND VOGLER (1975). Their subjects were male alcoholic inpatients at the hospital who had volunteered for the study. The selection criteria included a history of heavy drinking lasting more than five years. All subjects had experienced alcohol withdrawal symptoms but we are not told which symptoms, to what extent or how often they occurred, though it is likely that, having been admitted to hospital, their problems were not insignificant.

Subjects were each randomly allocated to one of four treatment groups. One of these was a comparison group who received standard hospital treatment including group therapy and AA meetings. All three of the remaining groups received three sessions of behavioural counselling lasting two hours each. This consisted of training alternative responses to the cues known to elicit heavy drinking, following a functional analysis of drinking behaviour. In addition, the subjects were given information about appropriate drinking styles, and regulated drinking practice was carried out. One of these groups also received videotape self-confrontation of their behaviour while intoxicated. A second group received 'modelling' treatment, where they viewed films in which the negative consequences of excessive drinking and the positive consequences of moderate drinking were portrayed.

Outcome was measured six months after treatment by estimating the number of days abstinent or drinking in a controlled way. Excessive drinking was defined as the consumption of more than about eight pints of beer or its equivalent over any consecutive two-day period. This information was based mainly on self-reports collected through a questionnaire of unknown reliability and information on hospital and prison incarceration was also collected from public records. While a trend appeared for the videotape self-confrontation group to do better than the other three groups, no significant differences emerged. Successes were defined as those who had experienced fewer than 20 per cent days of excessive drinking and by this definition, eleven out of forty subjects were successful, i.e. 27.5 per cent. No inferences regarding the relative efficacy of different treatments are possible from these data.

VOGLER, COMPTON AND WEISSBACH (1975) also carried out their first study with inpatients at Patton State Hospital. The 42 subjects were predominantly male, with a mean of more than five alcohol-related arrests, an average ten-year history of problem-drinking, and a mean pre-treatment drinking level of about 6.5 pints of beer per day. These subjects were randomly assigned to two groups. The first group received alcohol education, regulated drinking practice, BAC discrimination training, avoidance conditioning and behaviour counselling, which included stimulus control, problem-solving skills training, assertive training, relaxation training and social skills training. This group also received videotape feedback of their drunken behaviour. The second group only received alcohol education and the behaviour counselling. Once-monthly booster sessions were given to both groups over twelve months and a number of outcome measures were collected by blind assessors twelve months after the end of the main treatment programme, though booster sessions continued over this time. These measures included alcohol intake, number of days lost at work, number of days drunk, number of days drinking and amount spent on drink. No significant differences emerged between groups, but if the fact that the second group had a significantly lower pre-treatment alcohol intake was taken into account in the multivariate analysis, then the first group did reduce their alcohol consumption significantly more than did the other group. Of the 42 subjects in both groups, 33 per cent were abstinent at twelve months, 29 per cent were drinking in a controlled way (average intake less than the equivalent of two pints of beer per day and no more than one episode of uncontrolled drinking, where BAC levels exceeded 80 mg/100 ml), and the rest had relapsed. Follow-up information was based largely on self-reports, though family and friends were interviewed, particularly when inconsistencies appeared in the data. However, there appeared to be no formal procedure for dealing with contradictory information.

The success rate of 62 per cent for this group of seriously impaired alcoholics is extremely high (see Costello, 1975) and the fact that the more intensively treated group showed more improvement than the less intensively treated one, is an important finding. If this difference is a real one – and the fact that the analysis accounted for statistical regression to the mean suggests that it may be – then it must be concluded that some or all of the additional treatments received by Group One were effective. Which of avoidance conditioning, videotape feedback, BAC discrimination-training or regulated drinking practice were effective cannot be determined, though our discussion of these methods in Chapter 5 suggests that the last of these, regulated drinking, is likely to have been the most effective component. The fact that, despite a controlled drinking goal, 33 per cent of subjects abstained, is an interesting finding which we will discuss in the conclusions of this chapter.

In a second study with alcoholic outpatients, VOGLER, WEISSBACH AND COMPTON (1977a) conducted identical treatment programmes to those used in their 1975 study, again with two randomly assigned groups. The 26 outpatient alcoholics selected drank somewhat more than the inpatients of the previous study (approximately seven pints of beer per day on average), though they had fewer previous hospitalizations for alcoholism (a mean of 0.19), and fewer jobs lost through alcohol. However, they reported a mean of 9.5 previous alcohol-related arrests and were clearly suffering from serious problems.

It is unfortunate that the data on these subjects are combined with those from the 42 inpatients of the earlier study. Identical follow-up procedures were used and outcome was defined in a similar way. It appears that at twelve-months follow-up three of the twenty-six were abstinent (11.6 per cent), eleven were drinking in a controlled way (42 per cent) and twelve had relapsed (46.1 per cent). Insufficient data are presented to compare the randomly assigned groups of outpatients, perhaps because the numbers were so small. The authors conclude from the combined data of the two studies that 'wet' treatment – that is, giving patients practice in drinking – was effective only for inpatient alcoholics. From this we may infer that no significant differences existed between the two groups in this outpatient trial, since they received identical treatments. In summary, this study shows promising overall outcome results (53.6 per cent controlled drinking or abstinent) but fails to show any difference between groups.

POPHAM AND SCHMIDT (1976), at the Addiction Research Foundation in Toronto, integrated a moderate drinking goal into the routine group discussion methods traditionally used in abstinent-oriented clinics. No control group was used and the subjects were routine referrals to the clinic. Excluded were those who had been seen in other clinics of the same organization and for whom even moderate drinking was contra-indicated on the grounds of physical ill-health, and it is likely that these two criteria excluded the most severe cases. Relatively little relevant information about the clients is available except that they drank on average the equivalent of over eight pints of beer per drinking day.

Treatment consisted mainly of group discussions, with some teaching about the hazards of heavy drinking. Moderate drinking was suggested as being possible for most clients, though no attempts were made to persuade dissidents otherwise. Follow-up was completed at one year on 96 out of 150 consecutive cases but information was entirely based on self-report and it seems possible that those conducting the follow-up had also been involved in the treatment. Controlled drinking was defined as drinking less than an average of about three pints of beer per drinking day. At one year follow-up, 19 per cent of clients were in this category, and 9 per cent were abstinent. This does not include those lost to follow-up, but as we showed earlier in this chapter follow-up rates of 60 per cent to 70 per cent yield outcome results fairly representative of the total population treated.

By comparing these results with those of abstinence-oriented treatments in their clinic, the authors conclude that the effect of a moderation goal is to increase the proportion of controlled drinking outcomes, but not to raise the overall proportion of good outcomes. This study is useful in demonstrating the viability of a controlled drinking goal in a routine clinic setting but it does suffer many of the measurement problems of other studies, such as the reliance on self-report alone. On the other hand, one cannot conclude from this research that controlled drinking goals are interchangeable with abstinence goals since it is quite possible that particular treatments may be appropriate with particular goals. The main value of this work is to demonstrate that the goal of moderation is as potentially safe and viable as is that of abstinence.

The work of EWING AND ROUSE (1976) has been used by many as evidence against the feasibility of controlled drinking treatments (e.g. Seixas, 1977), though it appears that these commentators were concerned more with the apparently negative results of this study than with its scientific credibility. Subjects were selected on the basis of having failed with Alcoholics Anonymous and with total abstinence goals (Ewing and Rouse, 1972) and most of the 25 clients who appeared were referred by psychiatrists. They had been alcoholic for a mean of about 9.6 years, and they drank on average the equivalent of about 14 pints of beer per day.

The outpatient treatment consisted of avoidance conditioning, regulated drinking practice and self-monitoring. Group meetings were also held which some spouses also attended. Some social drinking with therapists took place, and discussions of drinking, drinking behaviour, putative reasons for drinking, consequences of drinking and alternatives to drinking were held. It is not clear whether this discussion took the form of a coherent behavioural programme, though this seems unlikely. Only 14 subjects completed at least six treatment sessions and these subjects were followed up between 27 and 55 months following end of treatment by treatment staff, sometimes by personal contact with the client and a family member or referring physician. Measures of drinking, relationships with family and friends, work history and health history were taken and conclusions were based on the *poorest* score at any point since treatment. Results are reported for the 14 clients who attended more than six treatment sessions and, not surprisingly, given the use of the poorest ever score as a criterion, most scored the lowest possible on all four measures. Nine of them were abstinent at follow-up, though none had abstained for the entire follow-up period and controlled drinking as the authors defined it was not apparent in any of their clients. The definition in question was *never* drinking to excess, since this judgement was based on the single poorest rating during follow-up.

The most obvious failing of this study is the criterion used for controlled drinking. Had one of their subjects drunk in a moderate fashion for four years, except for one day when he drank to excess, then he would have been classified as a failure. As Sobell and Sobell (1976) have shown, circumscribed relapses in the six months following controlled drinking treatment are to be expected and it is open to speculation as to how many of the subjects of this study were in this category. Another major fault of this study is that far from being a representative sample of alcoholics, these subjects were selected for having *failed* with Alcoholics Anonymous and total abstinence programmes. It is hardly fair to test the effectiveness of new treatments upon a group with such a poor prognosis. Thirdly, one must question the rationale for the treatment package. It appears that group psychotherapy of an unspecified nature was combined in an unsystematic way with a few discrete behavioural techniques. No mention is made of an overall coherent therapeutic programme and such shotgun eclecticism seems more likely to confuse than help the clients. In short, this paper is of little use in attempting to evaluate controlled drinking treatment effectiveness.

In one of the few studies conducted outside of the USA, CZYPIONKA AND DEMEL (1976) treated 20 chronic alcoholics at a clinic in Vienna where half were treated as outpatients and half as inpatients. Although no details of drinking histories, disabilities or alcohol dependence are given, half are described as 'gamma' alcoholics and half as 'chronic' alcoholics. Treatment was based loosely on that given by Lovibond and Caddy (1970) and consisted of between ten and fourteen sessions of avoidance conditioning and some regulated drinking practice.

A successful outcome was defined as one where the patient never exceeded a BAC level of 60 mg/100 ml, and a spouse or relative was interviewed at six months along with the patient in order to assess this. Exactly how these BACs were estimated is not made clear, and the reliability of the assessment interview is not reported. Of the 20 patients, one was by this definition controlling his drinking and four were successfully abstinent.

The authors conclude that these controlled drinking treatments are ineffective. However, their strict definition of controlled drinking eliminates those who relapsed just once or twice in the early months and, as was mentioned above, this is common among ultimately successful controlled drinkers. Secondly, this was by no means a replication of Lovibond and Caddy's (1970) study, as the self-control advice given by the latter authors was not given here. In fact, it appears that no aspect of the treatment dealt with anything other than drinking itself and no attempt was made to deal with the wider problems which may have elicited abusive drinking. Nevertheless, this is a useful study of the effects of the controlled drinking goal, and suggests that such a goal does not inhibit the achievement of abstinence for those patients who desire it.

SOBELL AND SOBELL (1973; 1976; 1978*b*) carried out one of the most methodologically sophisticated studies in the alcoholism treatment literature. Their subjects were all inpatients at Patton State Hospital, California who had volunteered to participate in a research programme. They were described as 'gamma' alcoholics, a significant number of whom had shown signs of physiological dependence such as tremors, blackouts and DTs. There was clear evidence of significant alcohol-related problems, such as arrests and divorces, for most of them.

The patients, all men, were allocated to either a controlled drinking (CD) or a nondrinking (ND) treatment goal according to three criteria which were evaluated in a 45-minute interview. Excluded from the CD group were those who could 'socially identify' with AA and those who requested abstinence.

Included were those who had social support for controlled drinking and/or successfully practised controlled drinking at some time in the past. It is important to note that there is no evidence that those in the controlled drinking group had any less severe dependence on alcohol than those in the nondrinking group. Within each group, random allocation was then made to experimental and control groups and four groups were thus compared:

CD—E : These received the full Individualized Behaviour Therapy (IBT) programme, with a controlled drinking goal.

CD—C : These men, while initially allocated to a controlled drinking goal, were then assigned to a conventional abstinence-oriented programme.

ND—E : These received the full IBT programme, oriented towards abstinence.

ND—C : These received the same treatment as the CD—C group.

Individualized Behaviour Therapy consisted of seventeen sessions which included as part of the treatment programme, videotape replay of drunken behaviours, electrical avoidance conditioning, stimulus control training, problem-solving skills training and regulated drinking of alcohol. The control treatment consisted of various combinations of group therapy, chemotherapy, AA, physiotherapy and other services.

The outcome measures are the most sophisticated used in any comparable study to date and include monthly self-reports of daily consumption, ratings on a three-point scale by a collateral (friend, relative or employer) of the patient's interpersonal relationships and adjustment to stressful situations, occupational status obtained from collateral sources, self-ratings of vocational status, an index of residential status and stability, use of outpatient therapeutic support and number of days incarcerated in hospital or prison. 'Controlled drinking days' were defined as those where less than the equivalent of approximately 3.5 pints of beer were consumed (Sobell and Sobell, 1978*b*), although in earlier studies (Sobell and Sobell, 1973) data were analysed using a more complex definition which subsequently proved to be unnecessary.

At one- and two-year follow-ups, information was collected by Linda Sobell, who had been involved in treatment. At two years, an assiduous tracking procedure succeeded in collecting information on 69 of the 70 clients – a truly remarkable feat. A three-year follow-up was also carried out by a team who were unaware of which treatment groups particular clients had attended (Caddy, Addington and Perkins, 1978). Sophisticated and reliable interviewing and coding procedures were used and information was collected on 53 of these subjects (76 per cent).

This research consists essentially of two separate studies, one comparing controlled-drinking oriented behavioural treatments with traditional treatment and one comparing abstinence-oriented behavioural treatment with traditional treatment. As we are concerned primarily with controlled drinking treatments, we will consider in detail the results of the first study only. A summary of results at one, two and three years follow-up is shown in Table 6.2.

What emerges from the results in Table 6.2 is a significant and long-lasting improvement in the drinking and general adjustment of those treated by behavioural methods. It is striking that the difference in the number of days functioning well between the two groups at the three-year follow-up is due to the higher number of *abstinent* days in the controlled drinking group and not to a higher number of controlled drinking days. In years one and two, the CD—E group *did* show a greater number of controlled drinking days, but in the third year the CD—C showed a dramatic increase from 5.81 per cent to 34.85 per cent days of controlled drinking.

Such positive findings in a well-designed study clearly merit close scrutiny, though a number of important caveats must be borne in mind when interpreting the results. Firstly, the CD—C control group received less individual attention than did the experimental group and differences may be due to this rather than to specific behavioural treatments. Secondly, this group had also volunteered for a research programme and had been chosen for a controlled drinking treatment, only to be referred back to AA and a traditional abstinence-oriented treatment regime. Indeed, the Sobells report that 42 per cent of them mentioned at one time or another that they felt somewhat rejected or resentful about not participating in the treatment programme (Sobell and Sobell, 1978*b*). This raises the possibility that differences in outcome are due to the control group having *suffered*, rather than to the experimental group having benefited. However, the fact remains that numerous other studies have used random allocation without any differences emerging between experimental and control groups (Emrick, 1975). One would have thought that had such 'rejection effects' been potent, significant differences between control and experimental groups in treatment research would have been common. Thirdly, intensive contact was maintained with all subjects for two years. Such active follow-up has been shown to be an important element in treatments (Costello, 1975) and it is possible that the experimental group benefited more from these follow-up interviews than did the control group. However, these differences are small and probably insufficient in themselves to account for the large differences in outcome between groups. Fourthly, while outcome measures were sophisticated, no systematic method was devised to resolve contradictory information between the clients and the friends, relatives and acquaintances who provided information about their progress. Fifthly, at the three-year follow-up, only 75.7 per cent of clients were traced. As we noted at the beginning of this chapter, many researchers have shown that it is those with the poorest outcome who are generally most difficult to find. However, as similar proportions of control and experimental subjects were lost, the remaining groups are comparable. Finally, considerable criticism has been made of the reliance on self-report data of alcohol consumption. But, as we have already mentioned, several recent studies have shown that such data can be quite reliable (Sobell, Maisto, Sobell and Cooper, 1979). Also, the existence of differences between groups on other measures, and on compound measures, lends

TABLE 6.2

A comparison of controlled drinking experimental (CD–E) and control (CD–C) groups on a number of outcome measures at one-, two- and three-year follow-ups

Measure taken over previous year	Year of follow-up	Outcome CD—E	CD—C	Measure taken over previous year	Year of follow-up	Outcome CD—E	CD—C
% Days drunk	1	14·0%	49·9%	Vocational	1	45·0%	23·7%
	2	12·3%	49·2%*	status (self-	2	70·0%	28·8%*
	3	5·1%	25·3*	evaluation)	3	85·0%	40·0%
				% who are improved			
% Days	1	45·3%	25·7%	Occupational	1	76·9%	46·7%*
abstinent	2	62·6%	36·5%*	status	2	75·0%	52·5%*
	3	66·0%	40·1%	(collateral evaluation) % having some work	3	84·6%	53·3%
% Days	1	25·2%	9·6%*	General adjust-	1	85·0%	34·2%*
controlled	2	22·6%	5·8%*	ment (collateral	2	87·5%	44·7%*
drinking	3	28·8%	34·8%	evaluation) % improved	3	–	–
% Days	1	15·5%	14·9%	General index	1	–	–
incarcerated	2	2·6%	8·5%	of outcome	2	0·86	0·48*
(hospital and jail)	3	0%	5·3%		3	0·84	0·66*
%Days	1	70·5%	35·2%*	Index of	1	–	–
functioning	2	74·5%	44·9%*	general adjustment	2	–	–
well (abstinent or controlled drinking)	3	94·8%	74·9%	(collateral evaluations)	3	0·84	0·66

Sources: Sobell and Sobell (1978); Caddy *et al.* (1978)
* Significant at least p < 0·01

support to the validity of the drinking reports. In short, although considerable methodological difficulties exist, we can accept on balance that there was a true difference between the two groups.

The puzzling findings that the control group increased greatly the number of controlled drinking days in the third year and that the experimental group were doing better then because of greater *abstinence*, are crucial to our understanding of how controlled drinking treatments work. It is possible that the new interviewers in the third year elicited information in a different way but, if so, why did this cause an increase in reporting of controlled drinking and not of other measures? An alternative explanation might be that controlled drinking tends to occur 'naturally' a few years following abstinence-oriented treatment. Both Orford and Edwards (1977) and Gerard and Saenger (1966) have shown this to be the case for some alcoholics. Another question is why men trained specifically to drink in a controlled way abstain on significantly more days than those who are treated in an abstinence-oriented programme? A possible answer to this is that some of the effective elements in the controlled drinking treatment were those which were not specifically directed towards controlled drinking. This argument is supported by the Sobells themselves who state: 'While the contribution of each component of the treatment procedure used must be evaluated experimentally, it is our contention that stimulus control sessions not only constituted the bulk of the treatment sessions, but were primarily responsible for the behaviour changes which later occurred' (1973, p. 69). This 'stimulus control' treatment was renamed 'problem-solving skills training' in later publications (Sobell and Sobell, 1978b) and consisted in fact of a combination of stimulus control training and problem-solving skills training. This contention by the Sobells is supported by some evidence. They note that very few subjects in the CD—E group actually received shocks for inappropriate drinking and that the subjects were equivocal in their ratings of the effectiveness of this part of the treatment. This is in agreement with most of the research on electrical aversive conditioning (see p. 154 above). Another element of the treatment which has not been proved effective was that of videotape replay of drunken behaviour, which earlier studies in Patton (Schaeffer *et al.*, 1971) found in some cases actually seemed to make patients worse. The final element in formal treatment was the practice of appropriate drinking, such as small sips, limited quantities, and diluted alcohol. The fact that very few clients were shocked for inappropriate drinking suggests that the shocks were giving *feedback* and information about drinking, rather than acting as unconditioned stimuli. The Sobells suggest that simple verbal feedback would suffice in modifying drinking responses, coupled with self-monitoring by the person of his own drinking. By exclusion, it appears that problem-solving skills training, stimulus control training, and regulated drinking together were the effective elements of treatment. As the first two of these need not be aimed specifically at controlled drinking, the finding that at three-years follow-up the CD—E group are doing better because they are abstaining on more days is less surprising. They have apparently learned how to solve stressful problems without recourse to drinking. The fact that they drank more often in a controlled way in the first two years, but not in the third year, suggests that the drinking practice sessions were valuable for the first two years of their recovery but less important in the long term.

Unfortunately it is impossible to compare usefully the CD—E group with the ND—E group who received the same kinds of treatment. The reason is that the latter were less likely to do well in treatment because they had been specifically selected in part for their lack of social support for controlled drinking. In general, however, the ND—E group were no better than their control group at both two- and three-year follow-up and this result can be interpreted in two ways. One interpretation is that these treatments are effective only where controlled drinking is a goal and where drinking training is given. The other is that the non-drinking groups were less likely to benefit from any kind of treatment because of their lack of social support, and that had the ND—E group been similar to the CD—E group, their outcome would have been at least as good, if not better. The answer to that problem lies in future research.

A final point we must deal with is whether the drinking reported by those treated was clinically acceptable. The criterion for a controlled drinking day was the consumption of less than about 3.5 pints of beer or its equivalent, and no subject in the CD—E group reported drinking more than about three pints on any day defined as such (Sobell and Sobell, 1978*b*). On average over the three years they exceeded three and a half pints of beer on just over 10 per cent of all days though in the last year this declined to about 5 per cent. While this number of 'drunk days' is undesirable, it must be contrasted with the average over three years of 42.9 per cent drunk days for the control group. By any reasonable definition, describing the CD—E group successes as controlled drinkers is clinically as well as statistically justified.

In summary, this study has produced results suggesting that a combination of problem-solving skills training and stimulus control training, together with regulated drinking during treatment, is an effective method of treatment when controlled drinking is the goal, though the effects are likely to be in the form of more frequent abstention. There are clear grounds for recommending such behavioural treatment towards controlled drinking on the basis of this study.

One of the few British projects on controlled drinking has been a residential programme run by the Alcoholics Rehabilitation Research Group in Birmingham under the directorship of Dr Hugh Norris. YATES (1979) carried out a study of two residential establishments, one operating a controlled drinking, and the other an abstinence policy. Referrals for this service came from a wide range of sources, including psychiatrists, social workers, families and friends, though the biggest proportion were referred by probation officers. 'Marked social, personal or intellectual impairment' constituted the only specified criteria for rejection. Refusal to abstain in the abstinence house resulted in exclusion, as did similar refusal during the first few weeks in the controlled drinking house.

No attempt was made to randomly allocate clients to the two houses, which were situated in different towns. The two sets of residents differed in that those in the controlled drinking house had had longer periods of controlled drinking, a shorter history of serious problem-drinking, less jobs lost through drinking and fewer days unemployed prior to admission. All clients had serious problems, reporting an average of 1.6 incidences of delirium tremens in the three months prior to admission. Those in the controlled drinking house reported slightly fewer solitary drinking sessions and fewer occasions of memory loss, although on most measures of dependence they did not differ from those in the abstinent house. On average, clients had been admitted to hospital for alcoholism 2.5 times, though 31 per cent had had no previous treatment for drinking. Only 22 per cent were married, and 38 per cent had been charged by the police in the last three months.

Treatment consisted of Personal Skills Training, a broad-based programme which attempted to help clients develop realistic long-term aims in their lives, and short-term goals to achieve them. Included in this was problem-solving skills training, self-management training and the development and rehearsal of appropriate alternatives to drinking. Social skills training also took place, and all of this was carried out in small group settings over the period of stay which was on average of ten weeks' duration. Written contracts between staff and individual patients were signed and follow-up meetings to discuss the implementation of the treatment to real-life problems took place.

While there was provision made in the planning of the controlled drinking programme for alcohol to be consumed, very little supervised practice actually took place. Initially residents in the controlled drinking house signed an abstinence contract which could be changed to a controlled drinking one when the staff felt that the client was successfully applying the principles of the Personal Skills Training. Only seven out of 23 who were followed up three months after the beginning of residence actually changed to controlled drinking contracts. Thus the differences in treatments between the two houses were more theoretical than practical, in the sense that those in the controlled drinking house were aware that controlled drinking was an acceptable target for the future.

Twenty-four clients from the abstinence house and twenty-three from the controlled drinking house who completed an intake questionnaire administered within the first two weeks of residence became eligible for follow-up in the first year. Follow-up data were collected at three-month intervals for up to one year following discharge by a researcher who had not been involved in treatment, but who knew which clients had been in which house. Only one of this group was lost in follow-up and at the time the report was written all the remainder had been successfully followed up for at least six months and almost 60 per cent for the complete year which included independent corroboratory information at twelve months after leaving. Controlled drinking as an outcome was a 'mutually negotiated term' between interviewer and client, with no explicit criteria. On average clients reporting that they were in this outcome category over the last three months drank about three pints of beer three days per week. One client out of the twenty-four in the abstinence house, and one out of twenty-two in the controlled drinking house, controlled their drinking for all four follow-up periods. Only one client in the abstinence house abstained for the entire twelve months. Four out of each house controlled their drinking for three out of four follow-up quarters, while three in the abstinence house abstained for nine months, as did two in the controlled drinking house. However, as twelve-month data was only available on 57.5 per cent of residents, the author classified outcomes by 'only including those individuals whose three-month periods in follow-up were dominated by one particular pattern, either abstinence or near-abstinence, controlled drinking or the three unsuccessful outcomes'. By this classification, 33 per cent were considered mainly controlled drinkers and 13 per cent were considered abstainers; 24 per cent were considered unsuccessful, leaving 30 per cent unclassifiable because of ambiguous results.

On first glance, the most striking conclusion from this research is that the goal of treatment had no apparent effect on outcome. The major differences between houses appeared to be in a greater number of drinking disturbances in the controlled drinking house, and a weaker community spirit there. As the author notes, however, very little of the treatment was specifically directed at controlled drinking, this being confined to seven of the clients signing controlled drinking contracts. A second important finding is the prevalence of periods of controlled drinking interspersed with other drinking outcomes. Only 41 per cent of the controlled drinking house residents and 58 per cent of the abstinence house residents did not report a single three-month period of controlled drinking. In general, more clients controlled their drinking for most of the time than abstained for most of the time.

Since this was not a properly controlled study, conclusions about the relative efficacy of the treatment regimes must be extremely tentative. Nevertheless, given that the controlled drinking house contained residents who had marginally less serious problems and were in favour of aiming for controlled drinking as a goal, the lack of difference in outcome must be taken seriously, as such clients should be more likely to be able to control their drinking (see p. 219 below). Some doubt must be cast on the method of assessment of controlled drinking without explicit criteria, and the poor response rate by collaterals is also a weakness. Nevertheless, this is a useful and interesting study, especially with regard to the questions it raises about the complexities and apparent disadvantages of operating controlled drinking policies in a residential setting. One cannot conclude on the basis of this study alone that the treatment goal has no influence on the type of outcome as this would be tantamount to 'proving the null hypothesis'.

LEWIS (1979) has described a controlled drinking treatment programme carried out within a routine inpatient setting, also in Birmingham. This was not a controlled trial and, because it was not conducted as a formal research project, many methodological criticisms can be made. Thirty-one patients were selected on the basis of not having any immediate intention to abstain and of coming from a social environment capable of accepting their controlled drinking. No information about the severity of their drinking problems is available, but the fact that they were inpatients suggests that they were relatively serious. Treatment consisted of education, regulated drinking practice, self-management training, contingency management and skills training, the last component including social skills and anxiety management training. Emphasis was also placed on helping the patients develop alternative pastimes to drinking. Between six and twenty-four months later, nineteen (61 per cent) of these patients were followed up by two nurses, one of whom had acted as a therapist. Interview assessments were made of the subject's drinking, but no criteria are given for defining controlled drinking. Self-ratings were made by the client of other areas of his life ranging from physical state to financial status. Of the nineteen patients followed up, eleven (58 per cent) were considered to be controlling their drinking, two (10 per cent) were abstinent, and six (32 per cent) were unimproved. The fact that 13 (68 per cent) patients reported no further use of helping agencies and the same number reported no legal problems, gives some support to the drinking outcome evaluation, as alcoholics' reports of such concrete and easily specifiable events are known to be highly reliable and valid (Sobell and Sobell, 1978*a*). In conclusion, this study clearly supports the notion that controlled drinking treatments are viable within a routine clinical setting.

MAXWELL, BAIRD, WEZL AND FERGUSON (1974) also included controlled drinking treatment within a routine hospital environment. In this particular ward, patients operated a self-governing system where an elected committee monitored the behaviour of the patients some of whom could, if they wished, opt for moderation as a goal of treatment. From within this group of controlled drinkers, volunteers for an avoidance conditioning programme, also aimed at controlled drinking, were selected if they showed normal electro-cardiograph readings and normal liver function. The twenty-five males selected were on average 43 years of age and most were long-term alcoholics who had previously been treated for alcoholism. None of these men was employed and only six had intact marriages.

Treatment was based on Lovibond and Caddy's (1970) procedure of BAC discrimination training together with electric shocks given when BACs exceeded 65 mg/100 ml. Only twelve of the twenty-five men completed twelve sessions, nine having either been discharged for excessive drinking or failing to return after weekend leave and four deciding to attempt abstinence.

Follow-up of these patients was carried out over an average of ten months, though it is not clear who carried out the assessment or which assessment procedures were used. According to unspecified criteria, eight of the twelve clients were described as controlling their drinking and all of these had remained out of hospital for a mean of ten months.

HEDBERG AND CAMBELL (1974) treated clients who had been referred to them at a Mental Health Centre in Forth Worth, Texas, for outpatient treatment of alcoholism. We are given no relevant information about the subjects other than that the forty-five men and four women were on average 38 years old, and that two-thirds of them had made a serious attempt to change their drinking patterns. All forty-nine who were treated were traced six months following the *beginning* of treatment.

Clients were randomly assigned to one of four treatments. These were systematic desensitization, covert sensitization, aversive conditioning and behavioural family counselling. All clients received 21 hours of treatment spread over six months. The treatment goal, whether abstinence or controlled drinking, was decided by the client and therapist according to unspecified criteria. Because treatment was spaced over six months, and the six month follow-up calculated from the *beginning* of treatment, there is actually no follow-up information, only end-of-treatment information. An Alcohol Questionnaire was used to measure drinking outcome but we are not told who gave this questionnaire, whether it was a reliable instrument or whether any attempt was made to cross-check self-reports with the reports of friends or family.

Results are presented in the form of 'goal attained', 'much improved', or 'no improvement'. No information about drinking levels or associated problems is presented. Of the thirteen clients aiming at controlled drinking, 62 per cent were considered to have attained that goal but numbers are too small to compare the effectiveness of the different treatments. Overall, however, when the results for both goals are considered, behavioural family counselling achieved the highest success rate though no statistical tests of significance were carried out.

Little can be concluded from this study other than that controlled drinking is a viable goal of treatment. The absence of proper follow-up, the poor specification of outcome, the general lack of information and the small numbers of those aiming at controlled drinking make any conclusions about the relative effectiveness of various treatments impossible. What does emerge however, is the ineffectiveness of electrical aversion therapy; when combining 'abstinent' and 'improved' outcome categories, this treatment produced a 25 per cent success rate, as compared with 87 per cent for the systematic desensitization and family counselling groups.

Controlled drinking treatments for clinic alcoholics: interim conclusions

With the exception perhaps of the Australian work (Lovibond and Caddy, 1970; Caddy and Lovibond, 1976), there is no doubt that the patients treated in those studies in our first category were 'real' alcoholics. The doubt about the Australian clients lies in the large number who were recruited through the media. However, reports of past hospitalization for 'most' of them suggests on balance that they were at least moderately dependent upon alcohol.

The question of whether authors' definitions of controlled drinking were clinically acceptable also arises. In at least one study (Mills *et al.*, 1971) they clearly were not. In another (Ewing and Rouse, 1976) the criterion for clinical acceptability of *no* episodes of intoxication *ever* was so stringent as to be absurd. Somewhere in the middle lies the Sobells' work where during the third year, controlled drinking subjects spent one day in twenty 'drunk' (drinking over 3.5 pints of beer equivalent), as compared to one day in three for those treated in a traditional abstinence-oriented unit. In relative terms, the success of the controlled drinking treatment is incontrovertible. In absolute terms, this frequency of drunkenness may be undesirable, but given that the traditional abstinence treatment considered appears to have resulted in more frequent drunkenness, appeal to absolute standards becomes academic and even misleading.

Of the fourteen studies of clinic alcoholics, eight made some attempt to allow for non-specific treatment effects by using a control group. Popham and Schmidt (1976), Ewing and Rouse (1976), Czypionka and Demel (1976), Yates (1979), Lewis (1979) and Maxwell *et al.* (1974) made no such attempt. Of the eight apparently controlled studies, one provided no follow-up data on their control group (Lovibond and Caddy, 1970), so that it was in effect an uncontrolled study. One of the remaining studies used such a broad definition of controlled drinking that the term was no longer meaningful (Mills *et al.*, 1971). Here the absence of detailed outcome information about the control group precluded critical examination of the authors' conclusions, so that the study must be rejected as methodologically inadequate. Another study (Hedberg and Cambell, 1974) included insufficient numbers aiming at controlled drinking for a comparison between groups to be made.

Five studies remain which are methodologically viable, though all are subject to methodological problems. The study by Baker *et al.* (1975) shows no significant differences between treatments, neither does the one by Vogler *et al.* (1977*a*). This leaves three studies which show effects, i.e. Vogler *et al.* (1975), Caddy and Lovibond (1976) and Sobell and Sobell (1976). In Table 6.3 is shown a summary of the methodological features and outcome data from the fourteen studies.

As can be seen from Table 6.3, we have tried to give each controlled study a crude rating of its methodological adequacy. One point is given for each of the following: at least six-month follow-up; drop-out rates for comparison groups within 10 per cent of each other; blind assessment; random assignment; control groups comparable to treatment groups on important variables, use of systematically derived corroborative evidence from collaterals, blood tests or official records. Thus a particular study can score a maximum of six. Only Vogler *et al.* (1975) and Sobell and Sobell (1976) achieve this maximum rating but when one looks at the treatment methods which appeared to differentiate the more successful from the less successful groups, only three are common to both studies. These are regulated drinking practice, avoidance conditioning and videotape replay of drunken behaviour. A glance at the results of Caddy and Lovibond's (1976) study, methodologically flawed though it is, provides further confirmation of the value of regulated drinking practice, as this, along with self-management training, appeared to significantly improve the success rate over aversive conditioning alone. The fact that self-management training was common to both the Sobells' and Caddy and Lovibond's more successful treatments suggests that this is also an effective form of intervention. While videotape replay of drunkenness and avoidance conditioning were also common to the more successful groups of Vogler *et al.*'s and the Sobells' research, our discussion of these methods above (p. 166 and p. 188) suggests that they were not likely to have been among the effective elements of treatment. Thus the effectiveness of regulated drinking practice is supported by all three studies, and the effectiveness of self-management training by two studies. The Sobells' study also strongly suggests the effectiveness of problem-solving skills training.

Obviously one cannot conclude from this that no other treatments are ever successful and it could be argued that differential treatment effects are due to the extra therapeutic time spent with the more successful groups. This is not likely, however, given the paucity of positive findings for intensive over minimal treatment in the literature (e.g. Emrick, 1975; Orford and Edwards, 1977). The possibility that these new treatments aroused 'therapeutic enthusiasm' on the part of patients and staff is a more realistic one (see Vaillant, 1979). However, there have been many more new treatments in the literature than positive results (Emrick, 1975) and this fact weakens

TABLE 6.3
Methodological features and outcome data: clinic alcoholic studies

Authors	length of follow-up (months)	no. of groups	follow-up rates within 10% of each other?	blind assessment?	random assignment?	comparable control groups?	systematic corroborative evidence?	methodological rating (if controlled study)	significant differences reported between groups?	treatment elements peculiar to more successful intervention	Percentage[1] of those who had received controlled drinking treatment, who were followed up, and who had: abstained	controlled their drinking[2]
Lovibond & Caddy (1970)	3–15	2	No	No	Yes	No	Yes	**	N/A	N/A	0	75 .
Caddy & Lovibond (1976)	6	3	Only for 2 groups	Yes?	?	?	Yes	***	Yes	SM;RDP	Gr 1 0 Gr 2 0 Gr 3 0	45 30 20
Mills et al. (1971)	12	2	Yes	No	No	No	Yes	***	Yes	N/A	Gr 1 30 Gr 2 20	Gr 1 40 Gr 2 0
Baker et al. (1975)	6	4	Yes	Yes	Yes	Yes	No	******	No	N/A	0	27.5
Vogler et al. (1975)	12	2	Yes	Yes	Yes	Yes	Yes	*******	Yes	BAC;AC; RDP;V	Gr 1 30 Gr 2 37	35 21

TABLE 6.3 continued

Study												
Vogler et al. (1977a)	12	2	?	Yes	Yes	Yes	Yes	*****	No	N/A	11.5	42
Popham & Schmidt (1976)	12	1	N/A	No	N/A	N/A	No	N/A	N/A	N/A	9	19
Ewing & Rouse (1976)	27–55	1	N/A	No	N/A	N/A	Yes	N/A	N/A	N/A	64[4]	0
Czypionka & Demel (1976)	6	1	N/A	No	N/A	N/A	Yes	N/A	N/A	N/A	20	5
Sobell & Sobell[3] (1976)	36	2	Yes	Yes	Yes	Yes	Yes	******	Yes	PSST;SM; RDP;V;AC	See text	See text
Yates (1979)	12	2	Yes	No	No	No	Yes	***	No	N/A	13	33
Lewis (1979)	6–24	1	N/A	No	N/A	N/A	No	N/A	N/A	N/A	10	58
Maxwell et al. (1974)	10	1	N/A	?	N/A	N/A	No	N/A	N/A	N/A	?	32
Hedberg & Campbell (1974)	0	4	N/A	?	Yes	?	No	*	No[5]	N/A	0	62

(1) Separate results for each group are presented only where a significant difference was reported.
(2) Based on individual authors' definitions.
(3) These results are based on a 3-year follow-up by Caddy et al. (1978). Only 2 treatment groups of the four studied could usefully be compared (see text).
(4) None had abstained during the entire follow-up period.
(5) In this case, insufficient clients aimed at moderation for comparisons to be made.

SM: Self-management training
RDP: Regulated drinking practice
BAC: Blood-alcohol discriminating training
AC: Avoidance conditioning
V: Videotape replay of drinking behaviour
PSST: Problem-solving skills training

this important argument. Only further replications will finally settle this question.

Two studies which were reasonably adequate methodologically produced negative results (Baker *et al.*, 1975; Vogler *et al.*, 1977*a*). Baker *et al.*'s (1975) study found no difference between any of three groups receiving self-management training, regulated drinking practice and, in some cases, videotape feedback, and a comparison group receiving traditional hospital treatment. Vogler *et al.* (1977*a*) found no difference between alcoholic outpatients receiving a wide range of treatments including problem-solving skills training, regulated drinking practice and self-management training, and another receiving only alcohol education and self-management training. The reasons for these negative results are open to speculation. Exercising suitable caution, it is fair to say that three out of five positive results from methodologically acceptable studies far exceeds the performance of alcoholism treatment studies hitherto reported (Emrick, 1975).

Yates' (1979) research, though not properly a controlled trial, produces another negative result which must be taken seriously. There are however two major findings which are of interest. The first, that no difference in type of outcome appeared between groups, might plausibly be explained by the lack of treatment aimed specifically at controlled drinking. In particular the absence of the kind of regulated drinking practice which we found to be common to the three successful outcome studies may be a factor. The second finding, that the majority of clients had at least one three-month period of controlled drinking in the twelve months, suggests on the other hand that they already had the requisite skills for, and practice of, drinking moderately, and that regulated drinking practice, in particular, would have been unnecessary. One possible resolution of these findings is to suggest that unless a client is made aware of the specifics of his drinking habits, and given an opportunity to consciously practise them, he will be unable in times of stress to replace his usual response to stress – i.e. drinking – with a more appropriate one. We are suggesting that such learning might only be useful in times when the client is feeling 'low', and is liable to have recourse to binge-drinking. The times when Yates' subjects were controlling their drinking might well have been times of relatively little stress though this hypothesis must await empirical scrutiny. The residential setting of this programme, where there was relatively little supervision and where a heavy drinking subculture appears to have emerged, also weighs against the success of the controlled drinking treatment and it is highly unlikely that the Sobells' and Vogler's clients were exposed to such an environment. For these reasons the results of this study do not seriously contradict the main conclusions of this review.

To concentrate overmuch on the search for significant differences in controlled studies is to run the risk of ignoring the wider findings of most of these studies with clinic alcoholics, which is that a substantial proportion succeed in controlling their drinking. If we ignore the study whose criteria for controlled drinking were too loose (Mills *et al.*, 1971), and those where the criteria were over-strict (Ewing and Rouse, 1976; Czypionka and Demel, 1976), the remaining ten studies for which there is relevant information show a mean controlled drinking outcome rate of 41 per cent. Of course, given the varying definitions of controlled drinking, and given that subjects in controlled drinking studies may tend to have less serious problems, this figure must be interpreted cautiously, but it does indicate that the rate of spontaneously resumed normal drinking of 5 to 15 per cent suggested above (p. 75) can be increased considerably by treatment. Furthermore, abstinence as an outcome remains fairly common (a mean of 15.3 per cent for thirteen studies), despite the controlled drinking goal. Thus, those who argue that controlled drinking treatments are dangerous because they discourage abstinence are not supported by this evidence. A study by Foy, Rychtarik *et al.* (1979), showing that controlled drinking training which included drinking in an inpatient setting had no effect on subsequent goal choice, lends support to the argument that those who seek abstinence will achieve it even if exposed to controlled drinking treatment. Two studies finding low rates of controlled drinking following treatment (Ewing and Rouse, 1976; Cyzpionka and Demel, 1976) have led their authors to conclude that controlled drinking treatments are ineffective. What they ignored, however, was that substantial proportions of their clients were actually abstinent at the time of follow-up (64 per cent and 20 per cent respectively), again implying that the goal of controlled drinking is no barrier to abstinence. Popham and Schmidt's (1976) conclusion that the effect of a controlled drinking goal is to increase the proportion of controlled drinkers but to leave the total number of successes unchanged is understandable given that they used only traditional group therapy methods in treatment. This present review has suggested that certain treatment methods do increase the likelihood of controlled drinking, with the implication that had Popham and Schmidt used such methods the number of successful outcomes would have increased.

One final point must be raised before ending this survey of studies using clinic alcoholics. Our discussion of the Sobells' work suggested that the significant differences between experimental and control groups at three-year follow-up were entirely attributable to an excess of abstinent days. This is not the case for Vogler *et al.* (1975) or Caddy and Lovibond (1976), the other two studies showing positive results. However, these reported only twelve- and six-month follow-up respectively, and the Sobell's found similar results during the equivalent period of their study. These results suggest that the effects of certain controlled drinking treatments in the first two years are likely to be an increase in the number of days spent controlled drinking as well as in the number of days abstaining but that the long-term effects may well be towards increased abstinence. This is a tentative suggestion only which must await further research.

The conclusions which may be drawn about controlled drinking treatments for clinic alcoholics are as follows:

1. Many seriously dependent alcoholics respond to certain controlled drinking treatments by successfully controlling their drinking.

2. The most effective treatments used so far appear to be problem-solving skills training, regulated drinking practice and self-management training.

3. There is no evidence that the controlled drinking goal is a barrier to successful abstinence.

PROBLEM-DRINKERS

We turn now to studies of a client population who in the main have not been exposed in the past to 'treatment' for alcohol problems and who typically are recruited by the unconventional means of advertisements in the media and compulsory court referrals.

LOVIBOND (1975) recruited 29 male drinking drivers aged between 19 and 66 from the court. Of these, 22 had had one or more previous drinking/driving convictions and they drank the equivalent of about 3.5 pints of beer per day on average. It is not clear whether or not they were under legal compulsion to attend the course, which consisted of eight to ten sessions lasting between two and two and a half hours. A control group matched for age, marital status, occupation, BAC at time of arrest and number of drinking/driving convictions was also selected and remained untreated. Treatment was similar to that given in other work by the author (Lovibond and Caddy, 1970; Caddy and Lovibond, 1976), and consisted of BAC discrimination training, avoidance conditioning, self-monitoring, self-management training and alcohol education.

Follow-up assessments were carried out by interviewers blind as to treatment condition between one and nine months after completion of training. The interviewers' reliability and validity are not reported and no mention is made of corroborative evidence for the self-reports. A 'complete success' was defined as a trainee reporting having exceeded a BAC of 50 mg/100 ml less than once per week, and 'moderately improved' were those who exceeded this at most once or twice per week. Significant differences appeared between training and control groups at follow-up, though this difference was much greater for those clients under 32 years of age. Eleven out of fourteen trainees under 32 were complete successes, as compared with two out of eight controls. Five out of fourteen trainees over the age of 32 were complete successes.

This study is seriously flawed in a number of respects. Firstly, the mean length of follow-up is not given, and could be as little as two or three months. Secondly, the danger of clients 'faking good' is particularly acute here, in view of the fact that they were told that 'a report of training undertaken would be furnished to the magistrate dealing with the case'. It is not clear whether the subjects believed such a report was outstanding at the time of follow-up. Thirdly, no corroborative information about the client's drinking was collected.

Vogler and his colleagues extended their original programmes with alcoholics to deal with problem-drinkers (VOGLER, WEISSBACH, COMPTON AND MARTIN, 1977b). These were referred mainly from courts, usually following drunk-driving offences (73 per cent). Some clients responded to newspaper advertisements, a few were referred by health professionals and the rest came from various other sources. Of 409 referrals, 103 'graduated' from the programme, and 80 of them were followed up. The definition of 'problem-drinking' in this case was 'a current amount and/or pattern of alcohol intake sufficient to produce legal, vocational or marital problems', though how these problems were defined is not made clear. While most clients had incurred several alcohol-related arrests, most of these were for drunk-driving, an offence most certainly not uniquely associated with other alcohol-related problems (e.g. Caddy, 1979). The mean pre-treatment consumption was also quite low, at an equivalent of about 3.5 pints of beer per day. These clients were randomly assigned to one of four groups. Group One received videotape feedback of drunken behaviour, discrimination training, aversive conditioning, assertion training, problem-solving skills training, counselling in the development of non-vocational interests and alcohol education. Group Two received the same, with the videotape feedback and aversion training eliminated. Group Three received only alcohol education, while Group Four received the same as Group Two, with BAC discrimination training eliminated.

Twelve-month outcome data were based mainly on self-report though collaterals were interviewed where inconsistencies appeared in the client's interview. No significant differences appeared between groups. Sixty-six per cent of the clients met the criteria of drinking less than about 16 pints of beer equivalent per week, and of having no more than one drinking episode per month where the BAC concentration exceeded 80 mg/100 ml. To summarize Vogler *et al*.'s findings, significant changes in drinking occurred in all four groups, but no differences emerged between them. This implies that for these problem-drinkers brief assessment and alcohol education were as effective as comprehensive behavioural programmes in reducing alcohol intake.

MILLER (1978), in the first of several studies, recruited clients partly through the media and partly through court referrals. The 32 males and 14 females who remained in treatment had a mean score on the Michigan Alcoholism Screening Test (MAST) of 13.75 which is well above its 'alcoholic' cut-off score of five (Selzer, 1971), though a pre-treatment mean daily consumption of the equivalent of about 3.5 pints of beer approached the 'problem threshold' defined above (p. 207).

A total of 46 clients were randomly allocated to one of three treatments: aversive conditioning alone, self-management training alone and a combination of avoidance conditioning, regulated drinking practice, self-management training and BAC discrimination training. Outcome was measured through self-report, data on record cards, and reports by friends or family and data were collected by interviewers blind as to treatment conditions. Those who were controlling their drinking (defined as not exceeding about 13 pints of beer per week where this report was not contradicted by a collateral) amounted to 50 per cent of those treated. A further 9 per cent abstained, but there were no significant differences in outcome between groups.

In an attempt to evaluate the effectiveness of a self-help manual, 26 of the clients were randomly chosen to be given one of these at the end of treatment. Three months later, this group were drinking significantly less than were the remainder who had not received it.

In order to assess further the effectiveness of this training manual, MILLER, GRIBSOV AND MORTELL (1979) recruited 35 clients through media advertisements, seven of whom dropped out or were not followed up. These eight women and 27 men were on average 40.4 years old and were drinking the equivalent of about five pints of beer on average per day prior to treatment. Following random assignment to two groups, one group received ten half-hour sessions of alcohol education, self-management training and training in the estimation of their BAC from external cues. The second group were simply given the same manual as were the clients in the previous study, which outlined the techniques applied to the first group. In addition they were given drinking record cards, one of which they were asked to send to the therapists each week.

Follow-up data consisted of the drinking records noted on the self-monitoring cards, as well as self-reports and interviews with significant others and if similar procedures to those in their previous studies were used, assessment was carried out blind. Unfortunately, only three months elapsed before the final follow-up, when no significant differences appeared between the two groups on any measure of outcome. However, the mean alcohol consumption had decreased to the equivalent of about two pints of beer per day and 42 per cent were considered as controlled drinkers by the definiton given by Miller in the prevous study. Thirteen per cent were abstainers, but no differences emerged between the groups.

MILLER, TAYLOR AND WEST (1979) combined the designs of the last two studies in comparing bibliotherapy, 'focused' treatment and 'multimodal' treatment. Clients were recruited through media advertisements offering '[treatment] not for alcoholics, but for those experiencing life problems relating to their drinking'. The 21 men and 20 women selected scored on average 17.5 on the Michigan Alcoholism Screening Test, and 37 per cent reported some morning drinking, while the mean history of problem-drinking was 9.5 years. The mean daily pre-treatment consumption rate was the equivalent of four pints of beer per day.

The basic design of this study was that the first group received only a manual, while the second received six sessions of treatment identical to that received by the treatment group in the previous study. Group Three received a 'broad-spectrum' programme which in addition to the treatment received by Group Two, included twelve sessions of relaxation training and social skills training. Group Four's regime was identical to that of the previous group except that the clients could choose three modules out of a 'menu' of ten to fill their twelve extra sessions. These modules included techniques ranging from systematic desensitization to insomnia management.

Follow-up assessment included self-reported drinking, measures of life-goal attainment, liver function tests, *in vivo* breath tests and collateral reports and were carried out by independent blind assessors between six and eight months following the end of treatment. No significant differences emerged on any measures between treatment groups except that Group One reported significantly more hours per week with a BAC exceeding 80 mg/100 ml. However subjects in Group One had reported a mean pre-treatment alcohol consumption of about double that of the other three groups. Significant reductions in consumption were reported for all three groups and 34 per cent were considered to be controlled drinkers. A particularly interesting incidental finding was that there were large differences in the success rates of nine therapists and the correlation between the accurate empathy of the therapists and their client success rate was very high.

A further study by these authors (TAYLOR AND MILLER, 1979) has produced similar results. Fifty-four clients similar to those recruited in the previous study, and who drank on average about five pints of beer daily, were accepted for treatment and were randomly allocated to four programmes. Forty-five began treatment and 41 completed it. The first two groups received identical treatments to those received by Groups One and Two, respectively, in the previous study. Group Three received self-management training, alcohol education, BAC estimation training and relaxation training individually, while Group Four received identical treatment in a group setting. Follow-up and outcome measurement procedure were the same as in the previous studies and no differences emerged between groups.

In another study by Miller and his colleagues MILLER, PECHACEK AND HAMBURG (1979) looked at the effectiveness of an educational programme where media-recruited clients were given ten 90-minute sessions of be-haviourally based self-control training in classroom groups of about ten people. The programme consisted of instruction in the whole gamut of behavioural methods including functional analysis, stimulus control, alter-natives to drinking, relaxation and social skills. The clients were on average 44.8 years of age, were well educated (14.4 years of schooling on average) and the majority were employed. Eighteen were male, and ten were female and the average reported duration of alcohol-related life problems was 8.5 years. The mean score on the Michigan Alcoholism Screening Test was 15.5. The mean pre-treatment consumption of alcohol was equivalent to about four pints of beer per day, and all this information suggests that these clients had mild but significant alcohol problems.

Follow-up information is available only for three months after treatment. Information was collected, as in previous studies by these authors, through interview, drinking-record cards, and reports by collaterals. Classification as 'considerably improved' required there to be a 50 per cent reduction in consumption, uncontradicted by collateral reports and 48 per cent of clients were in this category. However, only 14 per cent were categorized as controlled drinkers according to Miller's (1978) definition though the aver-age consumption had declined to the equivalent of about 2.5 pints of beer per day. While we have no way of knowing whether such an improvement is either clinically significant, long-lasting or attributable to therapeutic efforts, at least Miller *et al*.'s procedure is a fairly cost-effective package which reduces drinking levels considerably.

ALDEN (1980) viewed her intervention with problem-drinkers as a form of secondary prevention and she carried out three separate outcome studies in order to evaluate various types of intervention. (One of these had been reported in preliminary form elsewhere (Alden, 1978).) Most of the candi-dates for such programmes were recruited through the media; their mean age was 42, they had been drinking the equivalent of about 3.5 pints of beer per day. On average they reported having had problems with alcohol on and off for about four or five years. Follow-up results in all three studies were confined to measures of alcohol consumption, with about two-thirds of the clients supplying an informant who was asked about the client's drinking at follow-up. As no mention is made of blind assessment, it must be assumed that this did not take place.

The first study compared behavioural self-management – a wide range of techniques including stimulus control, stress management, rule setting, self-monitoring and instruction on the mechanics of slow drinking – with alcohol education. This consisted mainly of lectures and films concerning alcohol and its social and physical effects. At 15-month follow-up, those in the self-management group had consumed significantly less alcohol than those in the education group, though there were no significant differences in the number of controlled drinking days.

One of the treatments used in the second study consisted of ten sessions of self-management training aimed mainly at teaching appropriate drinking habits, self-monitoring and how to calculate BACs. This was compared with ten sessions which included, in addition to the aforementioned elements, a selection of procedures such as relaxation training, self-instructional training and assertion training. No significant differences emerged between groups at 12- or 24-months follow-up.

The third study compared behavioural self-management with a form of client-centred counselling on the one hand, and with a waiting-list control on the other. No follow-up data is yet available, though at the end of treatment significantly more in the self-management group had not exceeded a BAC of 80 mg/100 ml each week.

The apparent absence of blind follow-up in these studies together with a relative paucity of corroborative support for the self-report data make any conclusions extremely tentative. The major finding from the three studies is that alcohol education is ineffective compared with behavioural self-management counselling as a form of secondary prevention for problem-drinkers.

POMERLEAU, PERTSCHUK, ADKINS AND BRADY (1978) describe their clients as 'middle-income problem drinkers', who were recruited through medical referrals and media advertisements. Their median age was 44, they had 'problems with alcohol' for a median of eight and a half years, and had a median of two previous attempts at therapy. During the week prior to screening, they had drunk on average the equivalent of about five pints of beer per day. From this information it is clear that these clients did have significant problems with alcohol.

Seven out of 46 referrals were screened out because of depression, psychosis or other reasons, and a further seven failed to attend the first appointment after screening. The remaining 32 subjects were randomly assigned to one of two treatments. The first of these was a controlled drinking treatment involving stimulus control training, contingency contracting, regulated drinking practice, and covert conditioning. The second group received traditional insight-oriented group psychotherapy emphasizing group cohesion, confrontation of denial, and the channeling of 'intense emotions . . . into productive, future-directed activity'. A much more important difference between the two groups, however, was that the behavioural group paid a substantial fee in advance, together with a 'commitment fee' which could be earned back by following treatment instructions. In contrast, subjects in the traditional treatment group had only to pay for each session on arriving for that session.

At follow-up there was no significant difference in any outcome measures (self-reports of alcohol intake and liver enzyme tests) between groups. The only difference between them was that 43 per cent of those in the traditional group dropped out during treatment, while only 11 per cent of the behavioural group did so. While the authors attempt to use this fact in support of a controlled drinking goal – 'the effects of traditional therapy were mixed, helping those participants who were receptive, driving out those who were not' – a more parsimonious explanation is that they dropped out because they had much less to lose financially. It is extremely unfortunate that this use of fees so totally confounded the results, especially as the question of whether controlled drinking treatments are more likely to attract problem-drinkers and keep them in treatment is such an important one. Another confusing finding was that the reduction in drinking achieved by those in the traditional treatment group was entirely due to changes which occurred before treatment began, while in the behavioural group changes occurred during treatment. The authors interpret this as demonstrating that the results of traditional treatment were due to 'compliance with initial therapist demands made during the screening period', whereas the results of the behavioural group were somehow 'real' effects of treatment. An equally plausible interpretation would be that the screening interview and its demands were a much more cost-effective way of changing drinking habits than was a complicated behavioural programme. Indeed, there is considerable evidence for such a conclusion from the work of Orford and Edwards (1977).

This potentially valuable study was rendered almost useless by the confusion of treatment content and goal with the financial administration of the programmes. The authors' conclusion that 'behavioural treatment was more successful in several indicators of outcome' is simply not borne out if normal procedures of statistical significance are followed and this study does not help us to decide about the viability of controlled drinking treatments.

The defects of Pomerleau's work are not apparent in the only other study located where clients were randomly assigned to abstinence and controlled drinking goals. SANCHEZ-CRAIG (1980) recruited clients partly from the regular intake of the Addiction Research Foundation in Toronto and partly from newspaper advertisements. Subjects were excluded from the study who showed evidence of physical pathology, who had participated in Alcoholics Anonymous, who believed that alcoholism is a disease and who had more than a ten-year history of problem-drinking. In addition, the selected clients had to be 'naive to treatment for alcoholism' (*sic*), have no self-produced period of abstinence lasting more than six months in the previous two years and had to be able to provide two collaterals willing to report on the client's progress. Finally, the subject had to have maintained a job, a home or a stable relationship.

This highly selected group of clients were predominantly male, with a mean age of about 30 years. They reported about a five-year history of problem-drinking on average, and drank a mean of about the equivalent of eight pints of beer per drinking occasion. Their scores on the Michigan Alcoholism Screening Test averaged out at 19.45 and these facts suggest that the subjects did have significant problems. The 40 suitable subjects were randomly allocated to one of two treatment groups, the sample being reduced to 32 in order to match the groups on relevant intake variables.

The abstinence-goal group received problem-solving skills training, self-monitoring instruction and a form of cognitive therapy. The controlled drinking group received similar treatment but in addition were helped to develop rules and guidelines for moderate drinking, which were reassessed from week to week. Both groups received approximately six individual 90-minute sessions. Subjects kept drinking diaries, and the outcome information is based on their self-reported consumption during the three-week treatment phase. At this stage at least, the controlled drinking group drank approximately one third the amount of alcohol which the abstinence-oriented group drank (an average of about two pints of beer per occasion versus an average of over five pints of beer per occasion). They also drank on significantly fewer days and rarely drank heavily when compared with the abstinence-goal group. While no firm conclusions can be made until follow-up information is available, this study does provide some direct evidence that, for some, the aim of controlled drinking may be more effective than that of abstinence.

Controlled drinking treatments for problem-drinkers: interim conclusions

The literature on the treatment of less serious problem-drinkers is a relatively new one. It must first be asked, what are the problems experienced by the subjects of these studies, if any? Secondly, if the problems are trivial, are any reported drops in the consumption of alcohol in any way meaningful? Inextricably connected with these issues is the problem of cost-effectiveness, and only when these three questions have been resolved can we usefully consider the relative efficacy of different treatments.

Most of the research reviewed in this section provides some baseline information on the pre-treatment quantities drunk by the subjects. A few provide valuable information from the Michigan Alcoholism Screening Test; others provide data about alcohol-related arrests. As we discussed at the beginning of this chapter, there is some data upon which it is possible to base our judgements about the seriousness of various levels of consumption. At least two extensive and rigorous pieces of research have indicated that an average daily consumption of between about 3.5 and four pints of beer equivalent per day significantly increases the chance of alcohol-related problems, in particular morning tremor (Armor *et al.*, 1978; Edwards *et al.*,

1972). In this review therefore, we have taken seriously those studies whose clients drink more than this on average before treatment, assuming that other information regarding seriousness of alcohol problems is not provided. No studies are excluded using this criterion. Clinically significant changes will be defined as those which result in a consumption below this critical level, which is also significantly smaller than the pre-treatment intake.

Two questions regarding the level of problems and meaningfulness of changes in consumption have thus been answered. The third question – that of cost-effectiveness – remains, but this is a very large issue which will be discussed more fully in Chapter 8. Suffice it to point out that Fillmore (1974), on following up college students who had been problem-drinkers in 1953, found that about 33 per cent of them were still problem-drinkers 20 years later. These figures suggest that two-thirds of those treated for problem-drinking will 'grow out' of their problems by middle age. However, if some treatment is effective, presumably the third who remain problem-drinkers would benefit from it. If the treatment is sufficiently brief, then its cost-effectiveness is established; if, on the other hand, intensive and sophisticated intervention is necessary to produce change, the economics of treating a population with such a high spontaneous remission rate must be seriously questioned. Hopefully this review will help answer this question. The relevant studies are listed in Table 6.4 where the methodological ratings are provided as they were for the previous group of individual studies. Controlled drinking rates given in the table are based on authors' definitions which do vary widely.

Of the thirteen studies considered, five report significant differences between treatments. Alden (1980) found in her first study that a comprehensive behavioural programme aimed both at specific drinking habits and more general emotional and behavioural patterns was more effective than was a lecture and film-based alcohol education course. This may have more to do with the ineffectiveness of traditional educational methods than with the superior effectiveness of a comprehensive behavioural programme and Alden's failure to find significant differences between 'simple' and 'enriched' behavioural programmes in her second study lends weight to this argument. Her third study suggested that behavioural counselling was more effective than client-centred counselling, though no follow-up data are yet available. Sanchez-Craig (1980) reports another case of differential treatment effectiveness in a study where the interventions for the two treatment groups differed only in the goal of treatment. Unfortunately, follow-up is as yet unavailable, though the fact that those in the controlled drinking group drank significantly smaller quantities and on significantly fewer occasions during treatment suggests that for problem-drinkers the abstinence goal may be counter-therapeutic. It will be most interesting to see whether these differences are maintained over follow-up. As part of his larger study, Miller (1978) showed that alcohol consumption levels could be reduced considerably by giving clients a self-help manual in addition to behavioural treatment. This suggests that 'bibliotherapy' is in itself an effective element of treatment. Finally, Lovibond (1975) purported to show significant improvements for those in the behavioural treatment group. As we concluded in the discussion of his work, however, this study was so methodologically flawed that no confidence can be placed in this finding.

An analysis of these five studies suggests that the use of a self-help manual, the goal of moderation, and the use of behavioural self-management methods significantly add to the success of interventions with problem-drinkers. However, in neither of Alden's studies which show significant differences is it necessary to propose that intensive behavioural intervention was an essential part of the more effective treatment in order to explain the positive results; indeed, the failure by Miller and his colleagues – as well as by Alden herself – to find any significant differences between minimal behavioural intervention and a number of comprehensive self-management programmes suggests that such a proposition would be erroneous. It seems likely that Alden's first finding can be explained by pointing to the fact that the alcohol education course did not seem to address itself to the individual behaviour of the clients and did not offer them concrete advice relevant to their own personal circumstances. Alden's second significant finding could be explained by the fact that the client-centred counselling technique did not offer the kind of simple and specific advice which would be available for instance in a self-help manual.

Thus the present evidence suggests on balance that the use of a self-help manual, the goal of moderation, and a broadly behavioural orientation significantly add to the success of intervention with problem-drinkers. One example of the simple and brief treatment which seems to be as effective as more comprehensive behavioural programmes comes from Miller, Taylor and West (1979). To recall, they showed that brief assessment, a self-help manual and self-monitoring procedures were as effective as were 15 hours of individual behavioural treatment. However the intensive treatment given by the most empathic therapists produced higher success rates and that by the least empathic, lower rates of success. Such therapist variables have been neglected in the alcoholism treatment literature and this study shows that these are at least as important, if not more important, than treatment variables in determining outcome. Truax and Carkhuff (1967) have shown how central such factors are to effective psychotherapy with neurotic clients, and Harris and Lichenstein (1971) showed that similar variables were important in the treatment of cigarette smokers. Clearly those carrying out alcoholism treatment research must in future pay more attention to this area.

TABLE 6.4
Methodological features and outcome data: problem drinker studies

Authors	length of follow-up (months)	no. of groups	follow-up rates within 10% of each other?	blind assessment?	random assignment?	comparable control groups?	systematic corroborative evidence?	methodological rating (if controlled study)	significant differences reported between groups?	treatment elements peculiar to more successful intervention	Percentage of those who had received controlled drinking treatment, who were followed up, and who had: abstained	Percentage of those who had received controlled drinking treatment, who were followed up, and who had: controlled their drinking [1]
Lovibond (1975)	1–9	2	Yes	Yes	No	No	No	**	Yes	BAC;AC; SM;AE	Gr 1 0 Gr 2 0	57 6
Vogler et al. (1977b)	12	4	Yes	Yes	Yes	Yes	No	*****	No	N/A	0	66
Miller (1978)	12	3	Yes	Yes	Yes	Yes	Yes	********	No	N/A	9	50
Miller [2] (1978)	3	2	Yes	Yes	Yes	Yes	Yes	*****	Yes	Biblio therapy	Gr 1 ? Gr 2 ?	? ?
Miller, Gribsov & Mortell (1979)	3	2	Yes	Yes	Yes	Yes	Yes	*******	No	N/A	13	42
Miller, Taylor & West (1979)	6–8	4	Yes	Yes	Yes	Yes	Yes	********	No	N/A	5	34

TABLE 6.4 *continued*

Taylor & Miller (1979)	12	4	Yes	Yes	Yes	Yes	Yes	******	No	N/A	11	28
Miller, Pechacek & Hamburg (1979)	3	1	N/A	Yes	N/A	Yes	Yes	N/A	N/A	N/A	0	14
Alden (1980) (*a*)	15	2	Yes	?	Yes	Yes	Yes	*****	Yes	SM[3]	Gr 1 ?	?
(*b*)	24	2	Yes	?	Yes	Yes	Yes	******	No	N/A	Gr 2 ?	?
(*c*)	0	3	N/A	?	Yes	Yes	Yes	***	Yes	SM[3]	Gr 1 ? Gr 2 ?	? ?
Pomerleau *et al.* (1978)	12	2	No	No	Yes	Yes	Yes	****	No	N/A	6	66
Sanchez–Craig (1980)	0	2	N/A	No	Yes	Yes	?	**	Yes	Goal of moderation	N/A	N/A

(1) Individual authors' definition.
(2) This was a substudy of the main Miller (1978) study which used the same subjects.
(3) In addition to self-management training, a variety of other methods were used, according to the individual case. These included stress management, relaxation training and several others.

BAC: Blood-alcohol discrimination training
AC: Aversive conditioning
SM: Self-management training
RLX: Relaxation training
CT: Cognitive therapy
SST: Social skills training
AE: Alcohol education

A cautious conclusion from this review of controlled drinking treatments for problem-drinkers is that consumption levels can be significantly reduced from high-risk levels to acceptable levels by quite brief intervention by paraprofessional therapists. Indeed there is evidence that bibliotherapy and self-monitoring may be as effective as more intensive treatments. Whether even such minimal interventions are cost-effective with those clients whose consumption levels are already below the 'high-risk threshold', and whose alcohol problems are non-serious, must remain open to question.

With respect to treatments for problem-drinkers the following tentative conclusions appear justified:

1. Controlled drinking treatments significantly reduce the level of drinking of many problem-drinkers to non-problem levels.

2. Brief interventions are as effective as intensive ones in achieving this.

3. Self-help manuals together with self-monitoring procedures appear to be the least expensive and simplest effective intervention yet devised.

4. Abstinence appears to be an inappropriate treatment goal for most problem-drinkers (as defined p. 172 above). Such clients also rarely abstain following controlled drinking treatment.

SOME ANSWERS

Let us now return to the questions posed at the beginning of the chapter:

1. *Are any controlled drinking treatments effective?* Yes, in so far as they appear to increase rates of controlled drinking. As no study has yet employed a no-treatment control, questions about absolute effectiveness cannot yet be answered.

2. *Are some treatments more effective than others?* In the case of 'clinic alcoholics', problem-solving skills training, self-management training and regulated drinking practice appear to be more effective procedures, though others may also be effective. 'Problem-drinkers' appear to benefit from bibliotherapy and self-monitoring procedures and do not in general require intensive treatment.

3. *Are controlled drinking treatments more effective than abstinence treatments?* We cannot yet answer this question with respect to 'clinic alcoholics' in general, as the Sobells' clients were a selected group. There is some evidence that this is the case for problem-drinkers.

4. *Does the therapeutic goal have any influence on the type of outcome?* Yes. A controlled drinking goal in conjunction with appropriate treatment increases the likelihood of controlled drinking but does not appear to reduce abstinence rates greatly. This is true for both groups of clients. Abstinence as

a goal may actually *hinder* in the short term the reduction in a problem-drinker's alcohol consumption.

Many important questions remain unanswered. It is known that problem-drinkers probably benefit more from a controlled drinking goal, but it is not yet known whether this is the case for more severely dependent 'clinic alcoholics'. Orford and Keddie (1980) in Exeter are tackling this problem currently by randomly allocating such patients to abstinence and controlled drinking treatments. It has been concluded that problem-drinkers benefit as much from certain minimal treatments as from more intensive interventions but whether this is the case for clinic alcoholics is not clear. None of the studies dealing with this population included a minimal intervention – all compared one type of treatment with another. Orford and Keddie (1980) are also looking at this issue by randomly allocating the clients to minimal and intensive treatment, along the lines of the work of Orford and Edwards (1977), and Robertson and Heather (1980a) are also trying to answer this question.

There remain a host of unanswered questions about controlled drinking treatments and in particular the problem of whether certain goals are suited to certain categories of alcoholics or problem-drinkers is crucial. We will attempt to deal with this question in the next chapter.

7   Controlled drinking treatment practice

As a recent survey has shown (Robertson and Heather, 1980b), controlled drinking treatments are widely practised in a large proportion of alcoholism treatment agencies in Britain. In spite of this fact, there is a relative paucity of public debate about how to select clients for, and how to implement, controlled drinking programmes. This is partly because there is relatively little evidence upon which to base selection criteria and partly because of the heated opposition in many quarters to the whole notion of controlled drinking. We intend in the first part of this chapter to try to draw up some tentative guidelines in answer to the question, 'For whom controlled drinking?' and in the second part to discuss some of the issues in implementing treatment regimes which aim at the goal of moderation.

FOR WHOM CONTROLLED DRINKING?

In attempting to answer this question, we will draw on four main areas. The first of these is that research which looks at the characteristics of those clients who *choose* moderate drinking as a goal. The second is a body of evidence showing the characteristics of those who *achieve* moderate harm-free drinking. Thirdly, we will examine critically those *guidelines* for client-selection which have been proposed by various authors. Finally, a number of *hypothetical predictors* which on theoretical grounds might be expected to be related to the type of outcome will be discussed.

Predictors of goal choice

As was argued in Chapter 4, the prospect of total abstinence can be a barrier to change for some alcoholics and may even have detrimental short-term effects on the drinking of some problem-drinkers (Sanchez-Craig, 1980). Nevertheless, when given the choice, a substantial proportion of alcoholics do state that they would prefer to abstain. Pachman, Foy and Erd (1978) showed that in an alcoholism treatment clinic where 'the drinking goal is honoured by the staff to the extent that the patient's physical health permits it', 80 per cent of a group of 61 consecutive admissions chose abstinence while only 20 per cent chose moderate drinking. Those who chose controlled drinking differed from those opting for abstinence in reporting a shorter history of problem-drinking, in having had more education and in being more confident about achieving their goal. Kilpatrick *et al.* (1978) found no differences between the 63 per cent of chronic alcoholic inpatients in one hospital whom they found to favour abstinence and the 37 per cent who favoured controlled drinking, though as no measures of the length of problem-drinking or of confidence about achieving the goals were taken, these findings do not contradict those of Pachman *et al.* (1978). In a study of inmates of young offenders' institutions, Heather (1980) found a tendency for those boys classified as showing physical as opposed to psychological dependence to prefer abstinence rather than controlled drinking as a goal. In another study of hospitalized alcoholics, Cannon, Baker and Ward (1977) found that of 158 inmates who had had four rehabilitation programmes explained to them, one of which was aimed at controlled drinking, 29 per cent showed a preference for the non-abstinent regime. These men appeared to have somewhat more serious drinking problems than those choosing abstinence and showed less family and vocational stability. Foy *et al.* (1979) found that training inpatient alcoholics in controlled drinking methods had no influence on their choice of goal at the end of this treatment and that approximately the same proportion opted for controlled drinking in both abstinence and controlled-drinking groups (15 per cent). No differences emerged between groups on a comprehensive range of behavioural, psychometric and drinking-history measures except that those choosing controlled drinking were younger. As this was only one significant difference among eighteen comparisons, this result may well have been due to chance and the authors' conclusions that younger clients may benefit more from a controlled drinking goal is not justified on the basis of this evidence.

No clear conclusions are possible from this small group of studies on the goal choice of alcoholics. Between 15 and 37 per cent of inpatients state a preference for controlled drinking but no variables consistently differentiate this group from those choosing abstinence. This lack of consistency is perhaps understandable given the variety of ways in which the question, 'Which goal do you want to aim for?' can be asked, and given the number of implications which this can have for the individual, depending upon the setting. For instance, in a social climate where abstinence is overwhelmingly believed to be the only answer for an alcoholic, the client might fear that admitting he would like to control his drinking would be seen as a failure to face up to the problem.

One other possible reason for the fact that these findings are inconclusive may be that the most relevant variables have not been measured. A most important factor in whether an alcoholic feels he can control his drinking is possibly, as Sobell and Sobell (1973) have suggested, the extent to which he can expect family and other social support for such an attempt. Thus Yates (1979) found that significantly more of those alcoholics who answered 'yes' to the question, 'Do you ever feel you could learn to drink in a controlled manner?' had daily contact with their own family as compared with those who answered 'no' to the question. They also had daily or regular contact with their parents more often and were much more likely to be employed. Further research must be devoted to these issues; a preoccupation with objective life-history information and drinking symptoms obscures the fact that behaviour is heavily influenced by immediate environmental contingencies (see Chapter 5) and that such variables as current social support may emerge as being among the most important determinants of controlled drinking.

Predictors of controlled drinking outcomes

It is unfortunate that many authors of the controlled drinking treatment studies reviewed did not attempt to find predictors of outcome type. However, Vogler *et al.* (1977*a*) were able to combine the results of two previous studies (Vogler *et al.*, 1975; Vogler *et al.*, 1977*b*) to collect sufficient numbers of successful abstainers and controlled drinkers for comparison. A discriminant function analysis revealed that controlled drinkers were younger, had a shorter history of drinking problems, had lost fewer days from work in the previous year and had a lower pre-treatment alcohol consumption than abstainers. Popham and Schmidt (1976) also found that successful controlled drinkers were distinguishable from abstainers by a lower pre-treatment alcohol intake.

A notable finding in the Sobell's work (Sobell, 1978*a*) was that the only pre-treatment variable which predicted even a small proportion of the outcome variance was prior hospitalization for alcoholism, in that subjects who had fewer hospitalizations were more likely to engage in controlled drinking. Apart from early post-treatment functioning, assignment to the controlled drinking goal was the best predictor of a controlled drinking outcome. This finding contrasts with Yates' (1979) and Foy *et al.*'s (1979) conclusions that the treatment goal bears little relation to the type of outcome.

Miller and Joyce (1979) collected data from several studies on controlled drinking treatments for problem-drinkers carried out by Miller and his colleagues. Discriminant function analyses were conducted to determine the predictors of abstention versus controlled drinking at three-months follow-up for 141 clients. In comparison to abstainers, controlled drinkers had lower MAST scores, higher incomes and had had slightly more previous help for their drinking. They were also less likely to have had a heavy- or problem-drinking father, were more likely to be females and were less likely to label themselves as alcoholics.

One problem with these findings is that only 8.9 per cent of the subjects actually abstained. This is not surprising given the fact that most subjects were mildly handicapped problem-drinkers, who are, as was established in Chapter 6, less likely to abstain. Therefore, it is not possible to generalize from such a narrowly-defined population to alcoholics attending clinics; it is less clear in the case of this latter group what goal is appropriate and, as was shown in the last section, it is likely that a far larger proportion will opt for the goal of abstinence.

Yates (1979) found no differences between those who mainly controlled their drinking on follow-up and those who mainly abstained, on any pre-treatment or within-treatment measures. The only significant difference between the two groups was that controlled drinkers were in daily contact with their family or parents. Abstinence, bout drinking and continuous drinking were associated with significantly less contact with family, friends and parents. This concurs with Sobell's (1978a) observation that, when his subjects did drink moderately, it tended to take place in their own homes in the presence of other people who by implication were either friends or family members.

One major problem of many of the studies which attempt to find predictors of controlled drinking outcome is that subjects whose drinking is controlled are commonly compared with subjects whose drinking is uncontrolled, rather than with successful abstainers; variables predicting *outcome type* are thus confounded with those predicting *outcome success*. The fact that the predictors of moderate drinking emerging from these studies are those of chronicity, severity and social stability – which also predict outcome success – suggests that the two concepts may indeed be confounded. If Miller and Joyce's (1979) findings are excluded because of the unrepresentativeness of the subjects, only those controlled drinking treatment studies by Yates (1979), Popham and Schmidt (1976), and Vogler *et al.* (1977a) properly examine predictors of outcome type. Thus it becomes necessary to include studies of resumed normal drinking following abstinence treatment in order to search for potential predictors of abstinence versus controlled drinking outcomes. In doing so there is a danger of ignoring the fact that these predictors may not prove to be the same as those which emerge when more extensive controlled drinking treatment studies are carried out; the fact that Sobell and Sobell (1978b) showed allocation to controlled drinking treatment to overshadow all pre-treatment variables in predicting an outcome of successful moderation, must be borne in mind in this context.

Taking those studies reviewed in Chapter 2 which compared predictors of controlled drinking and abstinence outcomes, and including the studies by Yates (1979), Popham and Schmidt (1976) and Vogler *et al.* (1977a), Table 7.1 summarizes the predictors of controlled drinking versus abstinence outcomes which are currently available.

As is clear from the table, only five variables are found to predict controlled drinking in more than one study. These are low severity of drinking symptoms, lower pre-treatment alcohol consumption, regular employment, younger age, and less previous contact with Alcoholics Anonymous. There are contradictory findings for the variables 'previous arrests', 'marriage' and 'pre-treatment consumption'. Each of the other predictors are supported only by single studies.

TABLE 7.1

Predictors of controlled drinking outcomes, as compared with abstinence outcomes, following treatment for alcoholism

	Predictive of a controlled drinking outcome	Predictive of an abstinent outcome
1. Low severity of drinking symptoms	Orford *et al.* (1976) Polich *et al.* (1980)* Smart (1978)	
2. Fewer alcohol-related problems	Smart (1978)	
3. Younger age	Polich *et al.* (1980) Vogler *et al.* (1977a)	
4. Fewer previous arrests	Hyman (1976)	Bromet and Moos (1979)
5. Lower pre-treatment alcohol consumption	Smart (1978) Popham and Schmidt (1976) Vogler *et al.* (1977a)	Bromet and Moos (1979)
6. Married	Hyman (1976)	Polich *et al.* (1980)*
7. In regular employment	Hyman (1976) Polich *et al.* (1980)	
8. Prior abstinence		Anderson and Ray (1977)
9. Presence of post-treatment social support	Yates (1979)	
10. Greater previous contact with Alcoholics Anonymous		Polich *et al.* (1980) Anderson and Ray (1977)
11. Self-label 'alcoholic'		Polich *et al.* (1980)
12. Confidence about abstaining	Orford *et al.* (1976)	
13. Fewer days lost from work in previous year	Vogler *et al.* (1977a)	
14. Shorter history of drinking problem	Vogler *et al.* (1977a)	

* These findings refer to *relapse* following a given type of drinking outcome as opposed to remisson at one point in time. In these cases 'predictive of a controlled drinking outcome' should be read as 'predictive of relatively lower rates of relapse between 18 months and 4 years given this type of outcome'. 'Predictive of an abstinent outcome' should be read similarly.

Polich *et al.*'s (1980) study is of particular importance since it was the only one which looked at outcome stability and relapse. While differential relapse rates must influence differential outcome rates, the two are not synonymous and the former must be regarded as more significant and important pointers to selection criteria for controlled drinking treatment. However, one of the variables isolated by Polich and his colleagues, i.e. marital status, was found in one other study to be predictive of the opposite outcome, namely abstinence; thus for the time being this will be discarded in favour of the three other predictors which are not so contradicted, namely severity of drinking symptoms, employment and age.

Only one other variable both receives support as a predictive factor from more than one study and is not contradicted by another study, namely contact with Alcoholics Anonymous. Thus the following variables have emerged as the strongest predictors of a controlled drinking outcome:

- low severity of drinking symptoms;
- younger age;
- regular employment;
- less contact with AA.

However, two of the studies central to these conclusions included only men in their samples (Polich *et al.*, Orford *et al.*); hence we cannot apply them with confidence to female clients. In the second section of this chapter we will try to integrate these findings into a tentative model for selecting men for controlled drinking programmes.

Existing guidelines

At least three sets of working guidelines for the implementation of controlled drinking treatments have been proposed in recent years. These are by Miller and Caddy (1977), Sobell (1978*b*) and the National Council on Alcoholism (1980) in England and they are summarized in Table 7.2. The variables considered important by the authors fall into four main categories: wishes and attitudes of the client; physical and mental health; drinking history, and social environment. Some of the most important variables within these main groupings are discussed in detail below.

At least two authors have placed the *clients' wishes* high on the list of criteria used for determining a treatment goal (see Table 7.2): too little is known about the effects of ignoring these wishes on the drop-out rates from treatment programmes. If a client steadfastly refuses to consider abstinence, should one offer him help in reducing his intake, even if on every known predictor he is a poor bet for controlling his drinking and further drinking is liable to damage his health? On the other hand, should a young single man with relatively minor alcohol problems who wishes to abstain be helped towards this goal despite the fact that we know that he is much more at risk for relapse than if he moderates his drinking?

Such questions complicate the deceptively simple prescription that a client's wishes should be of prime importance in deciding upon a goal. Where his wishes run contrary to what one would advise on the basis of other factors such as employment status and age, some amount of informed advice and ethical persuasion are indicated. Where such attempts to persuade are

TABLE 7.2

Existing guidelines for controlled drinking treatments

Author	Indicators to controlled drinking	Contra-indicators to controlled drinking
Miller and Caddy (1977)	Patient's refusal to consider abstinence	Evidence of progressive liver disease such that any further use of alcohol could be life-threatening
	Strong external demands to drink (e.g. salesman who must drink with customers)	Evidence of other health problems which might be exacerbated by moderate alcohol use
	Younger patient with apparent 'early stage' problem-drinking (e.g. no history of physiological addiction)	Personal commitment to abstinence
	Prior failure to respond to reputable therapy oriented towards abstinence	Pathological intoxication: uncontrolled or bizarre behaviour following even moderate alcohol use
		Evidence of recent physiological addiction to alcohol
		Use of contra-indicated medication
		Current successful abstinence following a history of severe drinking problems
		Prior failure to respond to reputable therapy oriented towards controlled drinking

unsuccessful, therapists would appear to be justified in helping the client towards his chosen goal.

Perhaps the most obvious health factor which should be considered in relation to goal choice is that of *liver damage*. While biochemical liver function tests are frequently used as indicators of liver damage, they appear

TABLE 7.2 *continued*

Author	Indicators to controlled drinking	Contra-indicators to controlled drinking
Sobell (1978*b*)	Less chronic alcohol problems. Assessment based upon: (*i*) less pre-treatment ethanol intake than the average chronic alcoholic (*ii*) less likely to self-identify as having alcohol problems serious enough to warrant abstinence. (*iii*) available environmental resources to support controlled drinking	
NCA (ENGLAND) (1980)	Client wishes it	Client wishes it
	No evidence of physical dependence	Evidence of physical physical dependence
	No evidence of chronic physical damage	Evidence of chronic physical damage
	No evidence or history of chronically disabling mental illness	Evidence or history of chronically disabling mental illness
	Short duration of maladaptive drinking practices	Long duration of maladaptive practices
	Previous experience of sustained controlled drinking for six months or over	Previous experience of sustained total abstinence for six months or over

to have little value in predicting the extent of histological liver injury (Davis, 1980); liver biopsies appear to be the only accurate way of doing this. Nevertheless Davis recommends that all patients with elevated biochemical liver function test results should receive liver biopsies, with the exception of those who show isolated elevations of the liver enzyme gamma glutamyl transpeptidase. However, liver biopsies are expensive and time-consuming and do not appear to be used routinely in the majority of British Alcoholism Treatment Units for the purposes of screening for controlled drinking treatments (Robertson and Heather, 1980*b*).

Under the category of drinking history come several different but related variables, including the extent to which control or abstinence has been present in the past, prior levels of alcohol consumption, previous treatment experiences, levels of dependence and behaviour while intoxicated.

The extent to which *periods of control and abstinence* are present in the client's drinking history must, on *a priori* grounds alone, be an important issue when deciding upon a drinking goal. Given that previously well-learned behaviours are more readily reacquired than are less well-learned habits (e.g. Skinner, 1953), a client who has successfully abstained for long periods in the past would, depending upon many other factors, be better advised to abstain; the obvious corollary is that those who have exhibited long periods of controlled drinking in the past would be better advised to attempt to control their drinking. Whether a period of six months' abstinence in the past constitutes sufficient grounds for allocation to abstinence treatment (e.g. N.C.A., 1980) must depend upon many other factors, including the reasons for that period of abstinence and, more importantly, the client's own wishes and beliefs. The special case of *current successful abstinence* as a criterion for allocation to abstinence treatment (Miller and Caddy, 1977) also requires some qualification. Firstly, in the experience of the authors, there are some clients who abstain, but maintain that they have no intention of abstaining indefinitely. This can be for a number of reasons, ranging from the demands of parents or others with whom the client may be temporarily living, to the demands of a particular job or examination. For such individuals, some preparation for the time when drinking is likely to resume is indicated. This need *not* require the person to drink in the short term, however. In some cases where conflict exists between, for instance, a client and his parents about whether he should drink or not, some form of discussion with the two parties is called for. Otherwise, this unresolved conflict may well be a considerable source of strain, and may endanger whatever equilibrium has been achieved. It is also possible that a person may have successfully achieved abstinence in a particular environment, but intends returning in the future to a different setting where abstinence will be less easy to sustain. For instance, a seaman on extended shore leave who will be returning to sea, or a salesman temporarily in the office, are in this position. The course of action in these cases must be dependent upon the individual circumstances, and the possibility of preparing the client for controlled drinking in the new setting should not be excluded.

Pre-treatment *level of alcohol consumption* has also been suggested as a guideline for goal selection. Sobell (1978*b*) suggested that clients drinking less than the quantities typical of chronic alcoholics (e.g. see Armor *et al.*, 1978) are suitable for a non-abstinent goal. However, Polich *et al.* (1980) have shown that drinking symptoms such as relief drinking and morning tremor discriminate more readily between controlled drinkers and abstainers than do mean consumption levels, and hence these should be considered as more important factors in goal choice than simple consumption levels.

Such signs of *dependence* or *physiological addiction* (see Miller and Caddy, 1977) have already been discussed earlier in this chapter (see pp. 217–19), and have been shown to discriminate alcoholics who spontaneously resume normal drinking from those who choose to abstain. What must be noted nevertheless, is that in Polich *et al.*'s (1980) four-year follow-up of alcoholics, age and marital status were more powerful predictors of differential relapse rates for abstainers and controlled drinkers than was severity of dependence. Thus while this variable is clearly of great importance in determining goal choice, its importance should not be exaggerated. Furthermore, the fact that in the Rand four-year follow-up severely dependent alcoholics who were under 40 and unmarried tended to have *higher* relapse rates when abstaining, emphasizes that this variable must not be used as the absolute criterion for goal choice. The fact that the subjects in one of the most successful controlled programmes (Sobell and Sobell, 1978*b*) were severely dependent further strengthens this argument.

Similarly, there is also evidence from Polich *et al.*'s (1980) study that those who would exclude clients showing any signs of 'physiological addiction' are not justified in doing so on the basis of existing knowledge. Many of the subjects in this study who were more likely to relapse when abstaining *did* show signs of physical dependence; they *had* experienced morning tremor, relief drinking and a number of other 'symptoms' up to a total of nine times in the month prior to their last drink. Thus to exclude all those showing signs of physical dependence would not only exclude the majority of potential clients, but would also allocate to abstinence treatment many clients for whom this goal may be inappropriate.

Where the clients have *failed to respond to treatment* aimed at a particular goal, Miller and Caddy (1977) advise that treatment aimed at the other goal be attempted. However, where abstinence is advised because of failure in a controlled-drinking programme, the 'competence' of that regime must be ascertained; it is not unknown at some treatment centres for such 'treatment' to consist of no more than advice to 'cut down'. While this may be sufficient for some kinds of clients, it is clearly insufficient for many (see Chapter 6). Care must also be taken when assessing 'failure'; *increases* in problem-drinking shortly after the end of a controlled-drinking programme have been reported in many clients who are ultimately successful in controlling their drinking (Sobell and Sobell, 1978*b*).

The question of to what extent the *social environment* of an alcoholic favours or hinders a particular form of remission is an under-researched area which is of great potential importance. To take an extreme example, a Muslim living in a strongly Muslim environment would face considerable difficulties in attempting to moderate his drinking because of the opposition to any drinking within his culture. Similarly, a socially isolated unmarried alcoholic all of whose acquaintances are heavy drinkers may find extreme difficulty in drinking moderately. However, in most cases it may well be unclear what are the external social demands or, at least, how immutable they are. Where for instance a salesman has to drink with his clients as part of his job, it may not immediately be obvious whether he should try to conform to existing practices by drinking moderately, or try to change the expectations of his clients and not drink. In such cases, careful individual analysis of the demands and of other factors such as age and severity of dependence are necessary before a goal is decided upon. The question of which outcome the family of an alcoholic is likely to support is another complex one which must be carefully analysed at the individual level.

Hypothetical predictors of controlled drinking outcomes

While it has been possible to isolate some predictors of moderate drinking outcomes, it is likely that a large proportion of the outcome variance is as yet unaccounted for (Armor *et al.,* 1978). In this section, some variables are discussed which on theoretical grounds are implicated as possible predictors of outcome type.

Tolerance to alcohol may be an important factor in determining goal choice, but the phenomenon is both complex and inadequately understood (e.g. Gross, 1977; Le Blanc and Cappel, 1975; Kalant, Le Blanc and Gibbins, 1971; Maisto, Henry, Sobell and Sobell, 1978). Until the parameters of these processes involved in tolerance development are more clearly established, it is not possible to set out firm rules and guidelines upon which controlled drinking treatment practice can be based. However, trying to assess patterns of tolerance at the *individual* level may well be an essential component of effective controlled drinking treatment. Although tolerance can be measured in many different biological and psychological functions, it is arguably the individual's *experience* of tolerance effects in relation to the meaning of drinking for him which is the most clinically relevant variable. Even if this is not the case, routine measurement of these other tolerance variables may not yet be practicable, so that one is forced to consider phenomenological aspects. Among the subjective factors which can be considered is the individual's own past experience of tolerance. How much had he to drink in the past in order to enjoy pleasant effects? Did this vary from situation to situation and from mood to mood? If so, which situations or mood states were associated with low or high tolerance? As was mentioned above, tolerance is partly a learned phenomenon, and may emerge in some situations more than in others (e.g. Krasnegor, 1978). However, a subject's expectations may sometimes override any objectively measured tolerance effects, given that the experiences of drug effects are so much dependent upon psychological and social-context variables. Thus, for instance, the alcoholic who undergoes the as yet mysterious 'intrapsychic changes' which so often accompany recovery (e.g. Orford and Edwards, 1977; Armor *et al.*, 1978) may have the whole 'meaning' of drinking change for him such that he now expects that he will enjoy moderate amounts of alcohol despite the fact that he is highly tolerant. Whether such expectations in general override actual psychophysiological tolerance effects remains to be investigated experimentally, though in fact the two phenomena may not be conceptually distinct in some cases. We would suggest that future research on cognitive influences on intoxication should incorporate measures of tolerance so that some of these questions can be answered.

Until more systematic measures of 'subjective tolerance' are developed, it must be assessed less formally. The usefulness of such assessment is illustrated in the following example. An alcoholic reports in an interview that he experiences almost no intoxicating or tranquillizing effects from moderate doses of alcohol. If the individual's main motivation for drinking is anxiolytic, then one would predict that drinking this quantity would not be pleasurable for him and that control would be unlikely. If, on the other hand, the alcoholic reports that he can enjoy three or four pints of beer for reasons such as taste and conviviality, despite the fact that there are no intoxicating effects, one would predict that control would be possible.

As will be discussed later, a period of temporary abstinence before controlled drinking may prove advisable, especially for those severely dependent individuals who are also likely to be highly tolerant. A point which must be carefully considered is the fact that a few drinks are likely to have a much more intoxicating effect than they would have had in the past. The risk here is that this sudden and unexpected intoxication may result in much more severe drunkenness than usual, and perhaps also in uncharacteristic behaviour. It is possible that regulated drinking practice may help to forestall such 'slips' in some cases by making slower drinking more likely; it is when BAC levels rise quickly that blackouts, and hence possibly loss of control, are more likely (Nathan and O'Brien, 1971).

A common thread running through most of these hypothetical processes is the fact that the way in which the effects of alcohol are experienced is complex and idiosyncratic, and that refined individual analysis of these effects is necessary. An example of such work is the study of Litman (1974) of the different ways in which two alcoholics experienced craving. Similar studies of the behavioural, subjective and physiological effects of intoxication are long overdue.

The final topic in this section on hypothetical predictors of outcome type concerns the area of *brain damage* and *cognitive deficit*. These topics will be discussed at some considerable length because they are potentially of crucial importance to the understanding of alcohol problems. At least one study (Gregson and Taylor, 1977) has found cognitive deficit to be a significant predictor of outcome success and, given the low amount of outcome variance which is explained by the variables currently measured (Armor *et al.*, 1978), such findings warrant close scrutiny. Given also the relative complexity of the controlled drinking goal as compared with the abstinence goal, there is further reason to consider cognitive deficit and brain damage as potentially highly relevant to this area.

Recent findings have shown the existence of psychological deficits and cerebral atrophy in a much higher proportion of alcoholics than was previously assumed (e.g. Eckardt *et al.*, 1978; Guthrie *et al.*, 1979; Lishman, Ron and Acker, 1979). While these findings are of great importance for anyone trying to change the behaviour of alcoholics, there is a danger of drawing unjustified conclusions about the implications of these deficits for behaviour change, especially with reference to the question of which alcoholics could potentially control their drinking. The evidence must be considered critically with particular reference to the questions of what is the nature of such deficits, who is most likely to suffer from them and to what extent, and under which circumstances are they reversible.

If alcohol-related psychological deficits are in the form of a diffuse, non-specific reduction in intellectual abilities, then there is little cause to suggest that this should have any serious influence on outcome, as general intelligence has not emerged as an important determinant of outcome (e.g. Gibbs and Flanagan, 1977). One of the most recent studies (Lishman *et al.*, 1979) suggests that the damage is indeed non-specific, though Tarter (1975), in an extensive review of many studies of alcohol-related psychological deficit, concluded that there is no evidence for generalized cerebral deficit. The most promising hypothesis arising from his review was that the deficit is to a large extent caused by disruption of the frontal-limbic-diencephalic system and evidence from neuroanatomical, neurological and behavioural studies was cited to support this view. The evidence is not, however, conclusive. For instance, Lishman *et al.* (1979) found that alcoholics did not show a significantly greater number of perseverations on the card sorting test; and perseveration is one of the major features of the frontal lobe syndrome (Walsh, 1978). However, more studies support the existence of some form of frontal deficit than refute it and we must return later to discuss the implications of this evidence for treatment goal choice.

Who is most susceptible to such alcohol-related damage? There is some evidence that some forms of deficit are related to quite low levels of consumption. Parker and Noble (1977) found significant negative correlations between the average amount of alcohol consumed on one occasion and performance on some tests of non-verbal reasoning. Even among a subgroup of non-heavy drinkers consuming on average less than the equivalent of one and a half pints of beer per drinking occasion, there were significant negative correlations between this index of consumption and non-verbal abstraction abilities. No relationship was found between lifetime consumption of alcohol and cognitive performance after the effects of age had been controlled for, suggesting no strong cumulative effect of drinking. In a later study (Parker and Noble, 1980) regression analyses revealed significant relationships between consumption per occasion and non-preservative errors on the Wisconsin Card Sorting Test for men over the age of 42 but not for younger men.

While these findings are disturbing, there is no reason to suggest that the 'deficits' associated with moderate drinking are such as to interfere with the normal regulatory processes of behaviour. No frontal lobe deficits were apparent and the effects were related to current consumption alone – suggesting that they are not permanent. Given also that subjects had refrained from drinking only during the previous 24 hours, the differences may be related to the short-term toxic effects of the drug.

Parker and Noble's (1980) finding that older men's performance on one test was related to consumption, while younger men's was not, does fit in with evidence of the importance of age from other studies. In a study of male alcoholics in their mid-thirties, Grant, Adams and Reed (1979) found no differences in cognitive performance between alcoholics who had been abstinent for three weeks, a group who had abstained for six months, and a group of normal minimal drinkers, on several tests including the Halstead-Reitan battery and the Wechsler Adult Intelligence Scale. This runs so completely counter to the bulk of the evidence (Tarter, 1975) that one must look to the comparatively low mean age of the alcoholics (37) to explain this negative finding. However, deficits have been demonstrated in younger men (Lishman, Ron and Acker, 1979) though clear differences in the response to short-term abstinence did emerge in this study between alcoholics over the age of 43 and those younger than this. Finally, Eckardt *et al.* (1978) carried out one of many studies (Tarter, 1975) showing a relationship between cognitive deficit and the number of years of alcoholismic drinking. Eckardt *et al.* found that more than 15 years of such excessive drinking predicted deficits on a number of cognitive and psychomotor tests. Given that most alcoholics who have drunk excessively for that length of time will be relatively old, it may be that it is age as well as the amount consumed which is an important variable. Some support for this hypothesis comes from Wilkinson and Carlen (1980) who found no relationship between reported duration of heavy drinking and degree of cerebral atrophy measured by computerized tomography, but who did find a relationship between age and atrophy. However a contradictory finding does come from Guthrie and Elliot (1980) who found no relationship between age and memory impairment, and in all of these correlational studies there is the possibility that older subjects drink more *because* of their cognitive deficits as opposed to the deficits arising as a result of drinking.

To return to the question of who is most susceptible to alcohol-related cognitive deficits, the evidence suggests that older people may be more vulnerable. The figure of 40 ± 3 crops up in a number of studies as the period at which this vulnerability may increase. It is interesting that Polich *et al.* (1980) also come up with a figure in this range as the age above which a stable controlled drinking outcome becomes less likely; further research is necessary to determine whether the two phenomena are causally related.

Although at least one study suggests that malnutrition may lead to an increased susceptibility to alcohol-related cognitive deficit (Guthrie and Elliot, 1980), apart from age, there appears to be no way of predicting who is more likely to suffer such problems apart from by carrying out a neuro-psychological assessment. Furthermore, if the results are to have valid clinical and behavioural implications, then tests of frontal-lobe deficit should be included.

The third major question in this area is to what extent and under which circumstances the deficits are reversible. Talland (1965) showed that even one of the most severe forms of alcohol-related brain damage, Korsakoff's psychosis, could be ameliorated by up to two years' abstinence. Where 'normal' alcoholics are concerned, several studies have shown improvement up to two years after initial testing (e.g. McLachland and Levinson, 1974; Clarke and Haughton, 1975; White, 1965) though some have found no significant long-term improvement in abstainers as compared with drinkers (e.g. O'Leary *et al.*, 1977; Page and Schaub, 1977) and others have found only partial improvement (e.g. Guthrie and Elliot, 1980; Lishman *et al.*, 1979). One problem with studies which compare abstainers and those who have continued to drink excessively on follow-up is that the drinkers will in many cases be suffering from the short-term toxic effects of alcohol unless they have been hospitalized prior to follow-up testing. This bias would tend to exaggerate the apparent recovery rates of the abstainers. Whether or not abstention, as opposed to moderate drinking, is necessary for recovery is also an unresolved problem. In one study, Guthrie and Elliot (1980) found that partial recovery was apparent in both abstainers and those considered 'improved', while in another study (Guthrie *et al.*, 1979) only the abstainers showed some recovery. However, these results must be treated with extreme caution given that in the former study only 38 per cent of the group were re-tested and in the latter only 6 per cent of the total group were tested on all three occasions! Given the larger sample in the former group, we can have slightly more confidence in the finding that recovery is equally possible following moderate drinking as following abstinence. However the whole question of reversibility remains, for the time being, an open one.

What are the implications of the above findings for behaviour change in general and goal choice in particular? Firstly, fairly rapid recovery of some psychological deficit between three weeks' abstinence (e.g. Page and Schaub, 1977) and six weeks' abstinence (e.g. Clarke and Haughton, 1975), appears likely. Subsequent improvements are slower and some studies have found no such recovery. Such short-term improvements may be due to the waning of the immediate toxic effects of alcohol. Although only a small minority of alcoholics never drink following treatment (e.g. Polich *et al.*, 1980), a large proportion succeed in abstaining for the first few weeks (e.g. Hunt, Barnett and Branch, 1971) and it would seem advisable to ask alcoholics to abstain for a period of three to six weeks to allow at least partial recovery of cognitive deficit, irrespective of which treatment goal they are allocated.

The question of long-term deficit and its implication for a choice of treatment goal is less easy to answer. It seems likely that at least some of the deficit in some alcoholics is attributable to frontal lobe damage. For those individuals for whom this is the case, abstinence may be the optimal goal under some circumstances. The reasons for this lie in the nature of the frontal lobe syndrome, the characteristics of which include perseveration (e.g. Nichols and Hunt, 1940), difficulty in planning and regulating behaviour (e.g. Luria, 1973) and a difficulty in utilizing errors to modify subsequent behaviour (e.g. Konour and Pribram, 1970). This last problem is particularly important, especially in the light of the fact that these individuals can often recognize that they have made an error, but find it difficult to use this error to correct their behaviour (e.g. Luria and Homskaya, 1964). Thus one of the key features of the frontal lobe syndrome is the difficulty in regulating behaviour and in translating intention into action. In the light of this fact, it is possible that at least some of the apparently untrustworthy behaviour of alcoholics may be due to cerebral damage.

What implication does this finding have for goal choice? Given that the major difficulty for those who have suffered frontal damage is in carrying out planned action, it follows that they are likely to have more difficulty with complex plans than with simple ones. The plan 'I will never drink' is clearly a simpler one than the plan 'I will only drink so much under certain circumstances', and the former would appear to be the preferable option for those alcoholics suffering from this syndrome.

Having argued that frontally-damaged alcoholics should be directed towards abstinence, a number of practical difficulties emerge. Firstly, how does one identify this group? There appears to be no way of doing this other than by psychometric testing, as even the physical brain changes identified by head scanners do not correspond well with changes in function identified by psychometric testing (e.g. Lishman *et al.*, 1979; Wilkinson and Carlen, 1980). Although high proportions of alcoholics show *some* cognitive deficit, there is as yet no evidence about what proportion suffer from clinically significant frontal damage or about the drinking, nutritional or demographic characteristics of those who are handicapped in this way. A second problem is that frontally damaged clients will have almost as much difficulty in carrying out an intention to abstain as an intention to moderate their drinking. Hence, perhaps, the finding that intact cognitive functioning was an important predictor of abstinent outcome in one study of chronic alcoholics (Gregson and Taylor, 1977). It may be the case that the wishes and beliefs of the client together with the quality and availability of close social support in some circumstances outweigh cognitive variables in determining goal choice. Thus for instance, an alcoholic who has some frontal damage, who does not wish to stop drinking but who is willing to confine his drinking to when he is with his wife and who has been shown in the past seldom to drink excessively in his wife's company, might be helped towards his preferred goal of moderation.

In conclusion, the answers to the first question posed at the beginning of this discussion, namely, 'what is the nature of alcohol-related deficits', are that among more chronic alcoholics they tend to be frontal-lobe deficits, while among social drinkers and less chronic alcoholics they appear to be in the form mainly of deficits in non-verbal memory and non-verbal reasoning. In answer to the question, who is most susceptible to such deficits, it appears that those over the age of about forty, those suffering from malnutrition and those who drink relatively large amounts are most vulnerable. Finally, with respect to the question of reversibility, the evidence is so meagre that firm conclusions are impossible. Indirect evidence does suggest however that the damage is less likely to be cumulative and permanent in those under the age of forty. This fact lends support to the use of age as a criterion for selection for controlled drinking programmes. Selection on the basis of cognitive deficit would appear only to be justified where measures of frontal-lobe damage are included.

THE IMPLEMENTATION OF CONTROLLED DRINKING PROGRAMMES: TENTATIVE GUIDELINES

The logical progression from determining the characteristics of those who successfully control their drinking is to recommend some form of selection procedure. In this section the intention is to re-introduce some of the conclusions from the first part of the chapter into an outline of the issues and difficulties involved in operating treatments aimed at moderation; the problem of selection is only part of this. In making even highly tentative recommendations, there is a danger of stepping beyond what is justified on the basis of the existing evidence. Nevertheless, controlled drinking treatment is now sufficiently widespread that the need for some detailed working guidelines is indicated. In the following section, the issue of the client's wishes and beliefs with respect to drinking goals is considered, as well as those of significant others in his life. These are considered first because understanding, persuasion and behaviour change are likely to be difficult to achieve if the attitudes and wishes of the alcoholic and his family are not carefully considered. This is followed by a brief discussion of possible medical complications in view of the potential life-threatening consequences of moderate drinking under certain circumstances. Only after these two important issues have been discussed, is the question of selection on the basis of other variables considered. Secondly, some practical problems about implementing moderation-oriented treatments are considered: setting limits; dealing with relapse; reduced drinking in spite of harm; scepticism among family and friends; selection of treatment methods and the use of regulated drinking practice.

Issues in selection

The most immediate and important question which should arise in relation to the choice of treatment goal is, what are the client's *wishes, beliefs and attitudes* about this. It was shown at the beginning of this chapter that between 15 and 37 per cent of clinic alcoholics state a preference for a non-abstinent goal when asked to choose, though it was noted that these figures are likely to be influenced by the clients' perceptions of what the questioner believes. In many alcoholism clinics where an abstinence ideology prevails, clients may well expect disapproval if they state a wish for controlled drinking. It is also the case that such rates may vary widely from population to population and there are clear grounds for believing that problem-drinkers would opt mainly for controlled drinking. Knowing the high drop-out rate from alcoholism treatment programmes (e.g. Baekland and Lundwall, 1977) and assuming that drop-outs are more likely where a client's wishes and expectations are not fulfilled (see Parker *et al.*, 1979*a, b*), one must consider these to be of primary importance when considering which treatment goal is appropriate. Where these wishes conflict with what the therapist considers on the basis of the available evidence to be appropriate, it is up to him to present the evidence and attempt to persuade the client. Where this fails to change the client's mind, it may be necessary to conform to his or her wishes. In so doing the therapist might retain at least some influence over the client's behaviour.

There are some cases where the wishes and beliefs of an alcoholic are incompatible. For instance, a particular individual may on the one hand accept the tenets of Alcoholics Anonymous, yet on the other hand wish to control his drinking. In this case the therapist must attempt to help the client to change either his wishes or his beliefs in order to render them compatible. Another example of such incompatibility is the case of an individual who believes drinking alcohol to be sinful yet wishes to drink moderately; in this case some attempt must be made by the therapist to produce consistency in his beliefs before consideration of an appropriate goal. Where the client is unsure about what he should do, consultation with those closest to him may help him decide. If he and his close family and friends are presented with the evidence for which goal is most appropriate for him, he may be helped to come to a decision.

An extremely important question in relation to the client's expressed wishes and beliefs is the extent to which he is showing *denial* of the nature of his problems. The role of denial in the maintenance of alcohol problems and the importance of tackling denial in therapy have occupied a prominent position within traditional conceptions of alcoholism and its treatment (e.g. Moore and Murphy, 1961; McCarthy, 1956). However, recent work has suggested that denial is less common among alcoholics than has been generally assumed and that its importance has been exaggerated; Polich *et al.* (1980) found that alcoholics who were drinking excessively and harmfully did not differ substantially from abstainers in acknowledging that they were alcoholics and that drinking in the future would be damaging to them. Furthermore, Kilpatrick *et al.* (1978) found no significant difference between the proportions of those seeking controlled drinking treatment who denied that they had difficulty in controlling their drinking and the proportion of those seeking abstinence who denied this. Thus denial does not appear to be any more of a problem where controlled drinking is concerned than it is where abstinence is the goal.

The *wishes and attitudes of significant others* are also of paramount importance, and should be taken into account even where the client is quite sure which goal he wishes to attain; it is possible that when he hears the opinions and feelings of those closest to him that his wishes might change. Where for instance a husband is sceptical about his wife's intention to moderate her drinking, consideration of predictive variables such as problem severity and age would enable the therapist to decide how to advise the client.

Medical problems can also have considerable bearing upon the choice of goal. It is incumbent upon the medical practitioner responsible for a given client to decide whether the presence of such problems as liver damage, pancreatitis or brain damage makes even moderate drinking damaging to the person's physical health. However, as was noted earlier in this chapter, the criteria upon which to base such decisions are, in the main, not well-defined as yet. Furthermore, in many cases clients choose to ignore recommendations to abstain even when warned that they are endangering their health. Nevertheless where there are clear medical grounds for recommending abstinence, the case must be put forcefully and persuasively to the client.

Where there is some suggestion of physical damage, but where it is not apparent that lifelong abstinence is essential in order to prevent further deterioration, a period of temporary abstinence might be advised. What evidence there is suggests that there is a considerable improvement in cognitive function following approximately three to six weeks' abstinence (pp. 229–30 above), though full recovery may take considerably longer. Given also that a substantial proportion of alcoholics do manage to abstain for periods of a few weeks (e.g. Hunt, Barnett and Branch, 1971), temporary abstinence would appear to be both medically desirable and potentially achievable for a substantial proportion of alcoholics. While further research into the optimum period is vital, one medical authority recommends a period of three months (Thorley, 1980), and this may be a useful working target until further evidence is available. An additional advantage of such a period of temporary abstinence would be to help break existing drinking patterns and habits.

With less serious problem-drinkers, it may be advisable to reduce the period of recommended abstinence as it is well known that such clients abstain much less commonly (e.g. Miller and Joyce, 1979). Furthermore, Sanchez-Craig's (1980) work has suggested that the injunction to abstain may reduce short-term drinking far less than the injunction to drink moderately, though it is not clear whether this would also be the case where clients were being advised to abstain temporarily.

Following assessment of the client's wishes, beliefs and medical status, other relevant variables may be considered. Earlier in the chapter the variables of drinking symptom severity, age, employment and contact with AA were isolated as being important predictors of drinking outcome in men. Other variables such as social support and drinking history were predictive, but were supported by less evidence. Taking these four major variables in conjunction with the issues of client choice and medical problems, which have just been discussed, some form of provisional and tentative selection guidelines can be extracted. Prior contact with AA can be considered along with the client's wishes and attitudes, as confusion and conflict is likely if someone with strong AA connections is allocated to a controlled drinking goal. Medical screening may result in some clients agreeing that they should attempt to abstain, but those who continue to wish to moderate their drinking in spite of medical advice to the contrary may be, with the agreement of the physician, helped to achieve their goal. Figure 7.1 illustrates a *tentative* decision-tree for those men who, following assessment of their own wishes and beliefs, the wishes and beliefs of their families, and following informed medical advice about further drinking in relation to their physical health, still wish to control their drinking. What must again be emphasized however is that these are hints rather than inflexible rules. The variables in the diagram account for only a small proportion of the outcome variance (Polich *et al.*, 1980); when more of the variance is accounted for, a completely different set of predictors may emerge.

As can be seen in Figure 7.1, a period of abstinence between two weeks and three months is suggested. The time is variable because it must be adjusted to the individual case; where for instance the client agrees to abstain for a certain period but not for longer, to press for a full three months' abstinence might well result in his dropping out. Following an agreed period of abstinence, the client may be asked to reassess his goal choice, especially if he has successfully abstained for the full three months. It is possible that in some such cases the client will choose to remain abstinent and should be encouraged to do so.

Those clients who continue to wish to drink moderately can then be divided into those suffering low to moderate drinking symptoms and those suffering severe drinking symptoms. Among the symptoms which can be included in this assessment are frequency and intensity of withdrawal tremor, morning or relief drinking, morning craving and experience of impaired control over consumption (e.g. Edwards, 1977). Frequency of missed meals, amnesias and extended drinking bouts may also be included (e.g. Polich *et al.*, 1980). Like most dividing lines, the one for allocating clients to controlled drinking on the basis of their drinking symptoms is an essentially arbitrary one. The best that can be said is that those clients who have experienced the above symptoms only to a moderate degree or relatively infrequently, are best suited to a controlled drinking goal.

At the next level on the decision-tree in Figure 7.1 is age. The age of forty is chosen because Polich *et al.* (1980) found that men over forty were more likely to relapse when controlling their drinking. Further support for using this cut-off point comes from the evidence showing that drinkers over forty seem more susceptible to alcohol-related cognitive deficits than those under forty (see pp. 227–8 above). The final selection criterion is that of employment, which requires no further elaboration.

These three variables can be combined to form the decision tree. The two main decision alternatives are minimal or more-than-minimal intervention aimed at moderation. Minimal intervention might consist of assessment, advice, self-monitoring procedures and a self-help manual as used by Miller and his colleagues (see p. 201–4). It is only the group which is favoured for controlled drinking on *all three* of the major variables which is recommended for minimal intervention. All groups who are at risk on one of the variables (age, symptoms and employment) are allocated to more than

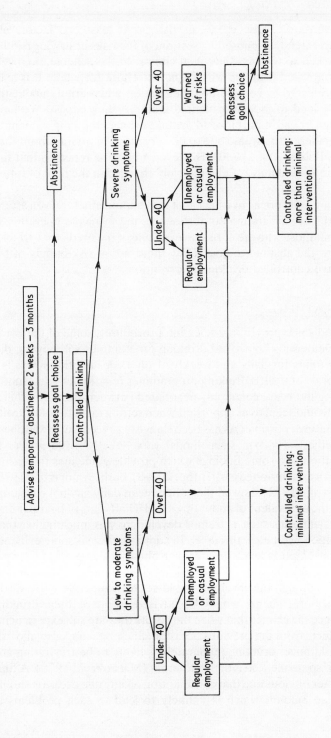

FIGURE 7.1
A tentative decision tree for those male clients wishing to control their drinking

minimal intervention. Those clients at risk on at least two factors are reminded, in an extended counselling session, of the risks in striving for this goal and are asked to reassess their goal choice. In this scheme, no one is rejected for controlled drinking who wishes it. Those for whom it is least suitable are subjected to considerable persuasion and warning about the risks but are helped to moderate their drinking if they persist. We have chosen to assign equal importance to symptoms, age and employment as there is little evidence to assume one to be very much more important than the other (e.g. Polich, *et al.*, 1980). However it must be repeated that this chart is provisional and may well be radically changed in the light of future research.

For those clients unsure as to which goal they should aim for, even after a period of abstinence or attempted abstinence, the principle operating in Figure 7.2 is that those who are at risk on even one of the predictor variables are allocated to the abstinence goal. Only those not at risk on any of the variables receive controlled drinking intervention.

ISSUES IN TREATMENT

Having outlined some provisional selection procedures, some of the issues related to implementing controlled drinking programmes will now be discussed. *Setting limits* for daily and weekly alcohol consumption levels is a feature of several controlled drinking programmes (e.g. Miller and Munoz, 1976). Drinking limits are commonly negotiated between client and therapist, though it would seem to us important when setting them to consult with close family wherever possible. As has been shown in a recent survey (Robertson and Heather, 1980*b*), such limits vary greatly from place to place, though there are some findings which provide guidelines for setting these limits. As was mentioned earlier (pp. 207–8), both Armor *et al.* (1978) and Edwards *et al.* (1972) showed that when mean daily alcohol consumption exceeded the equivalent of about three and a half pints of beer per day, the chance of symptoms such as tremor developing was much higher than when consumption was below this level. In addition, there is some evidence that alcohol consumption levels greater than about fifteen pints of beer per week result in a significantly raised risk of liver damage (Schmidt and Popham, 1975), though this level may be lower for women (e.g. Edwards, 1977). Furthermore, clients would be advised to space their drinking sessions to reduce the chance that when they drink they are still experiencing withdrawal effects from the previous occasion. Such 'spacing' also allows a reduction in tolerance; drinking moderately is likely to be frustrating and unsatisfying for someone who is highly tolerant (Maisto *et al.*, 1978). A final point is the rather obvious one that consumption on any one occasion should be limited to an amount which is unlikely to lead to such problems as

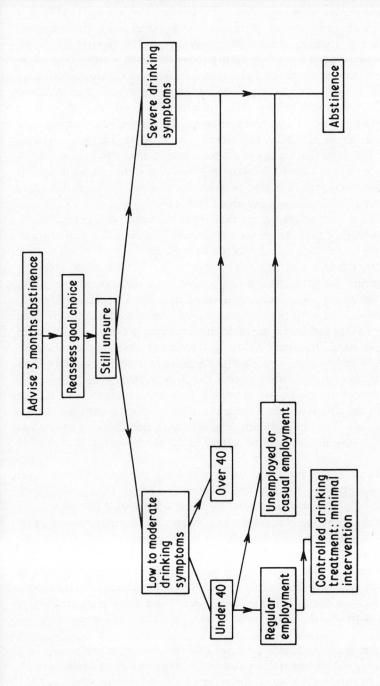

FIGURE 7.2

A tentative decision tree for those male clients unsure of which goal they wish to achieve

blackouts, hangovers or aggressive behaviour. As Gross (1977) has suggested that qualitatively different biochemical and psychological phenomena are apparent at BAC levels over about 200 mg/100 ml, clients should be discouraged from ever approaching this level – indeed far lower limits should preferably be set. For a man weighing twelve stones, drinking over a three-hour period, the absolute maximum he should drink to avoid reaching this maximum level is the equivalent of about six pints of beer (Miller and Munoz, 1976). Daily maximums may also be negotiated on the basis of whether or not the client experiences a threshold, i.e. a quantity drunk which if exceeded results in an experienced difficulty in stopping. A certain proportion of alcoholics report that they experience such a threshold which is commonly reported to be between the equivalent of three and five pints of beer (Robertson and Heather, 1980*a*).

How to deal with *relapse* is another important issue in operating controlled drinking regimes. There is a temptation to change the goal of treatment when a client fails to keep to the negotiated limits or practices, yet evidence from Sobell and Sobell (1978*b*) shows that bouts of excessive drinking during the first year after treatment were common among those who were ultimately successful in controlling their drinking. Hyman (1976) also showed that many of those who eventually became moderate drinkers did so after having suffered some additional drinking problems shortly after abstinence-oriented treatment. Thus it is probably advisable to 'ride out' such lapses without changing the goal of treatment unless it becomes clear that they are becoming chronic or that the client is beginning to express a desire to abstain. It may be useful to help clients to anticipate such lapses; encouraging the clients to regard them as learning experiences rather than as failures may also be helpful. In this way, the controlled-drinking equivalent of Marlatt's 'abstinence-violation effect' may be mitigated (see p. 138 above).

Some clients reject both abstinence *and* truly moderate drinking, yet continue to seek help. Should they be helped to achieve their own goals, even if these are, in the opinion of the therapist, unrealistic? The question of *reduced drinking* in spite of actual or potential harm is a difficult one. Clearly the therapist, physician, the client's family and the client must come to some decision about this. What must be borne in mind when coming to this decision is the fact that the majority of alcoholics do continue to drink at times in a harmful way and for therapists to reject from treatment those who do so may be unrealistic (cf. Pattison, 1976*a; b; c*). At least when the client is in contact with the therapist there is some possibility of influencing his behaviour.

The problem of *scepticism, criticism and mistrust* by other people in a client's life is another important issue. For instance wives can, quite understandably, be extremely worried when their husband returns home with the smell of alcohol on his breath. One way of minimising this potential strain is to negotiate drinking rules (see Chapter 5) with the client and his wife which make it easier for her to know how much and how often he is drinking. This may be done by agreeing with the client that he only drinks with his wife, or perhaps with another close friend or family member whom the wife trusts and who can be assured of telling her if her husband exceeds the negotiated limits.

The question of which *treatment methods* should be used is one which cuts across the problems of limit-setting, relapses and other issues. While it was concluded in Chapter 6 that problem-solving skills training, self-management training and regulated drinking practice apparently 'added' to the effectiveness of treatment programmes, it was impossible to conclude that other forms of treatment could not also be effective. Nevertheless, evidence from a number of sources suggests that *directive* forms of therapy are more appropriate for alcoholics (e.g. Gerard and Saenger, 1966; Costello, 1975). Furthermore, Davies (1980) has found that alcoholics attending clinics tend to expect that they be given advice rather than that they be counselled in traditional non-directive or psychotherapeutic ways, and Obitz (1975) showed that alcoholics showed a preference for directive over non-directive counselling. Furthermore, given that the focus of most controlled drinking treatments is, implicitly or explicitly, to have the alcoholic develop rules governing his drinking behaviour, it would appear that directive approaches are, on *a priori* grounds, more likely to achieve this than more circuitous non-directive methods.

This is not to say that psychotherapeutic methods are irrelevant to alcohol problems; clearly they are appropriate under certain circumstances. What appears to be the case is that at least some of the therapeutic time should be spent in giving advice and direction to the client. The use of printed material appears to be a highly useful adjunct to this part of the counselling (Miller, 1978). For those individuals with relatively minor problems, such as those typically seen in the 'problem drinker' studies reviewed in Chapter 6, brief advice, a manual and self-monitoring procedures would appear to be all that is necessary. Indeed there is a possibility that more intensive intervention could be counter-productive, either through 'labelling' the person as sick (e.g. Roman and Trice, 1968) or by exposing him to unnecessary therapy with an unempathic therapist whose clients actually may fare *worse* than those who receive only minimal treatment (e.g. Miller, Taylor and West, 1980).

Individuals with more serious problems are likely to require help in a variety of areas, and psychotherapeutic methods may be appropriate for some of these, and behavioural methods for others. With respect to alcohol consumption however, there is as yet no evidence that insight into dynamic reasons for drinking is a useful goal to strive for; less time-consuming and less esoteric approaches to drinking have been shown to be at least as effective, and possibly more effective, in changing drinking patterns. Problem-solving skills training and self-management training both deal with current everyday problems, and not with childhood conflicts and neuroses, this is possibly one reason why they have emerged as among the more effective forms of treatment.

Whether or not *regulated drinking practice* should be carried out should depend upon the individual circumstances of the client. Normally a client will be encouraged to drink with a safe person such as a particular family member, who may well, formally or informally, teach the client to drink moderately and appropriately. Where such support is unavailable or where the client finds difficulty in reducing his drinking under these circumstances, it may be necessary for the therapist to accompany the client when he drinks. Such 'coaching' is probably best done in as natural an environment as possible – preferably in the pub, club or house where the client intends to do most of his drinking. This will make generalization of these habits to outside of the therapeutic situation more likely.

What must always be borne in mind is that moderate drinking is not an end, rather it is a means to the end of a more satisfying and happy life for the client and his family. Gerard and Saenger (1966), Polich *et al.* (1980) and many others have shown that an improvement in drinking does not necessarily produce an improvement in adjustment and therapists must take care that they do not lose sight of this fact.

SUMMARY

The main question posed in this chapter is 'for whom controlled drinking?' In answer it is suggested that the wish to aim for moderation (present among 15% to 37% of alcoholic inpatients according to the available evidence) should constitute sufficient grounds for such a treatment except where contra-indicated by the presence of liver disease or other serious physical problems. However, advice should be given as to the appropriateness of goal choice by considering a number of variables. Unfortunately these criteria have been established with a population of mainly male alcoholics, and the characteristics favouring an aim of moderation among men are: low to moderate severity of drinking symptoms; younger age; regular employment and low frequency of contact with Alcoholics Anonymous. Clients with no strong goal preference should be allocated according to these criteria. While emphasizing that future research may throw up other important and relevant variables (e.g. cognitive deficits), tentative guidelines for the implementation of controlled drinking programmes are put forward.

8 Implications

In this final chapter we shall attempt to draw together and discuss the outstanding implications of the contents of this book for theory and practice in the field of alcoholism and alcohol abuse. The most immediate implications clearly have to do with such issues as the need for a greater flexibility in the response to alcoholism and the place of controlled drinking methods in the range of services available to the alcoholic. And we must not forget also the important implications for the prevention of alcohol abuse and for health education. Firstly, however, we shall consider the more theoretical implications of the evidence reviewed earlier in the book, especially in Chapters 2 and 3. These are of at least equal importance as the more practical issues to be dealt with later. Quite apart from the introduction of specific treatment methods and the implementation of new kinds of treatment programme, the evidence on which the principle of controlled drinking treatment has been based challenges the very foundations of traditional understandings of alcoholism and cannot be ignored. 'Controlled drinking' cannot be merely grafted on to existing knowledge or be made merely an appendage to existing treatment resources; its implications for the basic theory of alcoholism must be squarely faced up to.

PARADIGM CHANGE

The term 'paradigm' is one of the most overworked and confused in current parlance and Kuhn (1970) has admitted that he himself has contributed to this confusion. Nevertheless, we believe there to be some heuristic value in applying the notion of 'paradigm change' to recent events in the alcoholism field (cf. Heather, 1978). Basically, Kuhn rejects the naive understanding of science as a process of gradual and undimensional accumulation of knowledge and demonstrates instead that science proceeds by a succession of discontinuous paradigms which, while they are in force, regulate the direction of theory and research in the subject matter in question. In any field of scientific endeavour, Kuhn shows, there are periods of 'normal science' during which the concepts regarded as legitimate, the problems thought worth solving and, indeed, the standards by which correct solutions to these problems are recognized, are accepted with little or no dissent by the scientific community. Sooner or later, however, these periods of paradigm-regulated normal science are disrupted by the occurrence of *anomalies*, that is, by findings which cannot be predicted from and can find no place within the existing paradigm. Agitation resulting from these anomalous findings, which are incidentally the only true 'discoveries' of which science is capable, leads to a state of crisis in which the normal, technical, puzzle-solving activity of science breaks down and is replaced by a re-examination, often involving considerable bitterness and controversy, of the fundamental assumptions which shape the discipline. Out of the temporary confusion thus engendered emerges a new paradigm offering its own theoretical problems, evidential criteria and unique research methods. The response to this state of affairs is typically one of a polarization of the scientific community into two opposing camps, one defending the old paradigm and the other urging its replacement by the new. Eventually this dispute is resolved by the success, if its time has come, of the new paradigm and the discipline then enters the next normal period in which the achievements of the old paradigm are perceived in a new 'Gestalt'. Thus, in this last sense, progress becomes possible.

The major difficulty in applying Kuhn's (1970) analysis to the alcoholism field is that his examples are taken almost exclusively from the sciences of physics and chemistry which obviously possess a degree of coherence and technical sophistication not found in the human sciences. Added to this, until relatively recently alcoholism has shown a very low level of theoretical sophistication and a virtually inextricable entanglement of primitive theory and *ad hoc,* pragmatic therapeutic activity. For these reasons, it is not clear whether the disease view of alcoholism, which is obviously what is intended here by reference to the old paradigm, would actually qualify as a scientific paradigm in Kuhn's sense or is best regarded as representing the period of *prescientific* knowledge which precedes the application of scientific method proper. In similar vein, Pattison *et al.* (1977) have proposed that the disease view of alcoholism, with its heavy involvement of paraprofessional and lay personnel and its reliance on intuitive and subjective rather than analytic and objective styles of reasoning, constitutes a 'folk science', as described by Ravetz (1971).

Despite these considerable reservations, however, one of the attractions of the idea of paradigm change in the present context is that Davies' (1962) report of resumed normal drinking in former alcohol addicts fits so neatly with Kuhn's description of the disruptive, anomalous finding which precipitates a scientific revolution, especially so in view of the almost accidental nature of the finding commented on earlier (p. 22). Despite valiant attempts to do so, it has clearly proved impossible for the dominant disease perspective of alcoholism to accommodate or explain away this annoying but crucial finding. In historical terms, we think it will eventually become commonplace to observe that the discovery of resumed normal drinking opened the floodgates for a rush of further anomalous findings, particularly those emanating from experimental investigations of intoxication and described in Chapter 3, which could not be predicted from the dominant disease theory and which accelerated its downfall. The present position is that the disease theory is confronted by a mass of empirical data, which we have not been able to document fully in this book, which it cannot satisfactorily explain (cf. Pattison *et al.*, 1977).

This will be a convenient place to dwell briefly on the reasons for the tremendous hostility evoked by the finding of resumed normal drinking and by other assaults on the disease view of alcoholism. As we have already pointed out, the emergence of a new paradigm is nearly always accompanied by considerable acrimony among the scientific community. This is because authority, status and sometimes, perhaps, livelihood itself are at risk, as well as sincerely and deeply held convictions. However, there is an extra ingredient to the hostility involved here, one which is generated by features peculiar to the alcoholism field and which should not remain unspoken. As Roizen (1977) has pointed out, there is an especially intimate connection between theory and treatment in this field which is not shared by other human problem-areas. In the classical model of alcoholism originally propounded by AA and taken over in large part by the medical profession the treatment offered can be seen as precisely an acceptance of the theory of alcoholism held by those offering the treatment. The treatment can only be successful if the treated individual accepts, lock, stock and barrel, the theory which states that alcoholics are persons who possess a basic and pre-existent difference from other persons which prevents them from ever drinking in a normal fashion. In this way, treatment by Alcoholics Anonymous is like treatment by psychoanalysis or some other closed system of psychotherapy; one has to believe in it completely in order to benefit from it; scepticism regarding the theory is incompatible by definition with successful treatment. It is small wonder then that those who have themselves received help from AA or from derivative psychiatric services, and nobody would of course deny that there are plenty of these, are extremely hostile to the possibility that the AA theory of alcoholism might be wrong.

IRREVERSIBILITY: THE KEY ISSUE

In recent years the walls of the disease theory of alcoholism have been collapsing all around. The notion that alcoholism is a distinct entity and that alcoholics are different in some essential way from other drinkers has come under attack from several directions. To mention only one of these, there is strong evidence that the distribution of alcohol consumption in the population is continuous and unimodal, and not bimodal as would be expected if a discrete subpopulation of alcoholics were to exist (see, e.g. de Lint, 1976). We have also seen that in the most modern version of the disease conception of alcoholism, the Alcohol Dependence Syndrome, the postulation of a distinct entity has been explicitly abandoned, although it has been argued here (p. 19) that the assumption of a disease entity has been retained in disguised form. A further common feature of disease conceptions, the idea of a progressive deterioration in the 'symptoms' of alcoholism, has also been subjected to fierce pressure, chiefly from evidence that individuals experiencing problems with drinking do not by any means always get worse over time (see, e.g. Clark, 1976). Again this feature has been removed from the Alcohol Dependence Syndrome.

What then remains of the disease theory of alcoholism? What rearguard defence does it have to offer its critics? Some guidance as to an answer to these questions may be gleaned from Keller's (1976) revisit of the disease concept of alcoholism, especially since the author may be justly described as the leading contemporary defender of the disease theory faith. Large parts of Keller's discussion are devoted to an attempted rebuttal of various criticisms, real or imagined, of the disease theory of alcoholism. Finally, however, the reader is left with the conclusion that alcoholism is a disablement, a 'dysbehaviourism', or 'a behavioural disease' (*sic*). Thus, the conception of alcoholism as a disease is stripped of all meaningful content apart from the defining attribute that abnormal drinking leads to the disablement of the abnormal drinker. In fairness, it should be pointed out that this is consistent with Keller's (1960) much earlier definition of alcoholism as 'a chronic disease manifested by repeated implicative drinking so as to cause injury to the drinker's health or to his social and economic functioning'. We have already established in the discussion of Jellinek's work (p. 12) that the fact that abnormal drinking causes diseases cannot be used as a sole justification for calling the abnormal behaviour itself a disease. So, the proposition is that alcoholism is a disease because it is a 'dysbehaviourism' or because it results in injury to physical, social and economic functioning.

The important question here is why the attribution of dysfunction is regarded as sufficient grounds for alcoholism to be defined as a disease. If a normally skillful footballer is having an off day on the field, we may accuse him of 'dysfunctional behaviour' but we do not conclude, without further enquiry, that he is suffering from a disease! The attribution of dysfunction to an individual performance rests on complex social criteria referring to events far wider in scope than those which apply to the attribution of disease. To be sure, the presence of disease may be one cause of dysfunction, but disease cannot be inferred with any useful meaning from the presence of dysfunction; dysfunction is a larger concept than disease. It is interesting to compare Keller's (1960) definition of alcoholism quoted above with a definition of problem-drinking proposed by Cahalan (1970): 'Problem drinking is repetitive use of beverage alcohol causing physical, psychological or social harm to the drinker or to others.' In most essential respects the two definitions are identical and there seems to be nothing in Keller's, apart from the mere assertion of disease, which is not included in Cahalan's. Yet Cahalan's (1970) definition was arrived at from a perspective which specifically rejects a disease conceptualization of alcoholism. The simple point is that Keller's leap from dysfunction to disease is a conceptual error and a source of conceptual confusion.

This having been said, there is perhaps one way of saving Keller's (1976) disease conception of alcoholism. This is to insist that the dysfunctional aspects of the alcoholic's drinking are *permanent*, or at least long-lasting, properties of his behaviour. This is implied in Keller's use of the terms 'disablement' and 'chronic' but the implication is not clearly spelt out in his article and is confused by neologisms like 'dysbehaviourism'. Even here, the presence of permanent disablement is not a completely sure foundation for a disease conception since it is now being argued, for example, that mental retardation is not best regarded as within the province of disease in view of the superior consequences of regarding it as an educational rather than a medical problem (Kushlick, 1975). Nevertheless, the notion of alcoholism as nothing more or less than a relatively permanent disablement of the alcoholic individual, with associated physical, psychological or social harm, is a possible last-ditch defence for the disease theory of alcoholism.

Keller's (1976) article may also be employed here to discuss the merits of regarding alcoholism as a disease in the more specific sense of physical dependence on a harmful substance. Keller refers to research carried out by Gross (1977) which 'points tentatively to a neurophysiological basis for the alcohol-dependence syndrome', and appears to suggest 'the possibility of identifying an alcoholismic lesion'. If confirmed by further research, this work 'should satisfy the strictest reasonable criteria for the diagnosis of a physical disease' and 'will of course confound all the anti-disease conceptors'. But this does not follow. The justification for calling alcoholism a disease by equating it with alcohol addiction – as Keller would prefer to call it – is no less arbitrary and subject to discussion of its personal and social consequences than any other disease conception. After all, smoking is a behaviour which is undoubtedly maintained to some extent by pharmacological addiction and which clearly causes physical damage to the smoker. However, smoking is not generally regarded as a disease, partly because huge numbers of people would be thereby classified as sick and enormous legal and financial complications would arise. In the case of a disease conception of alcoholism which emphasizes physical dependence the crucial question is, how important is physical dependence in the treatment and prevention of harmful drinking. At the end of Chapter 3 we noted Shulman's (1979) argument that physical dependence may not be an important factor in treatment because it has little bearing on the probability of relapse after an extended period of abstinence. However, we also observed that if long-lasting neurophysiological changes resulted from prolonged excessive drinking, this could make relapse more likely and the presence and level of physical dependence considerably relevant to treatment. It was for this reason we stressed the need for research on the duration of the reinstatement element of the Alcohol Dependence Syndrome, its relationship to alcohol consumption and previous levels of dependence and its contribution to the relapse process. Thus, whether or not Gross' research will lead to a confounding of 'the anti-disease conceptors' very much depends on evidence as to the permanence, irreversibility and relevance to relapse of the putative alcoholismic lesion, if ever it is discovered.

In Chapter 1 we encountered another sense in which alcoholism had been designated a disease – that it was a mental illness in its own right or, at least, a symptom of mental illness. Numerous criticisms may be made of psychological disease conceptions of alcoholism (see, e.g. Jellinek, 1960; Armor *et al.*, 1978). However, the main argument here is not that psychological explanations are false but that, to the extent that they are valid, they should not be regarded as disease conceptions. Sarbin (1969) has shown that, both conceptually and literally in a historical sense, the notion of illness has been transferred *metaphorically* from its original somatic context to the area of experience and behaviour. Therefore, the central question with mental illness conceptions is, what are the consequences of applying this metaphor to the form of behaviour known as alcoholism. In other words, the problem of whether alcoholism should be regarded as a disease in the mental illness sense is not an empirical issue but one requiring an *a priori* decision. It is not a matter of showing that alcoholics come from disturbed families, make unusual responses on projective tests or give evidence of undesirable personality traits, but of debating the advantages and disadvantages of the personal and social consequences which flow from declaring them to be sick persons. This debate may be informed by evidence relating to these consequences but, to repeat, the question of whether alcoholism may usefully be construed as a form or symptom of mental illness is not in itself an empirical issue.

Earlier in this section we tried to show that the idea of an irreversible impairment, in virtue of which the alcoholic can never return to drinking normally, represents the only remaining defence for a disease conception of alcoholism. Even if this argument is not accepted, however, we would continue to maintain that irreversibility is the key feature of the disease theory of alcoholism, but this time on pragmatic rather than on theoretical grounds. In practice, the belief in the therapeutic necessity for total and lifelong abstinence, a necessity which logically entails the postulation of an irreversible deficit, is the belief which unites, more than any other, proponents of disease conceptions of alcoholism. It is the nature of this dominant treatment goal and its transformation into a widely promulgated 'abstinence ideology' which has had the greatest possible influence on the way in which alcoholism is popularly viewed in our society.

As this discussion has already made clear, the most meaningful question is, not whether alcoholism is or is not a disease, but whether it is useful to conceive of it as a disease. In this context, Jellinek's (1960) famous remark that 'a disease is what the medical profession recognizes as such' may be recalled. But surely, few nowadays would assert that the designation of a particular form of social deviance as a disease is the sole prerogative of the medical profession. In the areas of criminal, sexual and political deviance it is non-medical opinion which has been largely responsible for stemming the tide of medical imperialism and for placing the debate about the nature of this deviance, and society's response to it, in the arenas of psychological, sociological and political science where it belongs. The same process is now at work in the alcoholism field, since it is becoming increasingly obvious that the construing of deviant drinking as a disease has grave personal and social disadvantages. Robinson (1972) listed several undesirable consequences of Jellinek's (1960) wide-ranging definition of alcoholism most of which, as Room (1972a) correctly pointed out, apply to any disease conception. Some of these undesirable consequences will be mentioned later in the chapter.

Over and above any concrete disadvantages of the disease theory, the principal reason for rejecting its usefulness as a way of understanding deviant drinking is precisely that it cannot explain the mass of empirical evidence referred to in the previous section. And if the implications of this evidence were to be summed up in a single phrase, it would be that the phenomenon known as alcoholism does not betoken an *irreversible disease* but a *reversible behavioural disorder*. Thus arises the most outstanding disadvantage of continued adherence to the disease theory of alcoholism. To repeat, the crucial property of the dominant disease tradition, the property by which it stands or falls, is the postulation of an irreversible impairment underlying the alcoholic's destructive drinking. The overriding tendency of the evidence reviewed in this book is to show that the assumption of irreversibility can no longer be theoretically justified. Therefore, in our view, continued support for the disease perspective can only retard the development in theory and research of new and improved ways of changing the drinking behaviour of those who so request.

In case we are misunderstood on this score, we should like to make abundantly clear our belief that, even in the event of the wholescale demise of the disease theory, the medical profession will always and necessarily be centrally involved in society's response to alcohol abuse. This could not be otherwise in view of the physical damage caused by excessive drinking and the fact that it is to a greater or lesser extent maintained by mechanisms of pharmacological dependence. Moreover, there is absolutely no reason why medically trained personnel should not be responsible, as they are now and have been in the past, for effecting desirable behavioural change. This is not, or should not be, a question of interdisciplinary rivalry. But all this is a very different matter from the theoretical incompetence and practical disadvantages of disease conceptions of alcoholism.

What then is the new paradigm for alcoholism? The answer to this question is, we believe, transparently clear. It is a conception of alcohol abuse grounded in learning theory and beginning with the assumption that the drinking behaviour of the great majority of persons designated as alcoholic is, in principle and given sufficiently developed methods of instigating it, modifiable. This does not mean that drinking is *only* modifiable by therapy. There is now abundant evidence that radical changes in drinking behaviour can occur without any technical assistance (see Roizen *et al.*, 1978) and this is one of the important lines of evidence which has led to the emergence of the new paradigm. However, the assumption is that, with regard to alcoholics who seek help in changing their behaviour and who therefore presumably have failed to achieve this unaided, there exists no universal, theoretical barrier to the attainment of such change. A further fundamental assumption of the new paradigm is that there is no essential and qualitative discontinuity between the drinking behaviour of persons labelled as alcoholics and drinking behaviour in general. With respect to methods, the new paradigm will rely much more on well-designed experimental investigations and will be more responsive to properly collected empirical evidence of all kinds than has been the case in the past. Indeed, it was only by the introduction of scientific method into the alcoholism field, in the form of adequately conducted and objective follow-ups and controlled laboratory investigations, that the emerging paradigm became possible. It would go far beyond the remit of this book to attempt an elaboration of the details of the learning paradigm here. Suffice it to say that the learning theory foundations will not be restricted to simple Pavlovian and Skinnerian models of conditioning processes, although these models may continue to play a part. Rather, the appeal will be to more modern conceptions of learning which take full account of the cognitive interpretation and construction of experience and the interpersonal and wider sociocultural contexts in which experience is forged. In short, the new paradigm will constitute a genuinely sociopsychological, learning conception of alcohol use and abuse.

THEORETICAL IMPLICATIONS FOR TREATMENT GOALS

Having described in very broad outline the form of the new paradigm for alcoholism, we must turn now to the implications of this for the theoretical relationships between abstinence and controlled drinking treatment goals. In the past, the predominance of the disease theory has meant that total abstinence has been the *standard* solution to the problem of harmful drinking and, if controlled drinking were justified for particular kinds of cases, then exceptional circumstances were looked for. Perhaps the types of alcohol abuser suitable for controlled drinking were not 'real' alcoholics; perhaps they demonstrated only a minor degree of dependence on alcohol;

perhaps their youth, occupation or other personal and social circumstances were such that a target of abstinence was unlikely to be successful; or perhaps they simply refused to countenance a future existence without alcohol. Whatever the particular justification, abstinence was the rule and controlled drinking the exception. *It is our contention that this relationship should now be reversed.* We must emphasize, and this cannot be emphasized too forcefully, that we are speaking here in *theoretical* terms and are concerned primarily with research developments. Since any theory of alcoholism, or for that matter of anything else, is necessarily incomplete, treatment must proceed along careful and pragmatic lines and, if it is to be responsive to research findings, must pay more immediate attention to the results of clinical trials of new treatment methods, such as those described in Chapter 6, than to more basic research. Nevertheless, links must eventually be formed between treatment and theory and this is what we are attempting to do here.

The evidence reviewed in Chapter 3 showed that the theoretical foundations of permanent abstinence in the concepts of loss of control and craving could no longer be defended. In terms of Pattison *et al.*'s (1977) three major beliefs underlying the prohibition of normal drinking in the 'true' alcoholic, listed at the end of Chapter 1, the following conclusions are appropriate:

1. No pre-existent biogenetic defect which makes alcoholics in general react differently to alcohol than nonalcoholics has ever been discovered. The existence of such a defect is unlikely because under controlled laboratory conditions alcoholics do not typically demonstrate the loss of control and craving which would be predicted from such a hypothesis and because alcoholic drinking appears modifiable according to the same principles as normal drinking.

2. Although alcoholic drinking is to some extent maintained by the need to relieve withdrawal symptoms and although such withdrawal symptoms may become conditioned to internal and external stimuli thus strengthening the drinking response, it is unlikely that *permanent* physiological changes as a result of excessive drinking are responsible for the return to abusive drinking after a period of abstinence in the majority of alcoholics.

3. The belief of recovered alcoholics and of others involved in the treatment of alcoholism that alcohol addicts or severely dependent alcoholics are unable to return to harmfree, normal drinking has been contradicted many times by empirical evidence.

It is for these reasons that the abstinence treatment goal must now seek a new theoretical rationale which will consist in the enumeration of *exceptional* circumstances in which a return to normal drinking is not possible. We see these circumstances as being of two kinds:

A.   *Permanent abstinence.* Despite the evidence reviewed in this book, it is still possible that a few alcoholics are born with a physiological abnormality, caused by genetic or intrauterine factors, which makes them react differently to alcohol. If future research should discover the physiological basis of such an abnormality or abnormalities, it must then be determined whether its nature absolutely prohibits the further ingestion of any alcohol or whether some very limited drinking is still conceivable. However, permanent abstention could well be the only safe response in these cases. Of probably greater practical significance is the possibility that chronic excessive drinking causes permanent brain damage of a kind which interferes with the regulation of behaviour and the consequences of which are exacerbated by the effects of alcohol. Such a possibility has received some attention in Chapter 7. We hope that a great deal of future research will be devoted to this issue. It should be borne in mind, however, that the relationship between brain damage and further drinking is an empirical issue and that much more needs to be known about the reversibility or otherwise of cognitive deficits in alcoholics. Obviously there are many other kinds of physical damage which might prohibit further drinking but, unlike brain damage, these do not have theoretical implications.

B.   *Temporary abstinence.* As we suggested in Chapter 3, a large amount of research attention should now be directed towards the issue of the reinstatement of physical dependence after a period of abstinence. We need to know whether this hypothesized reinstatement is indeed a valid phenomenon, as seems likely on the basis of clinical impression, how long it lasts, and what its precise relationship with further drinking might be. The same kind of research analysis should be devoted to the effects of craving for alcohol based on conditioned withdrawal and to the temporary cognitive impairment caused by chronic excessive drinking. For these and possibly for other unknown reasons, it may well become apparent that a relatively protracted period of abstinence, of perhaps six months or one year, may be essential before controlled drinking is attempted by individuals described as severely dependent. It is highly relevant that, as was shown in Chapter 2, many alcoholics spontaneously adopt such periods of total abstinence before successfully resuming normal drinking. It is quite possible that the demand for permanent abstinence has been mistakenly based on the existence of physiological changes caused by excessive drinking which are reversible in the medium term and which do not therefore require a lifelong avoidance of alcohol.

IS THE DISEASE MODEL NECESSARY?

A recent influential report by the Royal College of Psychiatrists (1979) stated: 'Perhaps (in these terms) it would be best, in our particular society and at the present time, to look on alcohol dependence as a disease, but with the added insistence that society has to take an informed rather than a mechanical view of what is meant by that statement.' The purpose of this section is to assess the validity of this statement in relation to the practical implications it has for alcoholics and problem-drinkers.

To label an alcoholic as 'sick' is to provide him with some legitimation of his deviant behaviour – and this is clearly preferable to morally condemning him. Unfortunately there are undesirable side-effects of such a label, the most important being that the alcoholic is to some extent relieved of responsibility for his own behaviour. As the inculcation of such a sense of personal responsibility has been regarded as a crucial part of effective intervention with alcoholics (e.g. Orford and Edwards, 1977), the label may in this sense be counter-productive. A second possible side-effect of using this label widely is that alcoholics and problem-drinkers with relatively moderate problems and dependence upon alcohol may be deterred from contacting treatment services because their problems are insufficiently severe to conceivably be labelled as 'disease'. As such individuals have a far better prognosis following intervention than do more severe cases (e.g. Armor *et al.,* 1978; Orford and Edwards, 1977), this is of potentially crucial importance. Thirdly, beliefs such as 'one drink – one drunk' commonly associated with disease models may act as self-fulfilling prophecies for some alcoholics (e.g. Sobell, L.C. *et al.*, 1972). Fourthly, the advantages which may accrue to the chronic alcoholic labelled as 'sick' may well be outweighed by the disadvantages inherent in applying this stigmatic label to the less chronic alcoholic.

However, even if this last statement were not true, there remains the question of the extent to which the belief that alcoholism is a disease is actually generally held. A number of studies suggest in fact that public and professional attitudes in this context are at best ambiguous and at worst totally confused. For instance, Haberman and Scheinberg (1969) found that although a majority (64 per cent) of a sample of the general population subscribed to the notion that alcoholism is an illness, this amounted to little more than lip-service; this was illustrated by the fact that less than half of the respondents both subscribed to the illness notion and also attributed the clearly alcoholic behaviour of a fictitious character described to them as 'illness'. Furthermore in a survey of Scottish drinking habits, Dight (1976) showed that only 13–18 per cent of a sample of the general population mentioned illness or sickness when asked to define alcoholism; this suggests that a disease conception of alcoholism is not strongly held and provides support for Haberman and Scheinberg's suggestion that when endorsing this view of the problem, the respondents are paying lip-service to the notion. That one study should have shown a significant correlation between social desirability and subscription to the disease model is not surprising in the light of these findings (Tolor and Tamerin, 1975).

When the interview or questionnaire design allows apparently contradictory responses to be made, the public's beliefs about alcohol appear to be confused indeed. Several studies have shown how respondents frequently endorse both disease and moral conceptions of alcoholism simultaneously (e.g. Marcus, 1963; Meuller and Ferneau, 1971; Rix and Buyers, 1976). That this confusion exists is not surprising when the lack of consensus among professionals is considered. While Bailey (1970) found 85 per cent agreement with the statement 'alcoholism is a disease' among a group of social workers, Knox (1971) found that only 35 per cent of a group of 925 psychiatrists and psychologists endorsed such a notion. These differences may be in part due to the way in which attitudes are measured. Strong (1979) showed, in a series of open-ended interviews with a number of Scottish general practitioners, that clearly medical conceptions of alcoholism were not held by most of these doctors; rather they held ambiguous attitudes centred round the notion of 'will-power', social and environmental pressures, and simple personal choice. Rollnick (1978), using a repertory grid measurement technique, found similar confusion among a group of specialist alcoholism treatment professionals.

The evidence thus suggests that public and professional attitudes to alcoholism reflect the controversy and confusion apparent in the pages of the specialist journals. Insistent repetition of the statement 'alcoholism is a disease' may have succeeded in ensuring that lip-service is paid to this assertion, but more sensitive measurement of attitudes reveals that most people do not accept it at face value. Among the lay public, attitudes appear to be no more confused, and no less complex, than those of even specialist professionals. Rollnick (1978), for instance, showed how some members of the public rejected both disease and moral models while subscribing to an addiction model of alcoholism, suggesting that some researchers in this area appear to have far less sophisticated and differentiated views of alcoholism than do the non-specialist professionals and public whom they study. Given that disease models were an alternative to punitive moral approaches to alcoholism, is there a third alternative? The learning approach outlined in previous chapters may not be easily distilled into a particular slogan and it is unlikely, even if it could be, that it would supplant moral attitudes completely. Clearly a 'third' model must be found through which society can develop more appropriate responses to alcoholism in particular, and to other forms of social deviance in general. As the Royal College of Psychiatrists (1979) have pointed out: '[If society] is able to find a satisfactory way of looking at alcohol dependence, it may in the process have found an appropriate way of looking at much else besides.' The paradigm-change in the field of alcoholism, of which acceptance of the controlled drinking goal is only one aspect, makes it essential that we begin to try to find that 'appropriate way'. The evidence of the research reviewed above suggests that there is nothing to lose by involving the public and non-specialist professionals in such a search, without feeling obliged to throw a smokescreen of 'alcoholism is a disease' round our endeavours. To start with the premise that excessive drinking is a learned phenomenon, and to attempt to integrate the theories outlined in Chapter 5 into a convincing explanation of 'alcoholism' may be a useful first step in this direction. A more constructive interim slogan, if one is needed, might be 'alcoholics need help'.

If our conclusions about public attitudes towards alcoholism as a disease are accurate, the notion of controlled drinking should not be difficult for the public to accept. As was described earlier in Chapter 2, Hingson *et al.* (1978) showed that the widely publicized findings of the Rand Report had no appreciable effect on the attitudes or practices of the public, professionals or alcoholics themselves. The fear that wide publicity for the fact that controlled drinking is a viable outcome for some alcoholics might weaken the resolve of abstinent alcoholics does not appear to be justified on the basis of this admittedly limited evidence. Foy *et al.* (1979) showed that even being trained in controlled drinking methods over several weeks did not alter the proportion of alcoholics opting for abstinence, and this is further evidence that such fears are baseless. It may even be the case that more alcoholics will ask for help if it becomes widely known that abstinence need not be the only option.

IMPLICATIONS FOR TREATMENT AND EDUCATION

There are some who argue that 'treatment' for alcoholism does not work, and Emrick (1975) and Orford *et al.* (1976) are commonly cited to support this view. However, careful reading of both these studies leads one to make conclusions contrary to those frequently drawn. Although Emrick found no difference in abstinence rates between subjects in a number of different studies given minimal and those given more than minimal treatment, he did find that significantly more who had received more intensive treatment were classified as 'improved'. Orford *et al.* found that although there were no differences in outcome between minimally treated and intensively treated clients, more severely dependent alcoholics *did* benefit significantly more from intensive treatment than from minimal treatment (see Orford *et al.*, 1976; Table 1, p. 413).

It is however true that treatment is probably one of the least important determinants of recovery from alcoholism (e.g. Saunders and Kershaw, 1979; Orford and Edwards, 1977; Tuckfeld, 1976), and that major life circumstances such as marriage, employment, health and finance are of much more importance. Nevertheless, so long as alcoholics request help, and so long as treatment can be shown to have *some* influence on outcome, it cannot be dismissed. Furthermore, given that many of the learning-based treatments described in Chapter 5 attempt to manipulate some of the major life circumstances known to affect outcome, there are grounds for optimism about the effectiveness of such treatments – and the conclusions of Chapter 6 provide some support for such optimism.

Controlled drinking treatments are likely to add to the overall effectiveness of therapeutic interventions with alcoholics and problem-drinkers. Firstly, it is likely that a choice of goals will lead to fewer client drop-outs from treatment, given that client choice of treatment has been shown to increase success rates (Parker *et al.*, 1979*b*). Secondly, as was discussed in Chapter 4, it is possible that more clients will seek help if they know that they will not necessarily be required to abstain for life. Thirdly, controlled drinking treatments can be made available to problem-drinkers and alcoholics for whom abstinence is inappropriate and who are more likely to relapse if they abstain (see Chapter 7). Thus controlled drinking treatments allow us to do what has been advocated for many years – to intervene with those suffering less severe problems.

The conclusions about treatment for problem-drinkers in Chapter 6 suggest that extremely brief and cost-effective intervention with this population can lead to significant reductions in consumption to low-risk levels. Until relatively recently such problem-drinkers were not considered appropriate candidates for 'treatment' – probably quite rightly given the intensive and intrusive nature of many traditional treatment regimes. Now methods exist to intervene with this population in programmes with a format which straddles the boundary between treatment and education – and this meshing of two hitherto unco-ordinated and even conflicting intervention modalities constitutes a fourth major advantage of offering controlled drinking treatments.

Such treatments operate within a learning framework which is probably more acceptable to those suffering only moderate problems than is a 'sickness' framework. Learning is a valued enterprise within Western society – being 'treated' for non-physical problems much less so. This may lead to less severely handicapped problem-drinkers seeking help more readily. The fact that a learning approach to alcohol problems replaces the two discrete forms of intervention of education and treatment with a unidimensional one has many important implications. For instance, in recent years in the UK several 'safe drinking' campaigns have been mounted (e.g. see Leathar, 1979). Advice is given about how to drink safely, and sometimes the addresses of helping agencies are given; in the main, these agencies operate either by a disease model (e.g. Alcoholics Anonymous) or by a 'treatment' model (e.g. Alcoholism Treatment Units). There is a huge gap between the stage of simple written advice given on posters and leaflets and that of the potentially stigmatic panoply of treatment services. Some form of intermediate intervention is sorely needed. This has been provided in some parts of the USA, for instance by William Miller and his colleagues in Albuquerque (see Chapter 6), using brief advice sessions, self-help manuals and self-monitoring procedures. In the UK, a similar project with young offenders is under way in Tayside (Robertson, Manknell and Heather, 1980). Such 'community education' facilities are a natural consequence of a learning model of alcohol problems where treatment and education are not conceptually distinct and may potentially be implemented by paraprofessionals with a minimum of training.

It is unlikely, however, that the major obstacles to recruiting problem-drinkers with less serious problems will be completely overcome by the shift in orientation suggested here. Vogler, Compton and Weissbach (1976) in the USA and Cameron and Spence (1978) in Scotland have reported difficulties in recruiting such clients for controlled drinking programmes. Similar difficulties have led several researchers, including Vogler *et al.* (1976), to accept court referrals. These have tended to be drunk-drivers ordered by the courts to attend such programmes. Caddy (1979) in a review of these programmes concluded that those individuals compelled to attend benefited as much as those who attended voluntarily, though Room (1979) has pointed out the ethical difficulties of compulsory interventions. Among young offenders – who are at high risk for becoming alcoholic in later life (Robins, Bates and O'Neal, 1962) – there might be included in existing penalties a short course on controlled drinking for those committing drink-related offences. Preliminary findings of such a course developed by Robertson, Manknell and Heather (1980) suggest that offenders attending the programme do not in the main resent being compelled to do so. However, the ethical problems of combining social control procedures with therapeutic education are considerable and must be thoroughly debated before such compulsory intervention becomes widespread.

'Active' recruitment of problem-drinkers, or other individuals at high risk for becoming alcoholic, may be feasible without raising the spectre of legal compulsion. Employment-based programmes – especially in high risk industries such as distilling and journalism – might be suitable for the didactic interventions aimed at moderation described earlier. School-based programmes for high-risk groups, such as the children of alcoholics, might also be considered, though there are obviously considerable difficulties in this form of intervention.

Having dwelt at some length on possible innovative 'middle-ground' programmes which might bridge the gap between health education and more traditional treatment agencies, it is necessary to return to the issue of policies for treatment within existing treatment services – as these constitute the major response to alcohol problems at the present time. As Robertson and Heather (1980*b*) showed, although many treatment agencies offer controlled drinking treatment, it is in the main offered to a small proportion of drinkers. In other words, the abstinence ideology continues to pervade the alcoholism treatment services in the absence of theoretical or empirical support. Controlled drinking still tends to be relegated to the role of incidental intervention for an exceptional minority. Assuming, as we have in Chapter 7, that the client's wishes are the touchstone for goal selection, we can expect that *at least* 20 to 37 per cent of *hospitalized* alcoholics will opt for controlled drinking. Assuming that non-hospitalized outpatients will have less serious problems, and hence will be more likely to choose controlled drinking, this proportion is liable to be much greater within a comprehensive service, and may in many cases constitute a majority. Robertson and Heather showed that a small minority of agencies did indeed offer controlled drinking to the majority of their clients, and it is likely that, as the myths about abstinence become dispelled, this number will increase.

If the conclusions of Chapter 6 are valid, alcoholism treatment services should diverge in two directions, while being unified by a common learning theory of alcohol problems. On the one hand is the move towards brief, didactically-structured interventions carried out by non-specialist personnel in community settings; this will be aimed at those drinkers with less serious problems. On the other hand is a move towards specialist intensive treatment – which may in some cases require residential care – where certain more seriously handicapped alcoholics may be given various kinds of help including regulated drinking practice. The difference between this kind of intensive treatment and those hitherto practised is that it is based on a coherent, though imperfect, theory of alcoholism.

If such models of intervention are developed, it is incumbent upon those implementing them to evaluate their effectiveness, in order to avoid the danger of lurching from one set of myths and ritual practices to another. Linda Sobell and her colleagues (Sobell *et al.*, 1980) are currently attempting to develop ways of incorporating evaluative procedures into routine therapeutic practice and this in our view is the course which future developments in alcoholism intervention should take.

A HISTORICAL OVERVIEW

It may be appropriate to end this book with a broad historical overview of society's response to the problem of deviant drinking. For roughly the last 150 years the dominant method in European and American society for dealing with deviant behaviours of all kinds has been to label them as diseases. No doubt the attraction of the disease metaphor has been due in part to the achievements of medical science, especially during the last century, and to the prestige and authority of the medical profession in our society. But there may be deeper reasons than these. One outstanding feature of the disease approach to deviant behaviours is that they locate the 'fault', or the problem to be rectified, *inside* the individual; if the problem is to be solved, it is the responsibility of the sick individual to seek and co-operate with specific treatment given by medical or other specialists; normal society is not implicated and can proceed with its day-to-day business in the calm assurance that the problem will be receiving expert attention. There is an intriguing paradox here. For although it has been claimed that disease conceptions of alcoholism have been instrumental in removing responsibility from the alcoholic's shoulders, they also have the effect, as Beauchamp (1976) has pointed out, of blaming the alcoholic by making the deviant behaviour a question of individual capacities and abilities which he lacks. Perhaps this makes it more understandable that the disease perspective has not succeeded in lifting the stigma of alcoholism.

There are signs that, during the last two decades or so, the individualistic approach to deviance is breaking down as a result of our increasing under-standing of the social determinants of human behaviour. For example, it is now much less fashionable than it was to take a positivistic stance towards criminal deviance and locate the roots of criminal behaviour inside the individual criminal (see, e.g. Taylor *et al.*, 1973). As in many other respects, the alcoholism field is lagging behind. However, we must try to ensure that when the new learning paradigm for alcoholism fully emerges this learning will not be confined to an individualistic account of personal reinforcement histories but will be seen as an essentially social process. This is why it is so important to embrace the very widest implications of the evidence reviewed in this book. It must not be simply a matter of substituting 'controlled drinking' for 'abstinence' within an identical framework of individual treatment for individual alcoholics. In other words, in rejecting the disease view of alcoholism, we must also reject its deeper ideological tendency to shuffle off social responsibility for alcohol problems. Obviously, there will be very great difficulties in the way of this undertaking and Cahalan (1979) has outlined some of the bureaucratic obstacles and vested interests which will impede this effort. Nevertheless, it is to be hoped that the new paradigm will see the solution to alcohol problems as being much more a question of community responsibility and social policy than has been the case in the past.

There is one other residue of the past which is relevant to present concerns. We are not so foolish as to write off abstinence as a treatment goal for alcoholism. Indeed, we have stressed that there are often grounds which make it necessary and have tried to suggest ways in which these grounds might be more systematically and empirically formulated. Nevertheless, we do believe that an exclusive abstinence requirement is a reflection of 'abstinence ideology', and that this ideology is embedded in moral attitudes to drinking in our society. As implied earlier (p. 250), it is quite possible that good reasons for temporary abstinence have been caught up with moral forces to be transformed into bad reasons for permanent abstinence. Surely, anyone who has worked in the alcoholism field for any length of time cannot fail to be impressed with the difficulty of separating out rational, objective debate from the moral undertones which seem to pervade the discipline. Through its associations with the religious, social movements of the last century, the exclusive demand for abstinence is a fundamental expression of the Protestant tradition with the profound ambivalence of its attitude to hedonism and its specially reserved place for 'reformed sinners' (cf. Pattison, 1966). These are large generalizations, but no less true for that. It would be asking too much of society as a whole to abandon its moral attitude to drinking for, as Mandelbaum (1965) has informed us, all societies in human history have displayed powerful prescriptions and prohibitions on drinking behaviour; the use of alcohol may be tabooed, it is never ignored. But for those professionally or voluntarily involved in the alcoholism field the position is surely different. For those of us engaged in treatment, research and education concerned with the perplexing and tragic problem of alcohol abuse, the sooner we emancipate ourselves from the moralistic legacy of the past the better.

References

ALCOHOLICS ANONYMOUS (1939) *Alcoholics Anonymous*. New York: Works Publishing Inc.

ALCOHOLICS ANONYMOUS (1955) *Alcoholics Anonymous and the Medical Profession*. New York: Alcoholics Anonymous World Services Inc.

ALCOHOLICS ANONYMOUS (1965) *AA in Hospitals*. New York: Alcoholics Anonymous World Services Inc.

ALDEN, L. (1978) 'Evaluation of a preventive self-management programme for problem drinkers', *Canadian Journal of Behavioural Science*, **10**, 258–63.

ALDEN, L. (1980) 'Behavioural self-management: a new approach to the prevention of problem drinking', unpublished manuscript, University of British Columbia.

ALTERMAN, A.I., GOTTHEIL, E. and THORNTON, C.C. (1978) 'Variations in patterns of drinking of alcoholics in a drinking-decisions program', in Seixas, F.A. (ed.), *Currents in Alcoholism*, **Vol. 4.** New York: Grune and Stratton.

ANANT, S.S. (1968) 'Former alcoholics and social drinking: an unexpected finding', *Canadian Psychologist*, **9**, 35.

ANDERSON, W. and RAY, O. (1977) 'Abstainers, non-destructive drinkers and relapsers: one-year after a four-week in-patient group-oriented alcoholism treatment program', in Seixas, F. (ed.), *Currents in Alcoholism*, **Vol. 2.** New York: Grune and Stratton.

ARGYLE, M. (1967) *The Psychology of Interpersonal Behaviour*. Harmondsworth: Penguin Books.

ARMOR, D.J., POLICH, J.M. and STAMBUL, H.B. (1976) *Alcoholism and Treatment*. Santa Monica: Rand Corporation.

ARMOR, D.J., POLICH J.M. and STAMBUL, H.B. (1978) *Alcoholism and Treatment*. New York: Wiley.

ARMSTRONG, J.D. (1963) Comment on Davies, D.L. 'Normal drinking in recovered alcohol addicts', *Quarterly Journal of Studies on Alcohol*, **24**, 109–21.

BACON, S.D. (1973) 'The process of addiction to alcohol', *Quarterly Journal of Studies on Alcohol*, **34**, 1–27.

BAEKLAND, F. and LUNDWALL, L. (1977) 'Engaging the alcoholic in treatment and keeping him there', in Kissin, B. and Begleiter, H., *The Biology of Alcoholism*, **Vol. V.** New York: Plenum.

BAILEY, K.G. and SOWDER, W.T. (1970) 'Audiotape and videotape self-confrontation in psychotherapy', *Psychological Bulletin*, **74**, 127–37.

BAILEY, M.B. (1970) 'Attitudes towards alcoholism before and after a training program for social caseworkers', *Quarterly Journal of Studies on Alcohol*, **31**, 669–83.

BAILEY, M.B. and STEWART, J. (1967) 'Normal drinking by persons reporting previous problem drinking', *Quarterly Journal of Studies on Alcohol*, **28**, 305–15.

BAKER, T.B., UDIN, H. and VOGLER, R.E. (1975) 'The effects of videotaped modelling and self-confrontation on the drinking behaviour of alcoholics', *International Journal of the Addictions*, **10**, 779–93.

BANDURA, A. (1977) *Social Learning Theory*. New Jersey: Prentice Hall.

BANDURA, A. (1978) 'Self-efficacy: toward a unifying theory of behavioural change', *Advances in Behaviour Research and Therapy*, **1**, 139–61.

BANDURA, A. and SIMON, K.M. (1977) 'The role of proximal intensions in self-regulation of refractory behaviour', *Cognitive Therapy and Research*, **1**, 177–93.

BARCHHA, R., STEWART, M.A. and GUZE, S.B. (1968). 'The prevalence of alcoholism among general hosptial ward patients', *American Journal of Psychiatry*, **125**, 681–34.

BEAUCHAMP, D.E. (1976) 'Alcoholism as blaming the alcoholic', *International Journal of the Addictions*, **11**, 41–52.

BECK, A. (1976) *Cognitive Therapy and Emotional Disorders*. New York: International Universities Press.

BELASCO, J.A. (1971) 'The criterion question revisited', *British Journal of Addiction*, **66**, 39–44.

BHAKTA, M. (1971) 'Clinical applications of behaviour therapy in the treatment of alcoholism', *Journal of Alcoholism*, **6**, 75–83.

BIGELOW, G. (1973) 'Experimental analysis of human drug self-administration', cited in Miller, P.M. (1976) *A Behavioural Formulation of Alcohol Abuse*. Oxford: Pergamon.

BIGELOW, G. and LIEBSON, I. (1972) 'Cost factors controlling alcoholics' drinking', *Psychological Record*, **22**, 305–10.

BIGELOW, G., LIEBSON, I. and GRIFFITHS, R. (1974) 'Alcoholic drinking: suppression by a brief time-out procedure', *Behaviour Research and Therapy*, **12**, 107–15.

BLAKE, B.G. (1965) 'Application of behaviour therapy to the treatment of alcoholism', *Behaviour Research and Therapy*, **3**, 75–85.

BLOCK, M.A. (1963) Comment on Davies, D.L., 'Normal drinking in recovered alcohol addicts', *Quarterly Journal of Studies on Alcohol*, **24**, 109–21.

BLUME, S. (1977) Comment on the 'Rand Report', *Journal of Studies on Alcohol*, **38**, 163–8.

BOLMAN, W.M. (1965) 'Abstinence versus permissiveness in the psychotherapy of alcoholism', *Archives of General Psychiatry*, **12**, 456–63.

BORKENSTEIN, R.F., CROWTHER, R.F., SHUMATE, R.P., ZIEL, W.B. and ZYLMAN, R. (1964) 'The role of the drinking driver in traffic accidents'. Bloomington, Indiana: Department of Police Administration, Indiana University.

BRIDELL, D.W. and NATHAN, P.E. (1975) 'Behaviour assessment and modification with alcoholics: current status and future trends', in Hersen, M., Eisler, R.M. and Miller, P. (eds.) *Progress in Behaviour Modification*. New York: Academic Press.

BRIDELL, D.W., RIMM, D.C., CADDY, G.R., KRAWITZ, G., SHOLIS, D. and WUNDERLIN, R.J. (1979) 'The effects of alcohol and cognitive set on sexual arousal to deviant sexual stimuli', unpublished manuscript, Old Dominion University.

BROMET, E.J. and MOOS, R. (1979) 'Prognosis of alcoholic patients: comparisons of abstainers and moderate drinkers', *British Journal of Addiction*, **74**, 183–8.

BRUNNER-ORNE, M. (1963) Further comment on Davies, D.L., 'Normal drinking in recovered alcohol addicts', *Quarterly Journal of Studies on Alcohol*, **23**, 94–104.

BRUUN, K. (1963) 'Outcome of different types of treatment of alcoholics', *Quarterly Journal of Studies on Alcohol*, **24**, 280–8.

CADDY, G.R. (1979) 'The application of "state of the art" intervention and evaluation technology: prospects for the future of the alcohol and traffic safety countermeasures approach', unpublished manuscript, Old Dominion University.

CADDY, G.R., ADDINGTON, H.J. and PERKINS, D. (1978) 'Individualized behaviour therapy for alcoholics: a third year independent double-blind follow-up', *Behaviour Research and Therapy*, **16**, 345–62.

CADDY, G.R. and LOVIBOND, S.H. (1976) 'Self-regulation and discriminated aversive conditioning in the modification of alcoholics' drinking behaviour', *Behaviour Therapy*, **7**, 223–30.

CAHALAN, D. (1970) *Problem Drinkers: A National Survey.* San Francisco: Jossey-Bass.

CAHALAN, D. (1979) 'Why does the alcoholism field act like a ship of fools?' *British Journal of Addiction,* **74,** 235–8.

CAHALAN, D. and CISIN, I.H. (1968) 'American drinking practices: summary of findings from a national probability sample. 1. Extent of drinking by population subgroups', *Quarterly Journal of Studies on Alcohol,* **29,** 130–51.

CAHALAN, D. and ROOM, R. (1974) *Problem Drinking among American Men.* New Brunswick: Rutgers Centre of Alcohol Studies.

CAIN, A.C. (1964) *The Cured Alcoholic.* New York: John Day.

CAMERON, D. and SPENCE, T. (1978) 'Lessons from an outpatient controlled drinking group', unpublished manuscript, Crichton Royal Hospital, Dumfries, Scotland.

CANNON, D.S., BAKER, T.B. and WARD, N.O. (1977) 'Characteristics of volunteers for a controlled drinking training programme', *Journal of Studies on Alcohol,* **38,** 1799–1803.

CANTER, F.M. (1968) 'The requirement of abstinence as a problem in institutional treatment of alcoholics', *Psychiatric Quarterly,* **42,** 217–31.

CAPPELL, H. and HERMAN, C.P. (1972) 'Alcohol and tension reduction: a review', *Quarterly Journal of Studies on Alcohol,* **33,** 33–42.

CARROLL, J.F.X. (1980) 'Does sobriety and self-fulfilment always necessitate total and permanent abstinence?' *British Journal of Addiction,* **75,** 55–63.

CHICK, J. (1980) 'Is there a unidimensional alcohol dependence syndrome?' Unpublished manuscript, University of Edinburgh.

CLARK, W.B. (1976) 'Loss of control, heavy drinking and drinking problems in a longitudinal study', *Journal of Studies on Alcohol,* **37,** 1256–90.

CLARK, W.B. and CAHALAN, D. (1976) 'Changes in problem drinking over a four-year span', *Addictive Behaviours,* **1,** 251–60.

CLARKE, J. and HAUGHTON, H. (1975) 'A study of intellectual impairment and recovery rates in heavy drinkers in Ireland', *British Journal of Psychiatry,* **126,** 178–84.

COHEN, M., LIEBSON, I.A. and FAILLACE, L.A. (1972) 'A technique for establishing controlled drinking in chronic alcoholics', *Diseases of the Nervous System,* **33,** 46–9.

COHEN, M., LIEBSON, I.A. and FAILLACE, L.A. (1973) 'Controlled drinking by chronic alcoholics over extended periods of free access', *Psychological Reports,* **32,** 1107–10.

COHEN, M., LIEBSON, I.A., FAILLACE, L.A. and ALLEN, R.P. (1971) 'Moderate drinking by chronic alcoholics', *Journal of Nervous and Mental Disease,* **153,** 434–44.

COHEN, M., LIEBSON, I.A., FAILLACE, L.A. and SPEERS, W. (1971) 'Alcoholism: controlled drinking and incentives for abstinence', *Psychological Reports,* **28,** 575–80.

COLEMAN, J.W. (1976) 'The myth of addiction', *Journal of Drug Issues,* **6,** 135–41.

COMPTON, J.V. and VOGLER, R.E. (1975) 'Validation of the Alco-Calculator', *Psychological Reports,* **36,** 977–8.

CONGER, J.J. (1956) 'Reinforcement theory and the dynamics of alcoholism', *Quarterly Journal of Studies on Alcohol,* **17,** 296–305.

COSTELLO, R. (1975) 'Alcoholism treatment and evaluation. In search of methods', *International Journal of the Addictions,* **10,** 251–63.

CUTTER, H.S.G., SCHWAAB, E.L. and NATHAN, P.E. (1970) 'Effects of alcohol on its utility for alcoholics and nonalcoholics', *Quarterly Journal of Studies on Alcohol,* **31,** 369–78.

CZYPIONKA, A. and DEMEL, I. (1976) 'Kontrolliertes Trinken bei Alkoholkranken', *Zeitschrift für Klinische Psychologie,* **5,** 92–108.

DAVIDSON, W.S. (1974) 'Studies of aversive conditioning for alcoholics: a critical review of theory and research methodology', *Psychological Bulletin,* **81,** 571–81.

DAVIES, D.L. (1962) 'Normal drinking in recovered alcohol addicts', *Quarterly Journal of Studies on Alcohol,* **23,** 94–104.

DAVIES, D.L. (1963) Response to comments on 'Normal drinking in recovered alcohol addicts', *Quarterly Journal of Studies on Alcohol,* **24,** 321–332.

DAVIES, D.L. (1969) 'Stabilized addiction and normal drinking in recovered alcohol addicts', in Steinberg, H. (ed.) *Scientific Basis of Drug Dependence.* London: Churchill.

DAVIES, D.L. (1979) Conversation with D.L. Davies. *British Journal of Addiction,* **74,** 239–49.

DAVIES, D.L., SCOTT, D.F. and MALHERBE, M.E.L. (1969) 'Resumed normal drinking in recovered psychotic alcoholics', *International Journal of the Addictions,* **4,** 187–94.

DAVIES, D.L., SHEPHERD, M. and MYERS, E. (1956) 'The two-years prognosis of 50 alcohol addicts after treatment in hospital', *Quarterly Journal of Studies on Alcohol,* **17,** 485–502.

DAVIES, J. and STACEY, B. (1972) *Teenagers and Alcohol.* London: HMSO.

DAVIES, P. (1979) 'Motivation, responsibility and sickness in the psychiatric treatment of alcoholism', *British Journal of Psychiatry,* **134,** 449–58.

DAVIES, P. (1980) 'Treatment strategies and patient expectations of alcoholism treatment'. Paper read at the New Directions in the Study of Alcohol Conference, Southport, UK, May 1980.

DAVIS, F.T. (1976) 'Abstinence: goal for rehabilitation', *American Journal on Drug and Alcohol Abuse,* **3,** 7–12.

DAVIS, M. (1980) 'Alcoholic liver disease: what the practising clinician needs to know', *British Journal of Addiction,* **75,** 19–26.

DE LINT, J.E.E. (1976) 'Epidemiological aspects of alcoholism', *International Journal of Mental Health,* **5,** 19–51.

DE MORSIER, G. and FELDMAN, H. (1952) 'Le traitement de l'alcoolisme par l'apomorphine: étude de 500 cas', *Schweizer Archiv für Neurologie Psychiatrie,* **70,** 434–40.

DIGHT, S.E. (1976) *Scottish Drinking Habits.* London: HMSO.

DREW, L.R.H. (1968) 'Alcoholism as a self-limiting disease', *Quarterly Journal of Studies on Alcohol,* **29,** 956–7.

DREWERY, J. (1974) 'Social drinking as a therapeutic goal in the treatment of alcoholism', *Journal of Alcoholism,* **9,** 43–7.

DUBOURG, G.O. (1969) 'After care for alcoholics – a follow-up study', *British Journal of Addiction,* **64,** 155–63.

D'ZURILLA, J.J. and GOLDFRIED, M.R. (1971) 'Problem solving and behaviour modification', *Journal of Abnormal Psychology,* **78,** 107–26.

ECKARDT, M.J., PARKER, E.S., NOBLE, E.P., FELDMAN, D.J. and GOTTSCHALK, L.A. (1978) 'Relationship between neuropsychological performance and alcohol consumption in alcoholics', *Biological Psychiatry,* **13,** 551–63.

EDWARDS, G. (1977) 'The Alcohol Dependence Syndrome: usefulness of an idea', in Edwards, G. and Grant, M. (eds.) *Alcoholism: New Knowledge and New Responses.* London: Croom Helm.

EDWARDS, G., CHANDLER, J., HENSMAN, C. and PETO, J. (1972) 'Drinking in a London suburb: II: correlates of trouble with drinking among men', *Quarterly Journal of Studies on Alcohol,* Supplement No. 6, 94–119.

EDWARDS, G. AND GROSS, M.M. (1976) 'Alcohol dependence: provisional description of a clinical syndrome', *British Medical Journal,* **1,** 1058–61.

EDWARDS, G., GROSS, M.M., KELLER, M., MOSER, J. and ROOM, R. (1977) *Alcohol-related Disabilities.* WHO Offset Publication, No. 32.

EDWARDS, G., HAWKER, A., HENSMAN, C., PETO, J. and WILLIAMSON, V. (1973) 'Alcoholics known or unknown to agencies: epidemiological studies in a London suburb', *British Journal of Psychiatry,* **123,** 169–83.

EISLER, R.M., HERSEN, M., MILLER, P.M. and BLANCHARD, E.B. (1975) 'Situational determinants of assertive behaviours', *Journal of Consulting and Clinical Psychology,* **43,** 330–40.

ELKINS, R.L. (1975) 'Aversion therapy for alcoholism: chemical, electrical or verbal imagery', *International Journal of the Addictions,* **10,** 157–209.

ELLIS, A. (1962) *Reason and Emotion in Psychotherapy.* New York: Lyle Stuart.

EMRICK, C.D. (1974) 'A review of psychologically oriented treatment of alcoholism: I. The use and interrelationships of outcome criteria and drinking behaviour following treatment', *Quarterly Journal of Studies on Alcohol,* **35,** 523–49.

EMRICK, C.D. (1975) 'A review of psychologically oriented treatment of alcoholism: II. The relative effectiveness of different treatment approaches and the effectiveness of treatment vs. no treatment', *Quarterly Journal of Studies on Alcohol,* **36,** 88–108.

EMRICK, C.D. and STILSON, D.W. (1977) Comments on the 'Rand Report', *Journal of Studies on Alcohol,* **30,** 152–63.

ENGLE, K.B. and WILLIAMS, T.K. (1972) 'Effect of an ounce of vodka on alcoholics' desire for alcohol', *Quarterly Journal of Studies on Alcohol,* **33,** 1099–105.

ESSER, P.H. (1963) Comment on Davies, D.L., 'Normal drinking in recovered alcohol addicts', *Quarterly Journal of Studies on Alcohol,* **24,** 109–21.

EVANS, M. (1973) 'Modification of drinking', *Journal of Alcoholism,* **8,** 111–13.

EWING, J.A. and ROUSE, B.A. (1972) Cited in Sobell, M.B. and Sobell, L.C. (1978) 'Evaluating the external validity of Ewing and Rouse', *British Journal of Addiction,* **73,** 343–5.

EWING, J.A. and ROUSE, B.A. (1976) 'Failure of an experimental treatment programme to inculcate controlled drinking in alcoholics', *British Journal of Addiction,* **71,** 123–34.

FAILLACE, L.A., FLAMER, R.N., IMBER, S.D. and WARD, R.F. (1972) 'Giving alcohol to alcoholics: an evaluation', *Quarterly Journal of Studies on Alcohol,* **33,** 85–90.

FEINSTEIN, C. and TAMERIN, J.S. (1972) 'Induced intoxication and videotaped feedback in alcoholism treatment', *Quarterly Journal of Studies on Alcohol,* **33,** 408–16.

FESTINGER, L. (1957) *A Theory of Cognitive Dissonance.* Stanford:Stanford University Press.

FILLMORE, K. (1974) 'Drinking and problem drinking in early adulthood and middle-age', *Quarterly Journal of Studies on Alcohol,* **35,** 819–40.

FINGARETTE, H. (1970) 'The perils of Powell: in search of a factual foundation for the "disease concept of alcoholism" ', *Harvard Law Review,* **83,** 793–807.

FITZGERALD, B.J., PASEWARK, R.A. and CLARK, R. (1971) 'Four-year follow-up of alcoholics treated at a rural state hospital', *Quarterly Journal of Studies on Alcohol,* **32,** 636–42.

FLAHERTY, J.A., McGUIRE, H.T. and GATSKI, R.L. (1955) 'The psychodynamics of the "dry drunk" ', *American Journal of Psychiatry,* **112,** 460–84.

FOX, R. (1957) 'Treatment of alcoholism', in Himwick, H. (ed.) *Alcoholism: Basic Aspects and Treatment.* Washington DC: American Association for the Advancement of Science.

FOX, R. (1976) 'The controlled drinking controversy', *Journal of the American Medical Association,* **236,** 863.

FOY, D.W., MILLER, P.M., EISLER, R.M. and O'TOOLE, D.H. (1976) 'Social skills training to teach alcoholics to refuse drinks effectively', *Journal of Studies on Alcohol,* **37,** 1340–5.

FOY, D., RYCHTARIK, R.G., O'BRIEN, T.P. and NUNN, L.B. (1979) 'Goal choice of alcoholics: effects of training controlled drinking skills', *Behavioural Psychotherapy,* **7,** 101–10.

FREED, E.X. (1973) 'Abstinence for alcoholics reconsidered', *Journal of Alcoholism,* **8,** 106–10.

FREDERIKSEN, L.W. and MILLER, P.M. (1975) 'Peer-determined and self-determined reinforcement in group therapy with alcoholics', *Behaviour Research and Therapy,* **14,** 385–8.

FUNDERBURK, F.R. and ALLEN, R.P. (1977) 'Alcoholics' disposition to drink', *Journal of Studies on Alcohol,* **38,** 410–24.

GERARD, D.L. and SAENGER, G. (1959) 'Interval between intake and follow-up as a factor in the evaluation of patients with a drinking problem', *Quarterly Journal of Studies on Alcohol,* **20,** 620–30.

GERARD, D.L. and SAENGER, G. (1966) *Out-patient Treatment of Alcoholism: A Study of Outcome and its Determinants.* Toronto: University of Toronto Press.

GERARD, D.L., SAENGER, G. and WILE, R. (1962) 'The abstinent alcoholic', *Archives of General Psychiatry,* **6,** 83–95.

GIBBS, L. and FLANAGAN, J. (1977) 'Prognostic indicators of alcoholism treatment outcome', *International Journal of the Addictions,* **12,** 1097–141.

GILLIS, L.S. and KEET, M. (1969) 'Prognostic factors and treatment results in hospitalized alcoholics', *Quarterly Journal of Studies on Alcohol,* **30,** 426–37.

GITLOW, S.E. (1973) 'Alcoholism: a disease', in Bourne, P.G. and Fox, R. (eds.) *Alcoholism: Progress in Research and Treatment.* New York: Academic Press.

GLATT, M.M. (1967) 'The question of moderate drinking despite "loss of control" ', *British Journal of Addiction,* **62,** 267–74.

GLATT, M.M. (1976) 'Alcoholism disease concept and loss of control revisited' *British Journal of Addiction,* **71,** 135–44.

GOLDMAN, M.S., TAYLOR, H.A., CARRUTH, M.L. and NATHAN, P.E. (1973) 'Effects of group decision-making on group drinking by alcoholics', *Quarterly Journal of Studies on Alcohol,* **34,** 807–22.

GOODWIN, D.W., CRANE, J.B. and GUZE, S.B. (1971) 'Felons who drink: an 8-year follow-up', *Quarterly Journal of Studies on Alcohol,* **32,** 136–47.

GOODWIN, D.W., SCHULZINGER, F., MOLLER, N., HERMANSEN, L., WINOKUR, G and GUZE, S.B. (1974) 'Drinking problems in adopted and non-adopted sons o alcoholics', *Archives of General Psychiatry,* **31,** 164–9.

GOTTHEIL, E., CORBETT, L.O., GRASBERGER, J.C. and CORNELISON, F.S. (1971 'Treating the alcoholic in the presence of alcohol', *American Journal o Psychiatry,* **128,** 475–80.

GOTTHEIL, E., CORBETT, L.O., GRASBERGER, J.C. and CORNELISON, F.S. (1972 'Fixed interval drinking decisions. I. A research and treatment goal', *Quarterly Journal of Studies on Alcohol,* **33,** 311–24.

GOTTHEIL, E., MURPHY, B.F., SKOLODA, T.E. and CORBETT, L.O. (1972) 'Fixed interval drinking decisions: II. Drinking and discomfort in 25 alcoholics', *Quarterly Journal of Studies on Alcohol,* **33,** 325–40.

GRANT, I., ADAMS, K. and REED, R. (1979) 'Normal neuropsychological abilities of alcoholic men in their late thirties', *American Journal of Psychiatry,* **136,** 10–15.

GREGSON, R. and TAYLOR, G. (1977) 'Prediction of relapse in men alcoholics', *Journal of Studies on Alcohol,* **32,** 1749–60.

GROSS, M.M. (1977) 'Psychobiological contributions to the Alcohol Dependence Syndrome: a selective review of recent research', in Edwards, G., Gross, M.M., Keller, M., Moser, J. and Room, R., *Alcohol-Related Disabilities.* WHO Offset Publication, No. 32.

GUSFIELD, J. (1963) *Symbolic Crusade.* Urbana: University of Illinois Press.

GUTHRIE, A. and ELLIOT, W.A. (1980) 'The nature and reversibility of cerebral impairment in alcoholism: treatment implications', *Journal of Studies on Alcohol,* **41,** 147–55.

GUTHRIE, A.G., PRESLEY, A., GEEKIE, C. and MacKENZIE, L. (1979) 'The effects of alcohol on memory', unpublished manuscript, Tayside Health Board, Scotland.

GUZE, S.B., TUASON, V.B., STEWART, M.A., and PICKEN, B. (1963) 'The drinking history: a comparison of reports by subjects and their relatives', *Quarterly Journal of Studies on Alcohol,* **24,** 249–60.

HABERMAN, P.W. and SCHEINBERG, J. (1969) 'Public attitudes towards alcoholism as an illness', *American Journal of Public Health,* **59,** 1209–16.

HARPER, J. and HICKSON, B. (1951) 'The results of hospital treatment of chronic alcoholism', *Lancet,* **261,** 1057–9.

HARRISON, B. (1970) *Drink and the Victorians.* London: Faber.

HARRIS, D.E. and LICHTENSTEIN, E. (1971) 'The contribution of nonspecific social variables to a successful behavioural treatment of smoking', cited in Hodgson, R. (1980) 'Treatment strategies for the early problem drinker', in Edwards, G. and Grant, M., *Alcoholism: New Directions.* London: Croom Helm.

HAYMAN, M. (1955) 'Current attitudes to alcoholism of psychiatrists in Southern California', *American Journal of Psychiatry,* **112,** 485–93.

HEATHER, N. (1978) 'The crisis in the treatment of alcohol abuse', paper presented at 4th International Conference on Alcoholism and Drug Dependence, Liverpool.

HEATHER, N. (1979) *An Empirical Test of Sociological Theories of Delinquent Values Using Repertory Grid Methodology.* Ph.D. Thesis: University of Dundee.

HEATHER, N. (1980) Letter to the editor. *British Journal of Addiction,* **75,** 93–4.

HEATHER, N., EDWARDS, S. and HORE, B.D. (1975) 'Changes in construing and outcome of group therapy for alcoholism', *Journal of Studies on Alcohol,* **36,** 1238–53.

HEDBERG, A.G. and CAMPBELL, L.M. (1974) 'A comparison of four behavioural treatment approaches to alcoholism', *Journal of Behaviour Therapy and Experimental Psychiatry,* **5,** 251–6.

HINGSON, R., SCOTCH, N. and GOLDMAN, E. (1977) 'Impact of the "Rand Report" on alcoholics, treatment personnel and Boston residents', *Journal of Studies on Alcohol,* **38,** 2065–76.

HODGSON, R.J. (1979) 'Much ado about nothing much: alcoholism treatment and the Rand Report', *British Journal of Addiction,* **74,** 227–34.

HODGSON, R.J. (1980) 'Treatment strategies for the early problem drinker', in Edwards, G. and Grant, M. (eds.) *Alcoholism: New Directions.* London: Croom Helm.

HODGSON, R.J. and RANKIN, H.J. (1976) 'Modification of excessive drinking by cue exposure', *Behaviour Research and Therapy,* **14,** 305–7.

HODGSON, R.J., RANKIN, H.J. and STOCKWELL, T.R. (1979) 'Alcohol dependence and the priming effect', *Behaviour Research and Therapy,* **17,** 379–87.

HODGSON, R.J., STOCKWELL, T.R. and RANKIN, H.J. (1979) 'Can alcohol reduce tension?' *Behaviour Research and Therapy,* **17,** 459–66.

HORE, B.D. (1974) 'Craving for alcohol', *British Journal of Addiction,* **69,** 137–40.

HUBER, H., KARLIN, R. and NATHAN, P.E. (1976) 'Blood alcohol level discrimination by nonalcoholics: The role of internal and external cues', *Journal of Studies on Alcohol,* **37,** 27–39.

HUNT, G.M. and AZRIN, N.H. (1973) 'A community – reinforcement approach to alcoholism', *Behaviour Research and Therapy,* **11,** 91–104.

HUNT, W.A., BARNETT, L.W. and BRANCH, L.G. (1971) 'Relapse rates in addiction programs', *Journal of Clinical Psychology,* **27,** 455–6.

HYMAN, H.H. (1976) 'Alcoholics 15 years later', *Annals of the New York Academy of Sciences,* **273,** 613–22.

ISBELL, H. (1955) 'Craving for alcohol', *Quarterly Journal of Studies on Alcohol,* **16,** 38–42.

JAMES, J.E. and GOLDMAN, M. (1971) 'Behaviour trends of wives of alcoholics', *Quarterly Journal of Studies on Alcohol,* **32,** 373–81.

JELLINEK, E.M. (1946) 'Phases in the drinking history of alcoholics', *Quarterly Journal of Studies on Alcohol,* **7,** 1–88.

JELLINEK, E.M. (1952) 'Phases of alcohol addiction', *Quarterly Journal of Studies on Alcohol,* **13,** 673–84.

JELLINEK, E.M. (1960) *The Disease Concept of Alcoholism.* New Haven: Hillhouse Press.

JELLINEK, E.M., ISBELL, H., LINDQUIST, G., TIEBOUT, H.M., DUCHENE, M.D. MARDONES, J. and MACLEOD, L.D. (1955) 'The craving for alcohol: a symposium by members of the WHO expert committee on mental health and alcohol', *Quarterly Journal of Studies on Alcohol,* **16,** 34–66.

JONES, K.L. and SMITH, D.W. (1973) 'Recognition of the foetal alcohol syndrome in early infancy', *Lancet,* **2,** 999–1001.

JONES, R.W. and HELDRICH, A.R. (1972) 'Treatment of alcoholism by physicians in private practice: a national survey', *Quarterly Journal of Studies on Alcohol,* **33** 117–31.

KALANT, H., Le BLANC, A.E. and GIBBINS, R.J. (1971) 'Tolerance to and dependence on, ethanol', in Israel, Y. and Mardones, J. (eds.) *Biological Basis of Alcoholism.* New York: Wiley-Interscience.

KELLER, M. (1960) 'Definition of alcoholism', *Quarterly Journal of Studies on Alcohol,* **21,** 125–34.

KELLER, M. (1972) 'On the loss-of-control phenomenon in alcoholism', *British Journal of Addiction,* **67,** 153–66.

KELLER, M. (1976) 'The disease concept of alcoholism revisited', *Journal of Studies on Alcohol,* **37,** 1694–717.

KELLEY, H.H. (1967) 'Attribution theory in social psychology', in Levine, D. (ed.) *Nebraska Symposium on Motivation.* Lincoln, Nebraska: University of Nebraska Press.

KENDELL, R.E. (1965) 'Normal drinking by former alcohol addicts', *Quarterly Journal of Studies on Alcohol,* **26,** 247–57.

KESSEL, J. (1962) *The Road Back.* New York: Knopf.

KESSEL, N. and GROSSMAN, G. (1961) 'Suicide in alcoholics', *British Medical Journal,* **2,** 1611–12.

KESSEL, N. and WALTON, H. (1965) *Alcoholism*. Harmondsworth: Penguin.

KILPATRICK, D.G., ROITZSCH, J., BEST, C., McALHANY, D., STURGIS, E. and MILLER, W. (1978) 'Treatment goal preference and problem perception of chronic alcoholics: behavioural and personality correlates', *Addictive Behaviours*, **3**, 107–16.

KISH, G.B. and HERMAN, H.T. (1971) 'The Fort Meade Alcoholism Treatment Programme: a follow up study', *Quarterly Journal of Studies on Alcohol*, **32**, 628–35.

KISSIN, B., PLATZ, A. and SU, W.H. (1970) 'Selective factors in treatment choice and outcome in alcoholics', in N.K. Mello and J.H. Mendelson (eds.) *Recent Advances in Studies of Alcoholism*, Washington DC: US Government Printing Office.

KJOLSTAD, T. (1963) Further comment on Davies, D.L., 'Normal drinking in recovered alcohol addicts', *Quarterly Journal of Studies on Alcohol*, **24**, 727–35.

KNOX, K.M. (1971) 'Attitudes of psychiatrists and psychologists towards alcoholism', *American Journal of Psychiatry*, **127**, 1675–9.

KNOX, W.J. (1976) 'Objective psychological measurement and alcoholism: a review of the literature, 1971–72, *Psychological Reports*, **38**, 1023–50.

KONOUR, A. and PRIBRAM, K.H. (1970) 'Error recognition and utilization produced by injury to the frontal cortex in Man', *Neuropsychologia*, **8**, 489–91.

KRAFT, T. and AL-ISSA, I. (1967) 'Alcoholism treated by desensitization: a case report', *Behaviour Research and Therapy*, **5**, 69–70.

KRAFT, T. and AL-ISSA, I. (1968) 'Desensitization and the treatment of alcohol addiction', *British Journal of Addiction*, **63**, 19–23.

KRASNEGOR, N.A. (1978) *Behavioural Tolerance: Research and Treatment Implications*. Washington DC: NIDA Research Monograph 18.

KRYSTAL, H. (1962) 'The problem of abstinence by the patient as a requisite for the psychotherapy of alcoholism: II The evaluation of the meaning of drinking in determining the requirement of abstinence by alcoholics during treatment', *Quarterly Journal of Studies on Alcohol*, **23**, 112–21.

KUHN, T.S. (1970) *The Structure of Scientific Revolutions* (revised edition). Chicago: University of Chicago Press.

KUSHLICK, A. (1975) 'Some ways of setting, monitoring and attaining objectives for services for disabled people', Health Care Evaluation Research Team, Report No. 116: Winchester, Hants.

LANSKY, D., NATHAN, P. and LAWSON, D. (1978) 'Blood alcohol level discrimination by alcoholics: the role of internal and external cues', *Journal of Consulting and Clinical Psychology*, **46**, 953–60.

LAZARUS, A.A. (1965) 'Towards the understanding and effective treatment of alcoholism', *South African Medical Journal*, **39**, 736–41.

LEACH, B. and NORRIS, F.L. (1977) 'Factors in the development of Alcoholics Anonymous (AA)', in Kissin, B. and Begleiter, H. (eds.) *The Biology of Alcoholism Vol. 5, The Treatment and Rehabilitation of the Chronic Alcoholic*. New York: Plenum.

LEATHAR, D.S. (1979) 'The Scottish Health Education Unit's alcohol self-monitoring campaign: 1978', *Community Education*, Summer 1979, 12–15.

LE BLANC, A.E. and CAPPELL, H.D. (1975) 'Historical antecedents as determinants of tolerance to and dependence upon psychoactive drugs', in Cappell, H.D. and Le Blanc, A.E. (eds.) *Biological and Behavioural Approaches to Drug Dependence*. Toronto: Addiction Research Foundation of Ontario.

LEMERE, F. (1953) 'What happens to alcoholics', *American Journal of Psychiatry*, **109**, 674–6.

LEMERE, F. (1963) Further comment on Davies, D.L., 'Normal drinking in recovered alcohol addicts', *Quarterly Journal of Studies on Alcohol*, **24**, 109–21.

LEVINE, H.G. (1978) 'The discovery of addiction: changing conceptions of habitual drunkenness in America', *Journal of Studies on Alcohol*, **39**, 143–74.

LEVINSON, T. (1977) 'Controlled drinking in the alcoholic: a search for common features', in Madden, J., Walker, R. and Kenyon, W. (eds.) *Alcoholism and Drug Dependence*. London: Plenum.

LEWIS, P. (1979) 'Behavioural self-control of alcohol abuse: current status of a hospital-based controlled drinking programme', unpublished manuscript, All Saints Hospital, Birmingham.

LISHMAN, W.A., RON, M. and ACKER, W. (1979) 'Computerized tomography of the brain and psychometric assessment of alcoholic patients – a British study', unpublished manuscript, Institute of Psychiatry, London.

LITMAN, G. (1974) 'Stress, affect and craving in alcoholics', *Quarterly Journal of Studies on Alcohol*, **35**, 131–46.

LITMAN, G., EISER, J., RAWSON, N. and OPPENHEIM, A. (1977) 'Towards a typology of relapse: a preliminary report', *Drug and Alcohol Dependence*, **2**, 157–62.

LLOYD, R.W.J. and SALZBERG, H.C. (1975) 'Controlled social drinking: an alternative to abstinence as a treatment goal for some alcohol abusers', *Psychological Bulletin*, **82**, 815–42.

LOLLI, G. (1952) 'Alcoholism, 1941–1951: a survey of activities in research, education and therapy. *V*. The treatment of alcohol addiction', *Quarterly Journal of Studies on Alcohol*, 13, 461–71.

LOVIBOND, S.H. (1975) 'Use of behaviour modification in the reduction of alcohol-related road accidents', in Thompson, T. and Dockers, W.S. (eds.) *Application of Behaviour Modification*. New York: Academic Press.

LOVIBOND, S.H. and CADDY, G. (1970) 'Discriminative aversive control in the moderation of alcoholics' drinking behaviour', *Behaviour Therapy*, **1**, 437–44.

LUDWIG, A.M. (1970) 'On and off the wagon: reasons for drinking and abstaining by alcoholics', *Quarterly Journal of Studies on Alcohol*, **33**, 91–6.

LUDWIG, A.M., BENDFELDT, F., WIKLER, A. and CAIN, R.B. (1978) ' "Loss of control" in alcoholics', *Archives of General Psychiatry*, **35**, 370–3.

LUDWIG, A.M., LEVINE, J. and STARK, L.H. (1970) *LSD and Alcoholism: A Clinical Study of Treatment Efficacy*. Springfield, Illinois: Charles C. Thomas.

LUDWIG, A.M. and STARK, L.H. (1974) 'Alcohol craving: subjective and situational aspects', *Quarterly Journal of Studies on Alcohol*, **35**, 899–905.

LUDWIG, A.M. and WIKLER, A. (1974) 'Craving and relapse to drink', *Quarterly Journal of Studies on Alcohol*, **35**, 108–30.

LUDWIG, A.M., WIKLER, A. and STARK, L. (1974) 'The first drink: psychobiological aspects of craving', *Archives of General Psychiatry*, **30**, 539–47.

LURIA, A.R. (1973) *The Working Brain*. Harmondsworth: Penguin Books.

LURIA, A.R. and HOMSKAYA, E.D. (1964) 'Disturbance in the regulative role of speech with frontal lobe lesions', in Warren, J.M. and Akert, K. (eds.) *The Frontal Granular Cortex and Behaviour*. New York: McGraw-Hill.

McANDREW, C. and EDGERTON, R.B. (1969) *Drunken Compartment: A Social Explanation*. Chicago: Aldine.

McCARTHY, R.G. (1956) 'Alcoholism and the alcoholic', in *Exploring Alcohol Questions; No. 5*, New Haven, *Journal of Studies on Alcohol*, Inc.

McCRADY, B.S., PAOLING, J.J. and LONGABOUGH, L.R. (1978) 'Correspondence between reports of problem drinkers and spouses on drinking behaviour and impairment', *Journal of Studies on Alcohol*, **39**, 1251–7.

McLACHLAN, J.F. and LEVINSON, T. (1974) 'Improvement in WAIS block design performance as a function of recovery from alcoholism', *Journal of Clinical Psychology*, **30**, 65–6.

MACLEOD, L.D. (1955) 'The "craving" for alcohol', *Quarterly Journal of Studies on Alcohol*, **16**, 34–66.

McNAMEE, H.B., MELLO, N.K. and MENDELSON, J.H. (1968) 'Experimental analysis of drinking patterns of alcoholics; concurrent psychiatric observations', *American Journal of Psychiatry*, **124**, 1063–9.

MADDOX, G.L. (1964) 'High-school student drinking behaviour: incidental information from two national surveys', *Quarterly Journal of Studies on Alcohol*, **25**, 339–47.

MAHONEY, M.J. and ARNKOFF, D.B. (1978) 'Cognitive and self-control therapies', in Garfield, S. and Bergin, A. (eds.) *Handbook of Psychotherapy and Behaviour Change*. New York: Wiley.

MAI, N. (1975) 'Mathematical models for evaluation of therapies', in Brengelmann, J.C. (ed.) *Progress in Behaviour Therapy*. New York: Springer.

MAISTO, S.A., HENRY, R.R., SOBELL, M.B. and SOBELL, L.C. (1978) 'Implications of acquired changes in tolerance for the treatment of alcohol problems', *Addictive Behaviours*, **3**, 51–5.

MAISTO, S.A., LAUERMAN, R. and ADESSO, V.J. (1977) 'A comparison of two experimental studies investigating the role of cognitive factors in excessive drinking', *Journal of Studies on Alcohol*, **30**, 145–9.

MAISTO, S.A. and SCHEFT, B.K. (1977) 'The constructs of craving for alcohol and loss of control drinking: help or hindrance to research', *Addictive Behaviours*, **2**, 207–17.

MALETZKY, B.M. (1974) 'Assisted covert sensitization for drug abuse', *International Journal of the Addictions*, **9**, 411–29.

MANDELBAUM, D.G. (1965) 'Alcohol and culture', *Current Anthropology*, **6**, 281–93.

MANN, M. (1968) *New Primer on Alcoholism*. New York: Holt, Rinehart and Winston.

MARCONI, J.T. (1959) 'The concept of alcoholism', *Quarterly Journal of Studies on Alcohol*, **20**, 216–35.

MARCONI, J.T. (1970) 'Role of dorsomedial thalamic nucleus in "loss-of-control" and "inability to abstain" during ethanol ingestion', in Popham, R.E. (ed.) *Alcohol and Alcoholism*. Toronto: University of Toronto Press.

MARCONI, J.T., FINK, K. and MOYA, L. (1967) 'Experimental study of alcoholics with an inability to stop', *British Journal of Psychiatry*, **113**, 543–5.

MARCUS, A. (1963) *Alcoholism Questionnaire*. Toronto: Alcohol and Drug Addiction Research Foundation.

MARLATT, G.A. (1976) 'The Drinking Profile: A questionnaire for the behavioural assessment of alcoholism', in Mash, E.J. and Terdal, L.G. (eds.) *Behaviour Therapy Assessment: Diagnosis and Evaluation*. New York: Springer.

MARLATT, G.A. (1978) 'Craving for alcohol, loss of control and relapse: a cognitive-behavioural analysis', in Nathan, P.E., Marlatt, G.A. and Loberg, T. (eds.) *Alcoholism: New Directions in Behavioural Research and Treatment*. New York: Plenum.

MARLATT, G.A., DEMMING, B. and REID, J.B. (1973) 'Loss of control drinking in alcoholics: an experimental analogue', *Journal of Abnormal Psychology*, **81**, 233–41.

MATZA, D. and SYKES, G. (1961) 'Juvenile delinquency and subterranean values',

American Sociological Review, **26**, 712–19.

MAXWELL, M.A. (1950) 'The Washingtonian movement', *Quarterly Journal of Studies on Alcohol*, **11**, 410–51.

MAXWELL, W.A., BAIRD, R.L., WEZL, T. and FERGUSON, L. (1974) 'Discriminated aversion conditioning within an alcoholic treatment programme in the training of controlled drinking', *Behavioural Engineering*, **2**, 17–19.

MAYER, J. and MYERSON, D.J. (1971) 'Outpatient treatment of alcoholics: effects of status stability and nature of treatment', *Quarterly Journal of Studies on Alcohol*, **32**, 620–27.

MEICHENBAUM, D. (1977) *Cognitive Behaviour Modification*. New York: Plenum.

MELLO, N.K. (1972) 'Behavioural studies of alcoholism', in Kissin, B. and Begleiter, H. (eds.) *The Biology of Alcoholism Vol. II*. New York: Plenum.

MELLO, N.K., McNAMEE, H.B. and MENDELSON, J.H. (1968) 'Drinking patterns of chronic alcoholics: gambling and motivation for alcohol', *Psychiatric Research Report* No. 24. Washington, DC: American Psychiatric Association.

MELLO, N.K., and MENDELSON, J.H. (1965) 'Operant analysis of drinking habits of chronic alcoholics', *Nature*, **206**, 43–6.

MELLO, N.K. and MENDELSON, J.H. (1972) 'Drinking patterns during work-contingent and non-contingent alcohol acquisition', *Psychosomatic Medicine*, **34**, 139–64.

MENDELSON, J.H. and MELLO, N.K. (1966) 'Experimental analysis of drinking behaviour of chronic alcoholics', *Annals of New York Academy of Sciences*, **133**, 828–45.

MENDELSON, J.H., MELLO, N.K. and SOLOMAN, P. (1968) 'Small group drinking behaviour: an experimental study of chronic alcoholics', in Wikler A. (ed.) *The Addictive States*. Baltimore: Williams and Wilkins.

MERRY, J. (1966) 'The "loss of control" myth', *Lancet*, **4**, 1257–8.

MEULLER, S. and FERNEAU, E. (1971) 'Attitudes towards alcohol among a group of college students', *International Journal of the Addictions*, **6**, 443–51.

MILLER, P.M. (1972) 'The use of behavioural contracting in the treatment of alcoholism: a case study', *Behaviour Therapy*, **3**, 593–6.

MILLER, P.M. (1975) 'A behavioural intervention program for chronic public drunkenness offenders', *Archives of General Psychiatry*, **32**, 915–18.

MILLER, P.M., HERSEN, M., EISLER, R.M. and HILSMAN, G. (1974) 'Effects of social stress on operant drinking of alcoholics and social drinkers', *Behaviour Research and Therapy*, **12**, 67–72.

MILLER, P.M., HERSEN, M., EISLER, R.M. and WATTS, J.G. (1974) 'Contingent reinforcement of lowered blood alcohol levels in an outpatient chronic alcoholic', *Behaviour Research and Therapy*, **12**, 261–3.

MILLER, W.R. (1976) 'Controlled drinking therapies: a review', in Miller, W.R. and Munoz, R.F., *How to Control your Drinking*. New Jersey: Prentice-Hall.

MILLER, W.R. (1978) 'Behavioural treatment of problem drinkers: a comparative outcome study of three controlled drinking therapies', *Journal of Consulting and Clinical Psychology*, **46**, 74–86.

MILLER, W.R. and CADDY, G.R. (1977) 'Abstinence and controlled drinking in the treatment of problem drinkers', *Journal of Studies on Alcohol*, **38**, 986–1003.

MILLER, W.R., CRAWFORD, V.L. and TAYLOR, C.A. (1979) 'Significant others as corroborative sources for problem drinkers', *Addictive Behaviour*, **4**, 67–70.

MILLER, W.R., GRIBSOV, C. and MORTELL, R. (1979) 'The effectiveness of a self-control manual for problem drinkers with and without therapist contact', unpublished manuscript, University of New Mexico.

MILLER, W.R. and HESTER, R. (1980) 'Treating the problem drinker: modern approaches', in Miller, W.R. (ed.) *The Addictive Behaviours: Treatment of Alcoholism, Drug Abuse, Smoking and Obesity*. Oxford: Pergamon.

MILLER, W.R. and JOYCE, M.A. (1979) 'Prediction of abstinence, controlled drinking and heavy drinking outcomes following behavioural self-control training', *Journal of Consulting and Clinical Psychology*, **47**, 773–5.

MILLER, W.R. and MUNOZ, R.F. (1976) *How to Control your Drinking*. Englewood Cliffs, New Jersey: Prentice-Hall.

MILLER, W.R., PECHACEK, T.F. and HAMBURG, M. (1979) 'Group behaviour therapy for problem drinkers', unpublished manuscript, University of New Mexico.

MILLER, W.R., TAYLOR, C.A. and WEST, J.C. (1980) 'Focused versus broad spectrum behaviour therapy for problem drinkers', unpublished manuscript, University of New Mexico.

MILLS, K.C., SOBELL, M.B. and SCHAEFER, H.H. (1971) 'Training social drinking as an alternative to abstinence for alcoholics', *Behaviour Therapy*, **2**, 8–27.

MOORE, R.A. (1962) 'The problem of abstinence by the patient as a requisite for the psychotherapy of alcoholism. I. The need for abstinence by the alcoholic patient during treatment', *Quarterly Journal of Studies on Alcohol*, **23**, 105–111.

MOORE, R.A. (1968) 'The conception of alcoholism as a mental illness: implications for treatment and research', *Quarterly Journal of Studies on Alcohol*, **29**, 172–5.

MOORE, R.A. and BUCHANAN, T.K. (1966) 'State hospitals and alcoholism: a nationwide survey of treatment techniques and results', *Quarterly Journal of Studies on Alcohol*, **27**, 459–68.

MOORE, R.A. and MURPHY, T.C. (1961) 'Denial of alcoholism as an obstacle to recovery', *Quarterly Journal of Studies on Alcohol*, **22**, 597–609.

MOORE, R.A. and RAMSEUR, F. (1960) 'Effects of psychotherapy in an open-ward hospital on patients with alcoholism', *Quarterly Journal of Studies on Alcohol*, **21**, 233–52.

MOOS, R. and BLISS, F. (1978) 'Difficulty of follow-up and outcome of alcoholism treatment', *Journal of Studies on Alcohol*, **39**, 473–90.

MORSE, R.M. and SWENSEN, W.M. (1975) 'Spouse response to a self-administered alcoholism screening test', *Journal of Studies on Alcohol*, **36**, 400–405.

MUKASA, H. and ARIKAWA, K. (1968) 'A new double medication method for the treatment of alcoholism using the drug cyanamide', *The Kurume Medical Journal*, **15**, 137–43.

MUKASA, H., ICHIHARA, T. and ETO, A. (1964) 'A new treatment of alcoholism with cyanamide (H_2NCN)', *The Kurume Medical Journal 11*, 96–101.

MULFORD, H.A. (1964) 'Drinking and deviant drinking, U.S.A., *Quarterly Journal of Studies on Alcohol*, **25**, 634–50.

MULFORD, H.A. and MILLER, D.E. (1960) 'Drinking in Iowa: II. The extent of drinking and selected sociocultural categories', *Quarterly Journal of Studies on Alcohol*, **21**, 26–39.

MULFORD, H.A. and WILSON, R. (1966) 'Identifying problem drinkers in a household health survey', Washington, DC: Government Printing Office (Public Health Service Publication No. 1000, Series 2, No. 16, May).

NAGY, B. (1978) 'Alcoholics returning to social drinking', *Journal of the American Medical Association*, **240**, 776–7.

NARROL, H.G. (1967) 'Experimental application of reinforcement principles to the analysis and treatment of alcoholics', *Quarterly Journal of Studies on Alcohol*, **28**, 105–15.

NATHAN, P.E. (1978) 'Studies in blood alcohol level discrimination', in Nathan, P.E., Marlatt, G.A. and Loberg, T., *Alcoholism: New Directions in Behavioural Research and Treatment*. New York: Plenum.

NATHAN, P.E. and O'BRIEN, J.S. (1971) 'An experimental analysis of the behaviour of alcoholics and nonalcoholics during prolonged experimental drinking: a necessary precursor to behaviour therapy', *Behaviour Therapy*, **2**, 455–76.

NATHAN, P.E., TITLER, N.A., LOWENSTEIN, L.M., SOLOMAN, P. and ROSS, A.M. (1970) 'Behavioural analysis of chronic alcoholism', *Archives of General Psychiatry*, **22**, 419–30.

NATIONAL COUNCIL ON ALCOHOLISM (1980) *Draft Report of the Working Party on Treatment Goals*, unpublished manuscript, National Council on Alcoholism, London.

NICHOLS, I.C. and HUNT, J. McV. (1940) 'Case of partial bilateral frontal lobectomy', *American Journal of Psychiatry*, **96**, 1063–87.

NORVIG, J. and NIELSEN, B.A. (1956) 'A follow-up study of 221 alcohol addicts in Denmark', *Quarterly Journal of Studies on Alcohol*, **17**, 633–42.

OBITZ, F.W. (1975) 'Alcoholics' perception of selected counselling techniques', *British Journal of Addiction*, **70**, 187–91.

O'LEARY, M.R., RADFORD, L.M., CHANEY, E.F. and SCHAN, E. (1977) 'Assessment of cognitive recovery in alcoholics by use of the trail-making test', *Journal of Clinical Psychology*, **33**, 579–82.

ORFORD, J. (1973) 'A comparison of alcoholics whose drnking is totally uncontrolled and those whose drinking is mainly controlled', *Behaviour Research and Therapy*, **11**, 565–76.

ORFORD, J. (1978) 'The future of alcoholism: a commentary on the Rand report', *Psychological Medicine*, **8**, 1–5

ORFORD, J. and EDWARDS, G. (1977) *Alcoholism*. Maudsley Monograph No. 26. Oxford University Press.

ORFORD, J.and KEDDIE, A. (1980) Personal Communication.

ORFORD, J., OPPENHEIMER, E. and EDWARDS, G. (1976) 'Abstinence or control: the outcome for excessive drinkers two years after consultation', *Behaviour Research and Therapy*, **14**, 409–18.

PACHMAN, J.S., FOY, D.W. and ERD, M.V. (1978) 'Goal choice of alcoholics: a comparison of those who choose total abstinence and those who choose responsible controlled drinking', *Journal of Clinical Psychology*, **34**, 781–3.

PAGE, R.D. and SCHAUB, L. (1977) 'Intellectual functioning in alcoholics during 6 months abstinence', *Journal of Studies on Alcohol*, **38**, 1240–4.

PAREDES, A., HOOD, W.R., SEYMOUR, H. and GOLLOB, M. (1973) 'Loss of control in alcoholism', *Quarterly Journal of Studies on Alcohol*, **34**, 1146–61.

PAREDES, A., LUDWIG, K.D., HASSENFELD, I.N. and CORNELISON, F.S. (1969) 'A clinical study of alcoholics using audio-visual self-image feedback', *Journal of Nervous and Mental Diseases*, **148**, 449–56.

PARKER, E.S. and NOBLE, E.P. (1977) 'Alcohol consumption and cognitive functioning in social drinkers', *Journal of Studies on Alcohol*, **38**, 1224–32.

PARKER, E.S. and NOBLE, E.P. (1980) 'Alcohol and the aging process in social drinkers', *Journal of Studies on Alcohol*, **41**, 170–8.

PARKER, M.W., WINSTEAD, D.K. and WILLI, F.J. (1979a) 'Patient autonomy in alcohol rehabilitation. I. Literature review', *International Journal of the Addictions*, **14**, 1015–22.

PARKER, M.W., WINSTEAD, D.K., WILLI, F.J. and FISHER, P. (1979b) 'Patient autonomy in alcohol rehabilitation. II: Program evaluation', *International Journal of the Addictions,* **14,** 1177–84.

PARSONS, T. (1951) *The Social System.* Glencoe, Illinois: Free Press.

PATTISON, E.M. (1966) 'A critique of alcoholism treatment concepts with special reference to abstinence', *Quarterly Journal of Studies on Alcohol,* **27,** 49–71.

PATTISON, E.M. (1976*a*) 'Nonabstinent drinking goals in the treatment of alcoholism', *Archives of General Psychiatry,* **33,** 923–30.

PATTISON, E.M. (1976*b*) 'Nonabstinent drinking goals in the treatment of alcoholics', in Gibbins, R.J., Israel, Y., Kalant, H., Popham, R.E., Schmidt, W. and Smart, R.E. (eds.) *Research Advances in Alcohol and Drug Problems,* Vol. 3. New York: Wiley.

PATTISON, E.M. (1976*c*) 'A conceptual approach to alcoholism treatment goals', *Addictive Behaviours,* **1,** 177–92.

PATTISON, E.M., COE, R. and RHODES, R.J. (1969) 'Evaluation of alcoholism treatment: a comparison of three facilities', *Archives of General Psychiatry,* **20,** 478–88.

PATTISON, E.M., HEADLEY, E.B., GLESER, G.C. and GOTTSCHALK, L.A. (1968) 'Abstinence and normal drinking: an assessment of changes in drinking patterns in alcoholics after treatment', *Quarterly Journal of Studies on Alcohol,* **29,** 610–33.

PATTISON, E.M., SOBELL, M.B. and SOBELL, L.C. (1977) *Emerging Concepts of Alcohol Dependence.* New York: Springer.

PAVLOV, I. (1927) *Conditioned Reflexes.* London: Oxford University Press.

PFEFFER, A.Z. and BERGER, S. (1957) 'A follow-up study of treated alcoholics', *Quarterly Journal of Studies on Alcohol,* **18,** 624–48.

PIORKOWSKY, G.K. and MANN, E.T. (1975) 'Issues in treatment efficacy research with alcoholics', *Perceptual and Motor Skills,* **41,** 695–700.

PITTMAN, D.J. and TATE, R.L. (1969) 'A comparison of two treatment programmes for alcoholics', *Quarterly Journal of Studies on Alcoholism,* **30,** 888–99.

PLINER, P. and CAPPELL, H. (1974) 'Modification of affective consequences of alcohol: a comparison of social and solitary drinking', *Journal of Abnormal and Social Psychology,* **83,** 418.

POKORNEY, A.D., MILLER, B.A. and CLEVELAND, S.E. (1968) 'Response to treatment of alcoholism: a follow-up study', *Quarterly Journal of Studies on Alcohol,* **29,** 364–81.

POKORNEY, A.D., MILLER, B.A. and KAPLAN, H. (1972) 'The brief MAST – a shortened version of the Michigan Alcoholism Screening Test', *American Journal of Psychiatry,* **129,** 342–50.

POLICH, J.M., ARMOR, D.J. and BRAIKER, H.B. (1980) *The Course of Alcoholism: Four Years After Treatment.* Santa Monica: Rand Corporation.

POMERLEAU, O.F., PERTSCHUK, M., ADKINS, D. and BRADY, J.P. (1978) 'A comparison of behavioural and traditional treatment methods for middle-income problem drinkers', *Journal of Behavioural Medicine,* **1,** 187–200.

POMERLEAU, O., PERTSCHUK, M. and STINNET, J. (1976) 'A critical examination of some current assumptions in the treatment of alcoholism', *Journal of Studies of Alcohol,* **37,** 849–67.

POPHAM, R.E. and SCHMIDT, W. (1976) 'Some factors affecting the likelihood of moderate drinking by treated alcoholics', *Journal of Studies on Alcohol,* **37,** 868–82.

POPPER, K.R. (1959) *The Logic of Scientific Discovery.* London: Hutchinson.

QUINN, J.T. and HENBEST, R. (1967) 'Partial failure of generalization in alcoholics following aversion therapy', *Quarterly Journal of Studies on Alcohol,* **28,** 70–75.

QUIRK, P.A. (1968) 'Former alcoholics and social drinking: an additional observation', *Canadian Psychologist*, **9**, 498–9.

RACHMAN, S.J. and HODGSON, R.J. (1960) *Obsessions and Compulsions.* Englewood Cliffs, New Jersey: Prentice Hall.

RAKKOLAINEN, V. and TURUNEN, S. (1969) 'From unrestrained to moderate drinking', *Acta Psychiatrica Scandinavia*, **45**, 47–52.

RANKIN, H. and HODGSON, R. (1977) 'Cue exposure: one approach to the extinction of addictive behaviours', in Gross, M. (ed.) *Alcohol Intoxication and Withdrawal*, Vol. 3b. New York: Plenum.

RANKIN, H., HODGSON, R. and STOCKWELL, T. (1979) 'The concept of craving and its measurement', *Behaviour Research and Therapy*, **17**, 389–96.

RANKIN, H., HODGSON, R. and STOCKWELL, T. (1980) 'The behavioural measurement of dependence', *British Journal of Addiction*, **75**, 43–7.

RAVETZ, J. (1971) *Scientific Knowledge and Its Social Problems.* Oxford: Oxford University Press.

REINERT, R.E. (1968) 'The concept of alcoholism as a disease', *Bulletin of the Menninger Clinic*, **32**, 21–5.

REINERT, R.E. and BOWEN, W.T. (1968) 'Social drinking following treatment for alcoholism', *Bulletin of the Menninger Clinic*, **32**, 280–90.

RICHARDS, C.S. (1975) 'Behaviour modification of studying through study skills advice and self-control procedures', *Journal of Counselling Psychology*, **22**, 431–36.

RICHARDS, G.P. and BURLEY, P.M. (1978) 'Alcoholics' beliefs and attitudes to controlled drinking and total abstinence', *British Journal of Social and Clinical Psychology*, **17**, 159–63.

RIESMAN, D. (1950) *The Lonely Crowd.* New Haven: Yale University Press.

RILEY, J.W. Jr and MARDEN, C.F. (1947) 'The social pattern of alcoholic drinking', *Quarterly Journal of Studies on Alcohol*, **8**, 265–73.

RIX, J.B. and BUYERS, M. (1976) 'Public attitudes towards alcoholism in a Scottish city', *British Journal of Addiction*, **71**, 23–9.

ROBERTSON, I.H. and HEATHER, N. (1980a) 'Controlled drinking interventions with recent alcohol abusers: preliminary findings', in preparation.

ROBERTSON, I.H. and HEATHER, N. (1980b) 'A survey of controlled drinking practices in a sample of UK agencies', in preparation.

ROBERTSON, I.H., MANKNELL, S. and HEATHER, N. (1980) 'An Alcohol education course for young offenders: preliminary findings', in preparation.

ROBINS, L.N., BATES, W.M. and O'NEAL, P. (1962) 'Adult drinking patterns of former problem children', in Pittman, D.J. and Snyder, C.R. (eds.) *Society, Culture and Drinking Patterns.* New York: Wiley.

ROBINSON, D. (1972) 'The alcohologist's addiction: some implications of having lost control over the disease concept of alcoholism', *Quarterly Journal of Studies on Alcohol*, **33**, 1028–42.

ROBINSON, D. (1979) *Talking Out of Alcoholism.* London: Croom Helm.

ROBSON, R.A., PAULUS, I. and CLARKE, G.G. (1965) 'An evaluation of the effect of a clinic treatment program on the rehabilitation of alcoholic patients', *Quarterly Journal of Studies on Alcohol*, **26**, 264–78.

ROIZEN, R. (1977) Comments on the Rand Report, *Journal of Studies on Alcohol*, **38**, 170–8.

ROIZEN, R., CAHALAN, D. and SHANKS, P. (1978) ' "Spontaneous remission" among untreated problem drinkers', in Kandel, D. (ed.) *Longitudinal Research on Drug Use.* New York: Wiley.

ROLLNICK, S. (1978) 'Conceptions of alcoholism: a repertory grid study', unpublished Master's dissertation, University of Strathclyde.

ROMAN, P.M. and TRICE, H.M. (1968) 'The sick role, labelling theory and the deviant drinker', *International Journal of Social Psychiatry,* **14,** 245–51.

ROOM, R. (1972*a*) 'Comments on Robinson, D. '"The alcohologist's addiction" ', *Quarterly Journal of Studies on Alcohol,* **33,** 1049–59.

ROOM, R. (1972*b*) 'The social psychology of drug dependence', in *The Epidemiology of Drug Dependence: Report on a Conference, London, 1972.* Copenhagen: WHO.

ROOM, R. (1977) 'Measurement and distribution of drinking patterns and problems in general populations', in Edwards, G., Gross, M.M., Keller, M., Moser, J. and Room, R. (eds.) *Alcohol-Related Disabilities.* Geneva: WHO Offset Publication No. 32.

ROOM, R. (1979) 'Treatment seeking populations and larger realities', paper presented at Conference on New Directions in Alcohol Treatment, London, April 1979.

ROYAL COLLEGE OF PSYCHIATRISTS (1979) *Alcohol and Alcoholism.* London: Tavistock.

RUBIN, J.L. (1979) 'Shifting perspectives on the alcoholism treatment movement 1940–1955', *Journal of Studies on Alcohol,* **40,** 376–86.

RUBINGTON, E. (1968) 'The bottle gang', *Quarterly Journal of Studies on Alcohol,* **31,** 943–55.

RUBINGTON, E. and WEINBERG, M.S. (1968) *Deviance: The Interactionist Perspective.* New York: Macmillan.

SANCHEZ-CRAIG, M. (1980) 'A cognitive and behavioural strategy to teach abstinence or controlled drinking: preliminary results from an experimental study', unpublished manuscript, Addiction Research Foundation, Toronto.

SANCHEZ-CRAIG, M. (1980) 'Random assignment to abstinence or controlled drinking in a cognitive behavioural programme – short term effects on drinking behaviour', Addictive Behaviours, **5,** 35–9.

SARBIN, T.R. (1969) 'The scientific status of the mental illness metaphor', in Sarbin, T.R. (ed.) *Changing Conceptions of Mental Illness.* New York: Holt, Reinhart and Winston.

SAUNDERS, W.M. and KERSHAW, P.W. (1978) 'The prevalence of problem drinking and alcoholism in the West of Scotland', *British Journal of Psychiatry,* **133,** 493–9.

SAUNDERS, W.M. and KERSHAW, P.W. (1979) 'Spontaneous remission from alcoholism – a community study', *British Journal of Addiction,* **74,** 251–65.

SAUNDERS, W.M. and RICHARD, G. (1978) ' "In vivo veritas", an observational study of alcoholics' and normal drinkers' patterns of consumption', *British Journal of Addiction,* **73,** 375–80.

SCHAEFFER, H.H. (1971) 'A cultural delusion of alcoholics', *Psychological Reports,* **29,** 587–9.

SCHAEFFER, H.H. (1972) '12 Month follow-up of behaviourally trained ex-alcoholic social drinkers', *Behaviour Therapy,* **3,** 286–90.

SCHAEFFER, H.H., SOBELL, M.B. and MILLS, K.C. (1971) 'Some sobering data on the use of self-confrontation with alcoholics', *Behaviour Therapy,* **2,** 28–9.

SCHMIDT, W. and POPHAM, R.E. (1975) 'Heavy alcohol consumption and physical health problems: a review of the epidemiological evidence', *Drug and Alcohol Dependence,* **1,** 27–50.

SCHUCKIT, M.A. and WINOKUR, G.A. (1972) 'A short-term follow-up of women alcoholics', *Diseases of the Nervous System,* **33,** 672–8.

SEELEY, J.R. (1959) 'The WHO definition of alcoholism', *Quarterly Journal of Studies on Alcohol*, **20**, 352–6.

SEELEY, J.R. (1962) 'Alcoholism is a disease: implications for social policy', in Pittman, D. and Snyder, C. (eds.) *Society, Culture and Drinking Patterns*. New York: Wiley.

SEIXAS, F.A. (1977) 'Assessing "Emerging Concepts" ', *Alcoholism: Clinical and Experimental Research*, **1**, 281–3.

SEIXAS, F.A. (1978) 'Abstinence as a goal in the treatment of alcoholism', *American Journal of Drug and Alcohol Abuse*, **5**, 283–91.

SELZER, M.L. (1963) Comment on Davies, D.L., 'Normal drinking in recovered alcohol addicts', *Quarterly Journal of Studies on Alcohol*, **24**, 109–21.

SELZER, M.L. (1971) 'The Michigan Alcoholism Screening Test: the quest for a new diagnostic instrument', *American Journal of Psychiatry*, **127**, 1653–8.

SELZER, M.L. and HOLLOWAY, W.H. (1957) 'A follow-up of alcoholics committed to a state hospital', *Quarterly Journal of Studies on Alcohol*, **18**, 98–120.

SHAW, S. (1979) 'A critique of the concept of the Alcohol Dependence Syndrome', *British Journal of Addiction*, **74**, 339–48.

SHEA, J.E. (1954) 'Psychoanalytic therapy and alcoholism', *Quarterly Journal of Studies on Alcohol*, **15**, 595–605.

SHULMAN, G.D. (1979) Comment on Tournier, D., 'Alcoholics Anonymous as treatment and as ideology', *Journal of Studies on Alcohol*, **40**, 335–8.

SKINNER, B.F. (1953) *Science and Human Behaviour*. New York: Macmillan.

SKOLODA, T.E., ALTERMAN, A.I., CORNELISON, F.S.Jr and GOTTHEIL, E. (1975) 'Treatment outcome in a drinking-decisions program', *Journal of Studies on Alcohol*, **36**, 365–80.

SMART, R.G. (1978) 'Characteristics of alcoholics who drink socially after treatment', *Alcoholism: Clinical and Experimental Research*, **2**, 49–52.

SMITH, J.A. (1963) Comment on Davies, D.L., 'Normal drinking in recovered alcohol addicts', *Quarterly Journal of Studies on Alcohol*, **24**, 321–32.

SMITH, J.J. (1949) 'A medical approach to problem drinking', *Quarterly Journal of Studies on Alcohol*, **12**, 381–5.

SOBELL, L.C., MAISTO, S.A., SOBELL, M.B. and COOPER, A.M. (1979) 'Reliability of alcohol abusers' self-reports of drinking behaviour', *Behaviour Research and Therapy*, **17**, 157–60.

SOBELL, L.C. and SOBELL, M.B. (1975) 'Legitimizing alternatives to abstinence: implications now and for the future', *Journal of Alcoholism*, **10**, 5–16.

SOBELL, L.C. and SOBELL, M.B. (1978a) 'Validity of self-reports in three populations of alcoholics', *Journal of Consulting and Clinical Psychology*, **46**, 901–7.

SOBELL, L.C., SOBELL, M.B. and CHRISTELMAN, W.C. (1972) 'The myth of "one drink" ', *Behaviour Research and Therapy*, **10**, 119–23.

SOBELL, L.C., SOBELL, M.B. and WARD, E. (eds.) (1980) *Evaluating Alcohol and Drug Abuse Treatment Effectiveness: Recent Advances*. New York: Pergamon.

SOBELL, M.B. (1978a) 'Alternatives to abstinence: evidence, issues and some proposals', in Nathan, P.E., Marlatt, G.A. and Loberg, T. (eds.) *Alcoholism: New Directions in Behavioural Research and Treatment*. New York: Plenum.

SOBELL, M.B. (1978b) 'Goals in the treatment of alcoholism', *American Journal of Drug and Alcohol Abuse*, **5**, 283–91.

SOBELL, M.B., SCHAEFFER, H.H. and MILLS, K.C. (1972) 'Differences in baseline drinking behaviour between alcoholics and normal drinkers', *Behaviour Research and Therapy*, **10**, 257–67.

SOBELL, M.B. and SOBELL, L.C. (1973) 'Individualized behaviour therapy for alcoholics', *Behaviour Therapy*, **4**, 49–72.

SOBELL, M.B. and SOBELL, L.C. (1974) 'Alternatives to abstinence: time to acknowledge reality', *Addictions*, **21**, 2–29.

SOBELL, M.B. and SOBELL, L.C. (1976) 'Second-year treatment outcome of alcoholics treated by individualized behaviour therapy: results', *Behaviour Research and Therapy*, **14**, 195–215.

SOBELL, M.B. and SOBELL, L.C. (1978*b*) *Behavioural Treatment of Alcohol Problems*. New York: Plenum.

STEIN, N.L., NILES, D. and LUDWIG, A.M. (1968) 'The loss of control phenomenon in alcoholics', *Quarterly Journal of Studies on Alcohol*, **29**, 598–602.

STEINER, C. (1971) *Games Alcoholics Play*. New York: Grove Press.

STEINGLASS, P., WEINER, S. and MENDELSON, J.H. (1971) 'A systems approach to alcoholism: a model and its clinical application', *Archives of General Psychiatry*, **24**, 401–10.

STOCKWELL, T.R., HODGSON, R.J. and RANKIN, H.J. (1980) 'The experimental production and measurement of craving for alcohol', unpublished manuscript, Institute of Psychiatry, London.

STORM, T. and CUTLER, R. (1975) 'Notes toward the analysis of loss of control in normal and pathological drinkers', *British Journal of Addiction*, **70**, 151–5.

STORM, T. and SMART, R.G. (1965) 'Dissociation: a possible explanation of some features of alcoholism and implications for its treatment', *Quarterly Journal of Studies on Alcohol*, **26**, 111–15.

STRONG, P.M. (1979) 'The alcoholic, the sick role and bourgeois medicine', unpublished manuscript, Institute of Medical Sociology, Aberdeen.

STUNKARD, A. (1972) 'New therapies for the eating disorders: behaviour modification of obesity and anorexia nervosa', *Archives of General Psychiatry*, **26**, 391–8.

SUMMERS, T. (1970) 'Validity of alcoholics' self-reported drinking history', *Quarterly Journal of Studies on Alcohol*, **31**, 972–4.

TALLAND, G. (1965) *Deranged Memory: a Psychometric Study of the Amnesic Syndrome*. New York: Academic Press.

TARTER, R.E. (1975) 'Psychological deficit in chronic alcoholics: a review', *International Journal of the Addictions*, **10**, 327–68.

TAYLOR, C. and MILLER, W. (1979) 'Relative effectiveness of bibliotherapy, individual and group self-control training in the treatment of problem drinkers', paper presented at the Taos International Conference on Treatment of Addictive Behaviours, Taos, New Mexico, February, 1979.

TAYLOR, I., WALTON, P. and YOUNG, J. (1973) *The New Criminology*. London: Routledge and Kegan Paul.

THIMANN, J. (1963) Comment on Davies, D.L., 'Normal drinking in recovered alcohol addicts', *Quarterly Journal of Studies on Alcohol*, **24**, 321–32.

THOMAS, R.E., GLIEDMAN, L.H., FIZEUND, J., IMBER, S.D. and STONE, A.R. (1959) 'Favourable response in the clinical treatment of chronic alcoholism', *Journal of the American Medical Association*, **169**, 1994–7.

THORESEN, C.E. and MAHONEY, M.J. (1974) *Behavioural Self-Control*. New York: Holt.

THORLEY, A. (1980) Personal Communication.

TIEBOUT, H.M. (1963) Comment on Davies, D.L., 'Normal drinking in recovered alcohol addicts', *Quarterly Journal of Studies on Alcohol*, **24**, 109–21.

TIMNICK, L. (1980) *International Herald Tribune*, 25 January.

TOLOR, A. and TAMERIN, J.S. (1975) 'The Attitudes towards Alcoholism Instrument: a measure of attitudes towards alcoholics and the nature and causes of alcoholism', *British Journal of Addiction,* **70,** 223–31.

TRICE, H.M. and ROMAN, P.M. (1970) 'Delabeling, relabeling and Alcoholics Anonymous', *Social Problems,* **17,** 538–46.

TRUAX, C.B. and CARKHUFF, R.R. (1967) *Towards Effective Counselling and Psychotherapy.* Chicago: Aldine.

TUCKFELD, B. (1976) *Changes in Patterns of Alcohol Use Without Formal Treatment.* North Carolina: Research Triangle Institute.

VAN DIJK, W.K. and VAN DIJK-KOFFMAN (1973) 'A follow-up study of 211 treated male alcoholics', *British Journal of Addiction,* **68,** 3–24.

VAILLANT, G. (1979) 'The Doctor's dilemma', paper presented at Conference on New Directions in Alcohol Treatment, London, April 1979.

VOGLER, R.E., COMPTON, J.V. and WEISSBACH, J.A. (1975) 'Integrated behaviour change techniques for alcoholism', *Journal of Consulting and Clinical Psychology,* **43,** 233–43.

VOGLER, R.E., COMPTON, J.V. and WEISSBACH, T.A. (1976) 'The referral problem in the field of alcohol abuse', *Journal of Community Psychology,* **4,** 357–61.

VOGLER, R.E., WEISSBACH, T.A. and COMPTON, J.V. (1977*a*) 'Learning techniques for alcohol abuse', *Behaviour Research and Therapy,* **15,** 31–8.

VOGLER, R.E., WEISSBACH, T.A., COMPTON, J.V. and MARTIN, G.T. (1977*b*) 'Integrated behaviour change techniques for problem drinkers in the community', *Journal of Consulting and Clinical Psychology,* **45,** 267–79.

WAGMAN, A.M.I. and ALLEN, R.P. (1975) 'Effects of alcohol ingestion and abstinence on slow-wave sleep of alcoholics', in Gross, M.M. (ed.) *Alcohol Intoxication and Withdrawal: Experimental Studies II.* New York: Plenum.

WALL, J.H. (1936) 'A study of alcoholism in men', *American Journal of Psychiatry,* **92,** 1389–401.

WALL, J.H. and ALLEN, E.B. (1944) 'Results of hospital treatment of alcoholism', *American Journal of Psychiatry,* **100,** 474–9.

WALLERSTEIN, R.S. (1956) 'Comparative study of treatment methods for chronic alcoholism', *American Journal of Psychiatry,* **113,** 228–33.

WALSH, K. (1978) *Neuropsychology.* Livingstone: Churchill.

WATSON, J.B. and RAYNOR, R. (1920) 'Conditioned emotional reactions', *Journal of Experimental Psychology,* **3,** 1–4.

WEBER, M. (1930) *The Protestant Ethic and the Spirit of Capitalism.* London: Allen and Unwin.

WELLMAN, M. (1955) 'Fatigue during the second six months of abstinence', *Canadian Medical Association Journal,* **72,** 338–42.

WEXBERG, L.E. (1951) 'Alcoholism as a sickness', *Quarterly Journal of Studies on Alcohol,* **12,** 217–30.

WHITE, W.F. (1965) 'Personality and cognitive learning among alcoholics with different intervals of sobriety', *Psychological Reports,* **16,** 1125–40.

WHO (1951) *Report on the First Session of the Alcoholism Subcommittee: Expert Committee on Mental Health.* Geneva: WHO Technical Reports Series, No. 42.

WIENS, A.N., MONTAGUE, J.R., MANAUGH, T.S. and ENGLISH, C.J. (1976) 'Pharmacological aversive counterconditioning to alcohol in a private hospital: one-year follow-up', *Journal of Studies on Alcohol,* **37,** 1320–24.

WIKLER, A. (1971) 'Some implications of conditioning theory for problems of drug abuse', *Behavioural Science,* **16,** 92–7.

WILBY, W.E. and JONES, R.W. (1962) 'Assessing patient response following treatment', *Quarterly Journal of Studies on Alcohol,* **23,** 325–31.

WILKINS, R.W. (1974) *The Hidden Alcoholic in General Practice.* London: Elek Science.

WILKINSON, P.A. and CARLEN, P.L. (1980) 'Neuropsychological and neurological assessment of alcoholism', *Journal of Studies on Alcohol*, **41**, 129–39.

WILLIAMS, L. (1963) Comment on Davies, D.L., 'Normal drinking in recovered alcohol addicts', *Quarterly Journal of Studies on Alcohol*, **24**, 109–21.

WILLIAMS, R.J. (1948) 'Alcoholics and metabolism', *Scientific American*, **179**, 50–53.

WILLIAMS, R.J. and BROWN, R.A. (1974) 'Differences in baseline drinking behaviour between New Zealand alcoholics and normal drinkers', *Behaviour Research and Therapy*, **12**, 287–94.

WILLIAMS, T.K. (1970) *The Ethanol-Induced Loss of Control Concept in Alcoholism*. Ed. D. dissertation University of Western Michigan.

WILSON, G.T., LEAF, R. and NATHAN, P.E. (1975) 'The aversive control of excessive drinking by chronic alcoholics in the laboratory setting', *Journal of Applied Behaviour Analysis*, **8**, 13–26.

WINDHAM, G.O. and PRESTON, J.D. (1967). Cited in Stacey, B. and Davies, J. (1970) 'Drinking behaviour in childhood and adolescence: an evaluative review', *British Journal of Addiction*, **65**, 203–12.

WINTERS, A. (1978) 'Review and rationale of the drinkwatchers international program', *American Journal of Drug and Alcohol Abuse*, **5**, 321–6.

YATES, F. (1979) 'The use made of treatment: an alternative approach to the evaluation of alcoholism services', unpublished doctoral dissertation, University of Birmingham, UK.

Name index

Subject index